6/12

THE
OBAMIANS

THE
OBAMIANS

The Struggle Inside the White House to
Redefine American Power

JAMES MANN

VIKING

VIKING

Published by the Penguin Group

Penguin Group (USA) Inc., 375 Hudson Street, New York, New York 10014, U.S.A. • Penguin Group (Canada), 90 Eglinton
Avenue East, Suite 700, Toronto, Ontario, Canada M4P 2Y3 (a division of Pearson Penguin Canada Inc.) • Penguin Books Ltd,
80 Strand, London WC2R 0RL, England • Penguin Ireland, 25 St. Stephen's Green, Dublin 2, Ireland (a division of Penguin
Books Ltd) • Penguin Books Australia Ltd, 250 Camberwell Road, Camberwell, Victoria 3124, Australia (a division of Pearson
Australia Group Pty Ltd) • Penguin Books India Pvt Ltd, 11 Community Centre, Panchsheel Park, New Delhi—110 017,
India • Penguin Group (NZ), 67 Apollo Drive, Rosedale, Auckland 0632, New Zealand (a division of Pearson New Zealand
Ltd) • Penguin Books (South Africa) (Pty) Ltd, 24 Sturdee Avenue, Rosebank, Johannesburg 2196, South Africa

Penguin Books Ltd, Registered Offices: 80 Strand, London WC2R 0RL, England

First published in 2012 by Viking Penguin, a member of Penguin Group (USA) Inc.

10 9 8 7 6 5 4 3 2 1

LIBRARY OF CONGRESS CATALOGING-IN-PUBLICATION DATA
Mann, Jim, 1946–
The Obamians : how a band of newcomers redefined American power / James Mann.
      p.   cm.
Includes bibliographical references and index.
ISBN 978-0-670-02376-9
   1. United States—Foreign relations—2009–   2. United States—Military policy.   3. United States—Politics and
government—2009–   4. Obama, Barack.   5. Obama, Barack—Political and social views.   6. Obama, Barack—Friends
and associates.   7. Power (Social sciences)—United States—History—21st century.   8. Democratic Party (U.S.)—
History—21st century.   9. Presidents—United States—Biography.   10. Politicians—United States—Biography.
I. Title.
   E907.M325 2012
   973.932092—dc23   2011046331

Printed in the United States of America
Designed by Carla Bolte • Set in Granjon

For Caroline,

My wife and life partner:

May the coming decades we share

Be like the ones that have passed

CONTENTS

INTRODUCTION

L ate in the afternoon of Tuesday, March 15, 2011, President Barack Obama gathered with members of his National Security Council in the Situation Room of the White House. In Libya, Colonel Moammar Gaddafi was on the verge of slaughtering the civilians and ragtag opposition forces that had risen up against him. The Obama administration was confronting an urgent decision: whether to send out American warplanes over Libya in an effort to stop him.

Over the previous two weeks, French president Nicolas Sarkozy and British prime minister David Cameron had been imploring Obama to join them in setting up a no-fly zone over Libya, one that would prevent Gaddafi from using planes and helicopters to shoot at defenseless Libyans on the ground. The private messages British and French officials were sending to Washington went further than their polite public statements. They pointed out that Britain and France had been acceding to American requests for help elsewhere in the world. They had sent troops to fight in Afghanistan in the face of considerable domestic opposition. They had joined with the United States in imposing progressively tougher economic sanctions against North Korea and Iran. But Libya was in Europe's own backyard, and the message from America's closest European allies boiled down to this: We need you on this one.[1]

The National Security Council session opened with an intelligence briefing: Gaddafi's forces are now advancing rapidly eastward across the country, beating back the opposition. They are now approaching Ajdabiya, the last major city before Benghazi, and will probably reach there within a few days. Benghazi is Libya's second-largest city, the home base for opposition to the regime in Tripoli; that had been true in the past and was certainly true in Gaddafi's Libya. Intelligence officials predicted that Gaddafi, whose army had been rounding up and killing civilians elsewhere, would be at his most brutal in Benghazi.

Next, Mike Mullen, the chairman of the Joint Chiefs of Staff, laid out in detail the plans for a no-fly zone. That was what the British and French had asked for, and the March 15 meeting had been called to make a decision on that request. Obama's own cabinet was divided: Defense Secretary Robert Gates had been opposed to military action, while Secretary of State Hillary Clinton had been in favor.

But Obama suddenly took the deliberations in a new direction. He asked Mullen: "Will this no-fly zone stop the scenario we just heard about?" He was referring to the predictions of a possible bloodbath in Benghazi. No, replied Mullen. It could effectively take Libya's air force out of action, but Gaddafi would still have more than enough tanks and other heavy equipment on the ground to continue what he was doing.

Then why, asked the president, are we focusing on a no-fly zone? "This notion that we're going to put some planes in the air to fly over a massacre just doesn't make a lot of sense," he said. "We could feel really good about ourselves, on the right side of history, and the people would still get killed."

"I want more options," Obama concluded. The administration knew it needed to act quickly. The British and French were already pressing the UN Security Council for a resolution supporting a no-fly zone; if the United States didn't join them, it could be isolated, humiliated or blamed for inaction and any ensuing massacre.

It was late afternoon, and Obama said he had to leave. He and the First Lady were about to host an annual White House dinner for Combatant Commanders (many of America's senior military leaders) and their spouses. But Obama announced he wanted to reconvene the National Security Council later that night to hear what else he might do besides an ineffective no-fly zone.

The Pentagon was not caught unprepared. Officials there had begun looking at various plans for military action in Libya since early in the month, although the detailed planning had flagged a bit when Pentagon officials noticed Gates arguing in public against American involvement. National Security Adviser Thomas Donilon had already reviewed some of the plans. The possibilities had included everything from putting in ground forces to a no-fly zone to what some in the White House dubbed the "Dunkirk option"—sending ships to bring people out of Libya.

Obama's dinner began at seven p.m. He did not linger; the NSC meeting reconvened at nine. This time, he was presented with a range of military options. One was to use no American force at all, but simply to provide intelligence and other support for the French and British. Another was the no-fly zone. The third was to go beyond the no-fly zone by sending out planes to strike at Libyan military targets on the ground in a way that would stop their advance toward Benghazi.

They went around the table, debating the alternative approaches. Gates again voiced his reservations. Clinton was out of the country and not at the table, but had made her views known in advance. Finally, the president chose the third military option. Speaking to United Nations Ambassador Susan Rice, he said, "I want to call everyone's bluff up in New York. Go in tomorrow morning and say that we're not going to support this resolution for a no-fly zone, we're going to redo it to authorize the use of 'all necessary measures'"—a euphemism for military force—"'to protect civilians.' And, Susan, you have to basically say, 'That's the only thing we're going to support, because that's the only thing that's going to make a difference.'"

Obama's decision was momentous. He had sent American troops into war before—lots of them—to Afghanistan. But this was the first time he would send out American forces to initiate a new military conflict, one that was not already being waged at the time he took office. Obama was, moreover, engaging in humanitarian intervention: He was using force for the avowed purpose of protecting lives in a place that most officials acknowledged was not itself of compelling strategic interest to the United States; America's only arguable strategic interest on this issue lay in maintaining strong relationships with close allies who were supporting the United States elsewhere in the world.

What Obama did two days later was even more striking. After the Security Council approved the American proposal authorizing "all necessary measures" against Gaddafi, he called Cameron and Sarkozy and worked out what his own aides called a deal: At the start of the military campaign, the United States would use its unique military capabilities—the advanced planes, missiles and precision-guided munitions it has in greater numbers and with higher levels of technology than any other country—to demolish not only Libya's air defenses, but other military targets on the ground. Then, after a few days, the United States would step back and leave it to the British, French and other allies to continue the military campaign on their own. America would provide what the military calls ISR—intelligence, surveillance and reconnaissance. The rest would be up to others.

Less than forty-eight hours later, as Libyan forces were already on the outskirts of Benghazi, the United States and its allies launched what was known as Operation Odyssey Dawn: More than a hundred Tomahawk cruise missiles rained down on targets along the Libyan coastline, striking radar installations, air defense batteries and anything else that might be used against allied warplanes over Libya.[2] Immediately afterward, American planes struck again and again at tanks, armored vehicles, heavy artillery and other armor and weaponry. Gaddafi's forces were suddenly stripped of their principal advantage over the opposition.

There was no massacre in Benghazi. The rebel forces held the city. But the civil war was just starting. After the first few days, Obama kept American forces out of the combat, despite occasional British and French appeals for the United States to rejoin the air campaign.

Obama's decisions on Libya encapsulated, all at once, the two most distinctive aspects of his foreign policy.

First, Obama was not squeamish about employing American military power. His actions in the White House belied the stereotypes of weakness that Republicans have tried to pin on Democratic presidents and presidential candidates for four decades: that they are averse to the use of force.

In Libya, Obama decided to take stronger military action than U.S. allies had proposed. In Afghanistan, he greatly increased the American military presence, sending out more than 50,000 additional troops in his first year in office. In the war against al-Qaeda, he vastly stepped up the use of drones and special operations, such as the raid that killed Osama bin Laden. Meanwhile, in the realm of ideas, Obama took the occasion of his reception of the Nobel Peace Prize in 2009 to deliver a stunning defense of the concept of "just war," saying specifically that, as American president, he could not be Mahatma Gandhi or Martin Luther King Jr.

All of this was surprising to many Democrats, who had chosen Obama for the Democratic nomination in no small part because of his opposition to the war in Iraq. For them, Obama turned out to be the peace candidate who wasn't. Sometimes, as with the surge of forces to Afghanistan, Obama's willingness to use military power garnered more support from Republicans than from Democrats.

But Obama's actions were also disconcerting to the Republicans, who had trouble figuring out a consistent line of attack against the president. During Obama's first year, former vice president Dick Cheney had portrayed him as weak. In Obama's second year, Cheney began arguing that the Democratic president represented in many ways a continuation of George W. Bush's administration. In the third year, after the drone killing of Anwar al-Awlaki in Yemen, Cheney praised the operation, but called upon Obama to apologize for having supposedly accused the Bush team of overreacting to the September 11 attacks. Similarly, while running for the Republican presidential nomination, Newt Gingrich at first upbraided Obama for failing to establish a no-fly zone in Libya; then, after Obama did so and went even further, Gingrich said he would not have intervened at all.

Secondly, Libya also illustrated the other salient feature of Obama's foreign policy: his continuing effort to recast the United States' role in the world in a way that fit America's more limited resources. No other president since World War II had entered into a military campaign quite like the one in Libya, in which Obama helped start the operation and then willingly, indeed insistently, handed off the next six months of work to its allies. Costs were certainly a factor. For years, American politicians had been talking about the importance of "burden sharing" with its allies, but usually in the past, this came down to asking other countries to help pay for American-dominated operations. Obama went well beyond that.

In general, Obama turned out to be far less wedded than his predecessors to the idea of an enduring American primacy or hegemony in the world. Since World War II, American leaders had tended to take for granted the fact that U.S. military and economic power gave it the ability to shape the course of events around the globe. This was true of Democratic presidents as well as Republicans. It was Jimmy Carter who first declared that America had a strategic influence in the Persian Gulf; it was the Clinton administration that proclaimed the United States to be the world's "indispensable nation."

Like other leaders of both parties, Obama continued to say that America was the most powerful nation on earth. He, too, spoke of America's leadership role in the world. But in his speeches, Obama concentrated on other themes that hinted at a more modest American foreign policy than in the past. One theme was that it was time for the United States to focus on rebuilding its own nation at home, rather than other countries overseas. The other was the vague, subtle acknowledgment that America's dominance since World War II might not last forever, and that a new international order might be necessary.

"Our country has borne a special burden in global affairs," Obama said in one speech. "We have not always been thanked for these efforts, and we have at times made mistakes. But more than any other nation, the United States of America has underwritten global security for over six decades—a time that, for all its problems, has seen walls come down, and markets open, and billions lifted from poverty, unparalleled scientific progress and advancing frontiers."[3]

Obama voiced the same thought on other occasions, too. There was almost a wistful, elegiac tone to these passages. He made it sound as if this era was coming to an end.

———

Obama was the third Democratic president in a row to take office at the end of America's involvement in international conflict. Jimmy Carter took office after the end of the Vietnam War; Bill Clinton came to power following the Cold War. For Obama, it was the war in Iraq, still being fought as he came to the White House. George W. Bush's decision to launch that war had devastated America's image overseas.

At the time of his inauguration, Obama and his new foreign policy team faced a number of specific challenges: the continuing wars in Iraq and

Afghanistan, the nuclear programs of Iran and North Korea, the threat of terrorism from al-Qaeda, the rapid ascent of China, the downward spiral of America's relations with Russia. Obama wanted to close the prison holding detainees at Guantánamo Bay, Cuba. He sought to smooth over relations with Middle Eastern leaders such as Egypt's Hosni Mubarak, who had been upset by intermittent American efforts to promote democracy in his country.

More broadly, Obama needed to cope with the legacies of the two Georges—two men who, in different ways, cast shadows over Obama's foreign policy. One was Obama's immediate predecessor, George W. Bush. His war in Iraq and the widespread unpopularity of Bush at home and abroad meant that the new president faced a series of immediate problems. He needed not only to reexamine Bush's policies quickly, but to deal with expectations he would reverse nearly everything Bush had done, from the wars and antiterrorist practices to the prison at Guantánamo.

The second legacy was less obvious: that of George McGovern, the passionately antiwar senator who had won the Democratic presidential nomination in 1972. McGovern had gone on to overwhelming defeat, but in the process, his campaign had solidified inside the Democratic Party an antiwar base that would influence American politics for several decades.

Democrats running for president after McGovern had to reckon with this antiwar constituency in one way or another. Some embraced it, while others ran as various kinds of centrist Democrats, "new Democrats" or "third way" Democrats to distinguish themselves from the party's left wing. The Republicans, meanwhile, knew that even when they were divided among themselves, they could always attack the Democrats by summoning forth the specter of McGovern, using his campaign to caricature the Democrats as pacifists who lacked pride in America.

———

I began this book after Obama's election in 2008 because I was particularly interested in following how Obama and his foreign policy team would deal with the world. I had written about their immediate predecessors; in an earlier book, *Rise of the Vulcans*, I traced the backgrounds and ideas of George W. Bush's foreign policy advisers. Obama's presidential campaign in 2007–2008 was waged in contradiction to the Bush team. Starting as a state senator in Illinois, he had called Bush's war in Iraq "dumb." He had joined with antiwar forces within the Democratic Party at a time when most prominent Democratic leaders and candidates did not.

I wanted to see what happened when Obama and his new team took over after Bush. Could they bring about a new American relationship with the world, one that was less unilateral in approach and less reliant on American military power? I was interested in exploring the ideas, the assumptions and the people underlying Obama's foreign policy.

From the outset, the Obama foreign policy team differed from the one it replaced in several respects. At the cabinet level, officials did not have a common, shared history in dealing with the world, at least not by the standards of the Bush team. Indeed, they weren't all Democrats: Robert Gates, Obama's first defense secretary, was a holdover from the Bush administration, and James Jones, his first national security adviser, had spent his career in the military. Hillary Clinton, as secretary of state, had accumulated long experience in Democratic Party politics, but considerably less in the making of American foreign policy. Obama's first CIA director, Leon Panetta, similarly had a remarkably long track record in government but little in the field of intelligence or defense.

By virtually all accounts, the dominant influence on the Obama administration's foreign policy was the president himself. He was the main strategist. It was Obama's own ideas, sometimes changing over time, that have determined America's role in the world during his presidency.

But Obama has also relied heavily upon his own small, informal network of close aides. They did not hold cabinet-level positions, but in most cases worked closely with him during his 2008 presidential campaign. They had no previous experience in carrying out foreign policy at the State or Defense Departments, although some had worked on Capitol Hill. Obama installed these aides primarily on the National Security Council, and he often worked with and through them in formulating ideas and dealing with the foreign policy bureaucracies. I decided to focus primarily on this inner circle of aides not for the intrinsic importance of the jobs they held but because they were the ones who most closely share Obama's views, and were most involved in explaining his reasoning and enforcing his decisions. They provided a window into Obama's ideas and reasoning. It is these aides whom I call "the

Obamians." They were, in a sense, an extension of the president himself, the chief Obamian.

The Obamians self-consciously thought of themselves as a new generation in American foreign policy, and, indeed, in many ways they were. They were post–baby boomers, born in the 1960s and 1970s; they were infants or in elementary school (or, in one case, not yet born) during the Vietnam War. (Technically, demographers would classify Obama himself, born in 1961, as a late baby boomer, but few would question that he was of a different generation from Bill Clinton or George W. Bush, both fifteen years older.) The Obamians had not yet started their careers in government at the end of the Cold War. Obama had just turned thirty and graduated from law school at the time the Soviet Union collapsed, and other Obamians were in their teens or twenties. In deference to the Obamians' youthful approach and outlook, Secretary of Defense Robert Gates once quipped, "Jim [Jones] and Hillary and I have joked that we're of a different generation than those in the White House. While they're texting, we're on the cell phone or even a landline."[4]

The Obamians' formative experiences were the Iraq War and the financial crisis of 2008. Iraq brought forth an upsurge in anti-Americanism. The economic turmoil that had begun in Bush's final year—which led to America's growing unemployment and budget deficits—meant that the United States no longer had as much money to spend overseas as it had a decade earlier.

———

Obama's policies abroad are in many ways a clearer test of his own underlying ideas and choices than his policies at home. In most cases, he could not blame his foreign policy on Republican opposition or the need to make compromises—first because the Republicans have been so divided and scattershot in their views, but also because an American president doesn't need congressional support in foreign policy to the same extent as he does on taxes, budgets or health care. The reason for this is based in the Constitution: Congress has no role at all in the day-to-day execution of foreign policy and only a limited role in setting the overall direction. If anything, Obama increased presidential power over the Bush years, by choosing to carry out military action in Libya beyond the time limits set in the War Powers Resolution.

The one exception, in which Obama was clearly unable to achieve something because of congressional opposition, was his failure to close Guantánamo. But elsewhere—on Iraq and Afghanistan, policies toward Iran or China, drone attacks, killing Osama bin Laden, telling Hosni Mubarak to give up power in Egypt, intervening in Libya—the successes and failures were Obama's alone. In that sense, Obama's dealings with the rest of the world give a better sense of Obama himself, the people around him, his ideas and how he has (or has not) put them into effect.

The ultimate goal of this book is to look beyond the common perceptions and stereotypes about Obama's foreign policy. The conventional wisdom has varied: He's weak, he's strong; he's cautious, he's a risk taker; he's a continuation of Bush, he's a radical Kenyan anti-imperialist; he favors American decline, he's trying to preserve American power; he has made apology tours around the world, he has restored America's standing in the world. Beneath all of these slogans and epithets, there is a more complex reality—the blend of various events, people and ideas that made up America's relationship to the world in the Obama era. That is the story I seek to tell.

THE
OBAMIANS

Prologue

Nine days after Barack Obama was elected president of the United States, on a rainy mid-November afternoon in Washington D.C., several hundred people filed into the spacious downstairs ballroom of the luxurious Willard Hotel. The occasion was ostensibly a book party, but those who attended treated it as a political event. It was the first appearance since the election of the Democrats who would be guiding American foreign policy for the next few years.

The authors were Kurt Campbell and James Steinberg, who had worked on Bill Clinton's foreign policy team and could be expected to return to government again under Barack Obama. Their new book, which had been well timed to come out immediately after the election, was called *Difficult Transitions: Foreign Policy Troubles at the Outset of Presidential Power.* It sketched out what a president-elect and an incoming administration should do in its first few months. "Think carefully before reversing predecessors' policy decisions," the book advised at one point. "Before moving precipitously, the new president should make sure that well-developed alternatives are ready and clearly thought out."[1] Obama and his aides would sometimes ignore that warning in their first months in office—as, for example, when the president announced immediately after his inauguration that he would close the Guantánamo Bay prison within a year.

Obama had visited Washington only once since Election Day. He and his former campaign advisers were still working in Chicago, beginning to put together his new administration. He had already named Congressman Rahm Emanuel as his White House chief of staff, but had not yet said whom he might choose for the top foreign policy positions. The leading candidate for secretary of state was thought to be Senator John Kerry, the Democratic presidential candidate in 2004, who made no secret that he wanted the job. Or it might be a Republican senator, such as Richard Lugar or Chuck Hagel.

During a presidential transition Washington is a town of rumors and gossip, suspense and intrigue. Journalists and diplomats press to find out who will get which job. The young and ambitious want to know if they should put their names in, and if so, which influential people could put in a good word on their behalf. The lucky ones who get offered a position some-times worry if they should hold out for something grander in rank. Those eager to make money try to calculate whether it would be better to take a job in the administration or to capitalize on new lobbying opportunities in the private sector. The conventional wisdom is that if you want to make money, it is better to work as a lobbyist in the first years of an administration and take an appointment later on, rather than serving in government first and then going off to lobby. (After you leave government, you're covered by conflict-of-interest rules that limit how much you can lobby.)

Former secretary of state Madeleine Albright introduced Steinberg and Campbell at the Willard. She recalled how she had known Steinberg since the two of them worked as foreign policy advisers to Michael Dukakis's 1988 presidential campaign, and how she and Campbell had taken part in Asian diplomatic gatherings in the 1990s. As he talked about the book and an-swered questions, Steinberg flashed his genial but controlled smile, the one that gave little away and conveyed the assurance that he was surprised by nothing, that everything was working out well. Campbell displayed his self-deprecating wit: When he mentioned a "new generation" taking over Amer-ican foreign policy, he interrupted himself to say, "I'm not so new anymore." By Obama's standards, he wasn't.

The audience was listening, but with only one ear. The room was buzz-ing with gossip: Is Robert Gates going to stay on as Obama's defense secre-tary? What job will Bill Richardson be given—one in foreign or domestic policy? Why isn't Strobe Talbott at the book party today—does his absence mean he isn't interested in serving in the new administration? And the pe-rennial question for the Democrats: What job will they give to Richard Hol-brooke?

It was after the formal program had ended, when the audience had retreated to the rear of the ballroom for wine, snacks and rumors, that the word began to spread from one cluster of people to another. Have you heard? Do you know what ABC and the *Washington Post* are reporting?

The answer: Obama just met with Hillary Clinton in Chicago. He's talking to her about the job of secretary of state.

――――――

Obama's appointment of Hillary Clinton did not by itself determine the course of his foreign policy. Over the following years, Clinton's role and influence within the administration's internal decision making would be a work in progress—sometimes immense, sometimes less than she would have liked. She would handle most of the duties of secretary of state in admirable fashion and would, in the process, greatly increase her own standing in the Democratic Party, particularly with those who had originally supported Obama and opposed her in 2008.

Nevertheless, the decision to give her the job at State had implications that extended beyond Clinton herself. It was of profound significance for Obama's grassroots supporters, for perceptions of his new administration, for the Democratic Party and for the underlying politics affecting Obama's foreign policy over the following four years. In all these respects, the Clinton appointment was nothing less than a bombshell.

The origins of Obama's decision to appoint Clinton are by now as familiar as they are, ultimately, vague in detail. The standard version goes like this: Obama called Clinton to Chicago on that day, nine days after the election, and surprised her by saying he would like to appoint her secretary of state. She at first didn't think he meant it. "She was floored when he opened the door to that," asserted John Podesta, the veteran Democrat who headed Obama's transition team. Podesta was close to the Clintons and served as an intermediary. When Obama persuaded her he was serious, she then balked for several reasons, saying she was tired, that she had to pay off her campaign debt, that Bill Clinton's foundation, fund-raising and other activities would pose too many difficulties. She told Obama she wouldn't do it, reconsidered overnight and called him the next morning to accept.[2]

These accounts of Clinton's appointment should be viewed as incomplete. There are plenty of reasons to think Clinton was less than "floored" by Obama's postelection summons to Chicago. Richard Holbrooke told a friend he had learned in late October, before the election, that he would not be appointed secretary of state and that the job would probably go to Hillary Clinton instead. Podesta acknowledges that he began actively exploring the idea of the Clinton appointment in late October, in the two weeks before the election. The idea was "closely held," he recalled, but he talked about it either with Obama himself or with Peter Rouse, an Obama aide. If they were discussing it, even quietly, and if Holbrooke (himself a Clinton ally) had picked up the information, it is virtually impossible to believe Hillary Clinton was completely in the dark.[3]

Indeed, the origins of the Clinton appointment appear to date back much earlier. Some accounts have Obama starting to talk about Clinton as secretary of state in the summer and early fall. Asked about these, Podesta said, "It's possible that it's true. It may have been in the back of his [Obama's] mind. It was in the front of my mind. But we didn't start talking about it until October."[4]

What none of the standard accounts address is whether Clinton's appointment was the result of a deal, implicit or explicit, reached between the two Democratic rivals at the end of their bitter battle for the nomination. Clinton had withdrawn her candidacy in June, rather than challenging Obama all the way to the Democratic National Convention. She had then dutifully campaigned for him in the general election. Had Obama agreed to let Clinton have a top job in his administration, if she wanted, in exchange for finally dropping her primary challenge and helping him in the race against John McCain? There is no evidence on this subject one way or the other; it is something perhaps only the two of them know. No transcript exists of the secret one-on-one meeting between Obama and Clinton at the Washington D.C. home of Senator Dianne Feinstein on June 5, 2008, two days before Clinton finally conceded the primary race to Obama.

For Obama's most enthusiastic supporters, the Clinton appointment was difficult to accept. This was true both for rank-and-file volunteers and for some of Obama's senior campaign aides. Obama's grassroots supporters had of course spent months arguing to all who would listen that Clinton represented old thinking, the establishment, the Democratic Party elite— especially when it came to foreign policy, since the two candidates' views on domestic issues were not far apart. Now they learned, a couple of weeks after the election, that the State Department would be headed by the candidate they had so fervently denounced. Even worse, Clinton had her own network of friends and allies, one with deeper roots than Obama's. "I thought we were rid of these people," said one disappointed liberal Democrat who had long opposed the Clintons.

For some of the foreign policy experts who had advised Obama in the presidential campaign, the Clinton appointment was even more awkward. Under ordinary circumstances, some of them might have hoped to work in top jobs at the State Department. But how could Greg Craig, who had written the detailed memo saying Hillary Clinton "did not do any heavy-lifting" on foreign policy during Bill Clinton's administration, work as, say, deputy secretary of state under Clinton? How could Samantha Power, who had once labeled Clinton a "monster," take a job at the State Department in her field of human rights? Would Jeffrey Bader, who had worked as Bill Clinton's China specialist but then campaigned for Obama, feel comfortable in a role as assistant secretary of state for East Asia? The problems extended down throughout the Obama campaign's foreign policy team. "There are quite a number of, especially, younger folks who are moving from angst to anxiety to anger," said one Obama supporter during the transition. "After all, most of the jobs [for political appointments in foreign policy] are at the State Department."[5]

Apart from considerations of jobs and patronage, some critics also contended that the Clinton appointment was bad for foreign policy. They argued that Obama possessed a rare opportunity to show the rest of the world that the United States was turning a page after the Bush administration— and that Clinton could blur Obama's message. In the campaign, she had taken a different view from Obama on the Iraq War and about the idea of negotiating with adversaries like Iran. Would she now compromise his view of the world? Worst of all, how could Obama fire her? Moreover, critics asked, what did she really know about foreign policy, anyway?

Such critics often missed the point and, indeed, the underlying purpose of Obama's decision to appoint Clinton. It was a matter of long-term strategy, both for politics and also for Obama's foreign policy. Obama was removing Clinton from the Senate, where she would have been an independent power center, and putting her inside his administration, where she would find it far harder to oppose or criticize what he was doing.

Over the previous half century, three incumbent American presidents— Gerald Ford, Jimmy Carter and George H. W. Bush—had been voted out of office after one term. A fourth, Lyndon Johnson, decided not to run for reelection. All four of them had been challenged from within their own party. Hillary Clinton in the Senate under Obama would have been like Robert Kennedy in the Johnson years or Ted Kennedy in the Carter years— a magnet for intraparty opposition to the president.

To be sure, Hillary had been somewhat more hawkish on foreign policy issues than Obama, and thus less popular with the Democrats' liberal base. But that didn't mean much. If Clinton had stayed on in the Senate, it is not hard to imagine that, when Obama decided to send more American troops to Afghanistan, the groundswell of antiwar opposition within the Democratic Party might have still gravitated toward her, as Obama's leading opponent within the party. (A hypothetical first critical speech by Senator Hillary Clinton criticizing Obama on Afghanistan would not have needed to be dovish in its rhetoric. She might have said, simply, that his administration "lacked a plan" or "lacked a strategy" in Afghanistan, thereby winning support from the doves without necessarily joining them. After another speech or two, Hillary Clinton might have emerged as an intraparty opponent of the war, much like Bobby Kennedy.)

The Clinton appointment was a classic example of the famous old political axiom set forth by Lyndon Johnson when talking about J. Edgar Hoover that "it's probably better to have [a potential adversary] inside the tent pissing out than outside the tent pissing in." Even after recognizing this reality, Obama's early supporters were still unhappy. One line making the rounds during the transition was that Lyndon Johnson's line didn't apply: "The trouble is that the Clintons piss in all directions," one liberal Democrat said bitterly. "They're incontinent."

Over the long run, Hillary Clinton's appointment would work out much better than Obama's early supporters had feared. It would also work out well for Clinton, who would eventually come to be viewed as loyal, competent and (most important of all) a leader in her own right, operating independently from her husband. Obama's choice for secretary of state was not, however, a step toward dramatically new foreign policy, as he had promised during his presidential campaign.

———

None of Obama's senior campaign advisers in foreign policy got any of the top foreign policy jobs in his administration. Nor, for that matter, did others from the liberal wing of the Democratic Party. The positions of secretary of state, defense and treasury, the national security adviser and the director of the CIA were all filled elsewhere.

For secretary of defense, Obama decided to reappoint Robert Gates, the former CIA director George W. Bush had brought to the Pentagon to replace Donald Rumsfeld in late 2006. Gates brought to the Obama administration a wealth of experience and knowledge in foreign policy. Like Hillary Clinton, Gates also represented a sense of continuity with the past, even though Obama had attacked foreign policy insiders during his campaign.

Gates had once taken to the streets to join an antiwar demonstration, but the war in question was Vietnam, not Iraq. He had begun his government career in 1966 as a CIA specialist on the Soviet Union. Four years later, when President Nixon extended the Vietnam War into Cambodia, Gates, then twenty-five years old, protested. "I and virtually all of my friends and acquaintances in CIA were opposed to the war and to any prolonged strategy for extracting us," Gates later wrote. "Feelings among my colleagues—and nearly all of the men in those days were military veterans—were strong."[6]

Gates rose through the ranks at the CIA as a Soviet analyst and, consistently, a Cold War hawk. He served for a time as a Soviet adviser on Jimmy Carter's national security staff, working for Zbigniew Brzezinski. After returning to the CIA, he became a central figure in the Washington battles over Soviet policy in the late 1980s, when President Ronald Reagan and Secretary of State George Shultz believed that Soviet president Mikhail Gorbachev represented a fundamental change from past Soviet leaders; Gates, by that time the deputy director at the CIA, argued that Gorbachev represented continuity with the past and presided over the same old Soviet system.

President George H. W. Bush appointed Gates as first deputy national security adviser and then as director of central intelligence. It was during this period, in the elder Bush's administration, that Gates served most easily with colleagues whose views were closest to his own. His mentor was Brent

Scowcroft, Bush's national security adviser; he also worked closely alongside Colin Powell, whom Bush had appointed as chairman of the Joint Chiefs of Staff.

With Bill Clinton's election, Gates left the CIA. He went off to his lake-front home on Big Lake in western Washington, wrote a memoir and served as university president at Texas A&M until George W. Bush appointed him to replace Donald Rumsfeld as secretary of defense.

At his confirmation hearing at the end of 2006, Gates made no commitments to bring the American troops home from Iraq. Still, he earned praise for his willingness to admit that the United States was not winning the war. The Democrats, delighted by Rumsfeld's departure, did little to challenge Gates. One columnist mockingly summarized the mood of Congress at the time: "And so it came to pass, in the twelfth month of the sixth year of the reign of Bush, that a prophet came forth to deliver us from the war in Babylon."[7]

At the time Gates was sworn in, it appeared that the stage was being set for a gradual pullout from Iraq. Congress had set up an Iraq Study Group, made up of illustrious Americans of both political parties, to study the war and make policy recommendations. At the end of 2006, the group issued what was known as the Baker-Hamilton Report. It recommended phasing out the American military presence in Iraq, with most combat brigades out of the country by the beginning of 2008.

Instead of scaling back, however, Bush decided to escalate the war in an effort to turn it around. At the beginning of 2007, the president and his new defense secretary announced a "surge" in U.S. forces, dispatching more than 20,000 additional U.S. troops to Iraq. Bush also announced the appointment of a new military commander, General David Petraeus, the military leader most closely identified with the strategy of counterinsurgency. Within a year, American deaths in Iraq dropped to their lowest levels since the start of the war.

Thus Obama, in reappointing Gates as his own defense secretary, was keeping a knowledgeable, experienced hand on the job at the Pentagon. But he was also choosing someone who had helped to initiate and carry out for two years essentially the same approach in Iraq (more troops, counterinsurgency) that the Obama campaign and even the mainstream Democratic foreign policy elite had vigorously opposed during Bush's second term.

For two other top positions in his administration, Obama chose former military leaders. He picked James Jones, a former four-star general and commandant of the Marine Corps, as his national security adviser. Obama barely knew Jones, but he had come with high recommendations from foreign policy "wise men" such as Scowcroft. The job of director of national intelligence went to Dennis Blair, a former admiral who had been commander of U.S. forces in the Pacific. Jones and Blair reflected the distinct "anti-Rumsfeld" cast of the Obama administration. Both men had been critical of Rumsfeld's leadership of the military; during the Bush years each had been a potential candidate for promotion to chairman of the Joint Chiefs of Staff, but had been passed over by Rumsfeld.

There was a political component to the selection of Jones and Blair, just as there had been in the Clinton appointment. Taken together, Jones, Blair and Gates provided Obama with some cover for his decisions on defense and military issues. For more than three decades, ever since the Vietnam era, the Democrats had been obliged to defend themselves against recurrent Republican charges that they were soft or weak on national security. Obama himself had not served in the military and had run for president essentially as the antiwar candidate; thus, he might be vulnerable to the same old attacks. With a Bush appointee in charge of the Pentagon and with former military leaders for the National Security Council and the intelligence community, Obama could insulate himself. Moreover, Gates, Jones and Blair could help explain and defend Obama's decisions to the military and intelligence communities—and, if things went seriously wrong, could share the blame.

The result of all these choices, however, was that those who'd helped Obama in his presidential campaign were virtually shut out of the top jobs in his new administration. Obama had no one comparable to Secretary of State James Baker or Brent Scowcroft, who had been George H. W. Bush's longtime friends and associates. Nor did Obama have anyone like Zbigniew Brzezinski, Tony Lake or Condoleezza Rice, who had served as the top foreign policy advisers for the presidential campaigns of Jimmy Carter, Bill Clinton and George W. Bush, respectively, before going on, in each case, to serve as national security adviser in the White House.

From the Obama campaign team, only Susan Rice was given a senior position, as ambassador to the United Nations, a job two hundred miles away. Anyone holding that job has to battle (successfully, in Rice's case) for cabinet rank and a role in the Washington decision making. John Kerry, who had endorsed Obama at the pivotal moment when Obama lost the New Hampshire primary, did not get the appointment he sought as secretary of state. The Obama campaign's leading adviser on defense policy, former secretary of the navy Richard Danzig, did not join the new administration. There had been speculation Danzig might serve as Gates's deputy secretary of defense, but Gates made clear he thought it would blur lines of authority to have a senior Democrat (and potential successor) working right down the hall from him in the Pentagon.

On the other hand, Obama brought to the National Security Council a few younger, lesser-known aides who had been handling foreign policy for him during the campaign: Mark Lippert, Denis McDonough and Ben Rhodes. All of them were given jobs on the National Security Council, along with Samantha Power, another adviser close to the president.

The effect of these personnel decisions was that Obama had only distant relationships with those who held formal responsibilities for foreign policy, such as the secretary of state and the national security adviser, but he was extremely close to the former campaign aides on the National Security Council staff. It didn't take long for the word to spread throughout the top levels of the federal government: If you get a request from Jim Jones, he might or might not be speaking for the president. If you get a request from Denis McDonough, he's asking on behalf of the president himself.

———

On December 1, 2008, Barack Obama held a press conference in Chicago to introduce his national security team, including not only Clinton, Gates and Jones, but his other choices as well: Attorney General Eric Holder, Ambassador to the United Nations Susan Rice and Secretary of Homeland Security Janet Napolitano. Dressed in a dark suit with red tie, Obama towered over Clinton and Gates as the nominees read prepared statements. Gates's statement was terse, only six sentences long, as if he were in a hurry to get back to his Pentagon job. Clinton took the time to thank the voters of New York for her time in the Senate. The longest speech, predictably, came from Vice President–elect Joe Biden, who discoursed on his relationships with the members of the team.

Obama easily fielded questions about how he and his aides could work with Clinton after they had belittled her foreign policy credentials during the primaries. He accused reporters of "having fun" by dredging up anti-Clinton quotes made "in the heat of a campaign."[8]

The Obama team had already shrewdly deflected attention away from the politics of the Clinton appointment—whether, for example, Obama was appointing her to remove a potential source of intraparty opposition—by touting the idea of a "team of rivals." That phrase, taken from the title of Doris Kearns Goodwin's book on Abraham Lincoln's Civil War cabinet, gave a grand historical gloss to the uneasy merger of the Obama and Clinton teams, which everyone knew would be carefully scrutinized for any sign of discord.

Nevertheless, at the initial press conference Obama appeared considerably more comfortable with Clinton than, eight years earlier, George W. Bush had looked while announcing his appointment of Colin Powell as secretary of state (Powell proceeded to dominate the ensuing press conference). Bush's foreign policy team had been a genuine team of rivals; Obama's team was something less than that. As applied to the Obama cabinet, "team of rivals" was mostly a marketing concept for a Clinton appointment that would not go down well with the Obama faithful.

"In this uncertain world, the time has come for a new beginning, a new dawn of American leadership to overcome the challenges of the twenty-first century," Obama declared at the press conference. As so often during the campaign, Obama was promising a break with the foreign policies of his predecessors.

The prominent figures he appointed to his cabinet, however, were not new and they had strong ties to the policies of earlier presidents. Whether viewed together or separately, the appointments gave no clue as to what Obama thought a "new beginning" should be. They were talented people. But they were not a team, they were not close to Obama and, indeed, they did not necessarily know his goals or vision for where America was headed. Obama had campaigned against the foreign policy elite. As president, how-ever, he would rely on old Washington hands to help run the government. What Obama called the "new dawn of American leadership" began to look surprisingly similar to yesterday's dawn.

Obama was not putting his administration together in a vacuum. The president-elect was reflecting the influences and carrying the burdens of history. Over the previous four decades, the United States had been struggling to figure out its relationship with the rest of the world. And in domestic politics, the Democratic Party had been trying to iron out some sort of consensus on fundamental questions concerning American power and the use of force.

By appointing Clinton, Obama was seeking to reunify the Democrats. Yet the party's internal disagreements over foreign policy did not start with the two leaders' battle in the Democratic primaries of 2008. In dealing with the world, the Democrats had a long, tangled history of lessons learned and unlearned, of contradictions resolved or papered over, of issues pressed forward or discarded. Obama's foreign policy did not start from scratch. It was freighted with the legacy of the past and could best be understood against the context of the party's struggles over the previous four decades.

1

"A Look I Recognized"

In the fall of 2009, John Kerry, the Democratic chairman of the Senate Foreign Relations Committee, visited Afghanistan, where American troops were enmeshed in a nettlesome war that President Barack Obama was in the process of expanding. Kerry not only met with Afghan president Hamid Karzai, but took the time to travel around the countryside. Upon coming back to Washington, he reflected on what he had witnessed. As he stared out from inside an armored personnel carrier in Afghanistan, Kerry said, he saw on the faces of ordinary people "a look I recognized from forty years ago." Afghanistan and its people reminded Kerry of Vietnam. He repeated a line from the congressional testimony he gave in 1971, as a leader of the Vietnam Veterans Against the War. "How do you ask a man to be the last man to die for a mistake?" he had asked. Upon returning home from Afghanistan, Kerry remarked, "Thirty-eight years later, I keep that question very much in mind."[1]

For the Democratic Party, the war in Vietnam was not only tragic, but politically devastating. Between 1968 and 1988, the Democrats lost five out of six presidential elections. The only Democratic president of that era, Jimmy Carter, lasted only four years. The divisions caused by the war had caused core groups of Democrats to desert the party for the Republicans. It was not until Bill Clinton's election in 1992 that the party began to regain its footing.

And still the legacy of Vietnam lingered. When President Obama decided to send more troops to Afghanistan at the end of his first year in the White House, Obama and the younger members of his administration dismissed the comparison to the Vietnam War as irrelevant. "There are those who suggest Afghanistan is another Vietnam," said Obama in the speech at West Point announcing his decision; then he argued that it wasn't. "There are things to learn from previous military engagements, but the touchstone isn't always going to be Vietnam," observed his young aide Ben Rhodes.[2] Yet many members of his own administration had been preparing for the Afghanistan decision by reading books about Vietnam.

Kerry's flashback illustrates how Vietnam has endured as a starting point for older Americans in thinking about America's role in the world. A generation of Americans now in their sixties came of age during that war, in which more than 58,000 Americans died. Afterward, that war and the intense controversy that it engendered helped to define America's outlook and its assumptions about the world for decades. Whenever U.S. forces were sent into combat, American leaders talked about the importance of overcoming the "Vietnam syndrome"—meaning a fear of casualties and opposition to further U.S. military intervention overseas.

On college campuses, the war in Vietnam helped turn the children of conservative Republicans, like Hillary Rodham, into liberal Democrats. It also fostered a dark view of America's role in the world. Vietnam taught the lesson that even a supposedly small and limited war could eventually consume the United States and divert it from all other objectives. It demonstrated that military force could lead to disastrous results. Opponents of the war argued that there should be new limits on American power and the defense and intelligence agencies that wield it. The main lesson was that if America resorts to force at all, it had better do so carefully.

Vietnam had social and political ramifications that were not foreseen at the time. The war gradually led to the abolition of the draft, and that in turn had sweeping consequences for many other aspects of American life.

In the fall of 1969, demonstrations against Vietnam spread from college campuses to the American heartland. President Richard Nixon tried in various ways to undercut the growing strength of the antiwar movement. The one that succeeded was to do away with the draft. In April 1970, Nixon announced that he was reducing draft calls to zero and was meanwhile increasing the pay for military service. These were the first steps toward ending the draft. Three years later, the law authorizing conscription was allowed to lapse.

Liberal Democrats were divided about the draft. Senator George McGovern was in favor of abolition. For young men opposed to the Vietnam War, he said, "the draft is a source of torment that forces them to choose between participation in a war they sincerely oppose or a term in jail." By contrast, Edward M. Kennedy was strongly in favor; he predicted that an all-volunteer force would result in "poor people fighting rich men's wars."[3]

Once the draft ended, the Vietnam protests began to taper off. Future American presidents would find it easier to wage war overseas without so much domestic opposition. The public reactions to war become more muted, because relatively poorer members of American society were doing the fighting; they had less ability to make their views felt than the draftees and their families. Sam Brown, one of the organizers of the demonstrations against the Vietnam War, was asked in 2009 why there was so little organized opposition to the war in Afghanistan. "There's no draft," he replied.[4]

In electoral politics, the end of conscription meant that there were groups, even entire cities and regions of the United States, with little connection to the military or the people who fought in America's wars. For a short time after Vietnam, political candidates found that they could appeal to liberal audiences with a message that attacked the military and rejected the idea of patriotism. Writing of his Vietnam generation, the sociologist Todd Gitlin observed, "Indeed, it could be said that in the course of our political history, we lived through a very odd turnabout: the most powerful public emotion in our lives was *rejecting* patriotism."[5] However, as Democratic candidates appealed to antiwar audiences, Republicans and conservatives found in response that they could often win a greater number of votes with a message of patriotism, support for the military and a resentment of liberal elites. It often worked.

In 1972, George McGovern won the Democratic nomination for the presidency with a campaign based on impassioned opposition to Vietnam. He was scathing in his attacks on American policy and, indeed, its role in the world. "What we now present to the world is the spectacle of a rich and powerful nation standing off at a safe distance and raining down a terrible technology of death on helpless people below—the most incredible and murderous bombardment in all the history of mankind," McGovern said.[6] Specifically, McGovern promised that on the first day of his presidency he would stop all acts of force by American troops in Vietnam, and that within ninety days he would withdraw U.S. forces from the country. In his speech accepting the Democratic nomination, he made a broader appeal, with a line that came to define his candidacy: "Come home, America."

McGovern's campaign included a number of ambitious young college graduates who went on to serve in later Democratic administrations, including Obama's. Hillary Rodham worked for McGovern, registering voters in San Antonio while her future husband Bill Clinton served as McGovern's Texas state cocoordinator.[7] Greg Craig, Obama's first White House counsel, similarly served as state cocoordinator for McGovern, in Vermont. Dennis Ross, Obama's adviser on Middle East policy, worked for McGovern as a young graduate student in California.

However, the lessons these workers took from the campaign were mostly cautionary ones. McGovern's campaign never came close to winning the support of the American people. President Richard Nixon won 61 percent of the popular vote and 520 electoral votes to McGovern's 17, including only Massachusetts and the District of Columbia. The defeat was so overwhelming that no one, including those who worked for him, wanted future Democratic candidates to imitate McGovern. "The coalition that McGovern was trying to put together, which was essentially a coalition of people that felt left out and left behind, was never going to be the kind of coalition that could command a majority of the American people," reflected Craig many years later. "You really had to move to the center on some important issues to be credible."[8]

The McGovern campaign left the Democrats in a quandary on foreign policy and national security issues. On the one hand, the Vietnam War created a strong base within the party for candidates who favored peace, a more limited role for the military and a willingness to question America's role and actions abroad. On the other hand, these views usually represented a minority of voters, and as a result, the Republicans found that they could use foreign policy and defense issues to their own electoral advantage. The Democrats won the White House in years when domestic issues were paramount (Jimmy Carter in 1976, Bill Clinton in 1992) or when national security issues worked against the Republicans (Obama in the midst of the war in Iraq).

After 1972, the Democrats "would repeatedly be thrown on the defensive by the charge that they were weak on national security," writes Bruce Miroff, whose book *The Liberals' Moment* sympathetically describes and analyzes the McGovern campaign. "However much the horrors of the war in Vietnam are now widely acknowledged, it has been the heirs of Nixon who have had the upper hand on national security issues in subsequent presidential campaigns, and it has been the heirs of McGovern who have been caught up in an identity crisis of American patriotism."[9]

———

Antiwar forces had considerably greater success on Capitol Hill. Throughout the early and mid-1970s, Congress, where the Democrats held majorities in both houses, passed a series of legislative measures designed to prevent any future Vietnams. The broader goal was to restore the principle of constitutional limits on presidential power. The restrictions set down in the 1970s were far from airtight, but they would prove significant enough that even Barack Obama, nearly four decades later, would be obliged to grapple with them.

In 1973, overriding a veto by Nixon, the Democratic Congress passed the War Powers Resolution, which prohibited a president from deploying American troops overseas for more than sixty days without the authorization of Congress. In 1975, both houses of Congress launched investigations into the history of secret operations by the CIA agency, including attempted assassinations of foreign leaders such as Fidel Castro; in response, President Gerald Ford signed an executive order banning assassinations. Three years later, in the wake of revelations that the FBI and CIA had been wiretapping American citizens without warrants, the Democratic Congress passed the Foreign Intelligence Surveillance Act. It established special courts to review requests by the U.S. government for wiretaps.

In that era, the congressional Democrats were not only more numerous and powerful than the Democrats are today, but also more illustrious and, by today's standards, unimaginably more liberal. Among the sixty Democratic senators in the Ninety-fourth Congress, which took office in 1975, were Ted Kennedy, Walter Mondale, Edmund Muskie, Mike Mansfield,

George McGovern, Philip Hart, Frank Church, Birch Bayh, Gary Hart, Adlai Stevenson III, John Tunney and Joe Biden, among others. In the House, Speaker Tip O'Neill had 291 Democrats and only 144 Republicans, a majority of more than two to one.

Presidents of both parties chafed at and sought to circumvent these post-Vietnam restrictions on their authority. When Obama decided to intervene in Libya in 2011, he rejected arguments in Congress that he needed to comply with the War Powers Resolution of 1973. Before Obama ordered the killing of the Muslim cleric Anwar al-Awlaki in Yemen, Justice Department lawyers wrote a memo to explain why it did not violate the ban on assassinations imposed in 1976. When the Obama administration went to court in defense of the National Security Agency program to conduct surveillance of phone calls and e-mails without warrants, the law at issue was the Foreign Intelligence Surveillance Act of 1978.

By the end of the 1970s, however, the mood in Congress had begun to shift and the reform era came to an end. One of the best examples was Joe Biden, the young senator from Delaware. Like other Democrats outside the South, he had opposed the Vietnam War. Yet Biden was never closely identified with the antiwar movement; graduating in 1965, he was a little too old and too interested in electoral politics. "You're looking at a middle-class guy. I am who I am," he once quipped. "I'm not big on flak jackets and tie-dye shirts and—you know, that's not me."[10]

In the mid-1970s Biden participated in the congressional efforts to investigate the CIA and get it under outside control. A few years later, however, as the country was shifting to the right, he served notice at a Senate hearing that it was time to lay off. "The momentum is moving the other way," Biden told representatives of the American Civil Liberties Union. Yes, he agreed with their views, Biden said, but the issue of writing rules for the CIA did not have the same sort of popular appeal as opposing the Vietnam War.

"Let me tell you something, fellas," Biden declared. "The folks don't care. The average American could care less right now about any of this. . . . You keep talking about public concern. There ain't none."[11]

Intellectually, the Democrats were in ferment after Vietnam. The question was what they should say about America's future role in the world. On the political left, critics argued that liberalism was bankrupt, that America had become a national security state and that its economy depended on the continuing threat of war. Liberals were merely "the fig leaf for imperialism," wrote Marcus Raskin of the Institute for Policy Studies, the Washington organization that served as a home base for radical critiques of American foreign policy during and immediately after the Vietnam War.[12]

In the summer of 1976, Richard Holbrooke attempted to respond in an article in the journal *Foreign Policy*, for which he was the managing editor. Holbrooke's piece was entitled "A Sense of Drift, a Time for Calm." Holbrooke summarily rejected many of the ideas set forth in George McGovern's 1972 campaign. He denounced what he called "the Vietnam-based, guilt-ridden anguish of the left." The left-wing critique of the United States "is a cul-de-sac, a dead end, which could lead to isolation from the rest of the nation," Holbrooke asserted. He was particularly troubled by the belief "that because America has done some evil things, America itself is an evil force in the world."[13]

Holbrooke similarly dismissed the idea that America was in decline. He emphasized America's underlying strengths. "We remain, by a considerable margin, the most powerful nation on earth militarily," he observed. Its economic importance to the international economy might be relatively less than it had been after the end of World War II, but the United States still remained the world's economic leader. As for the Soviet Union, its power was overestimated. "History does not favor the Russians," wrote Holbrooke, with considerable prescience at a time when conservatives were raising alarms about growing Soviet power. He also dismissed the notion that the two superpowers, the United States and the Soviet Union, were equally on the wane. "I suspect that the differences between the two systems are so vast that they will respond differently to future challenges," Holbrooke observed.[14]

Holbrooke was attempting to speak for a new generation of centrist Democrats. The war had tarnished the reputations of the party elders who had run foreign policy in the Kennedy and Johnson administrations, such as Dean Rusk, Robert McNamara, McGeorge Bundy and Walter Rostow, the central characters in David Halberstam's bestseller *The Best and the Brightest*.

Foreign Policy, launched in 1970, became a vehicle for views that differed from those of the old foreign policy establishment. The leading writers included a group of men who would spend their careers switching between making government policy and writing about it: Anthony Lake, Leslie Gelb, Zbigniew Brzezinski, Joseph Nye, C. Fred Bergsten as well as Holbrooke, who began to run the magazine in 1972.[15]

Holbrooke's own role within the Democratic Party was a contradictory one: He was both a courtier to the old guard and careful challenger to it. He was intensely attracted to elites and the power they held, to fame and the journalists who could create it. As a young Foreign Service officer, Holbrooke had worked under Averell Harriman at the Paris peace talks aimed at ending the Vietnam War. He had grown up in Scarsdale, New York, next door to Dean Rusk, who eventually became the secretary of state for Kennedy and Johnson. Years later, when Clark Clifford, the Democratic elder from the Truman era, decided to write his memoir, he chose Holbrooke as his coauthor. Holbrooke did not seek to hide his ties to the old Democratic establishment; he boasted of them.

Yet Holbrooke had also served in Vietnam, saw the war go wrong there and forged close connections to other liberals disaffected with the war such as Lake, a former aide to Henry Kissinger, and Gelb, who had written the Pentagon Papers, the secret Defense Department study of the history of America's involvement in Vietnam. This group of Democrats accepted that American power still was, or at least could be, a force for good in the world. Lake dismissed the ideas of those on the left who believed that the United States was "inherently incapable of progressive action abroad."[16]

———

Quite a few of the ideas voiced by Obama, Hillary Clinton and other Democratic leaders today date back to this period of ferment in the 1970s. Today's leaders tend to believe their ideas are new and original, a response to events or trends of the twenty-first century, when in fact they were first aired by this group of liberal Democrats in the aftermath of Vietnam.

One was the idea of America's interdependence with other nations. This is often portrayed as a recent development. But in a 1976 book called *The Vietnam Legacy*, Anthony Lake—who would three decades later become Obama's first senior adviser on foreign policy—wrote: "Perhaps the greatest challenge to American foreign policy makers in the next generation will be to find constructive ways in which to cooperate with other nations at 'managing interdependence'—not only interdependence on security issues, but interdependence on questions of economic and ecological survival."[17]

Another was the idea of America as the "indispensable nation." Hillary Clinton used this phrase as Obama's secretary of state, explicitly borrowing the words used in the 1990s by Bill Clinton and his secretary of state Madeleine Albright. But the words didn't originate with them, either. In a 1976 article in *Foreign Policy*, Brzezinski wrote of "America the indispensable." Despite its defeat in Vietnam, he argued, American power remains "central to global stability and progress."[18]

During that period, Brzezinski argued that the United States should start to give a much higher priority to its relationship with its allies. He proposed "trilateral cooperation" among the United States, Western Europe and Japan. David Rockefeller, the chairman of Chase Manhattan Bank, took up the idea, and Brzezinski became the first director of a new Trilateral Commission, which sponsored regular exchanges among American, European and Japanese officials. One of its early members was the new governor of Georgia, Jimmy Carter, who had been seeking to develop trade for his state with Western Europe and Japan. Brzezinski had been looking for a "forward-leaning Democratic governor" to join the Trilateral Commission. When Carter said he was interested, Brzezinski told associates, "He's obviously our man." When Carter began to seek the Democratic presidential nomination in 1976, Brzezinski emerged as his leading adviser.[19]

That fall, after winning the Democratic nomination, Carter held a televised debate with President Gerald Ford. Holbrooke was in charge of preparing the briefing book for him. "Go back to domestic affairs time and again," the briefing book said. "We cannot be strong abroad if we are weak at home." That, too, became a frequent refrain for future Democratic leaders, especially Barack Obama.[20]

––––––––––

Carter was a one-term president who took over amid great hopes, but eventually became a symbol of American frustration. He did manage to achieve several noteworthy breakthroughs: He negotiated a Middle East peace agreement between Israel and Egypt, he established diplomatic relations with China and he won Senate approval of a Panama Canal treaty. Nevertheless,

Carter's final years in office saddled the Democrats with an image of ineffectiveness that would plague the party for years.

Inflation and interest rates in the United States shot up to 18 percent, largely as a result of increases in the cost of oil. Gas shortages forced Americans to wait in long lines to refuel their cars. In Tehran, the Shah fled the country. In November 1979, Iranian students and other radicals seized the U.S. embassy, where they captured and held more than fifty American hostages. Carter organized a rescue mission to try to free them, but it failed miserably.

Carter had managed to sound hawkish about the Cold War during his campaign, suggesting that the Ford administration was being naive. "We will not accept détente where the Soviets set the rules and define the priorities," he said.[21] With words like those, he had managed to win the support of more conservative Democrats. In the early years of his presidency, however, Carter pursued mostly conciliatory policies toward Moscow, in line with the views of his secretary of state Cyrus Vance, who made arms control his highest priority.

When the Soviets sent tens of thousands of troops into Afghanistan in December 1979, Carter adopted a far more confrontational Soviet policy, in line with the views of Brzezinski, his national security adviser. He approved new limits on technology sales to the Soviets, embargoed grain shipments, ordered covert action to support Afghan resistance groups, approved a new American military relationship with China, ordered a boycott of U.S. participation in the Moscow Olympics, asked for an increase in defense spending and declared the Persian Gulf a region of vital interest to the United States.

The result was a paradox: These retaliatory measures came too late in Carter's term to change perceptions of him as weak, but they also were strong enough to infuriate the Soviets. By the last year of Carter's term, recalled Anatoly Dobrynin, the Soviet ambassador to Washington, "Moscow so mistrusted Carter that it could not bring itself to support him even against Ronald Reagan."[22]

One of Washington's most determined Cold Warriors of that era, Robert Gates, argued later that Carter's Soviet policies were tougher than they were perceived to be. In a memoir published in 1996, Gates wrote that historians and political observers "have failed to appreciate the importance of Jimmy Carter's contribution to the collapse of the Soviet Union and the end of the Cold War." In fact, Gates said, Reagan's supposedly tough policies toward the Soviet Union merely built upon what Carter had started. "He [Carter] took the first steps to strip away the mask of Soviet ascendancy and exploit the reality of Soviet vulnerability," recalled Gates.[23]

Carter also left one other legacy that would have considerable impact on later presidents, particularly Democratic ones: his recognition of and intermittent emphasis on human rights as a legitimate element in American foreign policy. The idea didn't start with Carter, but with Democrats in Congress. During the Nixon and Ford administrations, Congressman Donald Fraser led the way in arguing that the U.S. government turned a blind eye to torture and intimidation of dissent by right-wing dictators like Ferdinand Marcos in the Philippines or the Shah of Iran because these leaders were allied with the United States against the Soviet Union. At the same time, more conservative Democrats charged that the Nixon and Ford administrations were too tolerant of political repression in the Soviet Union and Eastern Europe. Carter managed to win support from these disparate groups of Democrats by invoking the cause of human rights against both right-wing dictators and communist regimes.

The human rights policy was Carter's attempt to deal with some of the same problems that Obama would confront as president: the need to regain America's standing overseas in the wake of an unpopular war. Writing in 1978, Arthur Schlesinger Jr. argued that Carter's human rights policy "promised to restore America's international moral position, so sadly eroded by Vietnam, Watergate, support of dictatorships, CIA assassination plots, etc."[24] Carter sought to do so through his policies; Obama has relied more heavily on his own biography and his record of opposition to the war in Iraq.

———

Eventually, Carter's attempts to hold the Democratic Party together failed. The internal disagreements over Vietnam and the Cold War overwhelmed the party. Carter tried to come up with words, formulas and policies that would appeal both to liberals and to the more conservative Democrats who had supported Senators Hubert Humphrey and Henry "Scoop" Jackson, the most important leaders in the center and right wings of the party. (By this

time, most of those Democrats were clearly labeling themselves neoconservatives, thus differentiating themselves from the traditional conservatives in
the Republican Party.)

In 1976, these neoconservative Democrats lined up behind Carter. "We
didn't know what Jimmy Carter was going to be like," recalled Jeane Kirkpatrick, who had worked for both Humphrey and Jackson, in an interview
many years later. "He was from the Naval Academy, a businessman, all these
conservative symbols. So we couldn't say, 'Let's desert the party.'"[25] Once
Carter was in office, however, the neoconservatives complained that he repeatedly sided with the liberals and slighted their own views. The Democratic hawks were upset when Carter, in one of his early speeches, spoke of
an "inordinate fear of communism." Carter's appointments in foreign policy
were mostly from the center-to-liberal wing of the party; Holbrooke, Lake
and Gelb all went to work as senior aides to Secretary of State Cyrus Vance.
The neoconservatives gave the Carter team a list of names for possible appointments, but few of the suggestions were accepted.[26]

Over the course of the Carter administration, these Jackson-Humphrey
neoconservatives gradually abandoned the Democratic Party on foreign policy issues and found common cause with the Republicans. The leader in this
effort was Kirkpatrick. Writing in *Commentary*, the neoconservatives' counterpart to *Foreign Policy*, Kirkpatrick castigated Carter for undermining the
Shah of Iran (so she argued) by pushing him too hard to open up and liberal-
ize his regime. "A great weakness of liberal Democrats is that they don't learn
enough about the societies in which they operate before they set about dis-
mantling what is, and trying to encourage people to do something very different," wrote Kirkpatrick.[27] She maintained that the Carter administration
had pushed too vigorously for democratic change in a country that wasn't
ready for it. Ironically, this was essentially the same criticism that Democrats
would make in reverse about George W. Bush a quarter century later.

One reader of Kirkpatrick's article was Ronald Reagan, then preparing
to run for president again. He and his staff began to court her support, and
in 1980 she became the first neoconservative to endorse Ronald Reagan.
Other neoconservatives soon followed her. The Reagan campaign thus managed to bring together two groups of conservatives: the former supporters of

Barry Goldwater in the Republican Party and the former supporters of Humphrey and Jackson from the Democratic Party. The two groups often disagreed on what should happen at home, but shared similar visions of what America should do overseas, particularly during the Cold War.

The Carter administration also ran afoul of the military and intelligence communities in ways both substantive and symbolic. They were not accustomed to the reduced stature they were accorded in the years after Vietnam. General James Jones, who became Obama's first national security adviser, recalled with bitterness how he was required to wear civilian clothes when he worked as a lobbyist for the Marine Corps on Capitol Hill. In the Carter era, Jones reflected, "there was definitely a de-emphasis on wearing uniforms."[28] Both military and intelligence officials were rankled by Carter's efforts to cut their budgets and staff. The failure of the mission to free the hostages in Iran was viewed as a symbol of the low state to which the American armed forces had fallen after Vietnam. "On the whole, the vibrations coming out of the Carter White House were not comforting to the military profession," wrote Colin Powell, who served in the Pentagon under Carter. Although Powell considered himself nonpartisan, he admitted that he voted for Reagan, and he later became Reagan's national security adviser.[29]

This aspect of Carter's legacy meant that both Bill Clinton and Barack Obama, his two Democratic successors, often found themselves on the defensive in dealing with the military and the intelligence communities. Both were more careful and deferential than Carter had been. Both of them sought to install military officers in senior foreign policy jobs. Clinton tried to recruit Powell as his secretary of state; Obama gave top positions to several former military leaders.

When Reagan defeated Carter, the Democrats left the White House hoping to return quickly. Instead, they stayed out of power for twelve years, their longest period out of office since the similar twelve-year hiatus between Woodrow Wilson and Franklin Roosevelt.

———

With the migration of the neoconservatives to Reagan, the Democratic Party was firmly in the control of the liberals. There was less intraparty skirmishing than in the 1970s; the real policy disputes were now between, not within, America's two political parties. But the Democrats had to figure out how to win a presidential election again.

At one point in the middle of the decade, Joe Biden, who was then lining up to run for the 1988 Democratic presidential nomination, aptly summarized the obstacles the party faced. Biden was courting the liberal wing of the party, but he also argued that the Democrats needed to shake off a sense of drift and paralysis in foreign policy caused by its reaction to Vietnam. "The American people have grave doubts about the Republicans' lack of diplomacy, but they have grave doubts about the Democrats' willingness to back diplomacy with power," Biden told a conference of Democratic officials in 1986. "People think the Republicans are too tough but not very smart, and the Democrats are not tough enough."[30]

More than any other Democrat, Gary Hart, who ran unsuccessfully for president in both 1984 and 1988, tried to show that liberal Democrats of the post-Vietnam era cared about military issues and strong national defense. Hart had served as George McGovern's campaign manager in 1972 and went on to win a Senate seat in Colorado. On the Senate Armed Services Committee, he espoused the cause of military reform. He put himself forward as someone who knew how to make the Pentagon run more efficiently and how to buy weapons systems more cheaply. With this message, Hart could criticize the defense budget as wasteful, thus appealing to traditional liberals, and yet not sound as though he was simply opposed to the military or to the use of force.

"Gary came out of the McGovern world, where there was this deep mistrust of American power," recalled Will Marshall, a Democratic specialist on national security who was himself more hawkish than Hart. "His campaign was the first sign that the old politics of Democratic liberalism was eroding, and that there needed to be a new challenge to the traditional thinking about national security."[31]

In the late 1980s, Marshall and other moderate-to-conservative Democrats posted a new challenge to the liberal wing of the party. Analyzing the party's continuing losses, they decided that voters perceived the Democrats as hostile to mainstream values, quick to question America's motives overseas and reflexively averse to the use of military force.

Seeking to reverse these perceptions, they formed the Democratic Leadership Council, a new centrist organization within the party. Its members included a number of elected political leaders—most of them moderate-to-conservative Democrats who came from areas outside the Northeast and the West Coast, the traditional homes of Democratic liberalism. Among the early participants were the ambitious young governor of Arkansas, Bill Clinton, and the then hawkish Democratic senator from Tennessee, Al Gore.

"These were people who felt the Democrats' weakness on national defense was a real albatross when they had to go run for governor or senator," Marshall explained.[32] The DLC advocated strong support for the U.S. armed forces and an active role for the United States overseas. The organization soon became the driving force for those who sought to pull the Democratic Party back toward a more assertive foreign policy.

Liberal Democrats, meanwhile, waged several foreign policy battles against Reagan and his successor, George H. W. Bush, though with only middling success. The first, in the early 1980s, was the nuclear freeze movement, a drive to require both the United States and the Soviet Union to stop producing, deploying or testing nuclear weapons.

The freeze movement attracted extraordinary support from the grass roots, particularly on college campuses. One sympathizer was a Columbia University student named Barack Obama. Writing for a campus publication called the *Sundial*, Obama praised the efforts of the freeze movement. "By organizing and educating the Columbia community, such activities lay the foundation for future mobilization against the relentless, often silent spread of militarism in the country," Obama asserted.[33]

It was his first expression of his views on any foreign policy subject, and years later, his aides felt it was deeply felt and lasting. "The nuclear issue is really important to his background," observed Michael McFaul, who served first on Obama's National Security Council and then as his ambassador to Russia. In dealing with Russia, Obama gave considerably higher priority to nuclear issues than to the regime's steady weakening of political opposition. "He thinks you need a new START [arms control] treaty, no matter whether the Russians are a democracy or an autocracy, because these are dangerous weapons and we've got to control them—and in a way, that's a legacy from this 1980s era," said McFaul.

For a time, the movement was so powerful that Reagan went to extraordinary lengths to combat it. (The speech in which Reagan condemned the Soviet Union as the "Evil Empire" was delivered in 1983 as part of an attack on the idea of a nuclear freeze.) The results of this political skirmish were ironic and surprising. The antinuclear demonstrations eventually subsided, but the movement had a clear impact on Reagan himself. In 1984, Reagan began to change his rhetoric about the Soviet Union, and during his second term Reagan came out for dramatic reductions or even possible elimination of the Soviet and American stockpiles of nuclear weapons. Reagan's diplomacy took the steam out of the antinuclear movement, but through it the proponents of the freeze succeeded in getting some of what they had wanted from the outset.

After the end of the Cold War, the Democrats posed a new challenge to the Bush administration over the size of the defense budget. Within weeks after the Berlin Wall came down, Democratic leaders began suggesting that there should be what they called a "peace dividend," a transfer of money from the defense budget to pressing domestic problems.

"The choice of reducing our deficit, inoculating our children against disease and repairing our bridges and roads versus sending large sums to subsidize Japan and Europe should be an easy one," said Congressman Barney Frank.[34] But the peace dividend was far less than the Democrats wanted. The Democratic challenge prompted the Pentagon's top two leaders, Defense Secretary Dick Cheney and Chairman of the Joint Chiefs of Staff Colin Powell, who did not always see eye to eye, to unite in protecting the Pentagon from budget cuts.

One of the Democratic leaders in this search for a peace dividend was the chairman of the House Budget Committee, Leon Panetta of California. Ironically, two decades later, Panetta would emerge as defense secretary in the Obama administration, where he found himself warning regularly of the dangers of cutting the defense budget too much.

————

The Persian Gulf War, which most of the congressional Democrats determinedly opposed, became the last and, in some ways, the most significant foreign policy dispute between the two parties in the Reagan-Bush years. When Saddam Hussein sent Iraqi troops into Kuwait in August 1990, the

Bush administration sought authorization from Congress for the use of force to reverse the invasion. The request resulted in close votes that Bush won with mostly Republican support. In the Senate, only 10 out of 56 Democratic members voted to authorize the use of force; in the House, only 86 of 267 Democrats were in favor. The debate on Capitol Hill made clear that most Democrats still held to the core beliefs that had dominated the thinking of the liberal wing of the party since Vietnam. The Democrats exhibited a deep aversion to the use of force, even for the purpose of repelling one country's invasion of another.

"Personally, and I can speak for many members of our caucus, we are products of the Vietnam experience," said Representative Dick Durbin of Illinois. "We are really touched by the possibility that we may be repeating that experience."[35]

"The president says he's angry and impatient, but, God bless him, so are all of us. But is that a reason to send a whole generation to war?" asked Biden in the Senate debate. "The price is in body bags, in babies killed," said Barbara Boxer, then a member of the House of Representatives.[36]

At the time, the Democrats underestimated America's military capabilities and greatly overestimated the casualties that might result from a military campaign against Iraq. At one point, George Mitchell, the Senate majority leader, and House Speaker Tom Foley handed Bush a letter signed by eighty-one Democrats that contained a dire prediction: "We believe that the consequences [of military action against Iraq] would be catastrophic—resulting in the massive loss of lives, including 10,000–50,000 Americans."

Senator Edward Kennedy spoke of the need to "save thousands of American soldiers in the Persian Gulf from dying in the desert." More precisely, said Kennedy at another point, "we're talking about the likelihood of at least 3,000 American casualties a week, with 700 dead, for as long as the war goes on."[37] A handful of prominent Democrats decided to support the war, including Al Gore. But most of the party's most prominent figures voted against authorizing the use of force: Kennedy, Mitchell, Biden, Kerry and even Sam Nunn, the chairman of the Senate Armed Services Committee, a more conservative Democrat known for his expertise on defense issues.

Bush proceeded to assemble a broad coalition of forces from more than thirty other countries: not just Britain and France, but Egypt and even Syria.

The military campaign was quick and decisive. After an initial air campaign that employed new American technology, ground troops moved against Iraqi forces on February 23, 1991. The ground war lasted only one hundred hours before the Iraqi forces were in hopeless disarray and U.S. officials declared a cease-fire. The casualty figures were a mere fraction of what the Democrats had predicted: About 150 Americans died in combat and approximately the same number in noncombat accidents.

———

For the Democrats, the legacy of the Gulf War was profound. Their votes against the war served to fix their image as a party instinctively opposed to the use of force, no matter what the reason might be. Their fears of heavy casualties turned out to be exaggerated. Many Democrats were determined not to repeat the same mistake. More than a decade later, in 2002, George W. Bush asked Congress to approve the use of force once again against Iraq. The second time, the Democrats would go along. Once again, they found themselves overly focused on the last war, not the one at hand. At the time of the Gulf War, they had been too influenced by Vietnam; at the time of George W. Bush's Iraq War, they were thinking too much about their votes on the Gulf War. It would take Barack Obama to set them straight.

The Gulf War marked the end of an era. After nearly two decades, the post-Vietnam era was drawing to a close. The Democrats gradually began to rethink their views about the use of force and about America's role in the world. They had some time to do so, because with the collapse of the Soviet Union, the United States was the world's sole superpower. In the presidential election of 1992, national security was no longer the overriding issue it had been during the Cold War. Bill Clinton defeated George H. W. Bush and took office determined not to let foreign policy take up too much of his time.

2

"I'm Running Out of Demons"

B ill Clinton set the stage for Barack Obama. Both men took office determined to revive the American economy and, meanwhile, to adopt a
more modest role for the United States overseas. In both the Clinton and
Obama administrations, the Democrats grappled with questions of whether,
when and how to use military force. Obama followed Clinton's path in opting, after considerable hesitation, to send American troops into conflict for
the purpose of preventing the slaughter of civilians.

There were, however, striking differences between the two men and their
administrations, above all in the greatly different performance of the American economy during their time in office. Clinton governed in times that
were increasingly prosperous. Not coincidentally, as time went on, his foreign policy became increasingly assertive until, by the time he left office, he
seemed comfortable to have America take on a revised version of its old role
as superpower—the "indispensable nation," as he called it. Obama became
president in the midst of a financial crisis and spent most of his term trying
to restore the increasingly troubled American economy. As a result, Obama
sought to carve out a less assertive role for the United States, one in which it
occasionally demonstrated its continuing power and sought to preserve a
leadership role in the world, but relied far more on the support of other
countries. To understand the distinctive nature of the Obama administration, one has to understand how differently Clinton and the Democrats acted
and viewed American power in the 1990s.

In the decade after the Persian Gulf War, a swaggering new verb gradually
crept into the argot of American foreign policy: "to whack." It was used to
connote a quick, almost casual application of American military power,

aimed at bringing a recalcitrant country or its leader back into line—a demonstration of force, as if from a parent to an unruly child. When talking about the ruler of a problematic country such as Iraq or Yugoslavia or North Korea or Haiti, American officials, foreign policy experts and journalists would sometimes ask, "Do you think we're going to have to whack him?"

The word found its way from private conversations into congressional debates and the news media. Saddam Hussein was the leader Americans most often talked about whacking. A *New York Times* editorial during the 1992 presidential campaign said that President George H. W. Bush was "casting for a way to whack Iraq and boost his own political fortunes." Congressman Henry Hyde agreed. "I don't think Bush would hesitate to whack him," he said. In 1994, *Time* magazine asked: "Why not whack Saddam and be done with him?" Near the end of the 1990s, a Pentagon spokesman said of Saddam: "We whack him day after day in response to his challenges, and then he pulls back and goes down for a period and does nothing, and then he comes back up."[1]

"Whack" was distinctly a time-bound expression of the 1990s. The word would have made little sense during the Cold War, when there were two superpowers and Americans worried that any conflict, however minor, could lead to a much larger war. (No one talked of "whacking" Kim Il-sung in Korea or Ho Chi Minh in Vietnam, whether before, during or after the wars fought against them.) Nor would the verb "whack" survive too long past the 1990s. After the war in Iraq in 2003, the word seemed to disappear again. Americans gradually abandoned the language suggesting that military intervention would be quick, easy or cost-free.

———

The historic events of 1989 to 1991 had challenged many of the assumptions that liberal Democrats had held since Vietnam. Many had believed that American power was in decline, but with the collapse of the Soviet Union, the United States was left as the world's sole superpower. The far left had viewed American power and ideals as fundamentally malevolent, and liberal Democrats worried that the United States, while not inherently evil, was not a force for good, either. Yet after the fall of the Berlin Wall, Americans witnessed millions of people across Eastern Europe cheering for freedom and democracy. At the grass roots, Democrats instinctively opposed the use of force as dangerous or immoral; yet the Gulf War showed that military power could be both surprisingly successful and, indeed, popular enough to win public support.

Clinton was not himself from the liberal wing of the party. Although he had worked for George McGovern's campaign as a student, he quickly moved to the center once he started running for office. In 1990, he became chairman of the Democratic Leadership Council, the organization set up to counter the progressive wing of the party. Still, Clinton understandably spent most of his time not on foreign policy but on the domestic issues that interested him as governor of Arkansas.

Clinton avoided taking a position in the run-up to the Gulf War. Even after the war, during his 1992 campaign, he straddled the issue in the fashion that became a Clinton trademark; he said that if he had been in Congress he would have voted to authorize the war, but he also agreed with the liberal Democrats that Bush should have given more time for economic sanctions to work before launching military action.[2]

Clinton managed to attract back to the party some of the neoconservatives who had supported or worked for Ronald Reagan. The neoconservatives never liked Reagan's successor, George H. W. Bush. As a candidate, Clinton appealed to neoconservatives by speaking forthrightly of the importance of democratic values and attacking Bush for his foreign policy of realism. Indeed, one of the striking features of the 1990s, in retrospect, was that the neoconservatives frequently supported Clinton and were at odds with most of the congressional Republicans, who sought to avoid American entanglements overseas.

In Clinton's speech accepting the Democratic nomination, he promised "an America that will not coddle dictators from Baghdad to Beijing." (His mention of Baghdad referred to the U.S. policy during the 1980s of giving economic help to Saddam Hussein's Iraq in order to help strengthen it against Iran.) Clinton also upbraided Bush for doing too little to help keep the peace in Bosnia; he argued that the United States should ask for United Nations authorization to bomb Serbian targets there. At the peak of the fall campaign, Clinton charged that Bush "simply does not seem at home in the mainstream prodemocracy tradition in American foreign policy."[3] Thus, the Clinton campaign managed to get the support of all the disparate factions of the Democratic Party in foreign policy: antiwar liberals, centrist Democrats from the South and Midwest, and returning neoconservatives. All of them were eager to unseat Bush.

Yet foreign policy was not a significant factor in the election. Clinton's victory was nothing like, say, Reagan's in 1980 or Obama's in 2008, in which America's relationship with the world was a major issue. The lasting phrase from that election year was the Clinton campaign slogan, "It's the economy, stupid," which certainly implied that "it" wasn't foreign policy.

By 1992, the United States was less worried about national security than it had been for decades. "I'm running out of demons. I'm running out of villains," joked Colin Powell, then chairman of the Joint Chiefs of Staff, after the end of the Gulf War. "I'm down to Castro and Kim Il-sung."[4] The polls sometimes showed that on national security issues, there was still some lingering public uneasiness with the Democrats. Nevertheless, Americans felt secure enough in the world to give priority to the domestic economy and to elect Clinton.

———

The Democrats had been out of the White House for twelve years. They did not have a long list of people ready to take over the cabinet-level jobs. Clinton's first secretary of state was Warren Christopher, the deputy secretary in the Carter administration. The job of national security adviser went to Tony Lake, the director of policy planning in Carter's State Department.

The two men found themselves dealing with different issues and a changed world from the Carter years. After the Gulf War, America's military strength was taken for granted. The question that kept coming up was whether to use it in conflicts overseas that, no matter how serious, did not threaten the fundamental security of the United States. At Christopher's nomination hearing, he said he believed in the "discreet and careful" use of military force to maintain America's role as a world power. Those words were aimed at dispelling portrayals of him as someone whose skills lay primarily as a quiet negotiator. Yet Christopher went on to tell Congress that there were limits to what the U.S. military could do. "We cannot respond ourselves to every alarm," he said.[5]

Four months after Clinton took office, Peter Tarnoff, the new undersecretary of state, aroused a furor by declaring that the United States would no longer play the same leadership role in the world as it had during the Cold War. "It is necessary to make the point that our economic interests are paramount," said Tarnoff. "We simply don't have the leverage, we don't have the influence, the inclination to use military force. We don't have the money to bring about positive results any time soon."[6]

Clinton had already made clear that his administration's top priority was to revive the American economy, and Tarnoff was trying to describe a foreign policy in line with the new president. However, his words managed to touch on the sensitive issue of decline: whether the United States could afford to play the same dominant role in international affairs as it had in the past. The Clinton White House hurriedly disavowed Tarnoff's remarks, saying the United States would not retreat from its role as world leader.

It was a brief but revealing exchange: Tarnoff seemed to be suggesting that the United States would henceforth be merely one country among many, taking care of its own "paramount" interests rather than serving as the underwriter of global security. Even Obama, nearly two decades later and in the midst of dire economic times, was not willing to go that far.

One of the earliest critics of Clinton's foreign policy was Senator Joseph Biden. From his position on the Senate Foreign Relations Committee, Biden became a staunch proponent of U.S. military intervention in Bosnia to deter Bosnian Serbs from their campaigns of "ethnic cleansing" against Muslims. Three months after Clinton was sworn in, Biden upbraided the administration for not doing "a damn thing" to stop the Serbs from bombarding women and children in the Bosnian town of Srebrenica. Biden called for air strikes by the United States and its NATO allies. Other liberals in Congress, such as Senator Paul Simon, voiced similar sentiments.[7]

They were the vanguard of change for the Democrats. In the 1990s, Bosnia became a bellwether issue, gradually prompting liberals to offer new views on the use of force. As Biden demonstrated, some of the liberals who had opposed the use of force in the Persian Gulf were willing to support military intervention for the humanitarian purpose of preventing genocide in the Balkans. America was now viewed as, potentially, a force for good in the world, if only it had the will to act.

Although Clinton had taken a strong campaign position on Bosnia, after he became president he held off for a long time on military intervention. Powell, as the senior American military leader, argued repeatedly in opposition. It was during the early deliberations over what to do about Bosnia that Madeleine Albright, then Clinton's ambassador to the United Nations, famously asked Powell, "What's the point of having this superb military that you're always talking about if we can't use it?"[8] America's European allies did not support U.S. military action in Bosnia, either, because they worried that American air strikes could jeopardize their own peacekeeping forces on the ground. In the face of this opposition, Clinton wavered.

Meanwhile, questions about the wisdom of military intervention kept coming up elsewhere. In Somalia, the administration inherited and then extended a mission where American forces were used to help protect food shipments. But in October 1993, eighteen American servicemen were killed as they were trapped in Mogadishu, and Clinton quickly announced that he was pulling out the troops. In Haiti, Clinton succeeded in restoring an elected president to office only by dispatching what would have been an invasion force of 20,000 American troops. As these forces were in the air and on the way, Haiti's military junta finally gave up power.

In one notable instance, the Clinton administration simply sat on its hands. In the spring of 1994, militias in Rwanda conducted a rampage of mass murders in which hundreds of thousands of people were killed. The Clinton administration never seriously contemplated sending troops to stop the slaughter. In all these places, Clinton was worried about the public reaction to sending troops on humanitarian missions. Before he decided to send troops to Haiti, he grumbled to his old friend Taylor Branch, "This is a sack of shit."[9]

Eventually, in the summer of 1995, events in Bosnia forced Clinton's hand. Serb forces captured the Bosnian town of Srebrenica, rounded up the Muslims, set up firing squads and killed the men and boys. The Clinton administration quickly won NATO approval to launch air strikes against the Serbs, until Yugoslavian president Slobodan Milosevic and other parties agreed to come to peace talks.

———

Throughout this period, the Clinton administration was struggling to come up with the right words to explain America's strategy in dealing with the world after the Cold War. What was the underlying rationale? Tarnoff's controversial remarks offered one early formulation: The United States would no longer seek to maintain a leadership role. That idea was quickly disavowed; it would have been too jarring a change for the American public, for Congress, for foreign policy agencies like the Pentagon and CIA or, for that matter, for allies and friends (in NATO, Japan and the Middle East, for example) who were accustomed to American leadership.

In the fall of 1993, Lake offered a new concept: In the wake of the Soviet collapse, America's strategy would be one of "democratic enlargement"—to seek to expand "the world's free community of market democracies." But this idea failed to gain traction, in part because the word "enlargement" seemed so awkward. Albright offered another phrase: America's policy would be based on "assertive multilateralism." All these early efforts conveyed a more active role for the United States than the one originally suggested by Tarnoff.[10]

Finally, near the end of Clinton's first term, the administration came up with a phrase that stuck. During his campaign for reelection and again in the inaugural address for his second term, Clinton referred to the United States as the world's "indispensable nation." America, with its economic and military power, would help to resolve conflicts throughout the world; without the United States, the international order might fall apart. Albright took up and repeated these words when Clinton appointed her secretary of state, so often that they were later associated with her name.[11]

The idea of an "indispensable nation" laid out a strikingly active role for the United States. The phrase described both the existing state of affairs and the way things should be in the future: America would remain the world's leading power. It would not scale back its overseas presence and involvements, leaving it to other nations to handle international conflicts like Bosnia, as some of Clinton's Republican critics in Congress had urged. America would maintain its military bases, its overseas troop deployments, its willingness to dispatch American forces to places such as Panama and Kuwait, Haiti and Bosnia, Somalia and Kosovo. The United States would maintain its leading role in the world economic system, too.

Moreover, as the world's "indispensable nation" the United States would make its own decisions: It would not subordinate its policies to the United

Nations. America would try to work in concert with other countries, but, ultimately, it was up to the indispensable nation to decide what kind of military or economic power should be dispensed and to whom. "When our national security interests are threatened," said Clinton, "we will act with others when we can, but alone if we must. We will use diplomacy when we can, but force if we must."[12]

———

In late 1995, the Clinton administration sponsored a series of talks in Dayton that ended the Bosnian civil war. Clinton assigned the job of lead negotiator to Richard Holbrooke, whose brash style made him the right person to deal with Yugoslavian dictator Slobodan Milosevic and other leaders involved in the multifaceted conflict. "After all, everyone in the Balkans is crazy and everyone has a giant ego. Who else could you send?" joked Clinton afterward. Holbrooke was eager for the role, with all its drama and responsibility. As Holbrooke's old friend author David Halberstam later wrote:

> Holbrooke wanted the job for the most basic reason: it was the ultimate professional test. You were the man of the hour, all the attention was focused on you. Could you bring it off?[13]

After three weeks of frenetic diplomacy, Holbrooke succeeded in getting a peace settlement that ended the conflict. Yet within three years, another part of the Balkans was in turmoil: Serbian forces had begun a new round of ethnic cleansing campaigns against Albanians in Kosovo. This time, Clinton moved more quickly. In the spring of 1999, NATO forces carried out a series of air attacks on Serbian targets, including heavy bombardment of Belgrade, until, after nearly three months, Milosevic relented and accepted NATO's terms for peace.

Clinton's handling of Kosovo exhibited the distinctive characteristics of the Democrats' new approach to the world in the final years of the twentieth century. First, there was far less hesitation about the use of force, even overwhelming force, on behalf of causes deemed to be worthy. The targets were dictators who carried out campaigns of repression or were otherwise judged to have violated the international order. When Milosevic refused to back down in Kosovo, the Clinton administration sent Holbrooke to Belgrade to warn the Yugoslav president that the NATO bombing campaign he was about to witness "will be swift, it will be severe, and it will be sustained."[14] Milosevic was not the sole target of American military power. Three times in eight years, the Clinton administration took military action against Saddam Hussein in Iraq, though without mounting a full-scale invasion.

Secondly, the Clinton administration did not always seek approval of the United Nations for the use of force, as the elder Bush had before the Gulf War. The United States could not have won a vote at the UN Security Council, because the Russians would have cast a veto; they strongly opposed the use of force against Milosevic. Instead, military decisions were left in the hands of NATO—that is, the United States and its European allies. The Europeans themselves were increasingly divided. When Clinton bombed Iraq in December 1998, British prime minister Tony Blair supported him, but other European governments did not.

Thirdly, the Clinton administration generally relied upon one particular kind of military action: airpower, without the use of ground forces, in such a way as to minimize the risk of American casualties. Clinton wanted no more "Black Hawk Down" incidents where American troops might be attacked on the ground as they had been in Somalia.

Clinton's weapon of choice was often the cruise missile, which was used against Iraq and Serbia, as well as Sudan and Afghanistan, where, in 1998, the administration sought to retaliate for terrorist attacks by al-Qaeda. "If history offered a precursor to the use of air power during the Clinton era, it was Lyndon Johnson's bombing of North Vietnam, informed by vintage-1960s strategic theories positing the calibrated application of force to punish, draw lines, signal and negotiate," wrote one critic, the military specialist Andrew Bacevich.[15]

Adversaries like Milosevic recognized this fact and took it into their calculations. On the day Clinton started bombing Kosovo, he put out a statement saying, "I do not intend to put our troops in Kosovo to start a war." Later on, administration officials admitted this might have been a mistake; it seemed to encourage Milosevic to hold out against the air attacks simply by withstanding the punishment and keeping control on the ground. Clinton's aides originally thought it would take only a few days of bombing before Milosevic would give up. Instead, it took several months.[16]

Clinton's handling of Bosnia and Kosovo would serve as the backdrop for Obama's use of force in Libya. In both cases, liberals took the lead in calling for humanitarian intervention, and in both instances, military leaders initially opposed the use of force on grounds that there was no American strategic interest. In both cases, American presidents relied on airpower and made clear that the United States would not put troops on the ground. Both times, the opposing leaders—Milosevic and Gaddafi—were able to hold out for far longer than expected.

There was, however, a striking difference in America's role. In the Clinton years, America took the lead in the NATO military operation from start to finish. Under Obama, the United States joined the operation only on the president's condition that the allies who wanted America to intervene would themselves take on most of the military operation. Once that was understood, the United States then initiated the war, using the knowledge and techniques it had learned in the Balkans.

As time went on, the Clinton administration grew increasingly bold in other areas of foreign policy beyond the Balkans. Clinton decided to support and then press hard for the eastward expansion of NATO to Poland, Hungary and the Czech Republic. Russia objected repeatedly. President Boris Yeltsin at one point warned that Europe, after the end of the Cold War, was going to confront "a cold peace." Clinton went ahead anyway, recognizing that American power had increased and Russia's had decreased to such an extent that the Russians would have to go along. In doing so, Clinton effectively cast aside any suggestion that the United States and the West were in decline; rather, NATO showed the world the extent to which one of the two Cold War superpowers had triumphed over the other. NATO expansion also demonstrated a willingness to support the spread of democratic ideals, at least in Europe.

———

On Friday, May 29, 1993, about forty Chinese student leaders, dissidents and a representative of the Dalai Lama were all invited to join with President Clinton in the Roosevelt Room of the White House for what was portrayed as a landmark event: Bill Clinton was going to change American policy toward China. With the activists looking on, Clinton signed a new executive order that required China to make substantial, concrete improvements in its human rights policy within a year. If it didn't, it would lose its most-favored-nation trading status, which let Chinese goods be exported to America under the same low tariffs as other countries. "It is time that a unified American policy recognize both the values of China *and* the values of America," Clinton said that day. He seemed to be following through on his own campaign rhetoric about the "dictators" in Beijing.

But he would change his mind within a year. For Clinton, China was different. He came to judge China and its authoritarian regime by different standards than he used elsewhere. In Eastern and Central Europe, Clinton believed the United States should seek to establish and defend democratic institutions. But with China, he applied different principles, ones that amounted to a justification for American passivity: He argued that there was little the United States could or should do on behalf of democracy there, because prosperity and economic growth in China would lead inexorably to political change. "I just think it's inevitable, just as inevitably the Berlin Wall fell," said Clinton in one press conference.[17]

Where in Europe Clinton became increasingly more willing to challenge Russia, in dealing with Asia he became ever more reluctant to risk friction with China. Indeed, Clinton helped to create the conditions for China to become the economic goliath it is today—so much so that, a decade later, Obama would complain privately that the Clinton administration had been far too lenient in dealing with China on economic issues.

When he at first linked China's trade benefits to improvements in human rights, Clinton was merely doing what Democratic majorities in Congress had been advocating ever since the Tiananmen Square massacre of 1989. The leading forces in Congress at the time were Senate Majority Leader George Mitchell and a relatively junior congresswoman from California, Nancy Pelosi, both of whom had upbraided George H. W. Bush for not taking stronger action against China after Tiananmen. They began to support bills to impose conditions on China's trade benefits. In 1992 this legislation passed both houses of Congress, and Bush vetoed it. Clinton immediately denounced Bush's action as "unconscionable."[18]

Mitchell and Pelosi were present at Clinton's signing ceremony in 1993, smiling and accepting pens along with the Chinese dissidents and student leaders. At the time, it seemed as though the Democrats were uniting behind a new China policy. However, over the following year, American and multinational companies, fearing a loss of trade with China, mounted a powerful campaign to persuade Clinton not to take any punitive action against China and to drop the human rights conditions. They won high-level support within the administration, particularly from Robert Rubin, then the head of the National Economic Council. China became the crucial test of Clinton's relationship to the business community (which is of no small importance in presidential elections). In May 1994, Clinton announced he would renew China's trade benefits, even though it had not met the conditions he required in his executive order the previous year.

In backing down, Clinton reinforced China's sense of confidence and strengthened China's hand in dealing with domestic dissent. In the aftermath, Pelosi was furious with Clinton. "He said he was going to do something and he walked away, as if he was tossing away a used napkin," she said afterward. "We [the United States] should never, never have said we were going to do one thing and then not do it."[19]

The wrangling over China reflected a larger division among the Democrats on trade. In his first year in office, Clinton also won congressional approval first for the North Atlantic Free Trade Agreement (NAFTA) and then for another far-reaching agreement that set up rules for a new global trading system. Near the end of his second term, the Clinton administration reached a deal to bring China into this new entity, called the World Trade Organization. It was this agreement that Obama would come to question. The World Trade Organization opened the way for massive new foreign investment in China, yet the safeguards against trade abuses were inadequate and the loopholes were wide. Obama's complaint was that once China joined the world trading system under these loose rules, there was too little the United States could do to retaliate against China's mercantilist trade policies.

Organized labor, previously the dominant constituency in the Democratic Party, opposed the Clinton administration on all these various trade issues. In each instance, Clinton opted for expansion of trade, a cause supported strongly by the business community. In speeches and press conferences, Clinton repeatedly explained his actions as part of the larger process of globalization: Borders were becoming meaningless, international trade was becoming easier and quicker to carry out and the United States should get in line with the long-term trend.

Most of the Democrats in Congress opposed him on these issues. In the House of Representatives vote on NAFTA, for example, Clinton won the support of only 102 of the 258 Democrats; the bill passed because three-quarters of the Republicans (132 of 175) voted in favor. On Capitol Hill, the Democrats repeatedly raised questions about whether the cause of globalization might cause harm to American workers.

But at the White House, a different spirit prevailed. Apart from his initial stance on China, Clinton had been strongly in favor of trade and commerce from the time he took office. He immediately created a National Economic Council, supposed to be coequal to the National Security Council. He gave ever increasing weight to officials with ties to the financial community, particularly his three treasury secretaries, Lloyd Bentsen, Robert Rubin and Lawrence Summers. Rubin, in particular, was for a time the most influential member of Clinton's cabinet.

———

At the highest levels of the Clinton administration were two figures who would go on to work in Obama's cabinet: Hillary Clinton and Leon Panetta. Neither was closely involved in the day-to-day foreign policy operations at the time. During Bill Clinton's first term, Panetta was director of the Office of Management and Budget and then White House chief of staff, two positions in which his primary focus was the domestic economy. As First Lady, Hillary Clinton was in charge of the unsuccessful effort to pass universal health care; she played a powerful behind-the-scenes role in many of the administration's decisions and a ceremonial role on trips overseas.

Later on, during her presidential campaign against Obama, Hillary Clinton would assert that these efforts demonstrated her experience in foreign policy. But Greg Craig, who worked in the State Department during the Clinton administration, challenged her claims to experience in a memo he wrote after joining the Obama campaign. As First Lady, said Craig, "she did not sit in on National Security Council meetings. She did not have a security clearance. She did not attend meetings in the Situation Room. She did not manage any part of the national security bureaucracy, nor did she have her own national security staff. She did not do any heavy-lifting with foreign governments, whether they were friendly or not."[20] Her most tangible influence in foreign policy was in selecting personnel: She played an important role in persuading President Clinton to select Albright as his second secretary of state (over two other candidates, Holbrooke and Mitchell).

By the late 1990s, a younger group of Democrats began to rise to prominence in the Clinton administration—a new cadre of foreign policy officials with different perspectives from those (such as Christopher and Lake) whom Bill Clinton had brought in at the start of his administration. They had a less conflicted, more confident view of American power and of the U.S. role in the world. They found it easier to believe that the United States was a force for good overseas than the policy makers from the Vietnam era.

The views of this new cadre of officials were shaped by their own experiences under Clinton. They saw the conflicts in the Balkans as examples of American leadership and the prudent use of force. The slaughter in Rwanda, meanwhile, underscored what could happen if the United States and its allies failed to act. The expansion of NATO demonstrated how America's role as sole superpower could change the face of Europe and at the same time help to foster and solidify democratic change. The booming economy of the late Clinton years dispelled any notion that America was in decline.

By the late 1990s, there seemed to be few challengers in the world to American power. China was not yet the economic or military power it would became a decade later. Russia, under Boris Yeltsin, was generally friendly to the Clinton administration; in any event, Russia felt obliged to go along with American policies it didn't like, such as NATO expansion. To be sure, a murky terrorist organization named al-Qaeda had carried out a couple of attacks on American targets overseas, but nothing inside the United States. Most Americans had never heard of the group.

The Democrats serving under Clinton naturally hoped to stay in government in a successor Al Gore administration. When the Supreme Court ruled in favor of George W. Bush in the election of 2000, they found that they would instead have to turn over the White House to a new Republican president. Still, they had every reason to believe that whenever the Democrats returned to power, perhaps in four or eight years, the world would look much the same as it had when they left office on January 20, 2001.

3

Democrats in Exile

When the Democrats became the opposition party in 2001, few could have imagined what sort of upheavals their party would confront before they returned to power. The party leaders and grassroots Democrats were not particularly out of alignment with one another; both were aggrieved at the outcome of the previous year's election. The Democrats' leading spokespersons in foreign policy were, not surprisingly, the experienced hands who had just left the top jobs in the Clinton administration.

Not Bill Clinton himself: At the time, as he left office, he was in disgrace again for having granted several unseemly pardons to figures with whom he had personal connections, such as the financier Marc Rich. But Clinton's national security adviser Sandy Berger, his secretary of state Madeleine Albright and his UN ambassador Richard Holbrooke all remained active. They were charter members of the Democratic establishment, and it was taken for granted that the next time the Democrats took the White House, they would play influential roles in helping to shape a new administration's foreign policy team and ideas.

Democratic leaders didn't see the need for dramatically new ideas about America's role in the world, because they felt that, on the whole, things had gone well under Clinton. It wasn't as though the American public had rejected the Democrats' views on national security. After all, Al Gore would have won the presidency, had it not been for the Supreme Court; and the 2000 election hadn't turned on foreign policy, anyway. One organization called Alliance for American Leadership was formed to help perpetuate the foreign policy of the Clinton era: It favored an active American role overseas—the troop deployments, the bases, the alliances, the power.

In the early months of George W. Bush's presidency, the Democrats had opposed some of his policies. The new administration took a tougher position in dealing with North Korea than the outgoing Clinton team. Bush wanted to press ahead with missile defense, Ronald Reagan's pet project, and to withdraw from the 1972 Anti-Ballistic Missile Treaty. Yet on the whole, these were arcane disagreements between the two parties' foreign policy elites. The public wasn't paying much attention.

————

On September 11, 2001, after al-Qaeda hijacked planes and crashed them into the World Trade Center and the Pentagon, the Democrats immediately closed ranks behind Bush.

In Washington that morning, a congressional staffer named Denis McDonough parked his car as usual on New Jersey Avenue at about eight forty a.m. McDonough, then thirty years old, was a staff aide to Senate Majority Leader Tom Daschle, responsible for foreign policy, with an office in a basement room beneath the Capitol. When McDonough got there, the room was empty but a television was on.

He glanced at it and saw the image of a smoldering building. He figured the cleaning crew must have left the TV on a movie channel, and so he changed the station. But all the stations had the same image—of a fiery, crumbling World Trade Center tower—and McDonough realized this was no movie. Soon Daschle's chief of staff, Peter Rouse, stopped by to ask McDonough, "Who might have done this?" McDonough answered that it had to be al-Qaeda. "Who's that?" asked Rouse. McDonough didn't know much about the organization, but told Rouse there had been some stories about it in the *Washington Post.*

By the evening of September 11, McDonough, representing Daschle, began talking to the Bush administration about what Congress could do to help. McDonough found himself dealing with officials from the Bush team who would later become much more famous than they were at the time: Alberto Gonzales, the White House counsel, and John Yoo, a Justice Department lawyer. Within days, they had drafted a new law, the Authorization for the Use of Military Force Against Terrorists. It gave Bush the power he would use for the war in Afghanistan and other antiterrorist measures at home and abroad.

It was only in the following year that the Democratic leaders began to grow uneasy about granting too much authority to the president. Bush began to put forward new phrases and ideas laying the groundwork for unilateral American military action. He warned against an "axis of evil" of Iraq, Iran and North Korea; he spoke of the need for "preemptive action" to protect America's national security. The administration was clearly and openly moving toward war with Iraq.

The Democrats did little to slow down Bush's momentum. In the fall of 2002, when the Bush administration once again sought formal authorization from Congress for the use of military force, this time against Iraq, it rushed the legislation through Congress under many of the same speeded-up procedures as after the September 11 attacks. The administration claimed there was not enough time for hearings or a regular markup of the legislation. The Democrats went along, although McDonough, once again Daschle's representative in dealing with the Bush team, would reflect years later that the Democrats should have slowed things down and asked more questions. He realized, too late, that their acquiescence in this hurried process had been a huge blunder.

Most of the prominent Democrats in Congress, including Senators John Kerry, Hillary Clinton, John Edwards and Joe Biden, decided to support the Iraq resolution, casting votes that they would all find themselves obliged to justify for years afterward.

———

For the Democratic foreign policy elite, the Iraq War was a disaster both politically and for the ideas they had come to hold. The war reopened old divisions between the Democratic Party's leaders and the party's base. At the grass roots, the party included millions of liberals who, since Vietnam, had been instinctively skeptical about the use of force or other assertions of American power abroad. By contrast, many of the party's foreign policy hands, particularly the alumni of the Clinton administration, had a different outlook. They viewed themselves as heirs to the foreign policy traditions of Franklin Roosevelt, Harry Truman and John Kennedy, all proponents of national strength and an active leadership role for the United States.

The Clinton administration had put its imprimatur on the general idea of regime change in Iraq, though not by American military invasion. It had mistakenly believed, like the Bush team that followed it, that Saddam Hussein was continuing to develop weapons of mass destruction; that had been the conventional view right up to the Iraq War itself. Democratic leaders claimed to be merely accepting the views of the intelligence community. (On the eve of the 2003 war, former CIA director Robert Gates told *The New Yorker* magazine in no uncertain terms, "It's not ambiguous. Can Saddam produce these weapons of mass destruction? Yes.")[1]

So while the Democratic foreign policy hands were surprised by the Bush administration's determined drive to war in Iraq, some of them actively supported the idea and others were not intensely opposed. In the fall of 2002, before Congress voted to authorize the use of force in Iraq, veterans of the Clinton administration gave briefings to Democrats in the House of Representatives that strengthened the case for military action. Holbrooke told House Democrats he thought Saddam Hussein was the most dangerous man in the world. Albright argued that the strategies of containment and deterrence were no longer working in Iraq.[2] (They would later maintain they did not support the war in the way Bush fought it.)

The Democratic leaders acted almost as if they didn't know what they believed or what principles to apply. They were caught between two opposing forces with strong views—the Bush administration and the Democratic Party's own base. The Democratic foreign policy hands were not so enamored of military power as the Republicans, but they were not nearly as pacifistic as grassroots Democratic voters.

In their public statements, prominent Democrats temporized. They looked for narrow grounds or side issues on which to challenge the Bush administration, avoiding a direct attack on the wisdom, intellectual underpinnings or morality of invading Iraq. They questioned the timing or called for more diplomacy. Holbrooke, who had been Clinton's ambassador to the United Nations, wrote in 2002 that the Bush administration needed to go to the Security Council for its approval before going to war. Then, in early 2003, as Bush was preparing to go back to the UN for another vote approving force, Holbrooke wrote that there was no need to do so a second time. The thrust of all these efforts by the Democrats was to find a way to oppose Bush, but not the whole idea of the war.[3]

After the invasion of Iraq, senior Democrats once again struggled to find the right lessons and principles. Berger, writing in the spring of 2004, said that after the Democrats regained the White House, they would have to repair the damage caused by Bush and to restore America's "global, moral and political authority" in the world. But he made clear he wasn't proposing any diminution of America's active role in the world, which could include unilateral displays of force. "A Democratic administration will need to reaffirm the United States' willingness to use military power—alone, if necessary—in defense of its vital interests," Berger said.[4]

Bush, his political adviser Karl Rove and other Republicans noticed the Democrats' ambivalence and played on it mercilessly in the 2004 presidential campaign. When Kerry emerged as the Democratic nominee, the Republicans mocked him for his wavering positions on Iraq. Kerry at one point explained his 2003 vote against an $87 billion spending authorization for Iraq and Afghanistan by saying he had at first voted for the bill. Bush taunted him for always finding a new "nuance" in his position on Iraq. "Senator Kerry tried to explain his vote this way: 'I actually did vote for the $87 billion before I voted against it,'" Bush jibed. Eventually, this was reduced to an anti-Kerry sound bite: "I voted for the war before I voted against it."[5]

———

On September 22, 2002, John Podesta picked up the Sunday *New York Times Magazine* and saw a cover story about George W. Bush's deputy secretary of defense Paul Wolfowitz. Podesta was a regular Democrat's regular Democrat. He had been active in Democratic politics since the Eugene McCarthy campaign of 1968 and the campaigns of Ed Muskie and George McGovern in 1972. He had served as Bill Clinton's chief of staff during his final two years in the White House.

Podesta was fascinated by the profile of Wolfowitz, a leading intellectual force in the Bush administration, who at the time was arguing strongly for action to replace Saddam Hussein. Beyond Iraq, the article explored Wolfowitz's broader views in foreign policy. It spoke of his belief in democracy, of his "optimism about America's ability to build a better world" and his "almost missionary sense of America's role." Reading the piece, Podesta reacted with a mix of wonder and passionate disagreement. He told his wife, "You know, this guy actually has a coherent worldview. Unlike some of the other guys in the Bush administration, it's not just political for him." Then, cutting himself short, Podesta joked, "Of course, if this guy's worldview was right, the British would still be running India."[6]

The following year, Podesta launched a new project that was designed in part to develop ideas in foreign policy so that the Democrats could offer an alternative to Wolfowitz. With the help of several wealthy donors,[7] he launched the Center for American Progress, a Washington think tank designed to play the same role for liberals and Democrats as conservative organizations like the Heritage Foundation and the American Enterprise Institute had for the Republicans. The overall aim, Podesta said, was "to provide intellectual content to the progressive center."

Podesta's organization dealt with both foreign and domestic policy. At the time the Center for American Progress opened its doors, foreign policy was especially important, because the Iraq War was still raging and the Democrats were smarting from the criticism that they had failed to challenge Bush on Iraq.[8] One of Podesta's first hires was a former Pentagon official named Lawrence Korb. He had an unusual background for someone joining an avowedly liberal think tank: Korb had served in the Reagan administration as an assistant secretary of defense for manpower and logistics. He was a specialist on the budget and management aspects of the Pentagon, and he had come to the conclusion that the Pentagon was too big and wasted far too much money. After leaving government, he worked for think tanks like the Brookings Institution, where he regularly questioned the need for more military spending, more weapons systems, more troops and more bases overseas. He turned out reports proposing a more modest budget for the Pentagon.

Recruited into Podesta's new organization, Korb proceeded along the same lines, with studies and newspaper articles that challenged defense outlays and the logic used to justify them. "Trim Fat from Pentagon Budget to Help Pay for Katrina Relief," read the title of one typical op-ed. He took positions that were strikingly similar to the ones embraced by Barack Obama in his presidential campaign. One of Korb's reports called Afghanistan "The Forgotten Front," asserting, "Although the current [Bush] administration has portrayed Iraq as the central front in the 'global war on terror,' Afghanistan and the borderlands of Pakistan remain the central battlefield."[9]

In the fall of 2005, Korb published a study that urged the United States to begin withdrawing its troops from Iraq. "Most Iraqis do not want us there and they do not feel our presence makes them safer," the report said. The study was called "Strategic Redeployment," a phrase Korb had cleverly borrowed from the Republicans. When Ronald Reagan had decided to pull American troops out of Lebanon, he had called his action a "strategic redeployment," thus avoiding the sensitive word "withdrawal."[10]

These studies by Korb and others at the Center for American Progress fit in well with the views of the liberal base of the Democratic Party. The liberals had for decades been mistrustful of the Pentagon and in favor of a more subdued American role in the world. The reports usually had subtitles aimed specifically at a liberal audience: "A Progressive Plan for Iraq," "Towards a New Progressive Defense Strategy for America." However, this work attracted strikingly little attention in Washington's foreign policy community or inside the Pentagon. Korb showed up on the op-ed pages more often than he talked to generals and admirals. The Center for American Progress studies were setting forth the views of outsiders and were arriving at conclusions that the policy insiders would have predicted: Trim back the military.

———

After a couple of years, there was a curious change in the small, inbred world of Washington think tanks: Podesta became involved in setting up a second institution that was (though no one admitted it) a counterpart, almost a rival, to the Center for American Progress.

The driving forces were two relatively young defense specialists, Kurt Campbell and Michèle Flournoy, who had both served in the Pentagon during the Clinton administration. During Bush's first term, both had settled at the nonpartisan Center for Strategic and International Studies, a large, mainstream Washington think tank for defense policy. It serves both as a haven for ex-officials who have recently left government work and as a launching point for those who may want to serve in government in the future. CSIS imposes strict limits on the political activity of those who work there. Campbell and Flournoy chafed at the restrictions and talked to Podesta about doing something new.

"In what I viewed as a battle for the direction of the country, they [Campbell and Flournoy] were being wasted where they were," reflected Podesta years later. "They couldn't really build a program that was oriented to help an argument that would be adopted by Democratic policy makers and Democratic presidential candidates." Podesta wanted Campbell and Flournoy, as Pentagon veterans and mainstream defense experts, to help the Democrats overcome the recurrent charge that the party was weak on national security.

Campbell had even written a book on this subject. In it, he and his coauthor, Michael O'Hanlon, argued that the morass in Iraq gave the Democrats "an opportunity to gain substantial political ground and potentially even to trade places with Republicans in the competition for the loyalties of those who care the most about national security." The book sought to counteract what it called "blue-state bumper stickers: 'War Is Not the Answer.'" Campbell and O'Hanlon wrote, "Yet for most Americans, it depends on the question. Sometimes, war is the answer." [11]

Podesta at first talked about bringing Campbell and Flournoy into his own recently created Center for American Progress. But the pair wanted to run their own separate think tank, and Podesta went along, worrying that his own organization was too left wing for the community of specialists who devoted their careers to defense and the military. He wanted the Democratic Party to develop its own cadre of defense insiders.

So with Podesta's blessing and guidance, Campbell and Flournoy set up a new institution, the Center for a New American Security, devoted exclusively to military and defense issues. It recruited people who had served in the military or worked at the Pentagon and who knew the terminology, the studies, the internal processes. Flournoy, for example, was an expert on the Quadrennial Defense Review, in which the Pentagon reviews every four years where its money and resources should go. The Center for a New American Security was avowedly nonpartisan and had some Republicans along with the Democrats on its board, yet under Campbell and Flournoy's leadership, it was clearly devoted to developing policies and personnel for the next Democratic administration.

The result was that by 2007 the Democrats had two separate think tanks in Washington working on defense issues—one for the doves, the Center for American Progress, and one for more hawkish, establishment defense specialists, the Center for a New American Security. These two think tanks institutionalized the chasm in the Democratic ranks between outsiders and insiders, between rank-and-file liberals and the former Democratic officials and policy insiders who had served in the Clinton administration. Where the Center for American Progress published studies calling for cutbacks in the defense budget and withdrawal from Iraq, the Center for a New American Security developed new military strategies that would revitalize the Pentagon's ability to fight wars. After a couple of years, the Center for a New American Security became the leading institution for military specialists in favor of the doctrine of counterinsurgency—that is, fighting wars by protecting and developing close ties with the local population.

Podesta realized that his role in creating the second think tank was viewed as a slightly unfriendly act by some of his own staff. Korb, for example, was displeased. He pointed out that the Center for a New American Security was willing to accept donations from defense contractors, whereas his own Center for American Progress was not. Korb viewed the leaders of the rival CNAS as typical Washington game players, more hawkish than he was, less committed to progressive ideals, more accepting of the status quo.

A few years later, after the Obama administration came to power, several of the Democrats at the Center for a New American Security were appointed to top foreign policy jobs: Flournoy became undersecretary of defense for policy and Campbell the assistant secretary of state for East Asia and the Pacific. In an interview in early 2010, Podesta confessed that he was a little disappointed with CNAS. It had started out in the political center, maybe slightly left of center, he said. But he felt it had drifted to the right after Campbell and Flournoy departed and had gradually became just another mainstream Washington defense institution.[12]

Podesta's quest for a Democratic Wolfowitz was merely one example of a broader trend. In the years immediately after the invasion of Iraq, the Democrats were struggling to develop their own network of institutions to support progressive ideas. They had seen how Bush had put together a team of foreign policy officials, all veterans of past administrations, with deeply held views about America's predominant role in the world. That team had included the "Vulcans"—Dick Cheney, Donald Rumsfeld, Paul Wolfowitz and other officials who had worked alongside or under them during one or more Republican administrations.

During Bush's second term, the Democrats were searching for their own team of anti-Vulcans. They formed task forces, wrote reports and launched projects, all designed to bring together foreign policy specialists who had served in previous Democratic administrations and other Democrats from academia and think tanks. The very names the Democrats gave to these groups often conveyed the spirit of such endeavors. One group, for example, was called the Wilderness Initiative, aimed at helping Democrats find their way back to power from their years in exile. Another organization was called the Phoenix Project, named for the mythical bird that rose from the ashes to fly again. "The mission was, very directly, 'We need to be a counterpart to the Vulcans,'" explained one of the participants in the Phoenix Project. "The thinking was, 'We have to take over the ideas of the Democratic Party—we're the post-Vietnam generation.'"

But what ideas should these groups put forward? What should they say? It often seemed to be easier for the Democratic foreign policy specialists to explain what they *didn't* believe than what they did. In all these meetings and reports, a few themes came up over and over again. Problematically, they ran in opposite directions; it was almost as if the Democratic foreign policy establishment were running two different campaigns at once, one against the Republicans and another against the left wing of the Democratic Party.

On the one hand, they were opposed to Bush's policies and to the worldview of the neoconservatives. They believed the Bush administration had vastly overemphasized how much the United States should rely on military power—and, indeed, how much the use of force could accomplish. They felt that the Republican administration had given short shrift to diplomacy and to the importance of America acting in concert with its allies and friends around the world, rather than unilaterally.

Yet on the other hand, the Democrats involved in these meetings and reports also often sought to counter the arguments of antiwar forces within the party. They did not agree with groups like MoveOn, which often leaped from criticisms of the war in Iraq to a broader denunciation of America's role in the world. The Democratic foreign policy hands were not opposed in principle to the use of force. They believed in maintaining America's military strength, its power. They also felt that the United States was, in general, a force for good in the world and should maintain an active leadership role.

The participants in the Phoenix Project gave their final report the title "Strategic Leadership."

These beliefs were sincerely and deeply held, yet there was also a political dimension to them. It was the same motivation that had prompted Podesta to help set up the second think tank: The Democrats were eager to show that they were not somehow soft on national security. They wanted to demonstrate that they understood military issues and that they would be comfortable sending out American troops if that should be necessary. In the words of one participant, the Democrats thought they needed to overcome their "peacenik-y" image.

The books and studies of the Democrats in exile groped for some new formula or slogan for maintaining American power. The Republicans had been preoccupied with military power. Harvard University political scientist Joseph S. Nye, one of the Democrats' intellectual leaders, wrote about the importance of America's "soft power"—the influence of its intangible values, ideas, mass culture and educational institutions. In 2005, Podesta's Center for American Progress put together a proposed new national security strategy for the United States that was given the name "Integrated Power"; it called for a blend of military power and soft power. The book published in 2006 by Campbell and O'Hanlon was called *Hard Power*; it argued that while focusing on soft power, the Democrats shouldn't forget about the importance of old-fashioned American military power, either. Eventually, the Democrats came up with another phrase, "smart power," that conveyed well their conviction that the Bush Republicans had been dumb. Hillary Clinton would eventually make "smart power" the catchphrase for her first major speech as secretary of state.

Whatever the right adjective was, the Democrats' established leaders were still in favor of American power and they wanted to preserve it.

4

The Trout Fishers

Every August, America's many leading foreign policy experts gathered
together in Colorado for meetings of the Aspen Strategy Group. It was
a prestigious group of men and women who help to define and to try to
guide America's relations with the rest of the world. Current or former high-
ranking officials mingled with members of Congress, prominent academics
and journalists. The organization was bipartisan; the chairs were Joseph
Nye, a leading force in Democratic foreign policy, and Brent Scowcroft, the
former national security adviser to Republican presidents Ford and George
H. W. Bush. The Aspen membership included former Republican secretary
of state Condoleezza Rice and former Democratic secretary of state Madeleine Albright.

The group spanned the spectrum of mainstream thinking about American foreign policy. They were, above all, respectable. Aspen participants
were not too far to the left or right; there was no radical critic of the United
States such as, say, the late Chalmers Johnson, inveighing against American
empire, and there was no isolationist like, say, Pat Buchanan or Ron Paul,
urging that all U.S. troops simply be brought home. No, the visitors to Aspen
shared similar assumptions; they were senior practitioners, practical people
who dwelt within the realm of the possible. Each year they swapped ideas
about a single subject: energy or weapons proliferation, China or Europe.
Off hours, they relaxed in the cool climate and surroundings.

Among the Aspen participants were several friends from the Clinton
administration. These Democrats served not at the top ranks of government,
but one or two levels down. In their free time at Aspen, they liked to go off

fishing together in the streams nearby. Others at Aspen saw them as a network, a harmless clique. After a time, they were dubbed "the Trout Fishers."

The Trout Fishers were the Democrats' up-and-coming foreign policy team. They were in their forties and fifties, old enough to have played a significant role under Clinton, yet also young and ambitious enough to aspire to higher jobs when the Democrats returned to power. They were in the vanguard of the continuing efforts in Washington to figure out what the Democrats should say about the Bush administration and what the Democrats should do in foreign policy once they returned to office.

One of the Trout Fishers was Kurt Campbell, the stocky, quick-witted defense expert who, in the Clinton years, had been deputy assistant secretary of defense for Asia and the Pacific. Another was Jim Steinberg, the smooth, self-assured lawyer who had served as Clinton's deputy national security adviser. Another was Tom Donilon, the veteran political operative who had worked as chief of staff to Secretary of State Warren Christopher. A fourth was Tony Blinken, the Democrats' leading staffer on the Senate Foreign Relations Committee, who had worked on European issues on Clinton's National Security Council.

They were at the center of a larger cadre of former Clinton administration officials, most of whom had stayed on in Washington after the 2000 election, working at think tanks or on Capitol Hill, hoping to return to government someday. They knew one another, took part in many of the same meetings and study groups. Their ranks included Michèle Flournoy, a senior Pentagon official in charge of strategy in the Clinton years; Ivo Daalder and Philip Gordon, who had been European specialists in the Clinton administration; Daniel Benjamin, who worked on terrorism; Derek Mitchell, an Asia expert; Lael Brainard, in international economics; and Derek Chollet, who was talented at drafting speeches and policy papers.

The Trout Fishers represented the generation of Democrats who learned how to run foreign policy during the 1990s. They were eager to show that the Democrats were not a bunch of pacifists, that they understood national security issues and were willing to use American force where necessary—though sometimes in different ways and for different purposes than the Republicans. Among other things, the Trout Fishers believed in the use of military action for humanitarian purposes, such as to stop genocide or ethnic cleansing.

"Force should never be used as a first choice, but in some cases it may need to be used sooner rather than later, particularly when innocent lives are at stake or when grave dangers are emerging," said the report of the Phoenix Project, the 2008 document outlining a future Democratic foreign policy, which was signed by a small group of Democrats including Steinberg, Campbell and Blinken.

They were more optimistic in their outlook than the Vietnam generation and less defensive about American exercises of power. They assumed that the United States was and would remain the world's most powerful nation. They were not visionaries and, indeed, saw no need for visionaries. Above all, they saw themselves as experienced in government: The job of American foreign policy was to manage things well, to make deals, defuse crises and solve problems in ways so that the United States could maintain its leadership role in the world. They accepted the idea that America was the world's indispensable nation. "These Democrats believe in U.S. power," observed Morton Abramowitz, a former U.S. ambassador who served under both political parties. "They are internationalists. They are less unilateral in their approach than the Republicans, but to some extent of the same ethos."[1]

The Trout Fishers differed from Bush Republicans in their more modest views of what American military strength could accomplish. They believed that the United States couldn't simply coerce or order other nations to do whatever America wanted. Even at the height of American power, during the Cold War, the United States had found that it couldn't always get its way, not even with small and relatively weak nations like Cuba. They believed that economic power was as important as military power, if not more so.

The Trout Fishers believed America should lead the world in establishing general rules for an international order that everyone, including the United States itself, should follow. They did not believe in American "exceptionalism," if "exceptionalism" meant that the United States could exempt itself from the rules that applied to other countries. In their view, America needed to accept limits on its own power, not out of weakness, but because when other nations followed suit, the United States would help create a world of greater stability and cooperation that ultimately served American interests.

They believed strongly in the importance of America's military alliances and the institutions of collective security established after World War II, like NATO and the U.S.-Japan Security Treaty. They took part regularly in the exchanges that were part of maintaining these alliances. The Clinton foreign policy hands tended to know their way around Brussels and Tokyo, the cities at the center of America's alliances in Europe and Asia.

———

Some in the Trout Fisher generation had found reasons to endorse or at least go along with the war in Iraq. Days before the American invasion, Steinberg and Daalder signed a petition with more than twenty other foreign policy specialists who joined together "in supporting the military intervention. . . . The successful disarming, rebuilding and democratic reform of Iraq can contribute decisively to the democratization of the wider Middle East." Saddam Hussein had repeatedly defied United Nations resolutions, and Steinberg believed that the Security Council needed to act to enforce those resolutions if it did not want to lose all its credibility. He viewed the disagreements over Iraq within the Democratic Party as a reflection of a larger debate between liberal interventionists and liberal isolationists. "I'm definitely a liberal interventionist, when it comes to vindicating international norms," Steinberg said.[2]

He had plenty of company among people who thought of themselves as moderate to liberal. A few weeks before the war, Bill Keller, then a columnist for the *New York Times* and later the newspaper's editor, captured the prevailing mood in a piece headlined "The I-Can't-Believe-I'm-a-Hawk Club." Keller wrote, "We reluctant hawks may disagree among ourselves about the most compelling logic for war—protecting America, relieving oppressed Iraqis or reforming the Middle East—but we generally agree that the logic for standing pat does not hold." He pointed out that the "I-Can't-Believe-I'm-a-Hawk Club includes op-ed regulars at this newspaper and *The Washington Post*, the editors of *The New Yorker*, *The New Republic* and *Slate*, columnists in *Time* and *Newsweek*." In addition, said Keller, the club included prominent Democrats, including most of those who had declared an interest in running for president in the next election. (Eight years later, Keller would say that he was wrong and the invasion of Iraq had been a "monumental blunder.")[3]

The support for the war did not subside immediately after the invasion of Iraq, either. In the fall of 2003, fifteen Democratic foreign policy specialists banded together in a statement on behalf of what they called "progressive internationalism." This statement represented largely the views of the Clinton-era Democrats, the spirit of the Trout Fishers. It was endorsed by, among others, Flournoy, Campbell and Brainard.

"We . . . backed the goal of ousting Saddam Hussein's malignant regime in Iraq, because the previous policy of containment was failing, because Saddam posed a grave danger to America as well as his own brutalized people, and because his blatant defiance of more than a decade's worth of UN Security Council resolutions was undermining both collective security and international law," these Democrats said. While supporting the policy of regime change, they were critical of the way the Bush administration had carried it out. The United States should have done more to win international support and to plan for postwar reconstruction, they argued.

More generally, these Democratic foreign policy hands invoked what they called the Democratic Party's "tradition of tough-minded internationalism." A core principle of the party should be "national strength," their policy statement declared. "Democrats will maintain the world's most capable and technologically advanced military, and we will not flinch from using it to defend our interests anywhere in the world."[4]

This was, in short, a document aimed at counteracting any drift toward pacifism or isolationism within the Democratic Party. The signers sought to occupy a center ground between the left wing of their own party and the Republicans—or, as these Democrats phrased it, "between a view that assumes that our might always makes us right and one that assumes that because America is strong it must be wrong."[5]

In 2005, other centrist Democrats set up a youth movement aimed at encouraging a new generation of Democrats to support a strong national defense. It was called the Truman Project, named after the president who had created the institutions in which America responded to the Cold War. "Protecting national security will always require maintaining a robust capacity to use overwhelming force, including a strong military and intelligence apparatus," the group said on its website.[6]

Such views meant that the Democrats' foreign policy mandarins had a testy relationship with the party's antiwar wing. Former Vermont governor Howard Dean found them an inviting target when he campaigned for the Democratic nomination in 2004. He struck a chord by telling audiences, "I'm from the Democratic wing of the Democratic Party." (Dean had borrowed this line from the late senator Paul Wellstone.)

Some prominent Democrats on Capitol Hill were more willing to line up with antiwar forces. Senator Edward Kennedy was intensely opposed to the Iraq War. Steinberg, who had worked for Kennedy and observed his reaction to a range of foreign policy issues, had never seen his former boss so impassioned as he had been on Iraq. In early 2003, Nancy Pelosi, who had just become the House minority leader, came out squarely in opposition to the planned invasion. "I do not believe that going to war now is the best way to rid Iraq of weapons of mass destruction," Pelosi told the Council on Foreign Relations.[7]

In late 2003, Al Gore, once a Cold War hawk, joined with the Iraq antiwar movement and endorsed Dean for president. Gore had been outraged by the war and by the subsequent revelations of American abuses to Iraqi prisoners at Abu Ghraib. "An American policy of dominance is as repugnant to the rest of the world as the ugly dominance of the helpless, naked Iraqi prisoners has been to the American people," Gore said in a speech to the antiwar group MoveOn.[8]

It was not until 2005, after George W. Bush had won a second term in the White House, that the Democratic foreign policy elite began to take somewhat more aggressive stands against the war. The Trout Fishers began to creep leftward, toward the party's grass roots, because of changes both in Iraq and in American politics.

In Iraq, the war was going poorly. More than twenty months after the Bush administration had proclaimed "Mission Accomplished" in Iraq, there had already been 1,400 American soldiers killed in hostile action, nearly ten times the number in the Persian Gulf War of 1991. Even that figure understated just how bloody the Iraq War had become, because U.S. military medical teams had gotten much better at saving the lives of the seriously injured. Combat fatalities in Iraq represented 10 percent of the number of soldiers who had been severely wounded. In Vietnam and the Persian Gulf

War, the percentage of deaths had been much higher: about 24 percent of all Americans who were seriously injured had died in those earlier conflicts.[9]

Politically, Democratic leaders and foreign policy experts were under strong pressure from their own rank and file to present a stronger, clearer alternative to Bush on Iraq. To their considerable frustration, the Democrats had lost the 2004 presidential election after nominating John Kerry, who had voted to authorize the war before it was launched and offered cautious, ambiguous statements about it during his presidential campaign. By 2005, both wealthy contributors and grassroots groups such as MoveOn complained ever more insistently that the party's established leaders in foreign policy had been too accommodating in dealing with Bush.

At one session in early 2005, many of the Democrats' leading foreign policy hands gathered at the home of former secretary of state Madeleine Albright to talk about Iraq. An Iraq specialist, Kenneth Pollack, who had written a book supporting the invasion of Iraq before it took place, argued to Albright's group that the United States should not only continue the war but escalate it. More troops could turn the tide, he argued. In effect, Pollack was arguing for the surge that Bush would implement two years later.

The Trout Fishers and other assembled Democrats heatedly turned on Pollack and his hawkish views. Flournoy argued that the U.S. Army was stretched too thin and couldn't handle the strain. Blinken said more American troops couldn't reverse what was happening on the ground in Iraq. Pollack had been part of the Democratic foreign policy establishment; in the Clinton administration, he had been the National Security Council staff member responsible for Iran and Iraq. Starting with the Albright dinner, his views were no longer acceptable to the mainstream Democrats and he found himself increasingly shunned.[10]

———

The specific policy question confronting the Democrats throughout Bush's second term was whether Congress should set a specific deadline for the withdrawal of American forces from Iraq. The debate was similar to the one the Democrats would have a few years later concerning U.S. troops in Afghanistan. In both cases, antiwar forces urged that the troops be brought home quickly and on a fixed schedule. In both instances, military leaders warned that setting a deadline would encourage insurgent forces to hold out until after the Americans departed, and that a hasty withdrawal could lead to chaos.

At first only a handful of the most liberal Democrats called for withdrawal from Iraq. In January 2005, Senator Edward Kennedy called on Bush to start taking out troops "immediately"; that July, Senator Russell Feingold urged that all American forces be withdrawn within eighteen months. Other Democratic senators, however, including Hillary Clinton, Joe Biden and Minority Leader Harry Reid, refused to go along.[11]

But in the fall of 2006, Pelosi came out for withdrawal from Iraq within a year, and nineteen House Democrats sponsored a resolution to cut off funds for the war. In the congressional elections that November, the American public turned sharply against Bush, the Republicans and the war. The Democrats regained control of both the House and Senate, picking up thirty House seats. Pelosi became Speaker of the House. Commenting on the election results, Rahm Emanuel, who had been in charge of the Democratic Congressional Campaign Committee, explained: "Iraq was the driving force behind everything."[12]

———

Still, even the prominent antiwar Democrats lagged well behind the party's rank and file. Party activists and peace groups had been strongly against the Iraq War much earlier, and so had some local politicians. One of them was a state senator from Illinois, Barack Obama.

In the fall of 2002, Obama accepted an invitation to speak at a demonstration in Chicago against the war.[13] He had been a last-minute replacement for a University of Chicago political scientist, John Mearsheimer, and he shared the podium with several other speakers, including Jesse Jackson. At the time, Bush had just made clear in a speech to the United Nations his determination to move against Saddam Hussein. Congress was preparing to vote on whether to authorize the use of force. Obama was beginning to lay the groundwork for a campaign for the U.S. Senate.

Obama's speech that day proved to be a critical step in launching him to the Senate and then to the presidency. What he said would be recalled and recited again and again during his battle for the Democratic nomination in 2008. He called Bush's intervention in Iraq "a dumb war. A rash war. A war based not on reason, but on passion, not on principle, but on politics. I know that an invasion of Iraq, without a clear rationale and without strong international support, will only fan the flames of the Middle East, and encourage the worst, rather than best, impulses of the Arab world, and strengthen the recruitment arm of al-Qaeda."[14]

Obama went out of his way to emphasize, however, that he was not a pacifist. His characterization of Iraq as a "dumb war" clearly left open the possibility of a "smarter" war. In this sense, he was not giving the demonstrators what they expected to hear. "I stand before you as someone who is not opposed to war in all circumstances," Obama declared. He mentioned the Civil War, World War II and, finally, the Bush administration's action against al-Qaeda after September 11. "I would willingly take up arms myself to prevent such tragedy from happening again," Obama said.

Obama's speech set him apart from the elite Democrats. To be sure, there had been a series of caveats about other wars, but these would be either overlooked or dismissed as necessary hedging. Unlike the Trout Fishers, Obama had actually taken a clear, forthright and unequivocal position against the war in Iraq—before it occurred, not afterward.

———

The Trout Fishers were united more by their own friendship and similar worldviews than by support for any single presidential candidate. In the early stages of the 2008 campaign, Donilon supported Joe Biden, while Campbell lined up behind Hillary Clinton. Steinberg declined to endorse any one of the candidates, saying he would be happy to give advice to anyone who asked. A younger member of the network, Derek Chollet, went to work for John Edwards. No matter who they worked for, the Trout Fishers offered generally similar advice: Stay within the Democratic traditions of internationalism.

"Democrats will have to be more than the anti-Bush politicians to gain more lasting advantage than a temporary boost from the next election," wrote Kurt Campbell in 2006. "They will need the kind of idea-driven agenda and confident preoccupation with matters of national security that has generally been conceded to the GOP in recent decades. . . . After a hiatus, the Democrats are trying to get back into the national security game."[15]

Campbell and the Trout Fishers were foreign policy professionals. There were, however, plenty of Democratic voters who didn't play in the national security "game." They would have to render their own judgments in the 2008 election before the Trout Fishers could pursue their careers in government. The Trout Fishers were foreign policy mandarins without an emperor. They knew how government worked, but not how to win over voters. That wasn't their job.

5

The Obamians

Ben Rhodes was only twenty-three years old when the two planes hit the World Trade Center. Rhodes happened to be watching at the time, and the event was, in a roundabout way, the start of his rapid ascent. Within less than a decade, he would have an office in the White House as a senior aide to the president of the United States.

Rhodes had been working on a local New York City political campaign, helping out a candidate for city council. September 11 was the date of the city's 2001 Democratic primaries, and Rhodes happened to be standing at a polling place on the Brooklyn waterfront, with a clear view across to lower Manhattan as the events unfolded. He watched the towers collapse, then turned away and walked back to his home in Queens. With telephone and television service disrupted, all sorts of rumors were flying—the Pentagon had been hit, the Sears Tower in Chicago had been damaged, Camp David had been attacked.[1]

At the time, Rhodes was finishing a graduate program in writing at New York University and was trying to decide what to do with his life. He was on track for a career in publishing. That would have been a natural step for Rhodes, who had grown up on Manhattan's Upper West Side. But he had made no commitments, and after the September 11 attacks, he decided he wanted to get involved somehow in international relations. He began looking for work in Washington, perhaps in journalism. An editor at *Foreign Policy* suggested a different tack: to find a job as a speechwriter. "At a magazine like ours, you'll probably start out with the scrub work of fact checking," the editor explained, "but if you write speeches, you'll have a broader experience and actually learn about some of the issues."

The editor put him in touch with Lee Hamilton, the former Indiana congressman, who was running a nonpartisan Washington institution, the Woodrow Wilson International Center for Scholars. Hamilton was looking for a speechwriter. Rhodes had meanwhile been offered a job at a New York literary agency, where he imagined he would be working with fashionable women dressed in black and everyone would smoke incessantly while trying to write novels on the side. Rhodes found himself facing a choice: between culture and politics, between New York City and Washington D.C. He accepted Hamilton's offer and soon found himself drafting speeches, columns and op-ed pieces for his new boss.

During his thirty-four years in Congress, Hamilton had been one of the Democratic Party's most prominent leaders in foreign affairs; he had served as chairman of both the House Foreign Affairs Committee and the House Select Committee on Intelligence. He was a figure of probity—not an innovative thinker necessarily, but someone the party turned to for sensible, knowledgeable advice on foreign policy and how it related to American politics. With his crew cut hairstyle and his plain Midwestern speaking manner, he helped the Democrats to counteract the Republican-fueled stereotype that they were just a party of elitists from the East and West Coasts.

In the Reagan years, Hamilton had also headed the special congressional committee looking at the Iran-Contra scandal, in which the United States secretly sold arms to Iran and transferred the profits from these sales to pay for rebel forces in Nicaragua. Hamilton gained experience in the running of an investigation—how to question witnesses, how a final report should be written, how committee members deal with one another. As a result, in late 2002, when Congress set up a special commission to investigate the September 11 attacks, Hamilton was a natural choice to serve as the senior Democrat on the committee. Rhodes served as Hamilton's staff aide as the commission examined the intelligence failures that had led to al-Qaeda's successful terrorist operation. He later collaborated on a book Hamilton wrote with his Republican cochair of the committee, Thomas Kean.

In 2006, Congress set up another commission, the Iraq Study Group, to examine the war in Iraq and make recommendations about it. The Republican chairman was former secretary of state James Baker; once again, the senior Democrat and cochair was Hamilton, who brought Rhodes onto the staff. Rhodes helped to interview leading U.S. officials on Iraq. He visited Iraq with the commission. He then helped write the final report, which recommended that U.S. troops be shifted from combat to training and that combat troops be withdrawn from Iraq over a relatively short period of time.

Thus, at the age of twenty-eight, by circumstance and good luck, Rhodes had been closely involved in the official investigations of the two principal international events of the previous five years: the September 11 attacks and the war in Iraq. By then, he was passionately angry at the Bush administration and eager to work on a Democratic presidential campaign. At first, he wrote a few speeches for Mark Warner, the former governor of Virginia, but Warner dropped out. Rhodes next volunteered to work for the campaign of the candidate he liked best, Senator Barack Obama.

At the beginning of 2007, Obama was in the process of drafting legislation that would call for an end to the war in Iraq. It was a logical step to ask Rhodes, who had just been on the Baker-Hamilton Commission, to help write the legislation. Obama's bill, which never passed, would have stopped the Bush administration from proceeding with its "surge" of new American troops into Iraq. Rhodes found himself working alongside Democratic staff aide Denis McDonough, who was also helping Obama. Within a few months, McDonough and Rhodes both became full-time staff members for the Obama campaign, working together on foreign policy in a partnership that would last throughout the Democratic primaries and the general election campaign, into the White House and onto the National Security Council.

———

McDonough and Rhodes were prime examples of the Obamians—those who had not been closely involved in the making of foreign policy under Bill Clinton or any previous administration. They were Democrats, they were interested in America's role in the world and they had indeed worked on foreign policy in the past—but in Congress or in academia, not in the main executive branch agencies of the State Department, the Defense Department, the National Security Agency or the CIA. They were Obama's own team, his inner circle; they represented the relatively youthful, politically attuned side of Barack Obama's foreign policy.

Obama had many other advisers who already had held foreign policy positions in the executive branch during the Clinton administration. Yet both in the 2008 campaign and again in the Obama administration, these veterans were to discover that Obama relied to an unusual extent on his own informal network, the Obamians he had come to trust in his presidential campaign, such as McDonough and Rhodes.

Some of the Obamians had come up through fields like journalism or academia. Samantha Power had done a bit of both: She had been a journalist reporting in the Balkans in the 1990s, had written a book on genocide and had then worked on human rights policy at Harvard. Michael McFaul, another of Obama's early campaign advisers, was a specialist on Russia at Stanford.

The Obamians reflected the influence of Democratic congressional leaders who had operated outside the orbit of the Clintons. One of them was Tom Daschle, who as Senate majority leader had enjoyed the help of a large staff, a pool of Democratic aides he could lend or recommend to others. Another was Lee Hamilton; Rhodes was merely one of several former Hamilton aides who wound up working on foreign policy in the Obama campaign and administration. A third was Ted Kennedy; he would eventually endorse Obama over Hillary Clinton in the 2008 campaign, and several of his former staff members wound up working for Obama.

The viewpoint of the Obamians was subtly different from that of the Clinton veterans. They were not weighed down with the detailed knowledge of the policy decisions reached during the Clinton years. That background caused the Clinton veterans to have the perspective of insiders, with all the benefits and drawbacks that come with it. Insiders often find it more difficult to make unqualified statements (they know too much) or to launch a vituperative attack on the people in power (they held power themselves once, know when criticism is too harsh or unfair and are aware of the underlying continuities from any one administration to the next).

The Obamians tended to know less about the nuances and subtleties of an issue, and they were less concerned with practical details of governance. They were, however, more adept at providing a determined opposition to the Republicans, and much better at figuring out what to say in public about foreign policy. They found it easier to offer the broad perspective of outsiders.

The Obamians' first task was simply helping the candidate to win the presidency. Only then could they address the questions of how an Obama White House should deal with the world and the extent to which it would differ from the Bush administration.

———

Denis McDonough, who would rise to become Obama's close confidant and the National Security Council's second-in-command, was a vintage product of Capitol Hill. Throughout most of the decade after he finished college and graduate school, he had worked in a series of staff jobs for Democrats in Congress, learning the ways and politics of Washington, the foibles of various bosses, the virtues and rewards of loyalty.

McDonough had grown up in the small town of Stillwater, Minnesota, one of eleven children in a Roman Catholic family. He was a football star at St. John's University in Collegeville, Minnesota. After a couple years of teaching and traveling, he moved to Washington D.C. simply because his brother was already living in the city and he'd heard there were jobs available. He got in touch with college alumni in the Washington area, who recognized his name because of football. One of them was Cleveland Cram, then nearly eighty years old, a renowned veteran of the Office of Strategic Services and the CIA, who helped show McDonough around Washington. McDonough had been unsure whether he could succeed in Washington, but took heart that if Cram, who came from an even smaller town in Minnesota, could make it there, so could he.[2]

He enrolled in a master's program at Georgetown and searched for jobs on Capitol Hill. McDonough first landed an internship for the House Foreign Affairs Committee and soon afterward managed to gain a full-time job there. He specialized in U.S. policy toward Latin America, working for Hamilton, the committee chairman. Three years later, McDonough moved to the Senate as a foreign policy aide to Daschle. He was Daschle's point man for dealing with the 9/11 Commission.

After Daschle was defeated in the 2004 election, McDonough briefly moved to another congressional staff job for another Democratic senator. But when Daschle landed at the Center for American Progress as a senior fellow, McDonough followed him there. Before long, Daschle recommended several of his former congressional aides, including McDonough, to the ambitious young presidential candidate Barack Obama.

———

To the Obamians, the Vietnam War was a matter of settled history, nothing more. It did not induce in them a sense of nervous hesitation about overseas involvements and the use of force as it had for the liberal Democrats of the 1970s—nor, conversely, did it engender a perceived need to overcome the antiwar legacy of Vietnam, as it had for the Democrats of the 1990s.

When the Democrats of the Clinton era talked about their party's political vulnerabilities on national security, they meant people like George Mc-Govern and Michael Dukakis, who had gone down to defeat after the Republicans portrayed them as weak. The Clinton Democrats remembered all too well the series of elections during the Cold War in which the Democrats were attacked for being insufficiently hawkish.

By contrast, if one asked the younger Obamians a similar question about the Democrats' political problems on national security issues, their first association was to the "2002 syndrome." That was the shorthand phrase for the run-up to the Iraq War, when leading Democrats such as Senators Biden, Kerry, Clinton and Edwards had voted in favor of President Bush's request for authorization for the use of force in Iraq. For the Obamians, modern history started with the events of 2001–2002 and the Democrats' seeming compulsion to prove they were not a bunch of antiwar doves.

Thus, the Obamians' personal involvement in foreign policy began in a different era—in the 2000s, the decade of the September 11 attacks, the U.S. intervention in Iraq and, later, the international financial crisis of 2008. These events gave the Obamians a distinctly more modest and downbeat outlook on America's role in the world. The United States no longer seemed like a "hyperpower," a term coined by French foreign minister Hubert Védrine in the 1990s, when American military and economic power was at its zenith.

The United States no longer had seemingly limitless money to throw at international problems. The veterans of the Clinton administration who subsequently returned to office under Obama often reported they were surprised to discover the new financial constraints under which they had to operate. In 2010, one scholar, Michael Mandelbaum, labeled the United States the "frugal superpower."[3] The United States was still fighting two wars, in Iraq and Afghanistan, while at home it was seeking to overcome the worst economic decline since the Great Depression. America was preoccupied with how to pay for domestic needs and sought to minimize foreign involvements. Nor did the United States enjoy the same confidence in what military power could do as it had in the 1990s. The Persian Gulf War of 1991 had brought forth the "shock and awe" of new American military technology. But the wars in Iraq and Afghanistan had demonstrated how insurgencies can counterattack against conventional military power.

The Obamians viewed themselves as dealing with new realities and a different world from their predecessors. They scoffed at some of the reigning clichés, the stale language in which China and India were regularly termed "rising powers." To the Obamians, these countries were no longer rising powers; rather, they had already ascended. On issues ranging from economics to climate change, these countries were already established powers, helping to determine the outcome of issue after issue. At the summit on climate change in Copenhagen during Obama's first year in office, the key meeting was with the Chinese, Indians, Brazilians and South Africans.

Bill Clinton's generation had come to take it for granted that the United States was and would remain the world's dominant power. The Obama generation saw itself as struggling to hold on to that designation for another few decades. "What we're trying to do, frankly, is to preserve our leadership," observed Ben Rhodes. "We're not trying to preside over America's decline. What we're trying to do is to get America another fifty years as leader."[4]

———

The ultimate Obamian, of course, was Obama himself. Aides such as McDonough and Rhodes reflected the president's own views. Obama was as new to foreign policy as they were, and as little influenced by previous Democratic administrations.

Over the years, far too much has been made of how Obama's race and upbringing supposedly affected his thinking about the world. Political opponents, diplomats and journalists have sometimes speculated about the impact on Obama of his father's roots in Kenya or of his childhood years in Indonesia. Some have theorized that Obama had somehow been imbued with an "anticolonial" perspective and was hostile, or at least unsympathetic, to British and European traditions.[5]

There is little if any evidence to support this theory, and it represents an extremely selective interpretation of Obama's youth. His postprimary education included a private college-prep school in Hawaii, private colleges in Los Angeles (Occidental College) and New York City (Columbia), and law school at Harvard. Obama's secondary and higher education, in other words, was not radically different from that of, say, John F. Kennedy (prep school and Harvard), Franklin Roosevelt (prep school, Harvard and Columbia Law School), Richard Nixon (Whittier College and Duke Law School), Gerald Ford (University of Michigan and Yale Law School), George H. W. Bush (prep school and Yale), Bill Clinton (Georgetown and Yale Law School) or George W. Bush (prep school, Yale and Harvard Business School). If Obama's worldview was influenced by his upbringing—and even this is an open question—then surely those long years of elite American schooling must have counted for far more than the father he barely knew or his four years in elementary school overseas.

Instead, Obama's views of the world and of America's role in it were shaped to a far greater extent by his age and by the times in which he came to national prominence. Obama was the first president since Vietnam whose personal life and career were utterly unaffected by that war. Every president since Gerald Ford had tried, in one fashion or another, to declare an end to the Vietnam War or to put to rest its continuing impact. Ford had ended the American presence in Vietnam. Ronald Reagan and George H. W. Bush had both proclaimed the end of the "Vietnam syndrome," their term for the fear of military intervention and casualties. Bill Clinton had normalized diplomatic relations with Vietnam.

The war had nevertheless retained its potency in American political life. When Clinton ran for the presidency in 1992, he had to explain why he hadn't served in the military during Vietnam. When George W. Bush ran in 2000, his campaign was obliged to justify an assignment in the Texas Air National Guard that kept him out of Vietnam. In the 2004 presidential campaign, after the Democrats nominated a Vietnam veteran, the Republicans managed to raise questions about John Kerry's service on a "swift boat" in that war.

In the election of 2008, however, Obama, who was only thirteen years old when the last American troops came home from Vietnam, defeated a Republican candidate who was a Vietnam War hero and former prisoner of war. Vietnam had finally vanished from American presidential politics.

Obama was also the first American president in the modern era who neither served in the military nor was subject to the draft. In this respect, he was a fair representative of most other Americans under the age of fifty-five. Knowing nothing else, Obama could take as a given the existence of the volunteer professional army; military service was a career, not an obligation. The military could be seen as simply a constituency in American society— another big, powerful group with which Obama could try to reach compromise, bridge differences or find a centrist position. "He's not suspicious of the military, and he's not scared of the military," said Denis McDonough. "It's a vitally important institution that's part of this country and part of this government."[6]

Finally, Obama was the first president to come to the White House after George W. Bush's intervention in Iraq. The mere fact that he followed Bush provided Obama with considerable opportunity for improving America's relations with the rest of the world. In this respect, Obama had considerable success. He sought to avoid the rancorous relations Bush had with the leaders of France, Germany, Russia and other countries. During his second term, Bush had himself tried to smooth over the frictions caused by the Iraq War, but he was so unpopular that these belated efforts didn't have much impact; no elected president or prime minister in Western Europe could be seen as too close to Bush. After Obama's election, European leaders once again wanted to have their pictures taken alongside an American president.

The 2008 financial crisis affected Obama's foreign policy and America's international standing at least as much as the Iraq War. The impact of the financial crisis went far beyond the mere lack of money. The United States had far greater difficulty holding itself up to the world as an economic model. In the countries that were harmed by the financial crisis, some of the blame was assigned to the United States—legitimately so. In those few countries where the financial crisis did not hit so hard, such as China and Germany, there was a newly acquired sense of superiority to the American economic system.

President Clinton and his treasury secretary Robert Rubin had dominated international gatherings, regularly preaching the virtues of open markets, liberalization and deregulation. In the 1990s, Clinton confidently told President Jiang Zemin in public that China was "on the wrong side of history."[7]

During much of George W. Bush's presidency, Germany suffered from high unemployment and low growth. Many American descriptions of Germany in the years leading up to the financial crisis depicted it as a nation in decline, too willing to protect jobs and avoid financial risk. "Rather than embracing the challenge of making the sweeping changes needed to lay the groundwork for a globally competitive economy, their aim seems to be to try to hold back the forces of globalization and maintain as much of the old German model as possible," wrote one American columnist in 2004.[8]

After the financial crisis, German and Chinese government and business leaders were more likely to preach to the United States rather than the other way around. At international gatherings, Obama would not infrequently find that his requests went unheeded and his initiatives fell flat.

———

What the Obamians did not possess were detailed policy alternatives. Over the period from 2002 to 2008, they figured out how to criticize the Bush administration and what to say about Iraq. They came up with a few other ideas as well—stepping up the war in Afghanistan, attempting a new dialogue with Iran. But beyond these broad ideas, there was little in the way of concrete policy. They had not considered at any length what would happen if their initial ideas fell through—if, for example, engagement with Iran produced no results, or Congress didn't want to close Guantánamo, or if China turned out to be more assertive than it had been in the past.

Because the Obamians had so little experience in governing, they would have to rely on others for help and advice. They would need the veterans of the Clinton administration, as well as some old hands from government bureaucracies such as the CIA and the Defense Department. Their inexperience and their reliance on others hampered the Obamians' ability to bring about change. At times, the Obamians would illustrate the old aphorism by George Santayana that those who cannot learn from the past are doomed to repeat it.

6

"Join Us"

In a way, the Democrats' challenge to George Bush's foreign policy started to take shape without Barack Obama knowing about it, even before his first speech against the Iraq War. In the summer of 2002, Abner Mikva and Tony Lake, two prominent Democrats who had held senior jobs in the Clinton administration, together wrote an article entitled "What Rules Do We Play By?" Published as an op-ed in the *Boston Globe*, the piece denounced the security measures taken by the Bush administration in the aftermath of September 11.

"We are breaking away not only from our allies but from our own heritage on the most basic issues of human liberty and the rule of law," wrote Mikva and Lake.[1] They were particularly incensed by the detention camp set up at Guantánamo Bay to circumvent the legal requirements that would apply on U.S. soil. Their article demonstrated a desire for Democratic political leaders who would vigorously oppose and ultimately reverse what Bush had done.

The two men had different fields of expertise, Lake in foreign policy and Mikva in law. Lake was a former Foreign Service officer; he did an unhappy stint on Henry Kissinger's National Security Council staff and served as an assistant secretary of state under Jimmy Carter before becoming Bill Clinton's national security adviser. Mikva's career was even more distinguished: He had been a Democratic congressman, a judge on the U.S. Court of Appeals and White House counsel under Clinton. Both men were unapologetic liberals who cared deeply about ideas yet were also experienced in the ways of politics and government.

Mikva, with roots in both Chicago and Washington, had an extensive network of friends, ranging from Supreme Court justices to members of Congress to local Chicago politicians. He served as a mentor to many young, aspiring progressives, mostly those who were interested in law or politics. Obama was interested in both, and became one of the most ambitious and talented of Mikva's protégés. As a third-year law student at Harvard, Obama had declined Mikva's offer of a job as his law clerk in Washington, choosing instead to move to Chicago. But upon his arrival there, he got in touch with Mikva and began seeking career and political advice.

In late 2002, Lake visited Chicago to give a speech in which he argued that the camp at Guantánamo Bay was a big mistake. Mikva joined him at the event. Afterward, a woman in the audience told Lake about a local Chicago politician named Barack Obama, who she described as an attractive progressive candidate preparing to launch a long-shot campaign for the U.S. Senate. Could Lake offer him some advice on foreign policy issues? Lake agreed. Obama—who, as a state senator, had no compelling need to be conversant in foreign policy—called Lake from time to time during his Senate campaign to get background and to try out ideas for what he should say.[2]

After Obama won the Senate seat, Lake organized a dinner in Washington to introduce him to some foreign policy specialists he might call upon for advice. One of them was Susan Rice, who had worked for Lake during the Clinton administration. Obama got along well with her, and in early 2007, when he announced he was running for president, he picked the duo of Lake and Rice to take charge of foreign policy during the campaign.

———

Susan Rice is not related to Condoleezza Rice, George Bush's second secretary of state. During the Bush years, in fact, she occasionally joked that she was "the other Rice." Her political views could not be more different from Condi Rice, although she, too, had been a high achiever since childhood and was equally ambitious. A light-skinned African American woman, Rice is the daughter of two professionals, her father an economist and, for a time, governor of the Federal Reserve Board, her mother a Radcliffe graduate and scholar of education policy. She was the valedictorian of her class at National Cathedral School, one of Washington D.C.'s most prestigious private schools, and a three-letter varsity athlete and basketball star as well. A Phi Beta Kappa graduate of Stanford and a Rhodes Scholar, Rice holds a doctorate in international relations from Oxford, where she wrote a dissertation on peace-keeping in Zimbabwe.[3]

Rice was well connected in Washington. Her mother was a close friend of Madeleine Albright; the Rice and Albright families spent time together frequently during Susan's childhood. When Albright was appointed secretary of state in Clinton's second term, she brought Rice from the National Security Council to work for her as assistant secretary of state for African affairs. Rice was not yet thirty-three years old when she took that job, which gave her responsibility for directing the State Department's response to incidents such as al-Qaeda's bombing of the American embassies in Kenya and Tanzania.

When the Republicans came to power in 2001, she stayed on in Washington at the Brookings Institution, still so young that she was in a good position for a high-level job in the next Democratic administration or even the next two administrations. One former Clinton administration official recalled how, during a visit of foreign policy specialists to Hong Kong the following year, Rice sat at dinner questioning Jim Steinberg about how to advance in Washington; she wanted to broaden her interests so she could avoid being categorized as an Africa specialist.[4]

But there was more to Rice than sheer ambition. She had strong political views and was adept at finding ways to challenge the status quo. As an undergraduate at Stanford, she had helped set up a fund in which alumni donations could be withheld from use by Stanford until the university divested from companies doing business with South Africa's apartheid regime. She was, on many foreign policy issues, more liberal than mainstream Democrats such as Albright, Steinberg and most of her colleagues at Brookings. "Within Brookings, Susan Rice was the odd one out during the Iraq War," recalled Michael O'Hanlon, who worked with Rice there. "Many people didn't challenge the fundamentals of the war. She was among the minority who were against the war from the outset—who believed the war was wrong not just in execution, but in its entire concept."[5]

Like the grassroots Democrats, Rice argued that the Democratic foreign policy elite had been too slow, too hesitant and too reticent in criticizing Bush's war. In this respect, she shared the views of Lake, Mikva and Obama himself. She was a natural fit to work for Obama as he prepared to challenge Hillary Clinton for the Democratic nomination.

———

In January 2007, Michael McFaul took a phone call from his old friend Susan Rice. They had known each other for more than two decades: They had been classmates at Stanford and then Rhodes Scholars together at Oxford. Rice asked McFaul which Democratic candidate he was going to support for president. McFaul hadn't committed to anyone, but he'd done some work for John Edwards, the vice presidential nominee in 2004, and said he assumed he'd probably do so again.[6]

"Fuck that, man," Rice told McFaul, falling quickly into the vernacular she'd use with old friends. She had just signed up to work for Barack Obama, she explained, and was putting together a team of foreign policy advisers for his campaign. "Don't work with Edwards—that's ridiculous," said Rice. "Join us."

About thirty minutes later, McFaul got a second call, this one from Lake, whom he'd known only casually. Lake's pitch for Obama was even stronger. "I've known a lot of brilliant politicians and worked for some," he said. "You just have to trust me, this guy is going to be the next president, and he's the most talented person I've ever met."

McFaul signed up. At that point, he hadn't met Obama or read anything Obama had ever said or written about foreign policy, but he trusted the judgments of Lake and Rice. He went to an initial meeting of Obama's foreign policy team, held in Obama's new campaign headquarters on Massachusetts Avenue in Washington. Rice attended, along with Obama's Senate aides and a handful of foreign policy specialists.[7] The fledgling Obama advisers carved up the world, deciding which person would be responsible for which area. McFaul would do Russia; in that seemingly offhand way, McFaul set himself on a path that would lead to his becoming, two years later, the head of Russian affairs on the National Security Council, coordinating U.S. policies for dealing with Vladimir Putin and Dmitry Medvedev. Eventually, Obama would choose him as the American ambassador to Russia.

Jeff Bader, one of the country's most experienced diplomats in dealing with China, signed on with the Obama campaign team, too. As a young Foreign Service officer, Bader's first assignment had been in Katanga

Province in Zaire. But the State Department had brought him to Washington as an aide to Richard Holbrooke, at that point Jimmy Carter's assistant secretary of state for East Asia. He had never met Holbrooke before and never spent time on Asia, but the two men got along well. (When Bader was promoted to the rank of ambassador two decades later, he would pick Holbrooke to preside over the formal swearing-in ceremonies.)[8]

In 1979, after the Carter administration established diplomatic relations with China, Holbrooke picked Bader to be part of the new team of officials assigned to work at the American embassy in Beijing. Bader learned Mandarin and set off for Beijing in 1981. Over the next twenty years, he would rise through the ranks of the State Department with a variety of China-related assignments on both sides of the Pacific, a firsthand witness to the swings of the pendulum in U.S.-China relations. It was Bader who, working on the State Department's China desk at the time of the Tiananmen Square massacre, had instructed the American embassy to grant refuge and protection to Fang Lizhi, China's best-known proponent of democratic change. ("What are you doing?" a frustrated Bader shouted into the phone to U.S. officials in Beijing after they said they had at first turned away China's leading dissident.)

Bader had been head of the State Department's China desk during the Taiwan Straits crisis of 1995–1996, when China fired missiles in the seas near Taiwan and the Clinton administration countered by sending aircraft carriers to the region. He had worked on the NSC when Bill Clinton made the first presidential trip to China after Tiananmen, and had been at the U.S. Trade Representative's office when the United States finished negotiations to bring China into the World Trade Organization. He had left government in the early years of the Bush administration, working for a time for the private consulting firm headed by Sandy Berger, then at Brookings.

Bader was not a fan of Hillary Clinton and believed the Democrats would be better off with some other candidate in 2008. ("A lot of us associated with the Clinton presidency had great feelings of loyalty to Bill Clinton, but those didn't extend to Hillary," Bader told one reporter during the campaign. "I'm not a great believer in dynasties.")[9] In November 2006, Bader was invited to Barack Obama's Senate office to talk about trade issues. In a small meeting with only four people around a table, Bader was dazzled by Obama, not by his charisma but by his intellect. Bader had originally joined the Foreign Service with a sense of the United States as an inspirational force in the world, and he believed that with Obama leading the country, that spirit could be revived.

A few weeks later, shortly after Obama formally announced his candidacy for president, Bader bumped into Rice. The two had worked alongside each other as colleagues at Brookings. "Can I help?" he asked. Rice brought him in as the campaign adviser on China. He would become, two years later, the NSC's senior director for Asia, the Obama administration official responsible for relations with the world's most populous nation.

———

It went on like that. Obama's campaign foreign policy team was put together slowly and informally. Some people were actively recruited by their friends, as McFaul had been, while others volunteered, like Bader. Some of the advisers, such as Rice, gravitated to Obama because of his political views, believing he was the most progressive Democrat (or the one with the best chance of winning). Others, like Bader, were attracted more by Obama's personal qualities, or joined because they didn't like the idea of a Clinton restoration.

Many members of Hillary Clinton's foreign policy team had been senior officials in the Clinton administration. One dominant figure was Holbrooke, who had remained at the center of the Democratic foreign policy establishment for more than thirty years. Albright and Berger were also influential in the Clinton entourage; other supporters included former NATO commander Wesley Clark, former defense secretary William Perry and former secretary of state Warren Christopher. The only comparable senior hand on Obama's team was Lake, an idiosyncratic figure who'd been alienated from the Clinton crowd and tended to be considerably more liberal than his former colleagues.

Some of Obama's campaign aides believed he would lose, but worked for him anyway because they were eager to give him advice on the subjects on which they had spent their careers. Bruce Riedel, an expert on the Middle East and South Asia, had worked in the CIA for twenty-six years, with additional assignments at the Pentagon and on the National Security Council. He joined the Obama campaign in March 2007, when Lake called and asked him to come on board. He agreed.

"This will all be over soon," Riedel told his wife. "There's no way a guy named Barack Hussein Obama will be elected president of the United States."[10] Two years later, Riedel would direct President Barack Hussein Obama's first review of what he should do in Afghanistan.

———

What virtually everyone in the Obama campaign discovered was that Obama's closest advisers were not the ones who were, ostensibly, the most senior. There was a small inner circle, composed of congressional staff members who had worked on Capitol Hill either for Obama or for Tom Daschle.

"The key people are the Senate staffers," reported one source in the campaign. "They're the ones involved in the real decision making. Then the campaign brings out Rice or Lake to speak for the campaign."[11] It was a pattern that would be repeated in the White House, when Obama's first national security adviser, James Jones, and, for a time, Secretary of State Hillary Clinton discovered they held less influence within the administration than their job titles or their public roles would have indicated. The inner circle of Obama aides wielded surprising power. Most other aides assumed that this was the way Obama wanted it, enabling him to make the ultimate decisions.

At the beginning of the presidential campaign, the most important of the Senate aides was Mark Lippert, who had been in charge of foreign policy in Obama's Senate office. Lippert first worked on Capitol Hill for Senators Dianne Feinstein and Tom Daschle and then for the Senate Appropriations Subcommittee on Foreign Operations. In early 2005, Pete Rouse, Daschle's chief of staff, moved to a similar job in Obama's new office and brought in Lippert to help out.

Over the following two years, Lippert was the staff member at Obama's side on overseas trips to Russia, Iraq and Kenya, and the two men became good friends. In Iraq in early 2006, Obama and Lippert roomed together in what had once been Saddam Hussein's pool house and was now inside Baghdad's Green Zone. It was Lippert who provided Obama with the anecdote about Iraq that the candidate would repeat over and over again in the early stages of his presidential campaign. At a marine base in Fallujah, Lippert had wandered off with a colonel for a conversation out of earshot of Obama. Afterward, Obama asked what the colonel thought the United States should do in Iraq. Lippert's answer came in a single word: "Leave."[12]

In 2007, as Obama launched his presidential campaign, Lippert brought in his friend Denis McDonough, also a former Daschle staffer, to work with him on foreign policy. When the campaign needed a full-time speech-writer, the two then brought in Ben Rhodes, whom McDonough had known since their work on the September 11 Commission. Together, these three formed the nucleus of Obama's campaign inner circle on foreign policy. After Lippert, a navy reserve officer, was called up to active duty in Iraq, McDonough took over his job as the principal day-to-day foreign policy ad-viser. Lippert returned for the later stages of the campaign and the early months of the Obama administration, where he helped oversee the National Security Council staff. He left, officially for another tour of active duty in the military, but also because then national security adviser James Jones thought Lippert was undercutting him.[13] Once again, McDonough moved up to take Lippert's place.

Keeping the experienced hands at a distance from the decision making fit perfectly with the political message Obama wanted to convey. The Obama campaign wanted to show voters that he didn't rely too much on experts or veterans of past administrations, because these were the kinds of people who had led America astray. Obama was going to represent some-thing new. Let Hillary Clinton have campaign advisers like Holbrooke, who could usually be relied upon to bring up the way things had been done be-fore, the ghosts of past Democratic administrations. The Obamians were doing just fine, politically, as outsiders.

————

From the outset of his campaign, Obama pressed the theme that his foreign policy would be different. It would not be business as usual. He found ways to convey this message in ways that were both politically brilliant and, some-times, inaccurate. There were occasions when Obama outmaneuvered Hillary Clinton by staking out a position that he would not himself follow as president.

One noteworthy moment came at an early debate among the Democratic presidential candidates in Charleston, South Carolina, on July 24, 2007. Obama was asked a question posed by someone in a YouTube video: "Would you be willing to meet separately, without precondition, during the first year of your administration, in Washington or anywhere else, with the leaders of

Iran, Syria, Venezuela, Cuba and North Korea, in order to bridge the gap that divides our countries?"

"I would," Obama replied. "And the reason is this, that the notion that somehow not talking to countries is punishment to them—which has been the guiding principle of this administration—is ridiculous." Hillary Clinton immediately disagreed. "I will not promise to meet with the leaders of these countries during my first year," she said. "I don't want to be used for propaganda purposes. . . . I will use a lot of high-level presidential envoys to test the waters, to feel the way. But certainly, we're not going to just have our president meet with Fidel Castro and Hugo Chávez and, you know, the presidents of North Korea, Iran and Syria, until we know better what the way forward will be."[14]

The subsequent record of his administration shows that, on this issue, Obama came to realize he had been wrong. After he became president, Obama did not meet with the leaders of Iran, Syria, North Korea or Cuba, in Washington or anywhere else, not during his first year as president, or his second or third year, either. The leaders of these countries would have quickly accepted an invitation to Washington or a visit by Obama to their own capitals. Obama did "meet" Venezuelan president Hugo Chávez, but only for a brief conversation as they stood on the sidelines of an international meeting. In fact, as president, Obama has carried out a policy strikingly close to the one Hillary Clinton had advocated in the South Carolina debate: vigorous diplomacy, using presidential envoys, but no summit meetings with these leaders.

In the debate, Obama may have momentarily slipped into taking a stronger position than he'd intended. Later on, without admitting error, Obama and his aides would water down his promise considerably, employing a couple of verbal evasions that would have made Bill Clinton proud: Either they would leave out the word "leaders," saying that the Obama administration was willing to talk with these countries (presumably through lower-level officials), or they would mention the rulers but omit the word "meetings," asserting that Obama would be willing to carry out "diplomacy" with the leaders of countries like North Korea and Iran. These looser formulations glossed over the fact that Obama was specifically asked whether he would meet with the leaders and had said he would.

Immediately after the debate, the Clinton campaign and various news organizations challenged the position Obama had taken, arguing that it showed a lack of experience in foreign policy. He pushed back aggressively, insisting he had been right, and ordered his aides not to back down.

"We decided to be pugnacious, rather than defensive," recalled Obama's campaign manager, David Plouffe. He, David Axelrod and others on the Obama team depicted Clinton's position as "Washington salon foreign policy." The Obama team was happy to challenge the foreign policy establishment, knowing that its members were overwhelmingly supporting Clinton anyway. Obama himself went a step further, telling a reporter that Clinton, in her reluctance to meet foreign leaders, was following the foreign policy of George Bush and Dick Cheney.[15] As it turned out, her position was also the future foreign policy of President Barack Obama.

While wrong on the substance of the issue, Obama was shrewd about the politics. Virtually everything Obama was doing at that stage of the campaign was aimed at defeating Clinton in Iowa, the first contest for the Democratic candidates. The Obama team realized that antiwar sentiments were particularly strong in Iowa and had therefore emphasized his opposition to Iraq over and over again.

But Obama also needed to show that he was a serious candidate, that voting for him was more than simply a protest against the Iraq War. He was eager to demonstrate that his differences with Clinton extended beyond Iraq. Obama's advisers recognized that there were not many disagreements among the Democratic candidates on domestic policy, and so foreign policy would have to be the battleground.[16] The exchange about meeting with foreign leaders in Iran and North Korea gave Obama an opportunity to accomplish this larger purpose. He made it sound as if there was a fundamental disagreement about meeting foreign leaders, when there wasn't.

"We had clearly telegraphed how we stood apart from the pack with a stance that was timely and forward-looking," said Plouffe happily.[17] Obama's performance during the debate and the campaign's spin afterward were shrewd politics. As a predictor of what Obama would do as president, the entire event proved to be meaningless.

7

"To Track Down, Capture or Kill"

Not all of Obama's campaign commitments proved to be so ephemeral as the pledge to meet with foreign leaders. Obama staked out one position that differentiated him from the other Democrats and accurately presaged his policies as president: He promised to step up the war in Afghanistan and to take the fight against al-Qaeda into Pakistan. The very first step in his strategy against terrorism, he said, would be "getting off the wrong battlefield in Iraq and taking the fight to the terrorists in Afghanistan and Pakistan."[1]

"As president, I would deploy at least two additional brigades to Afghanistan," asserted Obama in a speech in Washington on August 1, 2007. As for terrorist groups across Afghanistan's border with Pakistan, Obama continued, "If we have actionable intelligence about high-value targets and President [Pervez] Musharraf won't act, we will." Obama promised that he would build up the capacity of the United States "to track down, capture or kill terrorists around the world."

At the time, these words tended to be written off as mere political posturing; many Obama supporters either didn't notice or persuaded themselves he wasn't serious. The usual argument went like this: *Obama had to say that. He needs to show voters he's not just a conventional dove. He came out strongly against the war in Iraq. Therefore, he needs to take a hawkish position on the use of force in Afghanistan and Pakistan.* A couple of years later, in his first year as president, Obama intensified both the war in Afghanistan and the use of drones and other cross-border raids into Pakistan. In 2011, he elected to send a SEAL team into Pakistan to kill Osama bin Laden, without telling any of Pakistan's leaders in advance. By that point, Obama's hawkish campaign statements seemed far more meaningful than they originally had.

Obama's ideas on Afghanistan and Pakistan reflected the thinking of Bruce Riedel, the specialist on the Middle East and South Asia who had signed on with the Obama campaign in March 2007 after spending most of his career in the CIA. Riedel had been arguing that the Bush administration relied far too heavily on Musharraf and other Pakistani military and intelligence leaders. When early in the campaign Obama began advocating a more aggressive stance toward Pakistan, Senators Hillary Clinton, Joe Biden and Chris Dodd chided Obama for his inexperience in foreign policy. Obama's statements are "frankly confusing and confused," said Dodd at a campaign debate in Chicago. "While General Musharraf is no Thomas Jefferson, he may be the only thing that stands between us and having an Islamic fundamentalist state in that country. . . . The reality is, if we lose him, then what we face is an alternative that could be a lot worse for our country."[2]

In response, Obama pulled out his trump card: his early opposition to the Iraq War that his opponents had voted to authorize. At the end of the Chicago debate, he recited as if spontaneously a line his campaign staff had worked out for him in advance. "I find it amusing that those who helped to authorize and engineer the biggest foreign policy disaster in our generation are now criticizing me for making sure that we are on the right battlefield and not the wrong battlefield in the war against terrorism," Obama said. The audience cheered.

Years later, Ben Rhodes, who as a young Obama staffer had helped draft these words, said he felt that this was a turning point in winning the Democratic nomination.[3] Obama not only deflected the attacks on his inexperience in foreign policy, but turned that inexperience into a virtue. His words reinforced the campaign's larger message that Obama was a young, energetic outsider who was not tied to the Democrats of the past.

In the fall of 2007, in an address timed to the fifth anniversary of Obama's first speech in opposition to the war in Iraq, Obama took this same theme a step further. He lashed out at "Washington groupthink," "the foreign policy elite" and "conventional thinking in Washington." This was good politics, helping further to distinguish Obama from the other Democrats.

While Obama was running against members of the Democratic establishment, some of them were campaigning against him, too. In the fall of 2007, Richard Holbrooke made phone calls to warn the Democrats' foreign policy hands that they would be wise to hurry up and endorse Clinton. Holbrooke informed them that Clinton would win the Democratic nomination and the general election, and that the jobs in her administration would go to those who had supported her. Those who opposed her would be out in the cold. It was a version of the classic old political line: *The train is leaving the station, and you'd better climb aboard.* Ironically, it was eventually Holbrooke who had to jump aboard the Obama train after Clinton's defeat. The Obamians remembered those Holbrooke phone calls for a long time, and not fondly. After Obama was inaugurated, one of Obama's campaign advisers said of Holbrooke: "We know who was making those phone calls."[4]

Holbrooke was not alone. In December 2007, Kurt Campbell, then serving as an adviser to Hillary Clinton, made an urgent appeal to his old friend Jeff Bader, encouraging him to abandon the Obama campaign. The Clinton team was just about to publish its extensive list of more than two hundred foreign policy advisers. Campbell appealed to Bader to switch sides and join the Clinton campaign. The two men had worked closely together in Bill Clinton's administration, and Campbell told Bader it was time for him to come back. Bader stuck with Obama.[5]

When Obama won the Iowa caucuses and established himself as the front-runner for the Democratic nomination, the animosity between the Obama campaign and the Clinton entourage deepened. Each candidate attacked the foreign policy credentials of the other. Obama pressed the theme that Clinton was tied to outmoded ways of thinking about the world, the sorts of ideas that had led to the war in Iraq. Clinton countered that Obama was inexperienced.

Clinton's line of attack was summed up in her television advertisement, distributed in February 2008 before the Ohio and Texas primaries, that asked whether Obama could be trusted to handle an international crisis. "It's three a.m. and your children are safe and asleep," the ad said, with horror film music in the background. "Who do you want answering the phone?" The Obama campaign countered by belittling Hillary Clinton's claim that she understood foreign policy by virtue of her previous experience as First Lady.

At the height of the primary campaign, one of Obama's closest advisers, Samantha Power, was forced to resign after going a little too far in her critique. In an interview overseas with *The Scotsman*, she said of Clinton: "She is a monster, too. . . . She is stooping to anything."[6]

———

Power possessed the most unusual background of any member of Obama's foreign policy team. She began her career as a freelance writer in Bosnia at the time of Serbian atrocities against the Muslims there. In years following she reported from Rwanda, East Timor, Sudan and Kosovo. Her first book, *A Problem from Hell: America in the Age of Genocide*, won the 2003 Pulitzer Prize. She eventually settled at Harvard, where she established the Carr Center for Human Rights Policy.

Power's outlook was formed in the 1990s, the direct result of her experiences in the Balkans. She believed in America as potentially a force for good in the world and, particularly, in the importance of strong action to prevent genocide. She had therefore become a proponent of the principle of humanitarian intervention; she was willing, at least in some circumstances, to support the use of military force to prevent mass slaughter. "We have to be prepared to throw some of our weight around in the interest of saving people," she explained.[7] Indeed, Power disagreed with the Clinton administration only in the sense that she would have gone further than it did on behalf of humanitarian goals. She pointed out that the Clinton administration had been far too slow to act in the case of Bosnia and negligent in its failure to stop the slaughter in Rwanda.

Power strongly opposed the war in Iraq, arguing that America's unilateral action against Saddam Hussein lacked legitimacy and had undermined international support for strong action against human rights. Nevertheless, some on the political left criticized Power's views on humanitarian intervention, claiming they served to provide an intellectual cover for military action by the United States or other Western powers. "Human rights has become, however inconsistently applied, the official ideology of the American empire," said one critic, David Rieff.[8]

Soon after coming to the Senate, Obama had called Power, told her he liked her book on genocide and asked to meet her. After a four-hour dinner, she agreed to work in his Senate office. She became a charismatic presence first on Capitol Hill and then in the Obama campaign: a celebrated author, tall, red haired and impassioned in her views and speech—so impassioned that, in the heat of the campaign, she momentarily slipped and said in public what others in the Obama campaign thought about Clinton in private.

She quickly apologized for the "monster" quote, pointed out how often she had expressed public admiration for Clinton in the past and stepped down from the Obama campaign. She would eventually return, however, to work in his administration.

———

At times, Obama and Clinton seemed to be in a bidding war to see who could stake out the stronger position on an issue, or the earlier position, or the one that might attract the most press coverage. In this competition, they wound up saying things that would bear little relationship to what the two of them would do once they were in office. On the subject of China, for example, Hillary Clinton said in the spring of 2008 that she thought President George Bush and other world leaders should boycott the opening ceremonies of the Beijing Olympics to protest its human rights policies and its unwillingness to take action against genocide in Sudan. Obama quickly followed suit. "If the Chinese do not take steps to help stop the genocide in Darfur and to respect the dignity, security, and human rights of the Tibetan people, then the president should boycott the opening ceremonies," said the Obama campaign in a prepared statement.[9] (At one point, in frustration, Bader privately groused, "Are these the Beijing Olympics or the Darfur Olympics?")

Shortly before the Pennsylvania primary, Clinton said she thought the United States should formally declare that China was manipulating its currency to help keep its exports cheap—which would have required the United States to take action against China in response. Obama quickly followed suit, saying he agreed. He told a union audience in Pittsburgh that the Chinese were "grossly undervaluing their currency, and giving their goods another unfair advantage. Each year they've had the chance, the Bush administration has failed to do anything about this. That's unacceptable. . . . And that's why as president, I'll use all the diplomatic avenues open to me to insist that China stop manipulating its currency."[10]

Voters who believed the candidates' statements on these issues would come to discover after the election that they were too credulous. Less than a year after she'd called for a boycott of the Olympics because of human rights abuses, Clinton announced she would not dwell on human rights issues in her first visit to Beijing as secretary of state. Under a 1988 law called the Omnibus Trade and Competitiveness Act, the Treasury Department is required to report to Congress every six months on whether any country with which the United States trades is manipulating the value of its currency. The Obama administration repeatedly declined to do so. Instead, Obama followed the same practice for which he had explicitly criticized the Bush administration: He looked the other way.

———

As soon as Clinton conceded defeat in early June of 2008, Obama moved quickly to establish his foreign policy credentials against John McCain. The Obama team knew that the Republican nominee was known for his Vietnam service and had taken a long-standing interest in foreign and defense policy in the Senate. McCain's candidacy had serious liabilities—above all the overwhelming public unhappiness with the Bush administration and the Iraq War—but Obama could capitalize on this vulnerability only by proving he could be trusted to deal with foreign policy and national security.

The Obama campaign's showpiece for demonstrating his credentials was the trip abroad he made in late July 2008. Obama was now the Democratic nominee, leading in the polls for the general election, and, in Western Europe particularly, he was already a hero for having opposed the war in Iraq early and often. His journey attracted close to the level of media attention of a Cold War summit or President Nixon's visit to China. Television networks sent their anchors; major newspapers were carrying two or more stories a day; even the most oblique or offhand remark was examined for meaning. The general excitement of the news coverage by itself seemed to confer upon Obama the status of a sitting president. The trip was destined to be a resounding success unless Obama made some major gaffe. He didn't.

———

One of Obama's early stops on this trip was Baghdad, where he had his first extended meeting with a man who would within a half year become a powerful influence over his military strategy: General David Petraeus, then commanding American forces in Iraq. Each man had more to gain than to lose by demonstrating amicable relations with the other, and both men had a coterie of press aides eager for flattering coverage. The result was a photo immediately transmitted throughout the world showing the two men together, smiling and happy, and pleasing to everyone but John McCain and his supporters.

In private, however, the two men were carefully feeling each other out. Petraeus described what sort of manpower and resources he would need in Iraq. In his detached manner, Obama offered an unusual response—a message that would presage, more than Obama could ever have known at the time, the budgetary dilemmas he would face as president. "Look, if I were in your shoes, General, I would be asking for everything you're asking for and more—and I totally understand it. But you have to understand that, from where I sit now as a senator, and from where I might sit if I'm elected president, is, we have ultimately different responsibilities.

"You're responsible for this battle space, and for getting everything you can get to succeed in your mission. My responsibility as a senator and possibly my future responsibility as president is going to be for the security of the country around the world and at home. And that means I have to make decisions about the allocation of resources and focus that have to take into account things that are not part of your responsibility. And so, there may be things that you want to do or think you need to do that we can't do when we factor them into the overall national security." [11]

This was not the sort of admonition that presidents ordinarily give to their commanders in a war zone. But Obama wasn't president yet and hadn't supported the Iraq War from the start. Petraeus did not seem put off by Obama's words. Afterward, the general told associates that he had been surprised because Obama had talked more like a centrist than a conventional liberal. [12]

Obama made a couple of other stops in the Middle East and then flew to Germany for the main public event of his trip. His foreign policy team had been working for weeks to arrange a speech before a large public gathering in Berlin that would demonstrate Obama's popularity in Europe. Their efforts had run into a series of complications, some of them caused by Henry Kissinger and the McCain campaign.

The original idea had been for Obama to speak before the Brandenburg

Gate, the monument that had become the iconic symbol of the city, of Germany's Cold War division and subsequent reunification. Ronald Reagan had delivered his 1987 speech calling upon Mikhail Gorbachev to "tear down this wall" in front of the Brandenburg Gate. At the time, some West German officials were unhappy with the idea of allowing it to be turned into a backdrop for Reagan's speech.[13] This same concern arose again when Obama's campaign sought permission for him to speak there.

By coincidence, U.S. officials had sponsored a series of July 4 events and entertainment in Berlin (ranging from Elvis Presley look-alikes to the Alvin Ailey dance troupe) to commemorate the opening of a new American embassy building. Quite a few prominent Americans, including George H. W. Bush and Henry Kissinger, had come to Berlin for the occasion. When Kissinger heard of the plans for Obama to speak in front of the Brandenburg Gate, he was annoyed: Obama was merely a candidate, not an American president, and his appearance there might make it seem as though the U.S. embassy was either supporting him or being used by others for partisan purposes.

From Kissinger, word of Obama's plans spread to the McCain campaign back in the United States. Not long after, Randy Scheunemann, McCain's principal foreign policy adviser, called the national security adviser to German chancellor Angela Merkel. He questioned why the German government was allowing its most revered symbol, the Brandenburg Gate, to be used for one of the two major-party candidates in an American political campaign. Merkel apparently agreed with this argument; she soon made clear in public her disapproval. "This kind of electioneering abroad is unusual," said Thomas Steg, Merkel's spokesman.[14]

The Obama team got the hint and quickly came up with a new site. He would speak at Berlin's Tiergarten, in front of the statue of the Winged Victory commemorating Germany's defeat of France in 1871. It was a huge open space, and the Obama team, headed by Denis McDonough, was apprehensive that a small crowd might make it look empty. The Obama campaign left nothing to chance. Bill Drozdiak, a specialist on German-American relations working for the Obama campaign, helped arrange to have two of the best-known German rock groups perform at the site as a lead-in to Obama's speech, thus providing an added attraction that would bring in many more young Germans.

When the day came for Obama's appearance, about 200,000 Germans showed up in the Tiergarten—a massive crowd, far bigger than the one at Reagan's speech twenty-one years earlier. Obama told the crowd he was "a proud citizen of the United States and a fellow citizen of the world." He reminded the audience of the divisions over Iraq between Europe and the Bush administration, and he promised to do better: "The walls between old allies on either side of the Atlantic cannot stand," Obama declared. The German audience cheered. Later, Peter Schneider, one of Germany's leading authors, reflected that the atmosphere at Obama's speech "felt almost like the day the Berlin Wall came down."[15]

The Obama campaign succeeded in getting what it wanted: a simple, clear demonstration of the candidate's popularity in Europe. The rally in Berlin had been designed to "visually demonstrate an important premise: the world was still hungry for American leadership, but of a different, more cooperative kind that only Barack Obama could deliver," wrote campaign manager David Plouffe.[16]

The McCain campaign felt obliged to counteract Obama's success in Berlin. McCain's first approach was to argue that by going overseas, Obama showed he was out of touch with ordinary Americans in places like Ohio. Soon McCain's team produced a campaign ad that showed pictures of Obama in front of cheering crowds and then suggested Obama was merely a celebrity, comparable to Britney Spears.

———

After the Democratic primaries, the Obama campaign took aboard some of Clinton's former foreign policy advisers. Obama appointed a new "senior working group" on national security, composed of many of the senior officials of past Democratic administrations. Madeleine Albright was at the head of the table, with other cabinet members from Bill Clinton's administration, such as William Perry and Warren Christopher, also taking part.[17] All three of them had endorsed Clinton over Obama. Notable for his absence was Richard Holbrooke, Clinton's leading foreign policy adviser, who would have to work a little harder to bring himself back into the good graces of the Obama camp.

But any focus on senior officials was inherently misleading. The truth was that there was no dominant figure within the Obama presidential campaign on foreign policy, no adviser who would play a weighty role for Obama comparable to the one the Vulcans had played in George W. Bush's presidential campaign.

Only a single aide on Obama's foreign policy team had held a cabinet-level job in a previous administration: Anthony Lake from the Clinton administration. He was, however, considerably older than everyone else; he turned sixty-nine during the primaries. While he was instrumental in putting Obama's team together, his influence waned as the campaign went along and the others grew increasingly confident of their own judgments. Obama's other top foreign policy adviser, Susan Rice, was considerably closer to the candidate both in age and mind-set. Rice, quick and articulate, appeared regularly on television as a spokeswoman for Obama on foreign policy. But she was not at the epicenter of decision making, either. When Obama and his political advisers David Axelrod and David Plouffe wanted something on foreign policy, they worked primarily through the former Senate staffers Denis McDonough and Mark Lippert. On foreign policy, the campaign was, essentially, leaderless except for the candidate himself. One high-level campaign aide described the process: "He gets the opinions, and he leaves most of the decisions until after the meetings, and then you hear about the decisions."[18]

The clearest demonstration of Obama's own instincts and operating style came when the foreign policy team dealt with the one crisis that emerged early in the general election campaign. In early August, fighting broke out between Russia and Georgia over two small provinces that were seeking independence from Georgia. Russia moved its troops deep into Georgian territory in a show of force that seemed to be aimed not only at Georgia but as a lesson to other neighboring countries such as Ukraine and the Baltic states.

McCain was quick to react. There were close personal ties between the McCain campaign and the Georgian government: McCain had known Mikheil Saakashvili, the president of Georgia, for more than a decade, and McCain's chief foreign policy adviser, Scheunemann, had been a Washington lobbyist for Georgia. "We've seen this movie before in Prague and Budapest," McCain said, recalling the Soviet invasions in Eastern Europe during the Cold War. Over the following days, McCain inveighed against Russia again and again.[19]

The Obama campaign was slower to respond and more detached when it did. At first, campaign officials merely called for a cease-fire and urged restraint on all sides. Only after a few days did Obama condemn Russia for moving its troops into Georgia. One explanation for his tepid response was that Obama was on his way to a vacation in Hawaii. Yet this was also more than a matter of timing: There were underlying disagreements within the Obama campaign about what position to take. Obama himself saw the events as part of a complex story that went beyond a simple narrative of Russian aggression; Georgia was not without fault in the events that had led up to the conflict, and Obama did not view Georgian president Saakashvili as an unalloyed hero or victim.

More broadly, Georgia brought out the underlying differences among Democrats between veterans of the Clinton administration and the Obamians, whose frame of reference was the war in Iraq. The Clinton-era Democrats had been in office at the time of the expansion of NATO. They believed that the United States should play a leadership role in the world and should protect Georgia from being bullied by Russia. The Obamians believed in a more modest role for the United States; they were mistrustful of any foreign policy that appeared too assertive or moralistic. One Obama adviser suggested that the candidate should talk about the importance of democracy, but was rebuffed. "It was clear that was an issue that was not going anywhere in the campaign," the adviser said. "I just saw that my view was a minority among the folks in the campaign, and certainly a minority when it came to Obama."[20]

Obama and his aides eventually reconsidered. His political aides pointed out that while most Americans didn't care much about Georgia, there were some constituencies who did: hundreds of thousands of Polish Americans, Ukrainian Americans and others of Eastern European descent, and they tended to live in swing states in the East and Midwest, such as Pennsylvania and Ohio.[21] Obama proceeded to ratchet up his rhetoric on Georgia so that, by the time of his first presidential debate in late September, his words sounded much like those of McCain: "[A] resurgent and very aggressive Russia is a threat to the peace and stability of the region." He said the United States needed to show solidarity with "all the fledgling democracies in that region—you know, the Estonians, the Lithuanians, the Latvians, the Poles, the Czechs."²²

———

The uneasiness about Obama's foreign policy credentials governed the choice of a vice presidential nominee. In late August, Obama announced that he had picked Joe Biden, the chairman of the Senate Foreign Relations Committee, as his running mate. The selection fit with a historic pattern in which presidential candidates who are governors or young senators turn to established Washington insiders as their vice presidential candidates: Bill Clinton/Al Gore, Ronald Reagan/George H. W. Bush, Jimmy Carter/Walter Mondale, John F. Kennedy/Lyndon Johnson. In Biden, the Obama campaign had a nominee who personified the Democratic Party's twists and turns on foreign policy over the decades: He had been a dove in the Vietnam era but a leading advocate of American intervention in Bosnia and Kosovo in the 1990s. He had voted against the Persian Gulf War in 1991, but had voted to authorize the use of force against Iraq in 2002.

———

On September 15, the investment bank Lehman Brothers filed for bankruptcy. Financial markets froze up and stock markets plunged both in the United States and overseas. Suddenly, the arguments about Russia and Georgia and even the far more intense ones about Iraq faded into the background. Obama and McCain were judged above all by perceptions of how they would handle the financial crisis. McCain came across as overexcited, Obama as calm; Obama benefited greatly from the comparison. Obama's aides believed that the Bush administration had unintentionally lent them a hand in the general election campaign against McCain. In his last years in the White House, Bush took the hard edge off his foreign policy; Vice President Dick Cheney and the hawks in the administration lost influence, while the more flexible policies of Secretary of State Condoleezza Rice and Defense Secretary Robert Gates were in the ascendance.

In the summer and fall of 2008, the Bush administration took two separate steps that Obama turned to his advantage. First, in negotiations over a new legal agreement covering American forces in Iraq, Bush acceded to Iraqi requests and agreed to a deadline to withdraw all U.S. troops by the end of

2011. Obama and other Democrats had long advocated setting a date for the American military to leave Iraq, a step McCain had opposed. Secondly, Bush launched new diplomatic initiatives with both North Korea and Iran. Rice met with her North Korean counterpart in Singapore, while Undersecretary of State William J. Burns talked with Iranian officials in Geneva.

The Obamians were able to point to these developments as showing that Obama's positions on foreign policy were not radical or dangerous, but merely ahead of their time. Look, they said, Bush is doing now what Obama has been suggesting since the very start of his presidential campaign. They portrayed McCain as more hawkish and more conservative than Bush.[23]

Again, the effect was to undercut McCain's efforts in challenging Obama's foreign policy credentials. McCain's decision to appoint Sarah Palin as his vice presidential nominee and her own utterances on foreign policy ("I can see Russia from my house") made it all but impossible to claim that he was the cautious, conservative candidate and that voting for Obama was too risky.

————

In retrospect, what stands out about the 2008 presidential campaign is how little the fierce disagreements over foreign policy mattered in the long run. At the time, it seemed as though the epic primary struggle between Clinton and Obama represented a choice between continuity and change. In voting for Obama, the Democrats were said to be opting for a fundamentally different approach to the world, one in which a new Democratic president would not only withdraw American troops from Iraq, but would also reverse most of the policies implemented by George W. Bush after September 11. After Obama won the Democratic nomination, there were once again expectations that the general election campaign against McCain would focus to a large extent on national security issues, between McCain the hawk and Obama the dove.

These perceptions turned out to be mostly wrong. The foreign policy differences between Obama and Clinton look, in hindsight, like artificial constructs. The Obama supporters who had attributed to Clinton everything wrong with Democratic foreign policy in the past were to discover, soon after the election, that she would be a central figure in the new administration. The Democrats' policy differences with the Republicans eventually began to blur, too. The Obama-McCain race turned far less on foreign policy than on the financial crisis. Once in the White House, Obama would leave in effect far more of the Bush administration's policies and programs than his supporters could have believed prior to his election. There was even some surprising continuity in personnel from Bush's Republican administration to Obama's Democratic one.

In the end, then, the 2008 campaign brought forth more changes in the style, rhetoric and perceptions of America's relations with the world than actual changes in policy. When it came to the actual substance of foreign policy, the change Obama's supporters thought they were voting for in 2008 was far greater than what they got.

———

Virtually everything Obama did in the presidential campaign seemed to work. On November 4, 2008, Obama won 53 percent of the popular vote and a clear electoral college victory over McCain.

The American public had turned to the Democrats in 1976, after the end of the Vietnam War. The country chose the Democrats in 1992, after the end of the Cold War. In 2008, once again, voters handed to the Democrats the task of straightening out America's role in the world in the wake of the war in Iraq.

8

CIA and the "Aw, Shit!" Campaign

On December 9, little more than a month after Election Day, the director of the Central Intelligence Agency gave President-elect Barack Obama a rather astonishing demonstration, a quick bit of show-and-tell. The CIA director, a bald-headed, bespectacled former air force officer named Michael Hayden, had flown to Chicago to brief Obama and his top aides for the first time on American intelligence operations around the world. Obama was accompanied by some of the leading members of his new team: Vice President–elect Joe Biden; James Jones, Obama's choice for national security adviser; Rahm Emanuel, the incoming White House chief of staff; Denis McDonough, Obama's campaign foreign policy adviser; and Tony Blinken, Biden's top foreign policy aide.

It was a long session, more than two hours. Hayden ran through America's covert intelligence activities, country by country and program by program, a *tour d'horizon* of the innermost secrets of American foreign policy. The Obama team listened carefully, even though it was a day full of distractions. Elsewhere in Chicago, the governor of Illinois, Rod Blagojevich, was being arrested.

Hayden saved the most sensitive part of his briefing for the very end.[1] It covered the CIA program for combating terrorists, the program known to intelligence officials as RDI—rendition, detention and interrogation. These were nice, antiseptic words for a tough reality: The CIA snatched up suspected terrorists around the world, turned them over to other countries or brought them to secret American-run camps, and tried to get them to talk. The program had been, for several years, the subject of international protests, congressional investigations, news stories and political attacks, including direct criticism from the successful Democratic presidential candidate. Barack Obama had, only a year earlier, called the Bush administration's interrogation program "an outrageous betrayal of our core values."[2]

Carefully, Hayden began to give an overview. He was talking about the policy of handing suspected terrorists over to friendly intelligence services in places like Egypt and Jordan, when Biden interrupted him.

As chairman of the Senate Foreign Relations Committee for the previous two years, Biden was more familiar with foreign policy issues than others on the new Obama team. Biden was polite but unmistakably skeptical. Come on, he said to Hayden. You turn these guys over to other countries so that they can be tortured. "Mr. Vice President, that's not true," Hayden answered. The CIA bore moral and legal responsibility for what happened to everyone subjected to rendition. "You can disagree with the policy, but we did not move them because they can be tortured," he insisted.

Though Hayden didn't explain it, this was as much a disagreement about semantics as about actions. The word "torture" carries serious legal implications. Torture is prohibited by, among other things, the United Nations Convention Against Torture, the Geneva Conventions and the Universal Declaration of Human Rights, all of which set down general rules for the treatment of prisoners. The Bush administration, from the president on down, had repeatedly held to the line that whatever had been done did not amount to "torture." And by extension, it stuck to the position that the policy of rendition, turning prisoners over to other countries, was not for the *purpose* of torture. Biden was speaking in plain English, Hayden in the CIA's standard legalistic formulations.

Soon, Hayden moved on to the subjects of detention and interrogation. Addressing the new Obama team, Hayden argued that the program was relatively limited in scope: Fewer than one hundred people had ever been detained under the CIA program. And of these, less than one third had ever had "techniques" applied to them—that is, special methods that exceeded or "enhanced" the usual methods of interrogation.

At that point, Obama pressed for detail. "What are the techniques?" asked the president-elect.

Hayden turned to another intelligence official at the Chicago meeting. He was David Shedd, a senior aide to Michael McConnell, the director of national intelligence. "Stand up, David," Hayden said.

Shedd obediently stood up. Hayden used him as a dummy. There were six "techniques" now allowed by the CIA program, he explained. He began to run through them, one by one.

Facial grab—Hayden moved to grab Shedd by the face. Torso grab—he feigned enveloping Shedd's whole body. Facial slap—he moved to slap Shedd's face with his open hand. Tummy slap—he directed an open hand to Shedd's midsection, without actually hitting him. These were four of the six approved "techniques" for CIA interrogators, Hayden explained. The other two, he said, were simply depriving the detainee of food and/or sleep (or at least making them so irregular as to destroy a detainee's sense of routine). Hayden could not demonstrate these ones. Shedd sat down.

To Hayden, the interrogation techniques he had shown to Obama were relatively minor. He had been CIA director for two years and took pride in the fact that he had scaled back the program. The CIA's secret detention centers, its so-called "black sites" overseas, had been emptied. Before Hayden arrived, there had been thirteen interrogation techniques, including the most controversial one of all, "waterboarding," which induced in the detainee the sense that he was drowning. Hayden had reduced the number to six, on the grounds that the United States didn't need the rougher ones like waterboarding because, by 2006, it knew more about al-Qaeda than it had in the immediate aftermath of September 11. Hayden sometimes spoke as though the CIA had adopted these limits on its own in a spirit of self-restraint, although the reality was that Congress and the news media had been subjecting the RDI program to ever growing scrutiny.

So the RDI program was not quite what it had previously been. But, of course, the whole concept of "minor" interrogation techniques was problematic. It raised the dilemma of severity: If you hit a suspected terrorist in the face or stomach gently, so that it didn't hurt too much, he probably wouldn't talk. On the other hand, if you hit him hard enough to cause intense pain, he might talk—but then this wouldn't qualify as "minor" interrogation.

Hayden's show-and-tell was over, as was the meeting itself. The president-elect thanked him for the briefing, without saying much about what he thought of it. He said he wanted to talk the issues over with Greg Craig, whom he had just appointed as White House counsel. "We're going to have to decide what to do about all of this," Obama said.

————

The session in Chicago was merely one step in a quiet campaign mounted by CIA officials during the period between Obama's election and his inauguration. Privately, Hayden and some senior intelligence officials had a name for it: the "Aw, Shit!" campaign. The idea was to make incoming Obama officials realize that they needed to be pragmatic; that the realities of American foreign policy didn't fit into the world as they had imagined it from the outside; that they couldn't live up to all their campaign statements and promises for change. Once Obama and his aides realized the hard truths of what American policy required—so it was hoped—the incoming officials of the new administration would say to themselves, "Aw, shit!" and abandon the positions they had taken before coming to office.

Meanwhile, Hayden himself was hoping to stay on in the job at the CIA. There were a few newspaper stories in December, quoting unnamed supporters of Hayden suggesting Obama keep him. Whether the job of CIA director should change hands with an incoming administration had been the subject of high-level debate in Washington. Shortly after the 1976 election, CIA Director George H. W. Bush, a Republican politician who had come to the intelligence agency reluctantly but then loved it, had tried to persuade President-elect Jimmy Carter that the job of running the intelligence community should be above partisan politics and that Carter should therefore keep him on. Carter quickly rebuffed him. The senior Bush came to believe in the general principle that the CIA should not change leaders with each incoming administration, and he held to it. As president, Bush kept the sitting CIA director, William Webster, on the job, and years later, in 2001, he encouraged his son George W. to stick with Bill Clinton's intelligence chief George Tenet.

Obama wasn't buying the idea that he should retain Bush's CIA director. For the president-elect and his top advisers, the question was not whether to replace Hayden, but with whom. They had a prime candidate: John Brennan, a veteran CIA official who was a Middle East specialist and former station chief in Saudi Arabia. Brennan had served as a senior aide to Tenet at the end of the Clinton administration and in the first year of the Bush administration, had helped set up the agency's National Counterterrorism Center and had then retired from the agency in 2005. He had also served as an adviser to the Obama presidential campaign, where he'd worked directly with foreign policy adviser Denis McDonough.[3]

In mid-November, Brennan flew to Chicago to meet Obama, and the two men talked for about an hour. Brennan was able to bond with him on the subject of Indonesia, where Brennan had traveled for a summer in college and where Obama had lived for a time in his youth. Brennan, who was neither a Democrat nor a Republican and generally mistrusted ideologies, concluded that Obama was pragmatic and appreciated the complexity of intelligence issues.

Like many other intelligence professionals, Brennan would have preferred that the job of CIA director carry a fixed term so that it didn't change over with each new president. He recommended to Obama that Hayden be kept on the job for purposes of continuity, at least for a period of six months or so. But there was little doubt the Obama people wanted Brennan, or that he would have taken the job. He was appointed head of the CIA's transition team for intelligence, assigned to figure out what issues and personnel questions needed to be addressed at the start of the new administration.

But soon the prospective Brennan appointment collapsed. When the plan to appoint him became public, there was immediate opposition, mostly from Obama supporters. Obama had promised a dramatic break from the policies of the Bush administration, but Brennan had been on the job as a top adviser to George Tenet when the agency's most controversial policies were adopted, including the creation of the Guantánamo Bay detention facility and the "enhanced interrogation" techniques. In public interviews after leaving the CIA, Brennan had supported the need for change in some of the agency's practices, such as waterboarding, but he had also defended the practice of rendition and other parts of the post-2001 programs. "We do have to take the gloves off in some areas," he had explained.[4] In a letter to Obama, a group of two hundred psychologists protested that Brennan's appointment "would dishearten and alienate those who opposed torture under the Bush administration."[5] Even if Brennan could win Senate confirmation, it appeared that any hearings on his nomination would attract new controversy at the beginning of the administration.

As a result, at the end of November, Brennan withdrew his name from consideration for CIA director. Instead, the administration brought him into the White House in a newly created position as special adviser for counterterrorism and deputy national security adviser, a position that did not require Senate confirmation. He would soon come to have more direct and frequent access to Obama than the CIA director or any other intelligence official, and in many ways more power as well.

That still left hanging the question of who would be CIA director. In early January, the Obama team came up with a surprise appointment from outside the intelligence community. He nominated Leon Panetta, an old Washington hand who had previously served Richard Nixon as a senior official in the Department of Health, Education, and Welfare and President Clinton as head of the Office of Management and Budget and White House chief of staff—with sixteen years in between as a Democratic congressman.

Although Panetta knew little of the internal workings of the CIA, he was perfectly positioned to protect the agency from attack. He knew well the ways of the White House, Congress and the budget process. He had many old friends dispersed throughout Washington, such as, for example, Speaker of the House Nancy Pelosi. ("We were in the House together, and we're fellow Italian Americans from California," explained Pelosi.)[6] Most significantly, during the early years of the Clinton administration, he had been a mentor in the White House to a young and tempestuous aide, Rahm Emanuel, who was now, fifteen years later, preparing to take on Panetta's old job as White House chief of staff.

At his confirmation hearing, Panetta promised what he called a "new chapter" for the CIA.[7] That particular metaphor was, as it turned out, revealing. He was not proposing to rewrite the entire book.

In early January 2009, Obama telephoned Hayden to inform him he was going to appoint Panetta to the job Hayden had been eager to keep. Still unsettled, however, was the question of what would happen to the interrogation techniques Hayden had demonstrated to Obama in Chicago. The CIA wanted to keep the program going.

A couple of weeks before Obama's inauguration, Hayden was summoned to a meeting with several members of the incoming Obama team to review the program. The key figure was Greg Craig, who was about to become Obama's White House counsel. Again, Hayden ran through the program, this time in more detail than he had with Obama in Chicago. He again stressed the modifications he had made in the program over the past two years. What you all think you have to do with this program to curb abuse, we already did that in 2006, Hayden told the others.

Greg Craig and Michael Hayden were both sixty-three but had little else in common. The CIA director was raised in an Irish American family in Pittsburgh, the son of a welder, and attended Duquesne University as a commuter student. He entered the ROTC program, chose the air force as a service and then intelligence as a career. Two years after leaving school, he found himself planning B-52 strikes over Vietnam. He spent his entire career in the military, in intelligence or usually in both at the same time.[8]

Craig, the son of a university educator, had graduated from Phillips Exeter Academy, a leading prep school, and from Harvard, where he had been a student government leader. One of his first campaigns, as leader of the Harvard Undergraduate Council, was to ask the university to ease the restrictions that barred women from men's dormitories after the early evening.[9] He had quickly moved on from parochial campus issues to the Vietnam War. When Hayden was planning B-52 strikes in Southeast Asia, Craig was among the moderate student leaders visiting Washington to meet with Secretary of State Dean Rusk to voice growing dissatisfaction with the war. (There was "no communication," Craig wrote afterward.)[10] After graduating from Yale Law School, Craig spent much of his adult life at one of Washington's most prestigious law firms, Williams and Connolly, where he represented a long and varied list of famous clients, including Kofi Annan, Konrad Bloch, Richard Helms, John Hinckley and the father of Elián González, who sought to get his son back from Florida to his home in Cuba. Craig also took time off from his law firm to work for Senator Ted Kennedy in the 1980s and the Clinton administration in the 1990s.

In short, Craig had worked for many years in the heart of Washington's liberal establishment, just as Hayden had been at the center of its military-intelligence community. They had different assumptions, different experiences, different values. Craig saw the need for change in the CIA's practices more than Hayden did. It would turn out that Craig also didn't agree with colleagues in the Obama administration, including Brennan, Panetta and Emanuel, all of whom were eager to prevent disruptive changes at the CIA. But that would come later.

———

On January 20, 2009, Barack Obama took the oath of office as the forty-fourth president of the United States. His speech was mostly about the nation's deep economic crisis. In the section about foreign policy, he declared that "we are ready to lead once again." He also said, "We reject as false the choice between our safety and our ideals." It was a vague but unmistakable reference to the Bush administration's interrogation and detention policies.[11]

The CIA waited to hear what the new administration would do in its first days in office. The rumors had been swirling: The new president was going to sign an executive order barring all humiliating and degrading treatment of detainees. The order would require the CIA and all other U.S. government officials to abide by the rules of the Army Field Manual, which sets out guidelines for noncoercive interrogation of all prisoners.

Hayden was trying to cultivate Craig, seeking to develop a friendship. The two of them had had lunch the week before the inauguration. Still, neither Hayden nor others at the CIA had been asked for formal comment on the draft executive order on interrogations, which the press was reporting Obama would sign soon.

After Obama was sworn in, Hayden called up Craig. "I hear the president's going to sign an executive order banning the CIA's interrogation techniques," he said. "True," replied Craig. "Well, Greg, not that you asked, but this is the director of central intelligence, officially nonconcurring," Hayden said. This was the Washington way of making sure that a dissent was formally recorded, so that no one could claim that a decision had been made unanimously or by consensus. Craig simply said okay, that he had already known the CIA director was opposed.

But Hayden wasn't finished. How about just adding a few words to the executive order, he suggested: All interrogation would be under the rules of the Army Field Manual "unless otherwise ordered by the president." That would at least leave a certain ambiguity, so that prisoners being questioned by the CIA wouldn't know how far the interrogators could go. Hayden was trying to preserve the CIA's authority through the time-honored loophole of claiming presidential authorization for something otherwise prohibited.

Craig thanked Hayden for his idea, but rejected it. On January 22, Obama's second full day in office, the president signed the executive order without the Hayden suggestion that would have undercut it. Obama did so with considerable fanfare, at an Oval Office ceremony in which he was joined by more than a dozen retired generals and admirals. At the same time, Obama took another action of equal significance and even greater symbolic importance to the international community: He ordered that the Guantánamo Bay detention center be closed and all its prisoners moved out in no more than a year.

"We believe we can abide by a rule that says, 'We don't torture, but we can effectively obtain the intelligence we need,'" declared Obama at the ceremony. Hayden immediately wrote a message to the CIA workforce, telling them the agency would abide by the new interrogation rules set by the Obama administration, just as the CIA had carried out the different rules set by the Bush administration. The message, which was immediately released to the press, said the CIA would comply "without exception, carve-out or loophole."[12]

Hayden made still one more try. The following day, he asked to see the new president after the regular morning intelligence briefing. There are some issues in the executive order that still need to be clarified, he said. The new rule applied to all "agents" of the United States, and Hayden said he assumed the intent had been to cover employees of the American private contractors that had been working for the U.S. government. But the wording was still a little vague. What if the CIA authorized a foreign government or a friendly intelligence service to capture someone and detain him? Did Obama's new executive order cover a foreign intelligence service? "Mr. President, if it does, I need to tell you that we don't have a partner service from Marrakesh to Bangladesh that is going to adhere to the conditions of confinement inside the Army Field Manual."

———

Hayden's effort to preserve the interrogation techniques was a classic example of the ways in which America's permanent government bureaucracies, like the CIA, maneuver to win over a new president and to preserve the status quo. Indeed, the dispute over interrogation was merely the opening skirmish in a much broader struggle over the degree to which the Obama administration would change the direction of American policy and how much it would accommodate to the existing order.

Within weeks, Hayden was gone, replaced by Panetta. Yet in a larger sense, the "Aw, Shit!" campaign lived on and, in quite a few instances, succeeded. Other intelligence officials continued to resist changes in the status quo, intrusions on the CIA's independence or efforts to investigate what the agency had done during the Bush administration.

The Obama administration decided to preserve—or, in some instances, expand—many parts of the counterterrorism program it had inherited from the Bush administration. Obama kept the CIA's program of rendition. He accepted and perpetuated the practice of indefinite detention, without trial or sentencing, for those prisoners believed to be especially dangerous terrorists. "I am not going to release individuals who endanger the American people," the president declared four months after taking office. "Al-Qaeda terrorists and their affiliates are at war with the United States, and those that we capture—like other prisoners of war—must be prevented from attacking us again."[13]

Even more important, Obama maintained and gradually expanded the practice known as targeted killing. Indeed, the following year, the president began to brag about how much better his administration was in this endeavor than the Bush administration. ("We have had more success in eliminating al-Qaeda leaders in recent months than in recent years," he said in one speech.)[14] Obama and his top aides were especially vigorous in their reliance upon unmanned drone aircraft to strike against al-Qaeda, making vastly more use of these drones than Bush. The Obama administration also expanded the geographical areas and the legal justification for these assassinations. On September 15, 2009, less than nine months after Obama had taken office, American commandos carried out a targeted killing of a figure linked to al-Qaeda in Somalia, far away from the area of combat for U.S. forces in Afghanistan or neighboring Pakistan.

While the Obama administration rejected the Bush administration's rhetoric about a "global war on terror," the change seemed to be mostly a decision not to put those four words together anymore while still preserving the concepts and using each of the words separately. Within a year of taking office Obama was repeatedly telling the country that the United States was "at war" with al-Qaeda. The Obama administration's formal National Security Strategy of 2010 called this effort "global."[15] And Obama's top aides talked about his intensified drive against terrorists: "Not only has he approved these operations, he has encouraged us to be even more aggressive, even more proactive and even more innovative, to seek out new ways and new opportunities for taking down these terrorists," said Brennan in one early speech.[16]

In some instances, the Obama administration decided on its own, even if reluctantly, to accept arguments for perpetuating Bush administration policies, particularly in the field of counterterrorism. After nine months on the job, Harold Koh, the former dean of Yale Law School who had joined the Obama administration as the State Department's legal adviser, quoted to friends the words of Mickey Mantle when he'd hit a home run one day while hung over from a night of heavy drinking. As the crowds cheered, Mantle had said, "Those people don't know how hard that really was." Koh applied Mantle's words to the sober work of trying to reverse the Bush administration. "I learned that the making of U.S. foreign policy is infinitely harder than it looks from the ivory tower," he admitted ruefully. "It is a lot harder to get from a good idea to the implementation of that idea than those outside the government can imagine."[17]

In other instances, after it had concluded all the reviews inside the executive branch, the Obama administration decided to go ahead and press for change, but then was forced to retreat in the face of political opposition from Congress, the American public or governments overseas. The most notable example was Guantánamo Bay.

When Obama announced his intention to close the Guantánamo Bay prison, some critics complained that the one-year time limit was too long. "It will be a great disappointment if concrete action takes anywhere near that long," wrote *Washington Post* columnist Eugene Robinson the following day. "An executive order becomes real when it is followed—promptly—by action."[18]

Obama couldn't come close to meeting the one-year pledge and, within eighteen months, would put the effort to close Guantánamo Bay on the back burner.[19] Congress repeatedly frustrated the idea by opposing the transfer of prisoners from Guantánamo to the mainland United States. In 2009, it restricted any transfers except for purposes of prosecution, and the following year it prohibited the use of any Defense Department money for transfers. Once it was clear the United States wouldn't itself take prisoners out of Guantánamo, it became much harder to persuade other countries to do so. By early 2011, the Obama administration had dropped the pretense that Guantánamo would be closed anytime soon. When asked at a congressional hearing where Osama bin Laden would be taken if he was ever captured, CIA Director Leon Panetta responded that he would probably go to Guantánamo.[20]

In the face of political resistance, the administration also retreated from its decision to transfer specific prisoners from Guantánamo to the United States for prosecution. Attorney General Eric Holder announced plans to bring Khalid Sheikh Mohammed, the architect of the World Trade Center attacks, to New York City for trial in federal court, along with four other Guantánamo prisoners connected to September 11. However, the administration had to drop the idea in the face of opposition from New York Democrats such as Senator Charles Schumer, from Mayor Michael Bloomberg, and from city real estate and business groups. They were worried the trial would require such heavy security that it could snarl traffic in lower Manhattan and virtually shut down the financial district for months.

Nothing provoked more controversy than the question of what to do about abuses during the Bush administration. At the time Obama took office, many civil liberties advocates and other liberal groups urged him to approve a formal, wide-ranging investigation of what had taken place in the Bush years, whether through criminal probes or through an independent truth commission. From the start, Obama rejected the idea. "We need to focus on the future," he said in an oft-repeated formulation. Trying to assess individual blame from the previous eight years, he argued, "can distract us from focusing our time, our effort and our politics on the challenges of the future."[21]

That disposed of the idea of a general investigation, but it still wasn't the end of the story. Over the following year, the actions of the Bush administration came up in several other contexts, in each case producing intense conflict, particularly with the CIA. In April 2009, Obama decided to release the "top secret" memos written in the Bush years by the Justice Department's Office of Legal Counsel that had authorized and justified the "enhanced interrogation" techniques. The memos had been requested in a federal court case. CIA Director Panetta and his four predecessors had all opposed the idea of making the memos public; so did Brennan. But all of them failed to persuade the president.[22]

A similar dispute broke out the following month over the question of whether to make public an extensive series of pictures of prisoner abuse by American military personnel. Some of the pictures were comparable to the ones of Abu Ghraib—snapshots by American soldiers of Iraqi prisoners in degrading situations. Others were even more explosive: They were taken by U.S. military investigators at the autopsies of prisoners who had died after alleged abuses while in custody. These pictures, like the memos, had been ordered to be turned over in a federal court case, and the administration at first said it would go along. American military commanders vigorously opposed the release, saying the photos would arouse intense anti-American sentiment in the war zones of Iraq and Afghanistan and thereby endanger U.S. forces. Defense Secretary Robert Gates agreed with this argument, and so ultimately did Obama.[23] Separately, the Obama administration began to invoke in court the "state secrets" doctrine to withhold information about national security. The new administration's brief movement toward transparency about the Bush years was beginning to subside.

Obama took on one more battle with the CIA. In the late summer of 2009, he supported Attorney General Eric Holder's decision to ask a special prosecutor, John Durham, to conduct a criminal investigation of possible illegal conduct by CIA agents while interrogating terrorist suspects. There was a case, for example, in which a CIA agent in Afghanistan had ordered that an uncooperative detainee be stripped naked, shackled to the concrete floor and left overnight without blankets. The next morning, he was found dead of hypothermia.[24]

This time, not four but seven former CIA directors joined with Panetta in urging Obama to stop the investigation.[25] They argued in a letter to the president that the CIA agents' conduct had previously been investigated and found to be legal in the Bush administration. "Those men and women who undertake difficult intelligence assignments in the aftermath of an attack such as September 11 must believe there is permanence in the legal rules that govern their actions," their letter said.[26] They did not address the question of whether some errant CIA agents might have transgressed even the expansive rules for interrogation set down by the Bush administration.

After the investigation was launched, Durham, a career prosecutor, vanished from public view for an extended period of time. He called a number of CIA agents before grand juries, heightening the anxieties at the agency. In mid-2011, on Panetta's final day as CIA director, the Justice Department announced that Durham had reviewed 101 cases involving interrogations of detainees by the agency or its contractors and had closed all but two of them. However, in those two remaining cases, one involving a detainee in Afghanistan and the other at the Abu Ghraib prison in Iraq, the Justice Department opened full-scale criminal investigations.[27]

———

Within less than a year after the inauguration, Greg Craig would be gone—in no small part because he had been willing to challenge the intelligence community too often. In early August 2009, while the Obama administration was in the last weeks of deciding whether the CIA abuse cases should be sent to a special prosecutor, an unusual story appeared in the *Wall Street Journal*. "White House Counsel's Job at Stake," read the headline. The story said that unnamed Obama administration officials were discussing Craig's "departure" as White House counsel.[28] This story, and others that followed it over the following weeks, said Obama administration officials were unhappy that Craig had mishandled Obama's efforts to close Guantánamo within a year. That explanation was both incomplete and highly misleading. It suggested vaguely that Craig had frustrated Obama's efforts to change the policies of the Bush administration. In fact, the reverse was closer to the truth: Craig had pushed too vigorously to break with the Bush administration on issues such as releasing the photos and Justice Department memos and investigating past abuses by the CIA. In the process, he had run up against some high-level adversaries in the intelligence community and the White House. At the top was Rahm Emanuel, who was especially close to Panetta and had probably played a role in winning him the job as CIA director.

"Greg Craig's a very good guy. Rahm just put him out to dry," observed a Washington official with long experience in national security. "What he didn't understand was, who gave Rahm Emanuel his first real job in government? If you're going to fight with a guy [that is, Panetta], you have to know who's in his corner."[29] Emanuel had been saying, even more insistently than Obama, that the new administration should not get bogged down in disputes over what had happened in the Bush years; from his perspective, such controversies could divert attention from the White House's top priorities, such as health care.

Craig was left without high-level political support. His longtime political patron, Ted Kennedy, had died of cancer in August 2009. The Clinton camp was certainly not going to rush to his defense; Craig was the author of the famous campaign memo arguing that Hillary Clinton had little experience in foreign policy. Indeed, one of the main reasons Craig had been appointed White House counsel was that Hillary Clinton had become secretary of state, thus ending Craig's hopes of landing a senior job at the State Department. (Some in the Clinton camp believed that Obama's inner circle had given Craig a prominent role in the presidential campaign primarily as part of a larger effort to win Kennedy's endorsement.)

Craig represented the legacy of Kennedy-style idealism within the Democratic Party, an outlook with its roots in the antiwar movement of the 1960s and 1970s. Obama, Emanuel and the aides around them had no strong identification with this strain of thinking. They thought of themselves as a new generation completely removed from the Vietnam era, a generation with its own ideals but also a different, pragmatic perspective on defense and intelligence issues.[30]

Craig stayed in his job for another three months. Near the end, his old friend Sam Brown—fellow leader of the Vietnam antiwar movement—sent him a note. If the administration doesn't give you another job, Brown told Craig, you should join those of us who are calling upon Barack Obama to refrain from sending new troops to Afghanistan and to gradually withdraw all American forces.[31]

But in November, Craig left quietly, and refrained from criticizing the administration. He moved to a different law firm. Within six months, he had a new client: Goldman Sachs.

In the early months of the Obama administration, the president and his aides regularly portrayed themselves as having made a fundamental break with Bush's policies. For their own part, Republican critics, led by former vice president Dick Cheney, chastised Obama for weakening American security by undermining the Bush policies.[32]

Over the following years, however, as it gradually became clear how much of the Bush administration's war on terror was being carried forward, the arguments of both parties shifted. By 2011, even Cheney was beginning to acknowledge that his early claims about the Obama administration jeopardizing national security had not been borne out. Cheney claimed a kind of gloating vindication from the fact that Obama had not closed Guantánamo, had stepped up the drone program and had continued other elements of the Bush administration's counterterrorism policies. "I think he has learned that what we did was far more appropriate than he ever gave us credit for while he was a candidate," Cheney said in one interview. "So I think he's learned from experience." Addressing a convention of conservatives, Cheney wondered aloud whether Donald Rumsfeld had had greater influence on Obama than Obama's own aides.[33]

For their own part, Obama administration officials shifted ground, too. Obama's aides still argued that they were different from the Bush administration. But they stopped talking about closing Guantánamo anytime soon. Instead, they often pointed out that they weren't the ones to open it, and that they had at least *tried* to shut it down. When asked about changes from the Bush era, Obama administration officials often pointed to the fact that the president had outlawed the CIA's "enhanced interrogation techniques" and required that all detainees be questioned under the rules of the Army Field Manual. This formulation was accurate; it was indeed a change in policy, and that was why Hayden had campaigned against it before Obama took office. Yet the Obama team didn't say that many of the "enhanced" techniques, including waterboarding, had already been abandoned, and that the CIA's secret "black sites" overseas had been emptied out, in 2006, during the final years of the Bush administration. Indeed, virtually everyone in the Obama administration interviewed for this book acknowledged that, in many policy areas, there had been considerable change from Bush's first term in office to his second, and that in fact the changes from the late Bush years to Obama's tenure were not so dramatic.

After a year in office, Obama's team came up with new formulations to justify the lack of change. When pressed to explain why there was so much continuity from Bush to Obama, they argued that there is always a lot of continuity from one administration to the next. The president was comfortable with not being entirely different from the Bush administration, they said. Or, on other occasions, they explained that the president's understanding of certain issues had evolved over time.

The CIA's "Aw, Shit!" campaign, started by Hayden after Obama's election, had failed to turn around Obama before the inauguration. But over the long term, it worked. Hayden left, but so did Greg Craig. There was no single scatological moment of the kind that Hayden had envisioned. But on many issues, the president's views "evolved," and the policies of his predecessor stayed put.

9

Afghanistan: Flip of the COIN

In the early days of the new administration, Bruce Riedel, the former intelligence analyst who had worked for Barack Obama's campaign, began to describe to the president the dangers of nuclear weapons falling into the wrong hands in a place like Pakistan. "That's scary," Obama told him. "But in the meeting I just had before this one, the Treasury people told me that virtually every bank in the United States could fail before the end of the month. Now that's *really* scary."[1]

It was a conversation that showed Obama's mind-set in the weeks after he took office. At other times, both earlier in his career and later in his presidency, he would demonstrate that he cared quite a bit about stopping the spread of nuclear weapons—too much so, in the eyes of hawkish critics. In the weeks after Obama took office, however, all foreign policy issues seemed of secondary importance. He was devoting most of his time and attention to domestic issues.

The American economy was in the most severe recession since the Great Depression. During the first three months of 2009, the economy contracted at an annual rate of 6.1 percent, after dropping 6.3 percent in the last quarter of 2008.[2] Unemployment was climbing month by month. The stock market kept dropping; having hit a high of 14,198 in 2007, the Dow Jones had fallen to 7,949 by the time Obama took office and it reached a low of 6,443 on March 6, 2009. Chrysler slipped into bankruptcy, and General Motors followed a couple months later.

After less than four weeks in the White House, Obama won congressional approval of his $787 billion stimulus package, the largest in history. Under George W. Bush, the government had already put trillions of dollars on the line to keep giant investment banks and insurance companies afloat.

Now the Obama administration did the same for the car industry, taking a majority share in General Motors, in effect nationalizing the company for a period of time, and firing GM's chief executive. For good measure, Obama also submitted the largest federal budget in history and began the process of overhauling the health care system. Later in his presidency, Obama's critics would sometimes accuse him of being weak, feckless or detached, but in those first months, it was the opposite: His detractors portrayed him as too powerful, too clever and too active.

———

Obama's first major decision in foreign policy, made amid the financial crisis less than six weeks after he took office, was to set a timetable for withdrawal from Iraq. The war had been the driving force behind his candidacy, and he fulfilled his campaign commitment, more or less. While running for office, he had promised to withdraw from Iraq in sixteen months, one combat brigade per month. On February 27, 2009, in a speech at the Marine Corps base at Camp Lejeune, North Carolina, he announced he would pull out all combat forces within eighteen months, by August 31, 2010, though at a slower pace in the first year and more rapidly at the end of the period. He promised to have all the remaining U.S. forces out of Iraq by the end of 2011.

Military leaders, including the Iraq commander Ray Odierno, had asked Obama to stretch out the timetable he had proposed as a candidate and, above all, not to withdraw too many troops in the early months, before the Iraqi elections scheduled for January 2010. Obama generally went along with these requests. In his address to the marines, he avoided dwelling on the old debates about the war and instead described Iraq as having cost too much and sapped America of energy and resources that could be used elsewhere. He said he had "taken into account the simple reality that America can no longer afford to see Iraq in isolation from other priorities: We face the challenge of refocusing on Afghanistan and Pakistan, of relieving the burden on our military and of rebuilding our struggling economy—and these are challenges that we will meet."[3] The specific mention of Afghanistan seemed at the time like just a passing reference, but it would come to mean much more in the following months.

This early action effectively removed Iraq as the most contentious issue in American life. Nearly 130,000 American troops remained in Iraq, but, mentally, America withdrew. With surprising speed, political leaders stopped talking about Iraq, stories about the war became ever less prominent in the newspapers and commentators turned their attention to other subjects. "As a political issue, Iraq has faded into the background, despite the sizable troop presence that remains there," wrote the *Washington Post*'s political reporter Dan Balz during Obama's first summer in the White House. The Republicans had little interest in dredging up the early debates about whether the Iraq War was justified, after the elections of 2006 and 2008 had shown that the public disagreed with them. The antiwar left was not eager to quibble over the details of withdrawal from Iraq when there were other issues that deserved attention. Most people saw no point in challenging Obama over the war he had inherited when he was already committed to ending it.[4]

Bush's intervention in Iraq had been a disastrous mistake: Obama never changed his view on that subject, which he had first put forward in 2002. It turned out, however, that in his last two years in office Bush had made two decisions on Iraq that made Obama's decision to withdraw easier. The first was Bush's agreement in 2008 to a broad status-of-forces agreement with the Iraqi government under which all American troops were to be taken out of Iraq by the end of 2011. Obama and his aides acknowledged that this decision by Bush had helped them (particularly during the campaign, when John McCain was opposing withdrawal). Bush's acquiescence in this deadline meant that, by the time Obama took office, the debate was not over whether to withdraw, but how quickly.

The other decision that had helped was the "surge" of U.S. troops in Iraq in 2007. When George W. Bush ordered the surge in January 2007, Obama and other Democrats opposed this action, which ran counter to the recommendations of the bipartisan commission headed by James Baker and Lee Hamilton. Obama never quite said that the surge had worked, but in his Camp Lejeune speech he singled out for special praise the American officials who had led it—military commanders David Petraeus and Ray Odierno, as well as Ryan Crocker, the U.S. ambassador to Iraq. Obama also spoke of the "renewed cause for hope" in Iraq and said the troops "got the job done," in effect praising the turnaround of the previous two years without explicitly mentioning his predecessor or the surge.[5]

With this action, less than two months into his presidency, Obama shifted his gaze away from Iraq. He and his aides avoided close involvement with Iraq, not wanting to leave too many fingerprints in case the final phases of the war went badly. Obama left most military decisions up to the Pentagon. Political issues were turned over to Vice President Joe Biden and James Steinberg, the deputy secretary of state. Everything seemed to be on track. In the fall of 2009, the president went several months without taking part in a meeting on Iraq, the issue that had won him the presidency.[6]

One of the principal reasons that Americans forgot about Iraq was that the war in Afghanistan quickly took center stage. Afghanistan was not Iraq, but the similarities were striking. The underlying political dynamics were the same. Just as with Iraq, progressives and independents generally opposed the war in Afghanistan while conservatives tended to support it. Military leaders, having fought in Afghanistan, were not eager to lose or to withdraw. General Petraeus, who had led the American forces in Iraq, eventually became the commander in Afghanistan. The military strategy of counterinsurgency, of which Petraeus had been the principal architect, was transported from Iraq to Afghanistan. In both wars, Petraeus worked under Defense Secretary Robert Gates, who had taken office a few weeks before the surge in Iraq. Quite a few of the news reporters who had covered the Iraq War were reassigned to Kabul, where they sometimes ran into the same military officers, development experts and intelligence officials who had served in the other war.

When Obama took office, the war in Afghanistan was going poorly. The American effort had been starved for lack of resources for six years, since Bush had diverted resources from Afghanistan to the invasion of Iraq. The American campaign seemed to have succeeded in 2001, when American forces helped oust the Taliban from control of the government in Kabul. Yet the war in Afghanistan never ended. Over the previous seven years, seven U.S. commanders had been in charge of it. When Obama arrived in the White House, he inherited a long-standing request from military leaders for additional troops, one that dated back three commanders. In late 2008, the new general in charge of Afghanistan, David McKiernan, sent an updated request to get 30,000 more troops by the end of 2009. The outgoing Bush administration had already cleared the way for 6,000 of these.[7]

The army was trying to import and adapt for Afghanistan the doctrine of counterinsurgency—the military acronym was COIN—that Petraeus had both devised and implemented. He had been the coauthor of a new Army Field Manual on the subject, published in 2006, and had then implemented the policy during Bush's surge in Iraq the following year. COIN meant that the army would focus its efforts on developing its ties to the civilian population, protecting ordinary Afghanis from the Taliban and thus winning their support and help for the war. In the fall of 2008, when McKiernan took charge on the ground in Afghanistan, Petraeus was elevated to the head of the U.S. Central Command, with responsibility for overseeing both Iraq and Afghanistan, and thus overseeing McKiernan's work.

"He [Petraeus] put forward this whole change movement within the military. We were almost like insurgents within the U.S government," said David Kilcullen, who was one of Petraeus's leading advisers, in an interview soon after Obama took office. "When I first arrived, we had to talk in whispers about stuff that is now commonplace. The conventional wisdom was totally unorthodox in '04, '05."[8]

Petraeus's ideas had some critics. There were those who thought the doctrine was a little too fashionable inside the army and the Pentagon. They grumbled that the army was by its nature a bunch of grunts trained to kill people, not to build sewer lines and speak Urdu. They also raised questions about whether the COIN doctrine would work well in Afghanistan. "Iraq had an urban, educated population, infrastructure, and bountiful natural resources, whereas Afghanistan has none of these," wrote Celeste Ward, a defense specialist.[9] But the COIN approach had seemed to work in Iraq and had attracted considerable support in Washington. Michael Vickers, the head of special operations at the Pentagon, liked Petraeus's ideas; so did Bob Gates and George Bush.

A counterintelligence strategy seemed to have some appeal for the Democrats. The doctrine meant that the army would focus less on killing and more on development work, less on the country's capital city or top leadership and more on winning over the people in the countryside.

America's two major political parties have displayed somewhat different tendencies when it comes to military conflict. The differences are not absolute, but they have emerged over time. The Republicans have tended to prefer big short wars or none at all. Since the beginning of the Cold War, the Republicans' ideas have focused on either using overwhelming force to win a war quickly (Dwight Eisenhower's doctrine of massive retaliation, followed by George H. W. Bush in Panama and the Persian Gulf) or, by contrast, in avoiding conflict altogether (Ronald Reagan pulling the troops out of Lebanon, George H. W. Bush staying out of Bosnia). The classic articulation of these ideas was the "Powell doctrine," set down in the aftermath of the Vietnam War, first by Caspar Weinberger, Reagan's defense secretary, and then by Colin Powell as chairman of the Joint Chiefs of Staff: The United States should go to war only with massive force, public support, well-defined goals and a good sense of how a war will end. (It was this doctrine that George W. Bush, Dick Cheney and Donald Rumsfeld violated in the Iraq War, because they assumed they would win as quickly and easily as in the Persian Gulf War. The younger Bush wrongly believed America's allies and friends would fall into line behind the United States; and then, worst of all, Rumsfeld wrongly persuaded others that, because of changing technology, "overwhelming force" could be reinterpreted downward to mean fewer troops.)

At least in the early stages of the Vietnam War, the Democrats were more willing to engage in the messy middle ground. Kennedy sent the first American troops to Vietnam and then Johnson escalated the war, step-by-step, yet occasionally pausing, ordering temporary halts in the bombing while tentatively exploring the chances for peace. In that era, the Democrats became intrigued with the possibilities of counterinsurgency. Indeed, one of the early proponents of COIN, during the war in Vietnam, was Robert F. Kennedy. In a speech to the International Police Academy in 1965, when he was in the Senate, Kennedy had observed, "In conventional war, the aim is to kill the enemy. But the essence of successful counterinsurgency is not to kill but to bring the insurgent back into the national life." [10]

There were also two aspects to counterinsurgency, however, that turned out to be not so appealing. The COIN approach seemed to mean that a war would require (1) more time and (2) more troops. It took time for an army trained for conventional warfare to reorient its own troops toward learning the doctrine of counterinsurgency and the culture of the country in which it fought. It also took time to retrain an army for counterinsurgency and then to gradually win over the support of the population. COIN requires lots of troops because it is far more manpower intensive to spread out through the countryside and win over a population than to shoot weapons from inside a protected city, bunker or armored vehicle. While the Iraq War had turned around under Petraeus, his counterinsurgency strategy had come hand in hand with the surge in American troop strength. One of the principal models for successful counterinsurgency, cited both by Robert Kennedy at the time of the Vietnam War and by Petraeus and others in the era of Iraq and Afghanistan, was the British campaign to overcome communist guerrillas in Malaya in the 1950s. That effort took roughly a decade.

In 2009, Barack Obama would accept, gingerly, some of the army's new COIN strategy. Only later would he struggle with its implications for how many troops the generals would say they needed in Afghanistan and how long the Americans would stay there.

———

Obama's first move on Afghanistan was to order a broad review of U.S. policy there and in neighboring Pakistan. For that, he turned to Riedel, the former CIA official who had been Obama's principal adviser on those countries during the campaign. After the election, he had returned to the Brookings Institution, determined not to get sucked into working in government again; he had already done that for decades. Obama knew of Riedel's determination to stay out of the administration, but he called Riedel and asked him to head up a brief review for the National Security Council of what should be done about Afghanistan and Pakistan. The review would be of limited duration, no more than sixty days. For that short period, Riedel was willing to come back into government.

Obama set the sixty-day limit for reasons well beyond his respect for Riedel's private life. He was scheduled to travel to Europe on April 3 to attend his first NATO summit with European prime ministers. He needed to tell them what his Afghanistan policy would be. European countries had their own troops on the ground in Afghanistan, but the Europeans generally faced considerable and growing domestic pressure to get out. Some of the European governments, such as Germany's, imposed severe limits on what the troops could do: They were required to avoid combat and refrain from offensive operations, and to concentrate on training, peacekeeping and reconstruction.

Keeping the Europeans on board in Afghanistan and furnishing them with airlift and other means of transport proved so arduous and time-consuming that some former American defense officials, upon leaving government, questioned whether it had been worth all the trouble, if the Europeans weren't going to fight anyway. The NATO mission in Afghanistan was formally called ISAF, shorthand for International Security Assistance Force. Some Europeans intellectuals, joking about their countries' reluctance to put troops in harm's way, confided that ISAF really stood for "Interested in Seeing Americans Fight."[11]

For the president to be ready for the NATO meetings in early April, Riedel's group needed to get something to him a week or two before that. But before the report went to the president, it would have to be discussed by what is known as the Principals Committee, comprised of cabinet-level officials, such as the secretaries of State, Treasury and Defense and the national security adviser. And before making its way there, the drafted strategy would have to go first through the Deputies Committee, the second-in-commands for State, Defense, NSC and other foreign policy agencies. That group meets more often than the principals and is responsible for approving a unified position within the bureaucracy.

Sometimes, in the middle of a crisis, this could all be done and a decision reached within hours, but for a full-blown review of long-term strategy, it usually took weeks. This was not new to the Obama administration; it was the process recent administrations had to follow as well. The bottom line was that although Riedel's review would last sixty days, he would need to come up with the draft of a new policy for Afghanistan and Pakistan within two or three weeks, certainly by the end of February.

In one respect, Obama couldn't even wait that long. General McKiernan was eager for additional troops in Afghanistan immediately. The war there couldn't wait for the April NATO meeting; the situation was continuing to deteriorate. On February 11, 2009, the day before Richard Holbrooke, Obama's special representative, was to arrive in Kabul for talks, the Taliban launched terrorist attacks at government buildings there, killing twenty-eight people. Six days later, while Riedel and his group were still hurriedly putting together the first draft of their report, Obama announced that he was ordering another 17,000 American troops to Afghanistan. It was the first time he would send troops into battle.[12]

The main officials taking part in the review, besides Riedel, were Holbrooke, Flournoy from the Pentagon and Petraeus, representing the uniformed military from the Centcom headquarters in Tampa. "There were a lot of egos in one room," said one participant, although both Riedel and Flournoy were by nature relatively modest.

Holbrooke had already moved to occupy as much bureaucratic turf as possible in his new job, immediately running into bureaucratic and diplomatic resistance in the process. Before Holbrooke took office, the Indian government had bristled at his proposed job description as special envoy for "Afghanistan, Pakistan and related matters"—a veiled hint that he might try to work out a solution to the dispute between Pakistan and India over Kashmir. Indian officials made their displeasure known to the new Obama team, and by the time Holbrooke's position was announced, the phrase "and related matters" was taken out, in effect removing India from Holbrooke's portfolio.[13]

For his own part, Petraeus had no small conception of himself, either. His view of the role of his Tampa-based Central Command for Afghanistan was no more limited than Holbrooke's view of his own civilian role. In late February, at the annual Munich security conference of defense officials from around the world, Petraeus joked of Holbrooke, "You know, it's every commander's dream to have an ambassadorial wingman who is described by journalists with nicknames like 'The Bulldozer.'" The audience laughed. Holbrooke didn't object to the word "bulldozer," since he'd been called that many times before and it probably made others in the government think twice before tangling with him. But he hated being called Petraeus's "wingman"—Holbrooke liked to be the center, not on anyone's wing. (Two months later, seeking to mollify Holbrooke, Petraeus made an appearance at Harvard and revived the line about Holbrooke the Bulldozer with a slight twist: "I'm very, very privileged to be his military wingman.")[14]

Ultimately, the first Afghanistan policy review was predetermined. The outcome was influenced in part by the shortage of time and the conflicting demands of the financial crisis, but above all by the positions Obama had taken during the campaign. He had been in the lead in his opposition to the Iraq War, repeatedly having made the argument that Iraq was a diversion from the war against al-Qaeda in Afghanistan and Pakistan. Since 2007, he had also been calling for more vigorous action to combat terrorists in Pakistan.

Now, in the first months of his administration, Obama seemed to be boxed in by his campaign rhetoric. He was not about to say, so soon after coming to the White House, that he would turn down the long-pending requests from military leaders for more troops in Afghanistan. Moreover, Riedel's report was being put together by officials whose views were generally in line with Obama's stated position. Riedel was a staunch proponent of much tougher American action in dealing with Pakistan's civilian leaders and intelligence service. Flournoy had helped run the think tank advocating counterinsurgency. Petraeus had written the book on that strategy. Holbrooke was no pacifist; he believed in the use and application of American military power on behalf of worthy causes, and he had been conversant in the ideas of counterinsurgency since serving in the countryside in Vietnam. Moreover, Holbrooke didn't mind if a widened campaign in Afghanistan and Pakistan, to be followed by determined diplomacy for peace, added up to an important role for him in the administration.

The result of all these forces was a review of Afghan policy that was rushed and less than thorough. Riedel produced a report that tracked with what he'd been saying for the past couple of years, and in fact what he'd written in a book, *The Search for al Qaeda*.[15] The report urged a stronger emphasis on changing the status quo in Pakistan by getting the country's leadership, including its intelligence agency, the ISI (Inter-Services Intelligence), to move against al-Qaeda leaders and forces on Pakistani soil.

The Riedel report also strongly embraced counterinsurgency. At the press conference announcing the results of the review, Flournoy returned again and again to core COIN concepts. "There is a shift in strategy toward emphasizing more bottom-up approaches in development and governance at the district and provincial level," she said. American and NATO troops would go to Afghanistan with "a couple of key missions in mind. First is protecting the population, reversing Taliban gains, creating secure environments that will allow other things to happen in the country."[16]

Obama announced that he was sending another 4,000 American troops to Afghanistan, in addition to the 17,000 he had already dispatched in February. The two new deployments within six weeks, at the beginning of a new Democratic administration, began to attract questions and a bit of opposition from within Obama's own party. To some Democrats, particularly older ones, this two-step seemed reminiscent of the incremental increases that brought the United States into Vietnam. House Speaker Nancy Pelosi told other Democrats in Congress to go along with the troop increases, on the grounds that they should give leeway to the new Democratic president. But she observed drily, in an interview two years later, "I have to admit that this wasn't what we had in mind."[17]

Within the Obama administration, the most senior official to register dissent was Vice President Joe Biden. He understood well the long-standing antiwar sentiments within the Democratic Party; he argued that more troops would mean more casualties and thus more unhappiness inside the United States about the war. It would become harder and harder to sustain public support, he maintained. Biden called for a strategy of counterterrorism rather than counterinsurgency: If the goal was to defeat al-Qaeda, Biden argued, then the answer was to step up the use of drones and special operations in Pakistan, not to keep on adding regular forces in Afghanistan. In early March, Leslie Gelb, who knew Biden well and had joined with him in trying to develop a strategy for Iraq, wrote an op-ed piece that argued against increasing troop strength or embracing counterinsurgency in Afghanistan. The piece was entitled "How to Leave Afghanistan."[18]

Others at the top ranks of the administration, however, starting with Obama, were persuaded that Biden's strategy wouldn't work. They argued that continuing the war in Afghanistan was necessary to overcome al-Qaeda. If the United States pulled out its troops and was defeated in Afghanistan, then the drones and other operations launched from Afghanistan into Pakistan would be for naught. Al-Qaeda could then simply move back across the border to a Taliban-controlled Afghanistan—much as it had moved from Afghanistan to Pakistan in late 2001 after American troops had dislodged the Taliban government in Kabul. On a Sunday talk show Obama explained, "We have to ensure that neither Afghanistan nor Pakistan can serve as a safe haven for al-Qaeda."[19]

Obama, in announcing the new strategy, left several important questions unanswered. These included the overriding questions of how many troops would be needed and for how long. The Riedel report had said the American strategy was to "disrupt, dismantle and defeat" al-Qaeda. It would take only a few drones to "disrupt" al-Qaeda, at least temporarily. What would it take to "defeat" it?

At the press conference to unveil Riedel's report, one reporter had asked about the American "exit strategy" in Afghanistan. Trying to duck the question by avoiding specifics, Holbrooke spoke vaguely about an exit strategy. Flournoy soon jumped in, uneasy with any talk of an American exit. The United States was making "a long-term commitment to assisting the Afghan people," Flournoy said. Two days later, Obama tried to shut down the discussion of a long-term presence. "It's not going to be an open-ended commitment of infinite resources," he said. "We've just got to make sure that we are focused on achieving what we need to achieve with the resources we have."[20]

In May, Defense Secretary Robert Gates, backed by General Petraeus, relieved McKiernan of his command in Afghanistan and replaced him with General Stanley McChrystal. Gates and Petraeus believed that McKiernan was too tied to conventional warfare and not the right general to carry out the strategy of counterinsurgency. Gates said he wanted someone with "fresh thinking" and "fresh eyes" to take charge of the forces in Afghanistan. At a press conference, he told reporters: "We have a new strategy, a new mission and a new ambassador. I believe that new military leadership is also needed."[21]

It would now be up to McChrystal to let Washington know what was needed to execute the counterinsurgency campaign.

10

"It's Not Like This Ghost in His Head"

One of the little-noticed rituals of American politics is the annual Veterans of Foreign Wars convention. Each summer, America's highest-ranking political leaders address the gathering. Republicans generally give speeches aimed at pleasing their hawkish supporters. Democrats use the occasion to show that they are not as dovish as they have been portrayed.

Year after year, the politicians' appearances have served as a bellwether showing where the United States is headed or what Americans are thinking. It was before the VFW, in August 2002, that Vice President Dick Cheney gave his first public speech laying out the case for war against Iraq, claiming without qualification that Saddam Hussein had resumed his quest for nuclear weapons. Cheney was seeking to rebut Secretary of State Colin Powell (who had been arguing that the United States should go to the UN Security Council for authorization of military action) and former national security adviser Brent Scowcroft (who had just come out against going to war).

Two years later, at the height of the 2004 presidential campaign, John Kerry spoke to the VFW and tried to show that he was in some ways more hawkish than President Bush. "Let me be clear: Like you, I defended this country as a young man, and I will defend it as president," said Kerry. "I will never hesitate to use force when it is required." An obscure group called the Swift Boat Veterans for Truth had just launched its television ads questioning Kerry's Vietnam War credentials. Kerry at first ignored the ads, but after getting a cool reception at the VFW convention, he changed his mind. Veterans at the convention repeated the Swift Boat charges that had been airing, without response from the Kerry campaign, for two weeks. Surprised and angered, Kerry decided to fight back one day later.[1]

At the VFW convention in 2008, John McCain challenged Barack

Obama's suitability to be commander in chief and chided him for failing to support the war in Iraq. The next day Obama showed up to rebut McCain and give his own version of the Democratic "I am not a dove" speech. America needed to be not just tough but both tough and smart, he told the VFW. Yes, he was against the Iraq War and wanted to end it, Obama said, but the reason was that it was diverting America's military strength from the war against al-Qaeda in Afghanistan and Pakistan. "As commander in chief, I will have no greater priority than taking out these terrorists who threaten America, and finishing the job against the Taliban," Obama declared. "For years, I have called for more resources and more troops to finish the fight in Afghanistan."[2] Antiwar liberals who were taken by surprise by Obama's actions on Afghanistan in the White House should have been paying closer attention to what he had said during the campaign.

In 2009, Obama attended the VFW convention for the first time as president of the United States. He had already increased the deployments in Afghanistan by more than 20,000 troops and had aroused stirrings of opposition within his own party in the process. This time, he carried his own rhetoric about Afghanistan one step further, arguing that the war there was fundamentally different from the one in Iraq. "This is not a war of choice. This is a war of necessity," Obama maintained. "Those who attacked America on 9/11 are plotting to do so again."[3]

———

By that time, in his first summer as president, Obama was heading toward another, far more extensive review of the war in Afghanistan, one that would last through the fall and would engender intense controversy both in public and within his administration.

In Afghanistan, General Stanley McChrystal, the newly appointed commander, had been surveying the field and talking to outside experts about what was required to implement the strategy of counterinsurgency that the Riedel report had recommended. When National Security Adviser James Jones visited Afghanistan in late June (with a longtime friend, Bob Woodward, in his delegation), McChrystal told him the war was going badly. Another general put it even more plainly: The U.S. military didn't have enough troops to carry out the mission in Afghanistan. Jones tried to discourage the idea of asking for more troops, but he and the White House were put on notice of what would be coming. In late August, McChrystal sent his assessment to Defense Secretary Robert Gates, describing the war in dire terms and asserting that if things didn't change, the United States would lose. Privately, McChrystal let Gates know he was going to need 40,000 more troops.[4]

Gates was worried. It reminded him of something he had seen before. During the 1980s, he had been the CIA's most senior specialist on the Soviet Union when Mikhail Gorbachev struggled with the Soviet military's request for tens of thousands of more troops in Afghanistan. That hadn't worked, and the Soviets finally withdrew.[5]

Other Obama administration officials were thinking about a different historical comparison: the Vietnam War. McChrystal's request for more troops and the administration's renewed internal debate over Afghanistan led to a "battle of the two books" within the U.S. government, with civilians brandishing one book, about Vietnam, while military leaders and defense intellectuals circulated another. That summer, both Jones and his deputy, Tom Donilon, had read a recent book called *Lessons in Disaster: McGeorge Bundy and the Path to War in Vietnam*. The book was initially a memoir of Vietnam by Bundy, national security adviser under Kennedy and Johnson, in collaboration with a scholar named Gordon Goldstein. When Bundy died with the book unfinished, Goldstein rewrote it as a history in which each chapter is a different lesson: for example, "Never Trust the Bureaucracy to Get It Right" and "Politics Is the Enemy of Strategy." (When Goldstein's book came out in 2008, the *New York Times Book Review* gave it front-page treatment, in a review written by Richard Holbrooke. The review carried the headline "The Doves Were Right.")[6]

The book was of obvious interest to Obama's national security aides, particularly at a time when they were increasingly worried about the military's efforts to obtain more troops for Afghanistan. Donilon, in particular, began recommending the book to others inside the administration, including the senior political advisers Rahm Emanuel and David Axelrod. When Emanuel tried to give a copy to the president, he found that Obama had himself already been reading it.[7] In the book, they found plenty of cautionary warnings about how a president and his advisers can drift gradually into an ever wider war by making short-term, ad hoc decisions without ever stepping back for a more extensive review.

Meanwhile, inside the Pentagon and in the larger defense community, a different Vietnam book began to circulate, putting forward a more positive view of the military and a more mistrustful view of what civilian leaders should do. The rival book was called *A Better War*, written by Lewis Sorley, a military historian, West Point graduate and Vietnam veteran. Sorley had argued that America's war in Vietnam began to succeed in its late years, when a new commander, General Creighton Abrams, adopted a strategy of trying to protect and develop ties with the local population. This sounded a lot like Petraeus's strategy of counterinsurgency.[8]

To Obama and his inner circle, the entire discussion of Vietnam was irrelevant, even silly. Indeed, rejecting Vietnam analogies lay at the core of the Obama team's self-image and political strategy. Obama and his confidants saw themselves, and were eager to portray themselves in public, as representing the first generation since the 1960s that was not influenced in one way or another by Vietnam. "There's a generational issue. The president's conception of power is not founded on Vietnam," said Denis McDonough. "This is the first president [since Vietnam] who's not trying to justify himself in the context of that very tumultuous period."[9]

Obama was born in 1961, at the tail end of the baby boom. In 1975, when the last American troops were evacuated from Vietnam, he was in the eighth grade in a college preparatory school in Honolulu. McDonough was eight years younger, born one year after the Tet Offensive. Ben Rhodes, Obama's foreign policy speechwriter, was still younger, born in 1977, well after the Americans had departed from Vietnam.

Susan Rice, born in 1964, remembered her annoyance when, working for John Kerry's campaign in 2004, she found American politics still bogged down in debates over who had done what in Vietnam. "What frustrated me about the 2004 campaign was, there we were, re-litigating, 'where were you in nineteen sixty-whatever?' as the big freaking issue between Bush and Kerry—you know, 'did you serve, did you not serve, what did your Swift Boat brothers think?'—and I'm thinking, what the hell does this have to do with me and the world we're living in today?" recalled Rice. "We just don't have that Vietnam hangover," Rice said about the Obama team. "It is not the frame of reference for every decision—or any decision, for that matter. I'm sick and tired of reprising all of the traumas and the battles and the psychoses of the 1960s."[10]

The Obamians were hardly the first Democrats to define themselves as having moved past Vietnam. Gary Hart did so in his 1984 presidential campaign; so did the Democratic centrists and liberal hawks who urged the use of force in the Balkans in the 1990s; and so did the Democratic senators who voted in 2002 to authorize the use of force in Iraq. Yet the younger members of Obama's team saw themselves as fundamentally different from those earlier Democrats: They thought of themselves as not just post-Vietnam, but post-post-Vietnam. They were reacting not merely against that war, but also against those Democrats who had first reacted against it or were influenced in any way by it. The Obamians were not going to be obsessed with events four or five decades old. Those who dwelled on the subject of Vietnam were perceived not merely as adversaries or wrong in their arguments, but simply as too old.

Of course, it didn't hurt that the theme of Vietnam's irrelevance also often fit with the interests of Obama and his inner circle. Obama had emphasized his relative youthfulness during the campaign, with good results: The election returns showed that Obama, like Gary Hart before him, had won unusually high percentages of young voters. In the primaries, Obama and his inner circle had portrayed Hillary Clinton as representing the Democratic establishment, the old guard, while the Obama team was fresh. In the general election, they had done little to discourage the notion that John McCain was aging, unfamiliar with modern-day technology and overly preoccupied with Vietnam.

After Obama reached the White House, the Obama advisers found themselves working with Democrats who had previously served in Bill Clinton's administration, or even Jimmy Carter's or (in Holbrooke's case) Lyndon Johnson's. They had to deal with civil servants and military leaders with many consecutive years in government for both political parties. Sensitive to charges that they might be too inexperienced, the Obama aides naturally embraced the bromides of all incoming political appointees—that fresh eyes helped, that the newcomers were more in tune with the mood of the country than the old hands and that the past was not always a good guide to the future. Vietnam symbolized the old disagreements within the Democratic

Party, ones they wanted to leave behind. Vietnam just didn't matter to them as it did to their predecessors. "It's not like this ghost in his [Obama's] head," Rhodes observed.[11]

Yet, of course, banishing the ghosts of Vietnam still didn't answer the question of what policy Obama should pursue in Afghanistan, and what he should say in response to McChrystal's request for more troops.

———

In mid-September, just as the Obama administration was beginning to hold meetings to decide what to do next in Afghanistan, McChrystal's report leaked out. Bob Woodward reported its central points in the *Washington Post*. That changed the policy discussions. The public was now aware that the administration was trying to decide whether to send tens of thousands more troops to the war, after Obama had already ordered two deployments earlier in the year. The decision could no longer be made in quiet deliberations and announced as a done deal, with careful packaging to minimize political fallout.

Antiwar groups and liberal Democrats in Congress were, not surprisingly, upset and angered. Most of them had originally supported Obama in the Democratic primaries because of his views against the war in Iraq. House Speaker Nancy Pelosi warned there was "serious unrest" among House Democrats about paying for a wider war in Afghanistan. In the Senate, John Kerry said he was very wary of a troop buildup "because of past experience [i.e., Vietnam] and because of some of the challenges that I see."[12] As the administration's discussions dragged on from September through October and November, Republicans launched their own salvos from different directions. Dick Cheney accused the Obama White House of "dithering" on Afghanistan, and the word "dither" seemed to stick, a favorite verb in future Republican attacks on Obama, whether on Afghanistan, Libya or domestic issues. (Less pejorative words for "dithering" would have been "cautious" or "deliberate." George W. Bush had been accused of the opposite: Critics called him "impulsive," although his supporters preferred "decisive.")

This time, Obama and his top aides accorded to Afghanistan the careful review it had not gotten in the president's first months in office. Obama and other senior officials were now all forced to confront the implications of the counterinsurgency strategy: How many troops would be required, and how long it would take, to protect the people of Afghanistan and win their support? McChrystal was telling the administration what it would take in military terms to carry out the ideas approved in the Riedel report. But shown the costs, administration policy makers were getting a serious case of sticker shock.

The administration now confronted the ambiguity of its stated goal to "disrupt, dismantle and defeat" the enemy. Which was it? And, moreover, who *was* the enemy? Was it al-Qaeda, or the Taliban? Would it be possible to split the Taliban, the political movement that had ruled Afghanistan before 2001, from al-Qaeda, Osama bin Laden's much smaller force of Saudis, Egyptians and other outsiders determined to attack the West? Were the Taliban of Afghanistan different from the Taliban that had emerged, alongside al-Qaeda, in Pakistan? Before each meeting of Obama's cabinet-level principals or their deputies, reams of memos were devoted to these and other subjects. "The whole motivation behind this second review was to narrow the concept of the mission," one participant explained.[13]

This time Biden won greater support within the administration when he again argued that the administration should emphasize a strategy of counterterrorism rather than counterinsurgency, relying more on drones and special operations instead of new deployments of ground forces. On the NSC, Donilon pressed for more scrutiny of whether McChrystal needed more troops. Emanuel worried about devoting too much money and attention to Afghanistan; as chief of staff, he had to pay attention to competing domestic issues such as health care. David Axelrod was skeptical, too.

All of them, including Obama himself, suspected military leaders were orchestrating a subtle campaign in the media and in Congress to win support for substantially more troops in Afghanistan, while the administration was still trying to decide whether to send any at all. The chief suspects were Petraeus, who had extensive contacts in the press corps, and Admiral Mike Mullen, the chairman of the Joint Chiefs of Staff.

In early October, Obama invited Gates and Mullen to a meeting in the Oval Office and informed them he didn't like what seemed like a concerted PR campaign. Obama's aides subsequently portrayed this meeting as historic.

As reported by author Jonathan Alter, the Obamians characterized this session as

> a presidential dressing-down unlike any in the United States in more than half a century. The commander-in-chief now undertook the most direct assertion of presidential authority over the U.S. military since President Truman fired General MacArthur in 1951.[14]

This hyperbolic comparison equated Obama's private complaint inside the confines of the White House with Truman's public firing of Douglas MacArthur, the Korean War commander who called for a wider war in Korea and the use of nuclear weapons against China. It also seemed to overlook other military/civilian conflicts of the past six decades, such as Eisenhower's warning about the "military-industrial complex"; Kennedy's clashes with military leaders during the Bay of Pigs and the Cuban Missile Crisis; Johnson's cowing of the generals during Vietnam; Defense Secretary Dick Cheney's warning to Joint Chiefs chairman Colin Powell before the Persian Gulf War to "stick to military matters";[15] and George W. Bush's decision to reject the advice of military leaders who did not favor the surge in Iraq. The fact that the Obamians viewed the president's warning to Gates and Mullen in such breathtaking terms was mostly a sign of their own inexperience.

During Obama's three months of meetings on Afghanistan, Gates gradually came around to supporting the McChrystal request, and Hillary Clinton did, too. During that period, the two often sided with each other in administration debates; they were happy to show that the secretaries of state and defense could work smoothly together, unlike their immediate predecessors, Donald Rumsfeld with Colin Powell and Condoleezza Rice. The Clinton-Gates combine helped to win over the president to sending more troops, despite the skepticism of other senior administration officials such as Biden, Donilon and Emanuel; the president was not prepared to override the recommendations of the secretaries of state and defense, the two departments primarily responsible for foreign affairs. At the end of the second review, Obama approved the deployment of 30,000 more American troops for Afghanistan, bringing the total to about 100,000, and also called on NATO allies to provide another 5,000 or more of their own.

Yet the extensive debate marked a turning point in the administration's thinking about Afghanistan. While sending more troops, Obama also began to back away from the full implications of a counterinsurgency strategy. He set limits both on the number of troops and the time they would spend in Afghanistan. Obama and his team became more careful in how they explained the war. Earlier, they had argued that the United States couldn't abandon Afghanistan because ordinary Afghanis, particularly women, depended on American protection. If the Taliban regained control of Afghanistan, it would once again order that women wear burkas and that girls be denied an education.

Shortly before Obama announced his new policy, some in Washington revived this argument, saying the Obama administration could get better support from the Democrats by talking about the impact on women of an American withdrawal. "If the target audience here is [congressional Democrats] Jane Harman and Nancy Pelosi and people like that, then Mrs. Clinton should be picking up the phone and saying, 'There's a national security aspect to this, but there's also a gender issue here that's very important,'" Bruce Riedel told one reporter.[16]

This was a serious argument, but it didn't square with Obama's new approach. He didn't want to justify his Afghan policy as a way of improving human rights or the ending the Taliban's medieval subjugation of women, because doing so would deepen America's long-term commitment to Afghanistan—it would be harder for the Americans to leave. Moreover, it would give new leverage to Afghanistan's president, Hamid Karzai, to resist American pressure, since he would know the Americans would stay in Afghanistan to support the people no matter what he did or didn't do.

Obama occasionally called in former national security advisers from both political parties, such as Republicans Henry Kissinger and Brent Scowcroft and Democrats Zbigniew Brzezinski and Sandy Berger, to ask them or brief them about pending decisions. One participant self-mockingly called these sessions the "old farts" meetings. At a session with the group in late 2009, before he announced his decision on Afghanistan, it was suggested that Obama point out how few Afghan girls had gone to school when the Taliban ruled the country, and how many millions more girls were being educated in the years since the Taliban fell. This argument was rejected: Obama's aides explained they didn't want to get involved in the task of "nation building." The U.S. forces were in Afghanistan on a limited mission to fight al-Qaeda, not to save Afghani women, said James Jones. One participant described the administration's thinking this way: "Once you use [nation building or protecting Afghan women] as an argument for why you're not running away [withdrawing troops], then it's very sticky, even ten years from now," explained one participant.[17]

As envisioned by the Obama administration, then, the war in Afghanistan was to be limited in scope and duration. These new ideas were in some tension with the military doctrine of counterinsurgency, which required time, patience and lots of troops.

———

Obama's speech on Afghanistan, delivered at West Point on December 1, 2009, was significant both for the policy it enunciated and also for the ideas and rationales the president put forward. He announced he was sending 30,000 more troops, thus exasperating the liberal Democrats who had been supporting him since the early stages of his campaign. However, Obama also said that he was setting a specific timeline for withdrawal of those troops: They would start leaving Afghanistan in July 2011. Critics, including Republicans and many in the military and defense community, were extremely unhappy with the deadline; they maintained that it would embolden the Taliban, allowing its forces to lie low until the American and NATO forces departed.

Obama had rendered a lawyerly solution, a compromise that gave McChrystal and the Pentagon most of the additional troops they sought, but seemingly for a limited time period. (The arguments over what the deadline meant would soon follow.) Obama also ordered the military to speed up the schedule of its troop deployments: faster in, faster out. It was Obama's own "surge." He had opposed the surge of troops to Iraq because he had opposed that war. He ordered a surge in Afghanistan, in hopes of succeeding quickly in a war he had long supported.

His West Point speech argued that the war was necessary to deny al-Qaeda a safe haven in either Afghanistan or Pakistan from which it could threaten America, its allies or the government in Pakistan. Obama told the public he could not accept a "nation-building project of up to a decade." This war was not going to be like the decade-long British campaign in Malaya in the 1950s, the model for winning back the support of the local population. In Afghanistan, America was going to do counterinsurgency in a hurry.

Obama brought up the subject of Vietnam, but only to dismiss its relevance for Afghanistan. Any comparison between Afghanistan and Vietnam depended upon "a false reading of history," he maintained. This was a response to antiwar liberals in Congress and the grass roots of the Democratic Party, but also, implicitly, to those within the Obama administration who had been reading up on Vietnam and trying to figure out the lessons to be drawn from that war. "Unlike Vietnam, we are not facing a broad-based popular insurgency," Obama claimed. "And most importantly, unlike Vietnam, the American people were viciously attacked from Afghanistan."[18]

Obama's speech went further, offering some broader themes that made him sound different from American presidents of the past. He said there were limits to what the United States could afford to spend in Afghanistan. A long nation-building project was a goal "beyond what we can achieve at a reasonable cost," Obama maintained. "The nation that I am most interested in building is our own." George H. W. Bush had been obliged to ask other countries to help pay for the war in the Persian Gulf, but there the issue had been burden sharing, not sheer affordability. The senior Bush never talked about "reasonable costs" the way Obama did.

It was in the West Point speech that Obama first hinted at a change in the international role America had been playing since World War II. The United States "has underwritten global security for over six decades," the president said, also noting that "we have not always been thanked for these efforts." Soon afterward, Obama said vaguely that America was entering a new age.[19] To America's old friends in Europe and Japan, these passages were unsettling. In the past, presidents had usually depicted America's leadership role in the world as enduring, not something of possibly limited duration. They generally vowed that America would do whatever it took, regardless of cost. Since the end of World War II, presidents tended to say that America's alliances, such as NATO and the U.S.-Japan Security Treaty, were what protected global security. Now Obama was abandoning the old formulas to say that, really, it was the United States that had been maintaining the international order—and yet it might not do so forever. "For the first

time, I can envision the United States returning to isolationism," remarked
one European journalist privately after listening to the West Point speech.[20]

———

Today, the question still comes up: Did Obama really believe in the merits
of the war in Afghanistan, a conflict he chose not merely to perpetuate but
to intensify? Around dinner tables and in casual conversation, Americans
offer a variety of purported explanations for why Obama was somehow pres-
sured or trapped into continuing the war. Obama's policy was said to be the
fault of the Republicans, or of the military, or the bureaucracy, or the dynamics of presidential campaigns.

One commonplace argument was that the war was a matter of politics
for the 2012 election: Obama felt he had to continue it because his Republican opponents would have crucified him for pulling out. Another frequent
explanation was that he didn't want to alienate the military. A third portrayed Afghanistan as a by-product of his campaign for the presidency in
2007–2008: As a candidate, Obama had called for stepping up the war in
both Afghanistan and Pakistan, but did so mostly for tactical reasons, to
show he was not a doctrinaire dove. In other words, this theory went,
Obama's hard line on Afghanistan was meant to offset his antiwar position
in Iraq; in doing so, he boxed himself in and, once in office, had to keep to
his campaign promises. Such cynical interpretations all start with the assumption that Obama of course must agree with antiwar critics that the war
in Afghanistan is morally unjust and strategically insignificant.

Some of these dismissive interpretations are clearly inadequate, because
they fail to take account of Obama's repeatedly professed views before he
ever got to the White House. Obama's positions in favor of a stepped-up war
in Afghanistan and a tougher stance toward Pakistan date back to the earliest days of his campaign, a time when he wasn't worried about his relations
with military leaders or about Republican attacks. He was, rather, thinking
about winning the Democratic primaries. He wanted to show that he was a
"credible" candidate; he did not want to be dismissed or marginalized in the
fashion of Dennis Kucinich.

Indeed, Obama's views on Afghanistan can be traced back even further,
to before his presidential campaign. In his 2002 speech against the Iraq War,
he had famously said he was not opposed to all war, only to "dumb war"

such as that in Iraq, which was an unnecessary diversion from fighting al-Qaeda. He took that position as a state senator and he stuck to it.

One of these cynical theories is harder to dismiss—that Obama came up with his position on the war in Afghanistan as political cover for his opposition to the Iraq War. That view can at least be squared with the available record of Obama's political speeches and statements in the seven years leading up to his presidency: Over the years, Iraq and Afghanistan seem almost joined together as polar opposites: dumb war/legitimate war. But if one were to accept the explanation that Afghanistan was merely a matter of politics, not principle, then that would raise the question of whether his early opposition to the Iraq War was politically motivated, too.

The more likely interpretation, consistent with the available evidence, is that before taking office, Obama believed in the legitimacy of the war in Afghanistan, and that during his first year he developed the more detailed justification that he offered at the end of 2009: If the United States did not step up the military efforts in both Afghanistan and Pakistan, then al-Qaeda would manage to find a safe haven in one country or the other; and from these sanctuaries would continue to threaten the United States. In short, the simplest explanation is that Obama meant what he said in escalating the war.

Every morning in which Obama was in Washington, he began his day with an intelligence briefing, just like other presidents in the modern era. The other senior officials who gathered with him for this daily White House ritual included Biden; Jones; Donilon; Denis McDonough; John Brennan; and Biden's national-security aide, Tony Blinken. After the briefing ended and the intelligence officials departed, this same core group stayed behind to talk about the administration's policies, both overt and covert: What should be done and by which agency or person. One of the regular participants in these small daily meetings acknowledged that what he witnessed was, in some ways, surprising. "This is not a president who is at all shy about the use of force," he concluded.

11

The Speeches: "Evil Does Exist"

In the early weeks of the Obama administration, one of the first internal debates was over where he should give an address aimed at Muslims around the world. The initial choice was Jakarta.[1] Obama's political aides figured that Indonesia, the country where he had lived for four years as a child, would give Obama an especially warm reception. Cheering crowds would greet him on his arrival, and the audience for this major speech would be unusually friendly. The television coverage would be tremendous.

But then the Obama team had second thoughts. Although Indonesia has more than 200 million Muslims, more than any other country, America's foreign policy problems were centered on the Middle East and South Asia. Indonesia was too far away. Its people are not Arab, its language not Arabic. If the goal of Obama's speech was to focus on the legacy of the war in Iraq and, more broadly, on America's relationship to the Islamic world, then Jakarta was the wrong venue. Moreover, if Obama gave the speech in Jakarta, the news stories would inevitably focus above all on Obama's own boyhood and his return to Indonesia. Biography was fine on other occasions; Obama had certainly not been reluctant to make his life story a central part of his presidential campaign. But the Obama team wanted the press coverage of this particular speech to focus on Obama's message, not his upbringing.

Within three weeks, the new White House team had decided the speech should instead be given in Cairo. It was the intellectual capital of the Arab world, at the heart of its conflicting currents. Egypt's leader, Hosni Mubarak, was America's friend. On the day after his inauguration, President Obama had made a series of phone calls to foreign leaders, and Mubarak was among the very first. At the grass roots, however, Egypt was not nearly so pro-American; a few of the leaders of al-Qaeda had come from Egypt, and many of the ideas that guided the jihadists had their roots in Egypt. Obama's aides, who had the same weakness for sports analogies that afflicts everyone else in American politics, wanted this event to look like an "away game," not a "home game."

Rarely does an administration spend four months writing and refining a single speech. Yet Obama and his team had just arrived in the White House, and they viewed the speech on Islam as the centerpiece of a broader campaign to improve America's standing in the Middle East. Obama was sending out a series of other signals. Less than a week after becoming president, he gave his very first television interview to Al Arabiya, a Middle East television network. In March, he sent a videotaped greeting to the Iranian people on the occasion of Nowruz, the traditional Persian new year. Some of these efforts later proved fruitless, notably the early overtures to Iran. But for a new president, they were worth a try.

Ben Rhodes drew the assignment to write the Cairo speech. As foreign policy speechwriter, he worked under Denis McDonough and Mark Lippert, the main message carriers and enforcers for foreign policy. At the White House, McDonough, Lippert and Rhodes worked so closely with Obama on foreign policy issues that they almost seemed like a single entity: the inner circle. The president talked with them before and after his meetings with his cabinet-level advisers, such as Secretary of State Hillary Clinton, Secretary of Defense Robert Gates and National Security Adviser James Jones. He tended to make his final decisions with these aides, and the aides were sometimes dispatched to inform State or Defense officials what Obama wanted or decided.

———

Looking for ideas and advice, Rhodes began to meet with Middle East specialists inside and outside government, with people in think tanks and some Muslim Americans. At one point, a graduate student who had worked with Rhodes on the September 11 Commission convened a dinner at her apartment with several young friends, all of them foreign policy specialists, to talk about what Obama should say. Dennis Ross, who had been President Bill Clinton's Middle East peace negotiator and was then serving as an aide to Hillary Clinton for Iran policy in the State Department, joined the brainstorming session. In keeping with the spirit of the mostly youthful gathering, Ross, then sixty-one years old, arrived on a bicycle.

Not all of Rhodes's discussions went so smoothly. The director of national intelligence, Dennis Blair, visited Rhodes seeking to offer his thoughts on what Obama might say in the Cairo speech. Blair had been an admiral, the commander of all U.S. forces in the Pacific; he had been a Rhodes Scholar and a White House Fellow and at various times a senior military aide for the National Security Council, the Joint Chiefs of Staff and the intelligence community. He was the military's version of a Renaissance man, but for Obama's aides, Dennis Blair was more a figure from ancient history. He'd graduated from the Naval Academy and went off for his first assignment on a guided-missile destroyer in 1968, before Denis McDonough was even born.

Blair urged Rhodes to think more about the strategic aspects of the U.S. role in the Middle East.[2] What message would the speech be sending to the leaders of the governments with which the United States worked most closely, including Egypt, Saudi Arabia and Jordan? What would Obama's speech convey to Israeli and Palestinian leaders? It was fine to talk about an ideal world in which Muslims, Jews and Christians got along together. But with what strategy and policies was the Obama administration proposing to accomplish that? Rhodes suggested that Blair didn't understand the larger purpose. The speech wasn't aimed at Middle Eastern rulers. It was meant to communicate with ordinary people in the Middle East. Blair left, and found himself cut out of the drafting process.

In midspring, Obama called in McDonough and Rhodes to tell them more specifically the ideas he was seeking to convey in Cairo. He hoped to alter America's relationship to the Islamic world. He wanted to talk about the history of the United States in the Middle East and to acknowledge the legacy of Western colonialism in the region. The speech should cover not only broad foreign policy issues (including Israel and the Palestinians), but also cultural issues such as women's rights.

The speech needed to explain not merely what Americans were *against* (al-Qaeda, violent extremism) but also what the United States stood *for*. And—so Obama and his aides thought at the time—this should not be just democracy, because quite a few people in the Middle East felt democracy represented a plot by the Western powers to regain political control of the Middle East. Moreover, George W. Bush had emphasized the importance of democracy to such an extent that the Obama team wanted to play it down.[3]

This last point soon proved to be controversial: Some within the administration argued that the United States shouldn't de-emphasize the theme of democracy. Ironically, a couple of years later, as Egyptians and others in the Middle East took to the streets to protest authoritarian rule, Obama and his aides would talk with pride about how they had actively promoted democracy in the Middle East. As evidence, they pointed to the few carefully worded passages in the Cairo speech that spoke gingerly about democracy.

———

In looking for a site, they turned down a suggestion that Obama go to the American University in Cairo. Although they didn't realize it at the time, the American University in Cairo had been the place where Bush's secretary of state, Condoleezza Rice, delivered a strong speech in 2005 calling for democracy in the Middle East. Mubarak had rebuffed that earlier appeal. Obama's aides decided that he shouldn't talk to an audience composed mostly of Americans or pro-American Egyptians. Seeking access to a broader range of Egyptian society, Obama's aides chose instead to speak at Cairo University, where American influence was limited.

On June 4, Obama stood before 3,000 guests at the university to call for a "new beginning" between the United States and Muslims around the world. American officials worked intensively to make sure what he said was given the widest possible distribution throughout the Middle East on television networks like Al Jazeera and on assorted websites. Obama repeatedly sought to smooth over tensions with the Islamic world. He acknowledged that these tensions had been "fed by colonialism . . . and also by a Cold War in which Muslim-majority countries were too often treated as proxies." He quoted from the Koran and talked of civilization's debt to Islam. He promised that America would not turn its back on Palestinian aspirations for "dignity, opportunity and a state of their own."[4]

In describing American values, Obama mentioned religious freedom: Western countries should not dictate "what clothes a Muslim woman should wear," he said, an oblique reference to France, which barred women and girls from wearing headscarves to school. He spoke of the importance of women's rights. In talking about economic development, Obama added an unusual note: "While America in the past has focused on oil and gas when it comes to this part of the world, we now seek a broader engagement." This idealistic portion of Obama's speech could be parsed as meaning either not much change (did the vague word "broader" mean that the United States would continue to care about oil while pursuing more "engagement," too?) or nothing at all (if the United States didn't focus on oil, then why was Saudi Arabia important to every administration, including Obama's?).

Yet Obama also coupled many of his points about how Americans needed to change with comparable ones about how Muslims should change their attitudes toward the United States. After winning applause with a line saying he would "fight against negative stereotypes of Islam wherever they appear," Obama quickly added:

> But that same principle must apply to Muslim perceptions of America. Just as Muslims do not fit a crude stereotype, America is not the crude stereotype of a self-interested empire. . . . We were born out of revolution against an empire.[5]

After noting that America was not at war with Islam, Obama then turned in the opposite direction: "We will, however, relentlessly confront violent extremists who pose a grave threat to our security."

Cairo thus carried forward the distinctive approach of Obama's most successful domestic speeches, the ones that sought to ease tensions, to find common ground between adversaries, to put forward ideals to which all should aspire and, finally, to position Obama himself in the middle ground, detached from the fray. Obama had sought to blur distinctions between red states and blue states in his speech to the 2004 Democratic National Convention, which first brought him to national prominence. His 2008 campaign speech on race in America, delivered in Philadelphia amid an uproar over his past ties to Reverend Jeremiah Wright, had spoken in a healing fashion about white and black in America. Now, in Cairo, he spoke in similar fashion about Americans and Muslims.

At home, the Republican and conservative reactions to the Cairo speech seemed to reflect considerable confusion. The political right was eager to attack Obama. But from which direction?

Some conservatives gloated that Obama represented little change from the Bush administration, far less than his admirers believed. On the day after the Cairo speech, the conservative *Washington Times* editorialized that Obama seemed to be "channeling George Bush." Obama said in Cairo that "Islam is a part of America"; Bush had said six days after the September 11 attacks that "America counts millions of Muslims amongst our citizens." In 2002, Bush had committed his administration to a two-state solution to Israel and Palestine and said it was "untenable for Palestinians to live in squalor and occupation." In Cairo, Obama said Palestinians "endure the daily humiliations" of living under occupation.[6]

On the other hand, other conservatives portrayed Obama not as a continuation of his predecessor but as a radical, wildly different from Bush and, indeed, from all other American presidents. Five days after its "same as Bush" editorial, the *Washington Times* published an op-ed column on the Cairo speech by Frank Gaffney, a foreign policy hawk who had worked in the 1970s and 1980s as an aide to Richard Perle. He asserted that Obama "not only identifies with Muslims, but may actually be one himself." As evidence, he said Obama mentioned "the Holy Koran" four times in his speech. If Obama were really a Christian, as he claimed to be, Gaffney wrote, then he would never have said he looked forward to the day "when Jerusalem is a secure and lasting home for Jews." (Gaffney did not seem to consider that this passage about Jerusalem could also be taken, by his own way of reasoning, as a sign that Obama was secretly Jewish.)[7]

These contradictory Republican reactions followed a pattern that would endure throughout the president's early years in office. When Obama continued Bush's antiterrorist policies, or intensified them (such as in the use of drones), conservatives exulted. When he did something the conservatives didn't like, he was then perceived and portrayed as an extremist, a socialist, a revolutionary, somehow alien to American traditions.

Liberal Democrats occasionally got tripped up in ideologically opposite contradictions. When they found that Obama unexpectedly carried on more than a few of the policies of the Bush administration, they lamented that he was a centrist, moderate Democrat unwilling to challenge the status quo. When Obama broke new ground, such as on gays in the military or in health care legislation, they rejoiced that he was willing and able to do what other presidents, even Democrats, had not.

———

Cairo got the most attention, but Obama's speech there was merely one of a series Obama delivered in 2009 that were aimed at setting out the new administration's goals and outlook in foreign policy. He spoke in Prague and Moscow, to Ghana's parliament in Accra and to the United Nations General Assembly in New York. Each of these events was different, but all the speeches contained similar themes.

One theme was nuclear weapons. In Prague, Obama pledged a commitment "to seek the peace and security of a world without nuclear weapons." (Carrying forward the slogan from his campaign, Obama added: "We must ignore the voices who tell us that the world cannot change. We have to insist, 'Yes, we can.'") Obama coupled this theme of nuclear abolition with another, sometimes more hawkish-sounding one: that the international community should act to stop Iran from developing nuclear weapons and to pressure North Korea, which already had them, to reverse course.[8]

In these early speeches abroad, Obama repeatedly emphasized the importance of the global economy, the need to prevent climate change and the dangers of violent extremism. He also talked about the importance of democratic government. Usually, his remarks on democracy were cautiously phrased and couched: He would introduce the subject by saying the United States did not want to "impose any system of government on any other nation." But there were flashes of strong rhetoric. "Africa doesn't need strong men, it needs strong institutions," he said in Ghana.[9]

Obama's speeches also possessed distinctive stylistic features. They were strikingly well crafted, each with a logical structure, a series of four or five points that Obama carefully delineated: "*. . . and that brings me to the fourth issue that I will discuss . . .*" Many of the speeches contained a few of the same buzzwords, the jargon that had become commonplace among foreign policy scholars and at think tanks around the world: The nations of the world were "interdependent," Obama regularly explained, and the pursuit of power was no longer a "zero-sum game." (On occasion, the Obama administration would uncomfortably find that other countries did seem to believe in zero-sum games, such as, for example, China on climate change and the value of its currency.) Obama and his aides acted as though these concepts embodied the distinctive views of their own new generation in foreign policy, one that had come of age after the end of the Cold War and America's dominance in the 1990s. Yet Zbigniew Brzezinski had begun referring to interdependence in the 1970s, and the Clinton administration talked regularly about win-win solutions and the lack of zero-sum games in the 1990s.

Often, Obama offered a dollop of his own biography, from which he drew lessons. "My grandfather was a cook for the British in Kenya, and though he was a respected elder in his village, his employers called him 'boy' for much of his life," he told the Ghanian parliament. "When I was born, segregation was still the law of the land in parts of America, and my father's Kenya was still a colony," he told graduating students at Moscow's New Economic School. "When you were born, a school like this would have been impossible, and the Internet was only known to a privileged few." [10] In Cairo, introducing a section on the shared interests of Americans and Muslims, Obama pointed to his own experience: "I'm a Christian, but my father came from a Kenyan family that includes generations of Muslims. As a boy, I spent several years in Indonesia and heard the call of the azaan at the break of dawn and at the fall of dusk."

In one sense, Obama's speeches seemed unusual, even premature. He was holding forth on foreign policy, often with admirable complexity, but he was doing so before he and his administration had a chance to get their feet dirty in a messy world. There was a slightly detached, antiseptic quality to his pronouncements. Taken together, they gave voice to noble ideals, but they seemed to presume that these ideals could provide solutions to the international conflicts they would face. The speeches didn't answer what would happen if Iran refused entreaties to give up its nuclear weapons program. They didn't explain how the United States should respond if Hosni Mubarak, its longtime friend, repressed an Egyptian movement toward democracy, or whether the United States should use force if Libya's Moammar Gaddafi was on the verge of slaughtering civilians.

Still, the speeches set forth with clarity what the administration wanted to do. They also served another purpose, one of overwhelming importance to the United States in 2009: Obama was seeking to repair America's relations with the rest of the world after the Bush administration's invasion of Iraq. In truth (as Obama administration officials sometimes freely volunteered in private), Bush himself and Condoleezza Rice had tried to turn things around themselves with more moderate policies in Bush's second term; but the job was virtually impossible for them to the extent that they succeeded at all, it was with leaders such as Germany's Angela Merkel and France's Nicolas Sarkozy—not with the general public in European countries or the Middle East. Obama's early speeches were pitched to audiences of educated people overseas, seeking to persuade, to find common ground, to reverse the entrenched perceptions of American unilateralism. One aide explained it this way: "We wanted to clear the air, to better position ourselves to be advocates again. To argue for other countries to do something, you need to have credibility. All that travel and all those speeches were trying to build American credibility around the world, in the person of Obama."[11]

Rhodes wrote most of the speeches. They reflected in part his own experience and the ideas he had gathered in Washington since 2001. One important influence upon the new administration's thinking was Lee Hamilton. In addition to Rhodes, other former Hamilton aides working in the White House included Daniel Shapiro, the National Security Council director for the Middle East, and Mara Rudman, who was working on the Middle East at the State Department.

Hamilton had served as a back-channel adviser to the Obama presidential campaign, both through his former aides and in private talks with Obama himself. The Obama aides who had previously worked for Hamilton felt the men shared a common worldview, a general sense of the limits of American power. Hamilton had long been a proponent of a policy of engagement with Iran. Separately, however, he had also favored intensive U.S. military strikes into Pakistan to combat al-Qaeda. Both of these positions became key points on which Obama, as a candidate, had sought to differentiate himself from Hillary Clinton. After Obama was elected president, these ideas on Iran and Pakistan eventually became among the most prominent and distinctive aspects of the new administration's foreign policy.

Before the Cairo speech, one columnist, Gerald Seib of the *Wall Street Journal*, asked several foreign policy experts what Obama should or would say. One of them was Hamilton. He came very close to the actual speech Obama delivered in both ideas and language. The central theme, Hamilton told the columnist, should be to show "respect for the Islamic world."[12]

Obama himself was involved to an unusual extent, not merely in giving overall guidance for the Cairo and other speeches, but in the fine-tuning as well. One aide recalled what happened when he accompanied Obama and his team to New York for an address to the United Nations. He was in his room at the Waldorf Hotel late one night when Denis McDonough summoned him, saying, with a sense of mystery and intrigue, "Come with me." They went to Obama's suite, where Rhodes was laboring over the wording of the speech. Obama walked in, and the aide was asked to explain his ideas to the president. They talked for nearly an hour. Obama left and came in one more time, dressed in a T-shirt, to give Rhodes another point he wanted in the speech. He said he was going off to watch ESPN, but a couple of hours later, Obama was still sending his aides e-mails with minor revisions and additions. The aide, not usually involved in this process, was astonished. "He takes these speeches extremely seriously," he said. "They put a lot of time into them."[13]

Obama's series of addresses culminated with one given near the end of the year that rightly attracted more attention than any of the others: his speech at the Nobel Peace Prize ceremonies in Oslo. There, Obama presented a brooding, elegantly phrased philosophical reflection on "just war," on America's role in the world, and on the history, morality and international law concerning the use of force. He also set forth some ideas that would provide justification for his decision in March 2011 to attack Libya. It was, under the circumstances, a startling message, both to the mostly European audience in Oslo and to some of the Americans back home who had helped elect Obama in 2008.

The Nobel Prize committee had awarded Obama the Peace Prize in October. Critics of the award—including not merely the Republican regulars, but others from across the spectrum—derided the choice, pointing out that Obama had completed less than a year in office and hadn't had a chance to do much. The citation by the Nobel Committee, however, justified the award essentially as recognition for Obama's speeches. It praised Obama's vision of a world without nuclear weapons (starting with the Prague speech) and "his extraordinary efforts to strengthen international diplomacy," of which the speeches in Cairo, Moscow and at the United Nations were the main examples. "For 108 years, the Norwegian Nobel Committee has sought to stimulate precisely that international policy and those attitudes for which Obama is now the world's leading spokesman," the citation said.[14]

As it happened, Obama was awarded the Nobel Peace Prize at the time when he and his administration were trying to decide whether to step up the war in Afghanistan. The Nobel ceremonies were scheduled for December 10. The West Point speech to explain Obama's decision to send tens of thousands more U.S. troops to Afghanistan had been scheduled for December 1. This created an odd juxtaposition: In late November, the Obama team was concurrently working on two major speeches, one on peace and one on stepping up a war. The president and his aides faced a delicate task squaring the ideas for the two speeches.

The West Point address was written by Rhodes, following the same process as for the other foreign policy speeches. The Nobel Prize speech was different. Aides put together a binder for Obama with collected readings, including some from the theologian Reinhold Niebuhr and from Michael Walzer, the philosopher who had written *Just and Unjust Wars* and other works on morality in wartime. Once the speechwriters circulated an initial draft, Samantha Power began to take part.[15] By virtue of her prior books, her *New Yorker* articles and her work at Harvard University, Power was, to intellectuals, the best-known member of Obama's NSC.

During Obama's first year, Power had not played a particularly prominent or active role in the administration—not surprising, since she had given birth to a child in April. She worked largely outside of the daily tumult: the endless paperwork flow driven by Tom Donilon, the communications and political arm of foreign policy run by Denis McDonough, the ideas and formulations of Rhodes, the overall supervision by Rahm Emanuel. One friend said she sometimes felt marginalized. She remained, however, close to

Obama, and her husband, the legal scholar Cass Sunstein, was also an old Chicago friend of the president's.

For the Nobel speech, Power at first weighed in with a memo, arguing that the speech needed to be better than the first draft then being circulated. She began meeting with Obama to contribute ideas and reactions. A few other people were brought in as well. Obama himself did quite a bit of the writing, which continued on the overnight flight from Washington to Oslo. Power accompanied Obama to the Nobel ceremonies. Afterward, she put up a large photograph of his handwritten draft on the wall of her office. Her pride was understandable: Many of the ideas in the speech bore her distinctive imprint, particularly his emphasis on the use of force for humanitarian purposes.

At the beginning of his speech, Obama paid homage to those "giants of history" who had won the Nobel Prize before him, such as Albert Schweitzer, Nelson Mandela and Martin Luther King Jr. Compared to them, the president said, "my accomplishments are slight." It was a graceful way to acknowledge the criticism that he hadn't done enough to deserve the award.

Then the speech very quickly changed direction, from peace to its opposite. "I am the commander in chief of the military of a nation in the midst of two wars," Obama said. "I'm responsible for the deployment of thousands of young Americans to battle in a distant land. Some will kill, and some will be killed." Within minutes, he offered the memorable passage at the core of his speech, one that spoke of the limited utility of pacifism and nonviolence to him as the leader of the United States:

As someone who stands here as a direct consequence of Dr. King's work, I am living testimony to the moral force of nonviolence. I know there's nothing weak, nothing passive, nothing naive, in the creed and lives of Gandhi and King.

But as a head of state sworn to protect and defend my nation, I cannot be guided by their examples alone. I face the world as it is, and cannot stand idle in the face of threats to the American people. For make no mistake: Evil does exist in the world.[16]

Instead of pacifism, Obama emphasized the old concept, dating back to early Christian thought, of "just war"—the idea that the use of force is morally justified in some situations. Obama described some of those circumstances, such as self-defense against an aggressor. He then interpreted the idea of "just war" in a much more expansive way:

> I believe that force can be justified on humanitarian grounds, as it was in the Balkans, or in other places that have been scarred by war. Inaction tears at our conscience and can lead to more costly intervention later. . . .
>
> [I]n a world in which threats are more diffuse, and missions more complex, America cannot act alone. America alone cannot secure the peace. This is true in Afghanistan. This is true in failed states like Somalia. . . . And sadly, it will continue to be true in unstable regions for years to come.[17]

There, in a few sentences in the Nobel Prize speech, was the rationale for Obama's decision fifteen months later for military intervention against Moammar Gaddafi's regime in Libya.

Finally, Obama's speech contained a few paragraphs about America's role in the world, aimed at overseas audiences, particularly Europe. In many countries, he said, there was "a deep ambivalence about military action today, no matter what the cause. And at times, this is joined by a reflexive suspicion of America, the world's sole superpower." But remember, the president went on, it wasn't just international institutions like the United Nations or NATO that brought stability after World War II:

> Whatever mistakes we have made, the plain fact is this: The United States of America has helped underwrite global security for more than six decades with the blood of our citizens and the strength of our arms. The service and sacrifice of our men and women in uniform has promoted peace and prosperity from Germany to Korea, and enabled democracy to take hold in places like the Balkans. We have borne this burden not because we seek to impose our will. We have done so out of enlightened self-interest. . . .[18]

Once again, as he had done less than two weeks earlier at West Point, Obama was abandoning past formulations stating that America's alliances and its friends had joined together to create the post–World War II order. Rather, that international order was based on the United States, its military and its armaments. By the same token, Obama's words also served as an implicit reminder that this order might not last, if the United States chose to stop underwriting it (because other countries were no longer willing to share the burdens) or if America was forced to abandon its role (because it was no longer affordable).

Obama's Nobel Prize speech was astonishing for the ways in which it challenged the perceptions of him and the ideas of his own core constituencies. The man who had just received the Nobel Peace Prize delivered a qualified defense of war. The American president who in mid-2008 had stood before cheering throngs in Berlin was now gently reminding Germans and other Europeans that the American military had helped bring about the stability and prosperity they had enjoyed for decades.

Finally, Obama's speech carried a particular impact, and an especially ironic one, back home. Obama had run as the peace candidate in the 2008 presidential election; now, his Nobel Prize speech represented an intellectual justification for the use of force. The Democrats had been upset by George W. Bush's emphasis on good and evil, and the "axis of evil." Now, while dropping the conspiratorial idea of an "axis," the Democrat they had chosen to replace Bush warned that "evil does exist in the world." In short, Obama's speech politely rejected many of the pacifistic beliefs that had held sway on the left wing of the Democratic Party since Vietnam.

12

The Scowcroft Democrats

While Obama's speeches were well written and inspiring, the policies he pursued as he began to deal with the world often didn't square with the speeches. It was almost as if the speeches came from one side of his brain and the policies from a different one.

In some instances, this was not his fault. Obama discovered that practical realities, among them the United States Congress, would not allow him to carry out what he had set out to do. The most obvious example was the failure to close Guantánamo. "I have ordered the prison at Guantánamo Bay closed by early next year," Obama had declared in the Cairo speech, and the Egyptian audience gave him a round of warm applause.[1] But it never happened. Congress, which at the time had a Democratic majority, refused to approve facilities in the United States to hold the Guantánamo prisoners. It also denied the use of federal funds to close the prison and objected to trials of Guantánamo Bay prisoners in the United States.

Obama ran into this problem on other issues, too. During the antinuclear speech in Prague, he pledged that "my administration will immediately and aggressively pursue U.S. ratification of the Comprehensive Nuclear Test Ban Treaty."[2] That didn't happen, either. Despite his words, his administration was neither "immediate" nor "aggressive" on this issue. Indeed, it turned out to be considerably less aggressive than the Clinton administration, which had actively pushed for ratification of the same treaty but lost a Senate vote fifty-one to forty-eight (a two-thirds majority in the Senate is required by the Constitution for adopting treaties). To get an idea of how "aggressively" the Obama administration was pursuing this, consider the words of Ellen Tauscher, the undersecretary of state for arms control, just over a year after

Obama's commitment in Prague. She was speaking to the foreign press in Washington:

> As you know, the President supports the United States Senate ratification and entry into force of the Comprehensive Test Ban Treaty. We have no specific timeline for its consideration by the Senate, but we are doing all the analysis necessary to determine how to best move the treaty forward. We expect the release of the National Academies of Sciences study reviewing the key technical issues underlying the Comprehensive Test Ban Treaty to be released shortly.[3]

For those not familiar with Washington's way of speaking, this is a seventy-five-word antonym for "aggressive." It is a way of saying, "Forget it" or "Don't even think about it anytime soon."

What happened to the test ban treaty? Obama discovered, if he hadn't known before, that sending it to the Senate would put some of its members, principally Democrats but also a few moderate Republicans, into the awkward position of casting a vote for which they might be attacked when they ran for reelection. John Podesta acknowledged that the timing for pushing forward with the Comprehensive Nuclear Test Ban Treaty kept slipping. "I don't know how they [administration officials] are going to do this. I say to them, 'What's the theory on this?' And I don't get one coming back at me."[4]

Podesta made an observation about the underlying politics, one that helps explain why Obama and the White House might, in fact, share some of the blame when Congress resisted or delayed action. He was speaking not just about the test ban treaty but, more broadly, about occasions when the United States was asked to sign treaties or approve other international rules that would in some way restrict America's power. "Building a world where there are restraints on power implies that you also will restrain your own power," he said. "And that in turn creates a world of greater stability and cooperation. The Democrats have supported this idea in the past, starting with Roosevelt and Truman, without being seen as wimps. It's a strength. But you have to *believe* it's a strength and sell it as a strength. You have to be forceful in articulating the idea and going after it." Podesta concluded: "If you do it from a crouch, you'll just get kicked in the head."

Those words were apt. There were times when Obama stood up to make strong speeches or promises overseas, and then back home went into a crouch alongside other crouching Democrats. The test ban treaty was hardly some fringe left-wing initiative. Since 2007, several of the most experienced officials in American foreign policy had been supporting the idea, including Republicans Henry Kissinger and George Shultz as well as Democrats William Perry and Sam Nunn, all of them among the nation's leading figures in foreign or defense policy. Still, the Obama administration crouched, unwilling to risk controversy and a Senate fight for a cause that the president, in his Prague speech, had endorsed and had promised to push quickly and vigorously.

———

There were other gaps between Obama's speeches and his policies that could not be blamed on Congress at all. The clearest example concerned whether the new administration should support the causes of democracy and political freedom overseas.

In Obama's string of 2009 speeches to foreign audiences, he almost invariably mentioned at some point the importance of democracy and freedom of expression. In Moscow, he spoke of "America's interest in democratic governments that protect the rights of their people." In Ghana, he declared that "we must support strong and sustainable democratic governments." At the United Nations, he called democracy and human rights "essential" and exhorted foreign leaders to "champion those principles which ensure that governments reflect the will of the people."[5]

He sometimes entered into discussions of democracy carefully and tentatively, seemingly afraid that the people he was addressing (or perhaps their countries' leaders) might disagree. On one occasion, in Cairo, he seemed to be momentarily surprised by the positive reaction. When he introduced the subject—"The fourth issue I will address is democracy . . ."—he plunged forward without pausing. The audience interrupted him with applause, causing him to stop. Shortly afterward, he said that speaking one's mind and having a say in how one is governed "are not just American ideas. They are human rights. And that is why we will support them everywhere." There was more applause, and moments later someone in the audience shouted, "Barack Obama, we love you."[6]

Yet during his first year, Obama's actions and policies seemed to give low priority to the goal of promoting democracy or human rights abroad. In Egypt, during the same period in which Obama spoke about democracy in Cairo, the new administration agreed to a demand by the regime of President Hosni Mubarak not to fund independent civil society groups unless they had government approval. In dealing with Burma, the Obama administration decided to begin meeting directly with leaders of the military government, although the regime continued to ignore the 1990 democratic election that would have ousted it from power and was still keeping Aung San Suu Kyi, whose party had won those elections, under house arrest.

The administration also seemed to de-emphasize the issue of human rights in China. Just before her first trip to Beijing, Secretary of State Hillary Clinton said differences over human rights shouldn't interfere with larger diplomacy. While the United States had to keep pressing China on human rights, Clinton said, the Obama administration needed to move on to other subjects. "We pretty much know what they are going to say," she explained.[7] In the fall of 2009, Obama declined to grant a White House meeting to the Dalai Lama, as his three immediate predecessors had, deciding instead to wait until after the president visited Beijing.

Of all the examples of the new administration's approach to democratic change, by far the most consequential involved the Green Movement in Iran. Obama had been advocating direct, high-level American engagement with Iran since the early stages of his presidential campaign. When he said in one debate that he would be willing to meet with the leaders of America's adversaries during his first year in office, Iran was at the top of the list. Within weeks after Obama was sworn in, he began sending out signals of his eagerness for a new dialogue with Iran. Those overtures continued right through early June, when the administration cabled American embassies and consulates that, in a departure from previous years, they should invite Iranian diplomats to their Fourth of July celebrations.[8] One part of Obama's Cairo speech was specifically aimed at Iran. He referred to its government by its formal title, "the Islamic Republic of Iran"—a gesture reminiscent of the time, in the early stages of the opening to China, when the Nixon administration stopped calling its government "Communist China" and instead, more respectfully, called it "the People's Republic of China." In dealing with

Iran, Obama said in Cairo, his administration was willing to put the past aside and "move forward without preconditions on the basis of mutual respect."9

A few days after returning from Cairo, Obama brought Dennis Ross, the administration's most experienced Middle East negotiator, directly into the White House. Obama had at first appointed Ross to be the czar for Iran policy at the State Department under Hillary Clinton; now Ross was being brought closer to the president and his team, with broader responsibilities. It seemed as though the stage was being set for far-reaching Middle East diplomacy centered on Iran.

It should be pointed out that even after Obama had decided to pursue engagement with Iran, he had alternatives to the specific policies he was pursuing. Iran was scheduled to have presidential elections in June. Obama might have delayed some or all of these overtures until after the election, so that he could see who won and what the next regime would look like. He might have started his diplomatic initiative with Iran at a slightly lower level, by having the early signals come from Ross, for example, or Hillary Clinton, or a deputy national security adviser or deputy secretary of state. (Nixon's earliest signals to China had come not from the president himself or from Henry Kissinger, but from Elliot Richardson, the deputy secretary of state.) Instead, through his speeches and his radio address to the Iranian people, Obama became publicly and closely involved, early on, staking his prestige before he could see how or indeed whether the Iranians would respond.

In the month between Obama's Cairo speech and the July 4 holiday, a series of tumultuous events in Iran made Obama's efforts to bring about an enduring reconciliation with Mahmoud Ahmadinejad's regime much harder, if not impossible. Iran held its presidential election on June 12. The turnout was higher than in past elections, about 84 percent of the electorate, and afterward both sides claimed victory. Ahmadinejad's principal opponent, Mir Hossein Mousavi, appeared to have extremely strong support in Tehran and other urban areas. "The people have voted for me," Mousavi declared. But when young supporters of Mousavi gathered together late that night to celebrate, they were met with tear gas. The following day, the interior ministry announced that Ahmadinejad had won the election handily, with 63 percent of the vote.[10] Mousavi and his supporters said they were convinced there had been massive vote rigging and that the election had been stolen.

Over the following days, hundreds of thousands of people took to the streets of Tehran in a series of demonstrations that would come to be known as the Green Movement or Green Revolution (Mousavi's opposition campaign had used green as its official color). The protests were larger than any in Iran since those that had led up to the fall of the Shah in 1979. The regime responded with force to get the protesters off the streets and with brutality toward those it locked up. By the government's own estimates, at least thirty-six protesters were killed; the estimates of opposition forces and independent observers ran into the hundreds. A video recorded the death of a young Iranian woman, Neda Agha-Soltan, who was shot as she was leaving a June 20 demonstration; the video spread around the world, making Neda the martyred symbol of the movement. There were documented instances of protesters being tortured in prison. One protester's father was asked to pick up his son's corpse in prison and was told his son had died from a preexisting condition. Medical reports showed that he had been beaten so severely that several bones were broken and that his toenails had been pulled out.[11]

Throughout the demonstrations, Obama said little. He did not side with the protesters, and he refrained from condemning the regime or challenging its legitimacy. When the violence against demonstrators escalated to the point where it was impossible for the president to ignore it, he read a statement saying that "the United States and the international community have been appalled and outraged by the threats, the beatings and imprisonments of the past few days." But even then, he made plain the administration's eagerness for engagement with Iran. "The United States respects the sovereignty of the Islamic Republic of Iran, and is not interfering with Iran's internal affairs," Obama asserted. He became vague when pressed whether there might be any consequences for the regime because of its brutal crackdown. "I think it is not too late for the Iranian government to recognize that there is a peaceful path that will lead to stability and legitimacy and prosperity for the Iranian people," he told reporters.[12] His frequent refrain was that he wanted to wait to see how events in Iran played out. Over the following month, in the face of the severe repression, the demonstrations subsided.

Obama's inner circle of White House advisers on Iran included Middle

East specialist Dennis Ross, Deputy National Security Adviser Tom Donilon, and Denis McDonough, who was responsible for disseminating the administration's point of view and guiding (if not controlling) the press coverage. This team put forward two underlying reasons for Obama's cautious, restrained, noncommittal responses to the Green Movement. The first concerned Iran's nuclear weapons program. The new administration had been trying since its earliest days to establish ties with the regime in order to negotiate an end to the nuclear program, and Obama didn't want to do or say anything that might jeopardize that. The second factor was that Obama and his team did not want to voice strong support for the demonstrators for fear that the protesters might be portrayed as tools of the United States.

Both of these were serious concerns, and they were deeply held. Still, the points were debatable, less clear-cut than administration officials maintained. One underlying premise was that, over the long run, the United States would need to work out a nuclear deal with the Ahmadinejad regime, and if it was strong, that might put Iran in a better position to negotiate. But others among Obama's advisers believed that if the demonstrations *weakened* Ahmadinejad, or if he fell from power, this might increase the chances of accommodation.[13]

It seems fair to ask, in light of what has happened since, whether Obama would have made the same decisions concerning Iran's Green Movement two years later. When Egyptian protesters took to the streets of Cairo in early 2011, Obama was considerably less stinting in his support of the opposition; rather, as the demonstrations grew, he pressed Egyptian president Hosni Mubarak to step down. He also began to support the idea of democratic change or reform throughout the Middle East. As the protests spread through the region from one country to another, Obama and Hillary Clinton sent signaled encouragement for Iranians to take to the streets. Clinton told reporters that the administration "very clearly and directly supports the aspirations" of those who protest against Iran's government. A day later, Obama urged Iranians not to be intimidated by the regime: "My hope and expectation is that we're going to see the people of Iran have the courage to be able to express their yearning for greater freedoms and a more representative government," he told a news conference.[14] By 2011, however, these words carried vastly less impact than they would have at the height of the Green Movement. Iran's protest movement had been eviscerated.

The circumstances in Egypt in 2011 and Iran in 2009 were different. In the two years since Obama had started diplomacy with Iran, the Ahmadinejad regime had repeatedly rebuffed his overtures and was still continuing its nuclear program. Egypt was a friend, not an adversary, and the United States, with its military ties to Egypt and its huge aid program, possessed vastly more leverage in dealing with Mubarak than with Ahmadinejad. Nevertheless, the contrast between Obama's approach to the protests in Ahmadinejad's Iran and Mubarak's Egypt was stark. The administration may well have sent out an undesired message to Iran, North Korea and other dictatorial regimes: If you want careful, respectful treatment from the United States, it helps to have a nuclear weapons program.

————

Throughout Obama's first year, the administration's downgrading of democracy and human rights became the staple of news stories, columns and even occasional anguished dissent from within the Democratic Party. In late 2009 James P. Rubin, who had served as a staff aide to Joe Biden in the Senate and as a senior adviser to Madeleine Albright at the State Department, wrote, "Over the past year, as the main contours of the new administration's foreign policy have been established, the principles of democratic values have been too often set aside."[15]

In a biting commentary that followed Hillary Clinton's trip to China, Leon Wieseltier of the *New Republic* observed acidly, "Idealism in foreign policy is so 2003."[16] That was an apt observation. By 2003, Wieseltier of course meant the time of the Iraq War. Certainly one of the driving forces behind Obama's (and Hillary Clinton's) initial unwillingness to emphasize the issues of democracy and human rights was that they and many other Democrats did not want to sound like George W. Bush. This was true both at home, where the Democrats had repeatedly challenged the Bush administration, and overseas, where the Iraq War had been intensely unpopular and Bush even more so. Since Bush had talked so fervently about the virtues of democracy (mostly after the Iraq War had gone sour), many Democrats had by 2009 settled on the virtue of not talking about democracy.

In particular, the views of Obama and his inner circle of aides had been shaped by their experiences over the previous decade, a period dominated by the war in Iraq. Most of the older Democrats had worked in the Clinton administration, a time when the United States had even used force to counteract human rights abuses (Bosnia, Kosovo) and when Bill Clinton had openly called for the spread of democracy and free markets. That was, however, a different era, immediately following the Cold War, when America's economic power was unchallenged and growing.

If there was any single individual most influential on the early foreign policy of Obama and his administration, it was not Bill Clinton, Jimmy Carter or any other Democrat. It was a veteran of three Republican administrations: Brent Scowcroft.

Over the previous four decades, Scowcroft's philosophy had remained relatively constant. He was a realist. He argued repeatedly that the United States should pay little or no attention to what happened inside a country's borders or how a government treated its own people. Instead, American leaders should focus on a country's actions overseas and in relation to its neighbors. These views were not uniquely Scowcroft's; in the Nixon and Ford administrations, he had served under Henry Kissinger, the modern-day apostle of realism, before eventually rising to become Ford's national security adviser.

In the past, Democrats had frequently attacked Scowcroft's views and had even mounted presidential campaigns against him. In the 1970s, Jimmy Carter had argued that under the Kissinger-Scowcroft brand of realism, the United States had become far too cozy with dictators such as Ferdinand Marcos and the Shah of Iran. In the late 1980s, after Scowcroft had returned to the job of national security adviser under George H. W. Bush, congressional Democrats such as Senate Majority Leader George Mitchell and Representative Nancy Pelosi had upbraided Scowcroft for his secret fence-mending trips to Beijing following the Tiananmen massacre. In the early 1990s, Bill Clinton had accused the George H. W. Bush administration of coddling dictators "from Beijing to Baghdad."

But many Democrats' views of Scowcroft changed a decade later, when he had strongly and publicly opposed George W. Bush's invasion of Iraq.

The Iraq War had separated Scowcroft from Kissinger, who regularly flattered presidents and tried to stay in good standing with each administration.

Liberal Democrats came to embrace Scowcroft in a way that they never embraced Kissinger. Scowcroft once joked about the shifting perceptions of him. "I think my views have changed very little," he observed in one 2002 interview. "Twenty-five years ago, I was a leading hawk. Now, I feel the same way about things, and I'm a leading dove, apparently."[17]

From the 1980s onward, Kissinger was based in New York, where he offered his Olympian analyses. Scowcroft, in Washington, was more closely involved in the day-to-day making of foreign policy. Kissinger had been the leading intellectual proponent of realism, but Scowcroft was its leading modern-day practitioner. Kissinger had long been a media celebrity and an openly self-centered personality, while Scowcroft came across as selfless and restrained, the insider's insider. By the time Obama took office, Kissinger was known mainly as himself and for his considerable role in history; Scowcroft had become Washington's gray eminence, the symbol of contemporary realism. He was revered in the foreign policy community, praised by columnists and honored and consulted by quite a few Democrats, including Barack Obama.

Scowcroft's influence over Obama's foreign policy was evident even before the new administration took office. During his campaign in 2008, Obama spoke approvingly of "foreign policy realism" and said he had "enormous sympathy for the foreign policy of George H. W. Bush."[18] During the transition, Scowcroft had recommended former Marine Corps commandant James Jones as Obama's national security adviser, and the president-elect, who hardly knew Jones, went ahead with the appointment.

The most powerful member of Obama's cabinet, Robert Gates, was especially close to Scowcroft, in some ways also a protégé. When Scowcroft had served as George H. W. Bush's national security adviser, Gates, nearly twenty years younger, had been his deputy. They had worked together during the invasion of Panama and Desert Storm in Iraq; afterward, with Scowcroft's blessing, Gates became CIA director in the administration's final year. They shared similar worldviews. Both were intelligent, sober and not given to flamboyance. "Scowcroft is just about Gates's father," observed someone who knew and had worked alongside both of them.[19] During the Obama years, the foreign policy hands outside government who usually knew best what Gates was thinking were Scowcroft and Colin Powell (whose run as chairman of the Joint Chiefs of Staff had coincided with Scowcroft's and Gates's time on the elder Bush's National Security Council).

Obama's speeches were elegantly phrased and full of idealism. But his own instincts seemed to tend toward Scowcroft's brand of realism—and particularly so during his first year in office. Obama did not want to sound like a moralist by talking too much about democracy. In Iran, he was not going to let the Green Movement in the streets stand in the way of his efforts at a rapprochement with the country's leaders. He hoped above all to persuade the Iranian regime to change its policies abroad, if not at home.

Obama's closest advisers, even those not involved in foreign policy, faithfully absorbed and transmitted his realist proclivities. When asked about Obama's view of foreign policy after more than a year in office, White House Chief of Staff Rahm Emanuel told a reporter: "Everyone always breaks it down between idealist and realist. If you had to put him [Obama] in a category, he's more realpolitik, like Bush 41."[20] A couple of months later, Denis McDonough observed, "Scowcroft is someone the president really admires."[21]

Scowcroft, in turn, offered frequent praise for Obama. When congressional Republicans criticized Obama for altering U.S. plans for missile defense in Europe, Scowcroft issued a statement of support. In an interview in the fall of 2009, Scowcroft gave high marks to the administration for changing the tone of America's relationship to the world. ("Now comes the difficult part, which is crafting policy," Scowcroft added.)[22]

For his part, Obama did not see himself as siding with the realists or even gravitating toward their views. He followed the same approach in foreign policy he often did elsewhere, which was to detach himself from two opposing camps or schools of thought, sympathize with each and insist the differences between them were less than believed. He sought to blend the two opposing perspectives, the realism of Kissinger and Scowcroft and the idealism of Woodrow Wilson.

"The president won't accept that he's in one of these camps," reported an adviser who spoke directly with the president. "He wants to be buddies with Brent Scowcroft, and he also wants to go out and give speeches about democracy. He thinks we can do both at the same time, and that he can transcend the whole debate."[23]

Obama was, after all, hardly the first person to resist being defined as either a realist or an idealist. Many other senior officials had trod down the same path, among them Madeleine Albright, Strobe Talbott and Condoleezza Rice. Those who sought to blur distinctions often tried to come up with phrases like "idealistic realism" or "realistic idealism," none of which ever took hold. The George W. Bush administration's first National Security Strategy, issued under Rice's supervision in 2002, had said it sought to bring about "a balance of power that favors human freedom"—a "balance of power" for the realists, "freedom" for the idealists.

Still, while Obama didn't identify himself as a realist, his administration's early actions and its internal debates usually showed the dominance of realist thinking. In the Situation Room at the White House, officials sometimes transmitted the view that those who spoke out for stronger action on behalf of democracy or human rights were "ideological," whereas realism was supposedly not. The prevailing attitude was that to be a realist, dismissing in advance the relevance of liberal values in foreign policy, was merely to be practical. When issues were framed in that skewed manner, thought one administration official, anybody would want to be a realist.

———

Gradually, a counterstrain began to develop among a collection of officials across different parts of the government who shared the view that the United States should give greater priority to democracy, political freedom and human rights in dealing with the rest of the world. In Obama's first year, these officials were often on the losing side of internal debates. They amounted to a minority school within the administration: They were admirers of Obama but less so of the realist direction of his foreign policy.

In most cases, these were individuals with strong convictions who had been strongly identified, through past experience and writing, with the causes of protecting human rights or fostering democracy. One of them was Samantha Power, who had begun her career writing about Serbian abuses in Bosnia. Another was Susan Rice, who as an aide for Africa policy had lived through the Clinton administration's failure to act against genocide in

Rwanda. A third was Anne-Marie Slaughter, the head of policy planning at the State Department. In Slaughter's previous position as dean of the Woodrow Wilson School of Public and International Affairs at Princeton, she had written frequently in support of the values of liberal internationalism.

A fourth was Michael McFaul, a unique case. At Stanford, in addition to his Russia scholarship, McFaul had been director of an institution called the Center on Democracy, Development, and the Rule of Law. The last book he had written as an academic, published while he was working in the Obama administration, carried a title that nicely captured his views: *Advancing Democracy Abroad: Why We Should and How We Can*. He had written the book for the specific purpose of persuading fellow Democrats of the continuing importance of democracy for American foreign policy, even after George W. Bush had seemed to make "democracy" a dirty word. McFaul had gone out of his way to get jacket blurbs praising the book from both a Democratic and a Republican secretary of state, Madeleine Albright and George Shultz. "The use of military force in the name of freedom's advance has not only produced limited results for democracy in Afghanistan and Iraq, but tainted all efforts—especially American efforts—to promote democracy around the world," McFaul wrote. "The Bush record, however, cannot be cited as a reason to abandon the project altogether."[24]

These four Obama officials, among others who quietly rejected the new administration's seeming drift toward realism, did not always think alike. Power and Rice, by virtue of their particular interest in problems like Bosnia and Rwanda, appeared to emphasize the importance of human rights more than democracy. They had also, of necessity, been required to think about the question of humanitarian intervention—how and under what circumstance force should be used to prevent genocide or particularly egregious abuses of human rights. McFaul, by contrast, focused less on humanitarian intervention and the use of force (concepts hardly relevant in dealing with a nuclear-armed Russia), devoting more attention to the question of how to spread democracy.

In the day-to-day, working-level debates within the Obama administration, these officials tended to find themselves on the opposite side from those who favored realist policies, such as Deputy National Security Adviser Tom

Donilon or Deputy Secretary of State Jim Steinberg. At the top level of the administration, too, a spirit of realism seemed to hold sway. In her early days as secretary of state, Hillary Clinton seemed uncertain of her role within the administration and eager to show she was no wild-eyed idealist (as Republicans liked to portray her). Vice President Joe Biden seemed to sympathize with those who favored an emphasis on democracy and human rights, but Biden was not the deciding voice in the administration; he'd been put on the ticket not to make foreign policy, but to demonstrate to voters that the Obama administration would have foreign policy experience. No one expected Secretary of Defense Gates to be anything other than a realist; the Pentagon is not typically the place from which to lead a campaign to spread democracy.

The antirealists did find some support and a sympathetic ear from one particular member of Obama's White House inner circle: Ben Rhodes. While Rhodes and Denis McDonough were often seen as a team closely allied within the administration, on the question of support for democratic movements abroad, some saw a shade of difference between the two men.

McDonough was intensely involved in the operational side of foreign policy, making sure that what Obama wanted was being carried out. On the National Security Council he worked particularly closely with realists like Donilon and Brennan. He was also in charge of the message and the political aspects of Obama's foreign policy. For Obama's domestic political advisers, it was important to show that the president was tough and hard-nosed in dealing with the world. McDonough was not without strong convictions of his own; he was certainly a believer in the general value of democracy and human rights, but he was above all an organization man for Barack Obama.

Rhodes was more idealistic, more reflective of the youthful spirit of the campaign, in which Obama's slogan was "Change We Can Believe In." He was also, as a speechwriter, more regularly preoccupied with the articulation of ideals. No matter what their foreign policies might be, American presidents don't usually explain them to the public in the idiom of realism. Even Richard Nixon called himself an admirer of Woodrow Wilson, saying in one speech that Wilson had taught Americans that "by not fearing to be idealists ourselves, we shall make the world safe for free men to live in peace."[25] And despite once famously quipping, about Bosnia, that "we don't have a dog in that fight," James Baker himself also stressed the importance of democracy and human rights in his speeches as secretary of state.

Democracy proponents like McFaul came to see Rhodes as their ally, an inner-circle advocate for their views. When Rahm Emanuel had described Obama in that newspaper interview as tending toward realpolitik, Slaughter shot off an anguished e-mail to Rhodes, saying, in effect, *Can't you make Emanuel shut up?* (There was little likelihood of that.)

For Slaughter and others, the problem was not so much that Obama was a realist, but that he and his administration were being characterized that way. They were convinced the perceptions were wrong, that Obama personally believed in the importance of human rights and democracy—that he was really on their side. McFaul became so upset with the characterizations of Obama as a realist that he began to compile a long list of all the speeches in which the president had mentioned the importance of democracy. He handed the list out to skeptics who used the R-word.

Later on, during the early stages of the Arab Spring, Obama's policies would come to match the rhetoric of his speeches. What had started as Mc-Faul's personal list attempting to prove Obama was no realist became, in 2011, a document representing the administration as a whole. The list was distributed proudly, to show that Obama had always given strong support for the cause of democracy. That information was of scant comfort to Iran's Green Movement, though, which had subsided following Obama's apparent indifference.

13

No Roosevelt, No Churchill, No Brandy

President Obama was going to do China differently. He and his aides didn't want to follow the wavering paths of earlier presidents such as Ronald Reagan and Bill Clinton. Both had suggested during their presidential campaigns that they would adopt more confrontational policies toward China. Neither had succeeded in doing so. These predecessors, the Obama team believed, had started with the hard line on China that they'd promised during their campaigns, only to discover that those initial policies were untenable. After a year or two they had fallen back on the more conciliatory approaches of those who had gone before.[1] The result had been to undermine America's credibility with the Chinese leadership (and, indeed, with other governments) by showing that strong words by American leaders were little more than posturing, that the United States did not carry through on its threats. Candidates for the presidency should try to resist the "siren song of tough promises to reverse their predecessors' soft approach" to China, two of Obama's advisers had written.[2]

Following this advice during the campaign, Obama tried to avoid tough talk on China. Sometimes he failed. At the peak of the primary battle, Obama found it necessary to follow Hillary Clinton's lead in proposing a tougher China policy. After Clinton called for a boycott of the 2008 Beijing Olympics, Obama did so, too. He also promised labor audiences, both in the primaries and the general election, that he would label China a currency manipulator. Still, China never became a preoccupying issue in Obama's campaign.

During the financial crisis in Obama's first months in the White House, the United States and China worked so closely together that there were occasional proposals they should collaborate as a "G-2," guiding economic policy throughout the world. "Even as the United States and China lead the way toward today's solution, they need to be shaping tomorrow's world economy," wrote World Bank president Robert Zoellick and the bank's chief economist, Justin Yifu Lin. The talk of a "G-2," however, aroused understandable mistrust among leaders of other major countries—Britain, France, Germany, Japan and India, for starters—who didn't like the idea of two economic superpowers making decisions about the international economy without them. Other critics argued that the United States and China did not agree on human rights or on international issues such as Iran, Burma and Sudan; there were too many inherent tensions between Washington and Beijing to make the idea of a "G-2" feasible.[3]

That was also the problem with a popular buzzword, "Chimerica," coined by author Niall Ferguson to convey the idea that America and China were becoming so interdependent—America the biggest buyer of Chinese exports, China the biggest purchaser of U.S. Treasury bonds—that their interests were blending together.

———

Talk of a "G-2" raised questions that extended well beyond China: How, and through what institutions, should the Obama administration deal with the world's leading powers? If the United States wanted to do business with several similar countries at once, or merely to think in conceptual terms about where the world was heading, how should major countries be grouped together? Where did China and India, Britain and Germany, Russia and Brazil fit in?

The most prominent international institution, the United Nations, reflects the power relationships at the end of World War II. Five countries—the United States, the Soviet Union, Britain, France and China—were given permanent seats and veto power on the Security Council. Virtually everyone recognized that this setup, more than six decades old, no longer fit the world of 2009. But repeated efforts at reform had been blocked by the countries happy with the status quo. China, relishing its role as the sole Asian nation on the Security Council, refused to support permanent membership for Japan or India. Britain and France didn't think much of the suggestion that there be a single seat for the European Union. Reforming the Security Council seemed like a long shot, not one Obama was prepared to take on in his early years.

Nevertheless, from the start of his administration, Obama began talking about other ideas for changing the outdated post–World War II order to give new weight to rising powers. At his first international summit in the spring of 2009, Obama declared at a press conference that the world could no longer be governed in the old, clubby fashion it once was:

> If it's just Roosevelt and Churchill sitting in a room with a brandy, you know, that's an easier negotiation. But that's not the world we live in. And it shouldn't be the world that we live in. And you know, that's not a loss for America. It's an appreciation that Europe is now rebuilt and a power-house; Japan is rebuilt, is a powerhouse. China, India, these are all coun-tries on the move. And that's good. That means there are billions of people who are working their way out of poverty. And over time, that potentially makes this a much more peaceful world.[4]

Since the early 1970s, the United States had been coordinating its inter-national economic policy in regular meetings with six other leading devel-oped, industrialized nations: Britain, France, Germany, Italy, Japan and Canada. This grouping, called the G-7 (later the G-8, after Russia was in-cluded), was a classic example of the old world dominated by Europe and the United States. Over the following three decades, it became impossible to explain the presence of Italy and Canada and the exclusion of many other important economic powers such as China, India, Brazil, Saudi Arabia, South Korea and Mexico.

In the fall of 2008, as the worst financial crisis since the Great Depression began to sweep the world, French president Nicolas Sarkozy and British prime minister Gordon Brown persuaded George W. Bush to convene a summit meeting in Washington of the leaders of twenty countries, including these economic powers and several others, such as Turkey, South Africa and Argentina. Bush agreed to go along with this meeting with considerable reluctance; it seemed like a major change that could dilute America's influ-ence, and by the time the summit was convened, Bush himself was prepar-ing to leave office.

Obama was far more enthusiastic. In 2009, he endorsed a fundamental change in which the meetings of the twenty governments that had first convened in the dying days of the Bush presidency (known, inevitably, as the G-20) would constitute "the premier forum" for guiding the world economy. The gatherings of the G-7 soon became a relic of a bygone era.[5]

Still, only a limited amount of business could be done at gatherings only a day or two long of the leaders of twenty governments. The G-20 was significant for having recognized new emerging powers and giving them a voice, but it was also at once both too big and too small—too big for easy discussion or decision making, but too small for other important countries that didn't make the cut, such as Singapore, Thailand and Nigeria.

In its day-to-day diplomacy, outside these large, formal meetings, the Obama administration was still often obliged, like its predecessors, to deal with individual countries. But in doing this, Obama's approach sometimes tried to offer a different perspective, one intended to reflect a changed world.

Throughout the Cold War and its immediate aftermath, American policy had rested on its series of alliance partners: above all, Japan and South Korea in East Asia, and the NATO countries in Europe. Either in these alliances or on its own, the United States was preoccupied with two major powers: the Soviet Union (or Russia) and China.

Early on, the Obama administration seemed to embrace a new concept: Its diplomacy would emphasize four emerging economic powers called the BRICs, or Brazil, Russia, India and China. (Later on, South Africa was sometimes added as a fifth country, conveniently taking up the letter *S*.) The idea originally came from Wall Street: In 2001, a Goldman Sachs economist invented the concept of the BRICs to describe the four emerging economies that he believed would play an increasingly important role in world markets.[6] By 2009, the term had become an addition to the jargon of foreign policy, and the Obama team began to talk about the importance of the BRICs in their speeches. In her first major speech as secretary of state, Clinton said that the Obama administration, while reinvigorating its traditional alliances, "will also put special emphasis on encouraging major and emerging global powers—China, India, Russia and Brazil, as well as Turkey, Indonesia and South Africa—to be full partners in tackling the global agenda."[7]

Over the long run, grouping together the BRICs proved to be of limited utility for the Obama administration. The idea was, in fact, of greater significance to the other countries, which began to hold meetings of their own, without the United States, to coordinate efforts to change the international financial system and to reduce dependence on the U.S. dollar.[8]

The underlying issue confronting the Obama team was that the BRIC countries were not all equal, and lumping them together didn't match reality. Brazil was a major and growing economic power, but not a military one. Russia had nuclear weapons but a shaky economy and a declining population. Above all of the others stood China, a country too important to be pigeonholed with the others. With the world's highest population, its second-largest economy and its fastest-growing military, China seemed to tower over the other BRICs. The Obama team could talk about groupings of countries, but increasingly, it would have to deal with China on its own.

———

No wonder the first nasty turf battle within Obama's cabinet was over China. The fight erupted in the two weeks after Obama's inauguration, and to those who weren't swept up in the fray, it had comical aspects. The combatants were Secretary of State Hillary Clinton and Treasury Secretary Tim Geithner.

In the George W. Bush administration, Treasury Secretary Hank Paulson had set up a regular series of meetings with Chinese officials, called the Strategic Economic Dialogue. Top-level American officials, headed by Paulson, began sitting down once a year in either Beijing or Washington for structured discussions with their Chinese counterparts. In the late Bush years, Paulson had become the principal American interlocutor with China.

As Obama's new treasury secretary, Geithner wanted to preserve Paulson's considerable authority. Geithner considered himself a China hand. His father, Peter Geithner, had run the Ford Foundation's extensive programs in Asia; among his other duties, the senior Geithner had overseen the program in Indonesia for which Obama's mother, Ann Dunham, worked.[9] As a Dartmouth undergraduate, Tim Geithner had learned Mandarin at Beijing University. He worked for Kissinger Associates, Henry Kissinger's consulting firm, and in the late 1990s had been closely involved in China policy as the Treasury Department's undersecretary for international affairs, working first for Robert Rubin and then for Lawrence Summers.

From the start, Clinton was opposed to letting Geithner head up the talks with China as Paulson had. She argued, plausibly enough, that she and the State Department should have the leading role. Under Paulson, she argued, the dialogue with China had focused too much on economic policy. "That's a very important aspect of our relationship with China, but it is not the only aspect of our relationship," Clinton said. The Obama administration wanted "a more comprehensive approach."[10] Just because her predecessor, Condoleezza Rice, allowed the Treasury Department to take the lead in dealing with China didn't mean that in the Obama administration Clinton must necessarily yield to Geithner.

They agreed to talk it over. When they tried to arrange a meeting, however, the bickering intensified. Geithner and Treasury officials insisted that they should host the get-together at the Treasury Department. No, replied Clinton, you come to us at the State Department. Finally Geithner relented and agreed to have lunch on Clinton's home turf. Even then, the wrangling persisted. How many State and Treasury officials would be on each side in the meeting? There was talk of inviting as many as twenty officials, perhaps ten per side, a full-bore interagency shoot-out. In the interests of harmony, the session was scaled back to a smaller lunch, and then to just the two secretaries, a more intimate meeting. So the State Department set up a small table, just big enough to accommodate only Clinton and Geithner. They finally broke bread together on February 2, 2009.

It was part of a big day for Clinton. The meeting with Geithner took place only a few hours before two lavish late afternoon and evening parties at the State Department, perhaps four hundred people each, to toast her warmly on the occasion of her swearing-in. There was little warmth at the lunch, however. Geithner still wanted to be in charge of the exchanges with China, but he lost out. The talks were renamed the Strategic *and* Economic Dialogue, making clear they were not just about economics, and Clinton was named cochair along with Geithner. In this cabinet tug-of-war, Clinton had both logic and politics on her side. She had won 18 million votes in the primaries and was the new head of the department that was, in protocol terms, the highest ranking in the cabinet. While Clinton did not get her way all the time in the Obama White House, on this she outweighed Geithner, who was nearly fourteen years younger. Moreover, the new Obama team was counting on Geithner to devote as much time and energy as possible to combating the recession and financial crisis that had engulfed the nation. For this task, no Mandarin was required.

The Obama administration's early China policy might well have worked in an earlier era. The idea was to forge a smooth working relationship early by minimizing conflict and avoiding the sorts of challenges from which it might be forced to retreat.

The veterans of the Clinton administration—not only Hillary Clinton but Tom Donilon, Jim Steinberg and Leon Panetta—remembered all too well how Bill Clinton had threatened China with a loss of trade privileges and then backed down a year later. If the Clinton administration had been more accommodating from the start, they reasoned, the Chinese regime might have responded with conciliatory policies of its own.

Thus, the Clinton alumni were trying to correct the mistakes of the 1990s. The problem was that the situation had changed. China possessed far greater economic and military power than it had when Bill Clinton was in the White House. In 2006, China passed Japan to become the world's largest holder of foreign exchange reserves. At the time Obama took office, China was fast approaching Japan as the world's second-largest economy, a milestone it passed during Obama's second year. The United States, meanwhile, was the world's largest debtor. China came through the financial crisis of 2008–2009 much more easily than many other countries, including the United States. Those changes had helped persuade many in China that America was not what it used to be.

Those who had worked for Bill Clinton and returned under Obama found that they were dealing with a different China. One official reflected with surprise after early meetings that his Chinese counterparts projected a sense of "ascendancy" that he had not seen in the Clinton years. Another Obama aide observed that Chinese officials were "much more worldly. They're much more sophisticated about what they're doing." During Bill Clinton's administration, China had been preoccupied with its immediate neighborhood in East Asia; in international conferences that didn't directly involve Asia, it had tended to stay in the background. By the Obama years, China cared much more about its global influence. There was an ongoing intellectual debate within China about whether the United States had entered into a state of permanent decline.

In this changed climate, the Obama administration's initial policy of avoiding conflict with China led not to greater accommodation, but to more insistent Chinese demands and further testing of American resolve. When the Obama administration sought to be conciliatory, Chinese officials seemed to take that as confirmation of American weakness and China's growing power.

On a number of issues, China pushed for changes in the status quo. During the Dalai Lama's ten previous visits to Washington dating back to 1991, Presidents George H. W. Bush, Bill Clinton and George W. Bush had all met with the Tibetan leader. But a few months after Obama took office, China made clear it did not want the president to meet with the Dalai Lama, at least not before Obama visited China near the end of the year. American officials then pressed the Dalai Lama's representatives to postpone a meeting with Obama, and in October, for the first time in eighteen years, the Dalai Lama visited Washington without seeing the president.[11] This episode led to a wave of criticism of Obama, and later on, his aides acknowledged they had made a mistake. "If you'd have told me how much that was going to upset people, we could have just done the meeting," a close aide to Obama admitted ruefully.[12]

Chinese officials also insisted that the Obama administration stop American arms sales to Taiwan. This was a particularly sore subject: During the Reagan administration, the United States and China had signed a communiqué in which these American arms sales would eventually be phased out. But no date was given, and the sales continued for more than a quarter century, through the presidencies of Reagan, Clinton and the two Bushes. Chinese officials pointed out (accurately) that even though these transfers had taken place fairly regularly, Beijing never gave its formal approval. In the first year of the Obama administration, China warned that it wanted the arms sales to stop, no matter how many times they had gone forward since Reagan's 1982 communiqué. The issue became one of China's highest priorities with the Obama White House. One administration official, who had hoped to talk with Chinese counterparts in Beijing about North Korea and economic issues, observed afterward that "the Chinese agenda was simple. It was Taiwan, Taiwan, Taiwan, Taiwan, Tibet, Taiwan, Taiwan, Taiwan."[13]

In late July of her first year, Hillary Clinton participated, with Geithner, in the new Strategic and Economic Dialogue with China. The two days of talks produced few tangible results. Instead, senior Chinese officials chose the occasion to put the Americans on the defensive by asking hard questions about when the United States would cut its budget deficit. In response, Geithner assured China that the Obama administration would bring down the deficit after the American economy recovered from the recession.[14]

Clinton had cause to wonder why she had fought so hard to get into these discussions. China usually transacts its most serious business in private, top-level talks, not in formal, structured dialogues among large groups of officials. Afterward, Clinton turned to other issues and, for nearly a year, remained in the background on China policy; Obama's own visit to Beijing would take center stage. By 2010, Clinton would reemerge as a leader in dealing with China, but in a different way and with a more assertive policy.

———

Obama's operating style on China mirrored his way of dealing with other policy areas and other countries, such as Egypt: The speeches and rhetoric didn't always match his private views or his policies. In public, he spoke in lofty terms, using the same New Age idiom of foreign policy he employed elsewhere, depicting a world of "win-win" outcomes and growing interdependence. "The pursuit of power among nations must no longer be seen as a zero-sum game," he told Chinese officials in the summer of 2009.[15]

China, however, was doing what it thought best for China, forsaking talk about broader global responsibilities. Obama's private views of China gradually became a bit more jaundiced. At one point during Obama's first year, when Chinese president Hu Jintao called him to make a point he had made before, in the highly scripted, stilted way that Hu did business everywhere, Obama afterward quipped, "I love the Chinese, because they're so predictable."

Obama was understandably far more concerned about China's impact on the American economy and the global economy than previous presidents. He saw the downsides of free trade as well as the benefits. "Let's just say he's no Adam Smith, okay?" said one aide. Obama was skeptical about the degree to which China felt bound by the rules of the global trading system in general and the rules of the World Trade Organization in particular. Obama made it plain to veterans of the Clinton administration that he felt they had allowed China to enter into the World Trade Organization under terms that weren't tight enough—thus allowing China to become a trading giant and leaving Obama with too little leverage when China flouted the trading rules. "He's asked us to answer, 'Did we fuck this up?'" admitted another official (Among the senior Obama aides who had worked on China's entry into the WTO in the late 1990s were Lawrence Summers, Timothy Geithner, Jeffrey Bader and Michael Froman.)[16]

Asian diplomats sometimes thought they detected an Asian style to the way Obama reacted to events, a pattern that, perhaps inevitably, some attributed to the years he had spent in Indonesia as a child. They noticed the ways in which Obama always maintained his self-composure and avoided displays of anger or emotion, his continual efforts to bridge differences, his reluctance to be forced to choose between opposing poles in an argument. There was also a certain Asian quality to the president's negotiations with China. "They push and push and push until you say no," Obama told those around him. "And then they stop pushing."

Chinese officials had their own worries about dealing with Obama inside their own country. There were ways in which Obama's persona and career were unsettling. China was not a country where Obama's biography was an easy subject. Would he talk in China about the importance of respecting and protecting ethnic minorities—a natural theme for the first African American president, and one Obama had already raised in other countries? That would not go down well with a government that claimed all ethnic groups—Hans, Tibetans, Uighurs and others—were already living in harmony. Would he talk about his background as a constitutional lawyer, or about the values Americans placed on the importance of law, due process and civil rights? That would not go down easily, either. Chinese leaders emphasized personal relationships over legal processes or abstract principles. Over the years, they had tended to get along poorly with American officials (such as Warren Christopher, Cyrus Vance and George Mitchell) who emphasized abstract rules and principles or who insisted that China should be treated like any other country.

When Obama finally made his first visit to China in November 2009, these undercurrents of mistrust made for an awkward trip. Chinese officials imposed a series of restrictions on what Obama could do, limiting his access to Chinese people outside the government. During the planning for his visit, American officials tried to arrange one event at which Obama could meet

with Chinese lawyers to demonstrate his belief in the rule of law. On a trip
to Russia a few months earlier, Obama had conducted a similar session with
representatives of a broad range of civil society groups. But China rejected
all suggestions for a meeting between the American president and Chinese
lawyers.

U.S. officials also proposed that Obama host a town hall meeting with
students in China, with the president alone on the stage taking questions, as
he had done elsewhere. During a presidential visit in 1998, Bill Clinton had
taken part in a similar event at Beijing University. Eleven years later, China
was more restrictive. Nothing was left to chance. Obama was permitted to
speak with students, but not on campus. He wasn't allowed to be alone on-
stage; instead, Chinese officials were there to introduce him and to take
questions to relay to him. American officials wanted Obama's speech to be
live-streamed in Chinese, but China would allow it to be seen only on Xin-
huanet, the website of China's official news service. The speech was broadcast on time delay, not live, and only in English, without translation into
Chinese. U.S. officials thought they had been promised that the speech
would be televised nationwide, as Clinton's had been in 1998. Chinese officials surprised them by allowing the American president to be seen only on
Shanghai television, not throughout the country.

In drafting Obama's remarks to the students, his aides followed an unusual model for a Democratic president: Ronald Reagan. On his only visit
to China, in 1984, Reagan first spoke at length about the enduring ties between the American and Chinese people, then moved gently to a description
of America's perspectives and values, its beliefs in liberty, freedom of speech
and freedom of religion. After studying Reagan's address, Obama's aides
structured his own speech in a nearly identical way: Like Reagan, Obama
spoke of the long history between the two countries, starting with George
Washington's dispatch of the ship *Empress of China* to pursue trade with the
Qing Dynasty. At the end of Obama's speech came his standard refrain
about how the world was becoming interconnected. Sandwiched in the middle came the sensitive subject of freedom:

> We do not seek to impose any system of government on any other nation,
> but we also don't believe that the principles that we stand for are unique

to our nation. These freedoms of expression and worship—of access to information and political participation—we believe are universal rights. They should be available to all people, including ethnic and religious minorities, whether they are in the United States, China or any nation.[17]

The thought was especially well phrased, but because of Chinese restrictions, it was heard by far fewer people in China than American officials had hoped.

Before leaving China, Obama granted a single interview to the newspaper *Southern Weekend*, which is based in Guangzhou. Chinese officials struggled to control the interview, trying to pick the topics, making sure that no controversial issues were raised. Obama was asked only seven questions, on obviously safe subjects such as his love of basketball. Nevertheless, when the interview was published, some readers found that the page with the Obama interview was ripped out of their newspaper, and it was also missing from the paper's website.[18]

At the end of Obama's visit, the United States and China issued a detailed, eleven-page "joint statement" of broad principles, pledging "a positive, cooperative and comprehensive U.S.-China relationship for the twenty-first century." The document was aimed at providing a new tone for the relationship, but it engendered more controversy than the Obama team had expected. Pentagon officials complained that the administration had allowed too much leeway for their Chinese counterparts to write the language about Taiwan, which emphasized "China's sovereignty and territorial integrity." Indian diplomats complained that another passage seemed to suggest the United States and China would team up to guide events in South Asia and mentioned both Pakistan and India on an equal footing. This language was in fact similar to what Bill Clinton had signed on his 1998 trip, soon after India and Pakistan had tested nuclear weapons. But that was precisely the sore point: The Indians felt that it wasn't the 1990s anymore, that India's relationship with the United States had changed and that India should no longer be equated with Pakistan.

By the end of the China trip, the Obama team was furious at the press coverage of it. The general feeling was that many of the stories were meant to fit into a preconceived narrative: that the United States, because of its growing debt, came to China as a supplicant; and that the United States was in decline and no longer accorded the same respect by China as it had been in the past. "This is no longer the United States–China relationship of old but an encounter between a weakened giant and a comer with a bit of its own swagger," reported the *New York Times*. "Washington's comparative advantage in past meetings is now diminished, a fact clearly not lost on the Chinese."[19]

Their attempts to alter these perceptions were not helped, however, by what soon followed. A month later, at the conference on climate change in Copenhagen, China scuttled the European and American efforts to set fixed numerical targets for reducing emissions by a particular date. In doing so, Chinese officials acted in ways that seemed to belittle Obama. Chinese premier Wen Jiabao sent a midlevel foreign ministry official to represent him at a meeting with Obama and other leaders, who had to wait while the Chinese official phoned the premier for instructions. At one point, during a session that also included officials from India, Brazil and South Africa, China's leading negotiator for climate change, Xie Zhenhua, wagged his finger at Obama and dressed him down in a heated tirade.

The following month, the Obama administration approved the sale of a new package of weaponry for Taiwan, one that amounted to less than Taiwan had requested. China responded in an unprecedented fashion. It announced that it would impose commercial sanctions on any American company taking part in these arms sales—meaning that any company involved would lose its business in China.[20]

By that point, in the first months of 2010, unhappiness with China's actions had reached into the highest levels of America's foreign policy elite. Harvard professor Joseph Nye—a Democrat who had held a series of senior foreign policy jobs in the Carter and Clinton administrations—was prompted at one point to depart from his usually restrained style. Sending an underling at Copenhagen to meet with Obama and other heads of state was "insulting," Nye said.

"To have a Chinese underling point his finger and shout at the U.S. president is very insulting behavior. And these things don't necessarily happen by accident." For good measure, Nye added, China had also sent a lower-level official, without instructions, to a separate meeting with the Americans, British, French, Germans and Russians to talk about Iran. That, said Nye, was "also insulting."[21]

Gradually, a consensus was emerging that the Obama administration would have to switch course and get firmer in dealing with China. Obama's incoming policy of avoiding conflict hadn't worked in the way that Obama and his aides had hoped, but instead had been taken as an opportunity for China to seek changes in the status quo.

And so the Obama administration's China policy followed roughly the opposite trajectory from the Clinton and Reagan administrations—it started off conciliatory in Obama's first year and then began to toughen.

———

With Russia, the Obama administration was occasionally more successful. The Bush administration, in its final years in office, had such poor relations with Vladimir Putin that there was plenty of room for improvement.

Less than two weeks after Election Day in 2008, Russian president Dmitry Medvedev visited Washington to take part in the G-20 meetings on the financial crisis. Medvedev didn't meet with Obama then, but he wasn't shy about delivering a message that would surely be passed to the president-elect: There was "no trust" between the United States and Russia, he told a group of Americans active in foreign policy, including Madeleine Albright and Brent Scowcroft. With Obama's election, he said, "I believe we have great opportunities to restore relations. . . . There can be a new foundation."[22]

Dressed immaculately in a blue suit, white shirt and maroon tie, Medvedev was, on the surface, more Westernized than any previous Russian official. He was four years younger than Obama. Indeed, he was the first truly post–Cold War Russian leader, much as Obama was the first such American president. Neither had started his career in government or politics before the Berlin Wall came down. At that time, in 1989, Obama was still at Harvard Law School, while Medvedev had just graduated from Leningrad State University and was staying on to complete graduate work in the law department.

Bill Clinton had visited the Soviet Union as a student during the height of the Cold War and, as governor, was active in the debates over Cold War foreign policy within the Democratic Party. George W. Bush had not been involved in the Cold War on his own, but had experienced it through his father's career as CIA director, vice president and president; moreover, virtually all of the younger Bush's advisers, from Dick Cheney and Donald

Rumsfeld to Colin Powell and Condoleezza Rice, had devoted most of their careers to the Cold War. By contrast, Obama had little connection to the Soviet era, in either his family life or his career.[23] He first set foot in the former Soviet Union in 2005, after his election to the Senate, on a mission to Russia and Ukraine with Senator Richard Lugar to observe what was happening to the former Soviet nuclear complex. Obama's impression was that it was aged and decaying. He described former Soviet officials "presiding over remnants of the past, their institutions barely relevant to nations whose people had shifted their main attention to turning a quick buck."[24]

Medvedev also seemed to have little personal connection to the Cold War. His grandfather had been a local Communist Party official, one who had fought in the Bolshevik Revolution, but his father had been a chemist, apparently divorced from politics. Medvedev had not risen through the ranks of the Communist Party, like Boris Yeltsin and Vladimir Putin, nor through the KGB like Putin. As a law student in Leningrad, he was among those pushing for democratic change in the final days of the Soviet Union.

But then again, there was Medvedev's relationship with Putin, the career KGB officer and hardened veteran of the Cold War. Putin had served as Medvedev's patron since the early 1990s and was responsible for bringing him from St. Petersburg to Moscow, where he was a top aide to President Putin. When he was legally obliged to give up the presidency, Putin stage-managed the election of Medvedev to succeed him. (In the presidential balloting in 2008, Medvedev won 70 percent of the vote—nearly twenty points higher than Obama, and yet also a relatively low percentage when compared to the purported election returns of the Soviet era.) Putin took the job of prime minister and, despite Medvedev's victory, remained easily the most powerful man and the ultimate decision-making authority in Russia. In 2011, Putin removed any question about that by announcing that in 2012 he would become Russia's president once again, replacing Medvedev, who would become prime minister.

Nevertheless, Obama and his aides decided early on to devote most of their attention to Medvedev and to treat him as an independent actor in the hopes he might become one. They occasionally voiced the hope that Medvedev, while highly dependent on Putin in many ways, would not serve merely as Putin's puppet in the way he was sometimes described.

Obama first met Putin in Moscow in July 2009. They talked for nearly three hours. Putin spent most of the first hour talking bitterly about the Bush administration: how George W. Bush and Condoleezza Rice had treated him with disrespect; how things could have gone differently; how the United States and Russia could have developed a different and more positive relationship after the September 11 attacks. The conversation was polite, but the Obama team came away with the impression that Putin was an old-school believer in zero-sum games, antithetical to the Obama team's preferred worldview of win-win solutions.

Medvedev seemed far more attuned to Obama's way of thinking. By virtue of his title as Russia's president, Medvedev would go to summit conferences for heads of state that Putin did not attend. Obama had met him prior to Putin, at an international gathering in London in the spring of 2009. Like Obama, he projected an air of detachment and didn't seem to view the world as good guys versus bad guys. He was interested in economics, in technology, in bringing Russia into the age of Google. He didn't spend time complaining about or trying to reverse recent history. When asked about the expansion of NATO into Central and Eastern Europe, Medvedev answered simply that whatever he and other Russians thought, the existing institutions would remain in place. "I'm a realist," Medvedev liked to say—a self-identification that must have warmed Obama's heart.[25]

Obama's pitch to Medvedev was phrased in the terms of a realist—that there were many areas in which the United States and Russia could cooperate, because it was in both countries' national interest to do so. One major issue, early on, was the U.S. air base at Manas in Kyrgyzstan, the only American base in Central Asia. It was of surpassing importance to the United States, because it was at the heart of what was called, in shorthand, the NDN—the Northern Distribution Network to supply American troops in Afghanistan. Although most U.S. military supplies for the war moved through Pakistan, an increasing share came through the northern route, and after the Obama administration's decisions to send more troops to Afghanistan, the base took on even greater significance. In early 2009, the president of Kyrgyzstan suddenly announced plans to close the American facility, immediately after a meeting in Moscow in which the Russians had promised him the extension of \$2 billion in loans.[26] The Obama administration got the obvious message: It was Russia, not Kyrgyzstan, that wanted the base closed.

At their first meeting, Obama argued to Medvedev that what America was doing in Afghanistan was in Russia's own interest: The United States was trying to defeat a group of radical Islamic fundamentalists who would otherwise challenge Russia itself. "Tell me how this is not in Russia's self-interest, too," Obama asked.[27] Two months after this Obama-Medvedev meeting, Kyrgyzstan changed its mind and decided it would keep the base open. In turn, the Obama administration agreed to increase the rent it paid to Kyrgyzstan from $17 million a year to $60 million and to add additional millions for economic development.[28] Russia provided all of the fuel used for the American base; if Russia had decided to cut off that fuel, the base would have had to cease operations within less than two weeks. That never happened, and the base continued to function as a principal transit point for American troops and supplies into Afghanistan, a symbol of quiet new cooperation between Washington and Moscow.[29]

For its part, Russia derived important benefits from Obama administration policies. In the fall of 2009, the United States announced that it would drop the Bush administration's plans to deploy a missile defense system based in Poland and the Czech Republic. Administration officials said it would be replaced by a mostly ship-based system that would be located closer to Iran and designed specifically against Iranian missiles. That change was welcome news for Russia, which had viewed the earlier Bush plan as directed at itself. In this climate of implicit bargaining, each side got other things it wanted, too. Russia went along with resolutions by the UN Security Council for economic sanctions against North Korea and Iran, measures aimed at halting their nuclear weapons programs. The Obama administration supported Russia's entry into the World Trade Organization.

During Obama's first month in office, Vice President Joe Biden came up with a sentence to describe what the new administration was trying to do. "It is time to press the reset button and to revisit the many areas where we can and should be working together with Russia," Biden had said. The word "reset" was repeated again and again until it became the Obama team's early, all-purpose, one-word description of its Russia policy. Obama tried to collaborate with Russia on a wide range of issues and lessen the rancor that had prevailed throughout most of the Bush administration. At the beginning of Obama's term, Tom Donilon had said the administration's relationship with Russia "shouldn't feel like 1974," when the two adversaries had met primarily to talk about Cold War issues like arms control. In that respect, the Obama administration succeeded.

But the "reset" went only so far. Russia did not ease its continuing efforts to eviscerate any serious, organized political opposition to Putin and his regime, whether in national politics, the provinces or the news media. Obama administration officials acknowledged ruefully that their attempts to promote greater democracy in Russia did not bring forth any qualitative change.

There were a series of debates within the Obama administration about how far to go in pressing Russia to be more tolerant of dissent—arguments that took place in the Situation Room of the White House and even overseas. The divisions among Obama's aides were relatively predictable: Michael McFaul pressed for strong action to try to open up Russia's political system; Ben Rhodes often sympathized with McFaul's views. On the other side were realists like Donilon, who often prevailed in the internal debates over Russia policy, in no small part because Obama himself often supported the realists.

However, McFaul and his allies won an occasional round. On Obama's trip to Moscow in the summer of 2009, the president agreed to hold two meetings with opposition leaders and with representatives of Russian civil society. He also did a series of interviews with opposition newspapers. (These were precisely the kinds of events Obama later tried to hold in China, prompting the Chinese regime to impose severe restrictions on his trip there.)

Obama refused to acknowledge the choices or trade-offs. He wanted to do business with Russia, on the basis of national interests, and also to promote democratic change on occasion, when he could. He did just enough to convince both sides of the internal debate to believe that he was really on their side.

———

Near the end of Obama's first year, he held his first state dinner. The event not only received extensive media coverage that night and the morning after, but stayed in the headlines for weeks for a reason that had nothing to do with foreign policy. Two Washington socialites, Tareq and Michaele Salahi, crashed the party, causing recriminations over how they'd gotten past security into the White House and were able to mingle, uninvited, in a room with Obama and the most senior officials of his administration.[30]

The brouhaha over the Salahis overshadowed the underlying strategic significance of the event. This was Obama's first state dinner, and he chose to hold it for Indian prime minister Manmohan Singh. It was intended to symbolize the importance India held in the eyes of the Obama administration.

Of the BRICs, India was the one with which the United States had the greatest confluence of interests, particularly on security issues. The two nations were natural if unofficial partners. Both could work together in efforts to combat terrorist groups in Afghanistan and Pakistan. Both could keep a wary eye on China's growing military power. Both Americans and Indians regularly insisted that their deepening relationship was not directed at any other country (i.e., China)—in much the same fashion that, in the 1970s, the Nixon administration and China regularly insisted that their new relationship was not aimed at any other country (i.e., the Soviet Union). These demurrals were rarely believed. Henry Kissinger once told Richard Nixon that China and the United States had become "tacit allies."[31] In the Obama administration, that same description applied to America's ties to India. The two countries shared intelligence and coordinated strategy with one another.

It didn't hurt that India was also a democracy, in obvious contrast to China. When it came to India, the realists within the Obama administration and the proponents of democracy joined together. The realists saw India as a counterweight to China's growing power, and the idealists saw India as a counterexample to China's one-party state. The state dinner at the White House was merely a fleeting display of a relationship that flourished, out of the public eye, in secret meetings of intelligence and national security aides. As its problems with Pakistan or China cropped up, the Obama team repeatedly looked to India for advice, insights and help.

To Obama and his inner circle, the rise of these new world powers was not merely the subject of speculation about the future. It was already a fact of life, one they confronted from their very first days in office. In that sense, Obama's first years differed from those of Clinton, back when the United States had seemed to be the world's unchallengeable superpower.

"People keep talking about how the United States needs to prepare for the 'rise' of India and China," mused Ben Rhodes one afternoon. "When we came into office, they had already risen, you know? When we went into the [climate change] conference in Copenhagen, China already had dozens of votes in its pocket, and Obama found himself dealing with the Chinese, the Indians, the Brazilians and South Africans. . . . You can't deal with climate change unless China's there. You can't deal with a global economy unless China and Brazil and India are at the table. You can't deal with international peacekeeping operations unless India is going to provide the troops for it."[32]

The days when Churchill and Roosevelt could sit down over a bottle of brandy and settle the world's problems were long gone. Obama often found himself dealing with a host of emerging powers, configured in a variety of ways on a variety of issues. The rooms were more crowded, the conversations less intimate. The Cold War doctrine of mutually assured destruction may have been more potentially disastrous than this new world order. But it was a lot simpler.

14

"Iran, Iran, Iran and Iran"

One of the most important members of Obama's foreign policy team during its early years was a trim, dapper lawyer named Stuart Levey. While his official bureaucratic function was as an obscure undersecretary of the Treasury, Levey was the point man for the Obama administration's efforts to stop the nuclear weapons programs of North Korea and Iran.

His background made him the odd man out on the Obama team. Levey did not come from any of the various Democratic networks that had melded into the Obama team; he was neither a Trout Fisher from the Clinton years, like Tom Donilon, nor a true Obamian like Denis McDonough. Rather, Levey was a holdover from the Bush administration, a Republican—and not just any Republican, but one of the young lawyers who had gone to Florida after the 2000 election to work for George W. Bush against Al Gore in the disputed recount. Nor did Levey come from the Scowcroft network of Republican realists, like Bob Gates. His intellectual and social ties put him closer to the neoconservatives. As an undergraduate at Harvard, he had studied under Martin Peretz, the staunchly pro-Israeli onetime owner of the *New Republic*; after graduating from Harvard Law School, he had clerked for U.S. Circuit Court judge Laurence Silberman, a prominent conservative jurist.[1]

Whatever his political connections, Levey was also smart and creative in a nonpartisan way, as the Obama inner circle quickly came to realize. During Bush's second term, Levey had come up with approaches for dealing with North Korea and Iran by squeezing their ability to do business overseas. Tim Geithner, Tom Donilon and Rahm Emanuel asked him to stay on for another six months under Obama. After that, he kept offering to step down and they kept persuading him not to. Levey served with Obama for more than two years, nearly as long as Gates, another holdover from the previous administration. He was certainly the only member of the winning side in *Bush v. Gore* to work in the Obama administration.

While Obama and other senior advisers promoted the idea of new talks and other forms of engagement with Iran and North Korea, Levey worked alongside them to pursue the other, tougher side of the Obama policy: economic sanctions.

———

The Democrats have wavered back and forth over half a century over economic and trade sanctions, depending on the issue, the country involved and the strength of the business community inside the Democratic Party. Sometimes the Democrats have embraced the idea that sanctions are an effective way to add muscle to American foreign policy or to convey disapproval of unsavory regimes. On other occasions, Democrats have elevated to high principle the argument that sanctions are counterproductive or somehow improper, or even the old shibboleth that "sanctions never work."[2]

President Kennedy imposed broad, general trade embargo on Cuba in 1962. After the seizure of American hostages in Iran, Jimmy Carter froze Iranian assets in the United States. In the 1980s, Democrats in Congress strongly supported sanctions against South Africa's apartheid regime, rejecting claims by President Reagan that the United States should instead pursue a policy of "constructive engagement" with South Africa's white leadership. The Democratic Congress also pushed unsuccessfully for George H. W. Bush to cut off China's trade benefits in the United States if it failed to meet a series of human rights conditions.

During the Clinton administration, however, the Democrats shifted ground. In general Clinton was able to muster unusually strong support from the business community, and his opposition to sanctions was one of the main reasons for his success. The decisive issue was China, which American companies had come to see in the 1990s as the world's last big undeveloped market. In 1994, Clinton rejected the efforts of Democrats in Congress (including George Mitchell, Richard Gephardt and Nancy Pelosi) to impose conditions on the approval of China's trade benefits. Instead, Clinton opted for what he (and, before him, George H. W. Bush) called a policy of "engagement"—thus applying to China policy the word Reagan had earlier used for dealing with South Africa's apartheid regime. By the mid-1990s business groups were lobbying for a more generalized policy of lifting or easing American sanctions throughout the world, from Iran to Burma to Cuba. They, too, used "engagement" as a code word that meant "no sanctions": The United States should seek to promote change through contacts, dialogue or interaction rather than sanctions, the business groups argued. An organization of American corporations and trade associations formed in the 1990s to lobby for the lifting of economic sanctions took the name USA Engage.[3]

Bill Clinton's views underscored a curious phenomenon: In recent decades, Democrats ironically have sometimes been more probusiness than Republicans when it comes to trade sanctions and export controls. One reason is that the Republicans have so strongly favored the business community on the fundamental questions of domestic economic policy, such as taxes and regulation, that they are relatively safe from attack on foreign policy concerns. "The Democrats don't help the business community as much in domestic politics as the Republicans, so the Democrats are more sympathetic to the business community overseas," observed Gary Milhollin of the Wisconsin Project on Nuclear Arms Control, a nonpartisan group that seeks to limit the spread of nuclear weapons and long-range missiles.[4]

Milhollin has for years lobbied for strict export controls and tight sanctions against countries that are trying to develop missiles or weapons of mass destruction. He has been frequently disappointed by both political parties, but, since the 1980s, particularly by the Democrats. He is among the few in Washington who think of Jimmy Carter as having been an unusually strong president. Carter, a former nuclear technician in the navy, took strong measures—including the use of sanctions—to prevent Pakistan and India from developing nuclear weapons. In the 1970s, other Democratic leaders such as Senator John Glenn were also in the vanguard on the issue of nuclear proliferation. Milhollin mourned what he saw as a decline in liberal and Democratic support for vigorous action to stop the spread of nuclear weaponry and missiles. "Whatever happened to the old 'ban the bomb' crowd?" he wondered.

As a candidate, Barack Obama had made "engagement" the central theme of his foreign policy, the issue that distinguished him from Hillary Clinton and John McCain. During his campaign, he pointed to Iran, specifically, as a prime candidate for engagement. Once in office, Obama wasted little time: In his first months on the job, he sent out his series of signals of his eagerness for a new relationship with Iran. Obama also pursued various forms of "engagement" with many other countries: North Korea, Burma, China, Russia, Venezuela and Sudan.

Yet for Obama, "engagement" seemed to have a different meaning than it had had when Reagan was dealing with South Africa or Bill Clinton with China. In those earlier instances, "engagement" was a substitute for economic sanctions. For Obama, these were not mutually exclusive; as usual, Obama rejected the idea that it was necessary to choose between opposites. He was in favor of talks, diplomacy and other interaction; at the same time, he also favored putting pressure on a regime through economic sanctions. That was where Stuart Levey came in.

In Bush's second term, Levey had come up with a new method of applying economic pressure on a regime. In the past, U.S. officials had sought to do this through a general trade embargo, such as the one against Cuba. The problem with that approach was that it was hard, sometimes impossible, to get other governments to join in a broad, general embargo. American officials had also tried to impose more narrow, carefully targeted sanctions against individual companies, in hopes of deterring them and others. That didn't work so well, either. The business communities, at home and abroad, didn't like measures that could impinge on trade.

In 2004, the Bush administration set up a unit in the Treasury Department called the Office of Terrorism and Financial Intelligence and brought in Levey, then working at the Justice Department, to run it. The importance of the new office was that, for the first time, the Treasury Department was given full status in the intelligence community. It had firsthand access to the wealth of information gathered by the CIA, the National Security Agency and other agencies concerning financial transactions, such as wire transfers. Treasury could even "task" (assign) the intelligence community to target the money flows to and from a particular company or individual.

Levey's innovation was to take this new information and concentrate in particular on international banks that might be involved, knowingly or not, in money flows used to finance terrorist groups, such as in purchasing weapons of mass destruction or in other illegal activities. The Bush administration imposed sanctions on Banco Delta Asia, a bank in Macao that the North Korean government used for laundering counterfeit money. The sanctions required other companies and banks to stop doing business with Banco Delta Asia, thus cutting off its access to the international financial system. There was a run on the bank, and other banks in Macao and elsewhere began to cut off business with the government and companies of North Korea.

The approach worked so well that Levey soon turned his attention elsewhere, notably to Iran. He began traveling around the world, meeting bankers for private, informal discussions. He would approach a particular bank and explain how the money that flowed through it was being used for illicit or improper activities—North Korean counterfeiting, for example, or Iran's nuclear and missile programs.[5] When bankers claimed, as they often did, that they had no knowledge of these activities, Levey would show them the detailed evidence: Here's how money from illegal counterfeiting flowed into a North Korean company or bank, and from there into your bank. Here's how money flowed from your bank to an Iranian bank and from there to a specific weapons program or to the financing of a terrorist organization. In doing this, Levey made ample use of information collected by U.S. intelligence agencies about financial transactions around the world.

Levey wasn't actually imposing new sanctions. In many cases, the sanctions were already on the books, either in individual countries or in United Nations resolutions. Levey was merely informing a bank about ways in which it was involved in financing shady or illegal conduct. The implicit threat was that if a bank continued to do business in the same way, its reputation was at risk. It might be publicly exposed. In the worst case, the bank might be subjected to further sanctions and lose its ability to operate in the United States or elsewhere around the world.

When this quiet approach was successful, an international bank would quietly shut down its business with the Iranian or North Korean firms. Levey also found a snowball effect: Once a few banks refused to deal with North Korean or Iranian institutions, other banks would also become increasingly reluctant to do so, for fear of being seen as having looser international standards than their competitors. Levey managed to get banks in Europe, Australia, Canada, Japan and South Korea to cut off their ties with Iranian banks and other entities. The sanctions, and the implied threats to enforce them specifically on international banks, made it much more difficult for Iran to gain access to the technology and foreign investment it needed. After a few years, Levey concluded that, despite the conventional wisdom that "sanctions never work," in fact they seemed to be working fairly well.

From the outset, as Obama pressed forward his policy of engagement, his administration was also quietly exploring the possibilities for tightening sanctions. Cables released by Wikileaks show that on March 2, 2009, barely six weeks after the inauguration, a Treasury Department official named Charles Glaser, working for Levey, gave an overview of the Obama policy to a gathering of European officials in London. He started off with the new policy of engagement with Iran. According to the cable, he then added: "However, 'engagement' alone is not likely to succeed."[6] Along with the efforts at conciliation, there would need to be some "sticks," some punitive measures, to demonstrate to Iran the consequences if it failed to stop developing nuclear weapons.

Thus, from the start an underlying purpose of Obama's engagement policy was to help the United States win greater international support for tougher action, such as economic sanctions, than the Bush administration had been able to obtain. Indeed, Obama's initial attempts at engagement with North Korea and Iran were generally a flop: Neither was willing to rein in its nuclear weapons program. But these failed efforts helped to buttress the case for international sanctions by demonstrating that engagement by itself had failed, or that it wouldn't accomplish much. The Obama team was able to win greater European and other international support for sanctions than had ever been obtained by the Bush administration.

North Korea was one of the clearest examples where the new Obama administration adopted fairly quickly a tougher policy than the Bush administration. In George W. Bush's final two years, he and Secretary of State Condoleezza Rice had given leeway for an assistant secretary of state, Christopher Hill, to carry out extensive talks with North Korea. Hill reached a much debated interim agreement in which the North Koreans agreed to shut down a nuclear reactor in exchange for concessions from the United States.

When the Obama administration began holding its first meetings on North Korea, it was examining the possibilities for further diplomacy and further engagement. The initial discussions were about "how to enter into negotiations, and what had worked and not worked in previous administrations," according to James Steinberg, deputy secretary of state.[7]

But whatever early hopes the Obama administration had for engagement didn't last long. On April 5, 2009, North Korea fired a long-range missile, attempting to put a satellite into orbit. The test failed when the third stage of the rocket went not up into space but down into the Pacific Ocean. Nevertheless, the test served to show the world that Kim Jong-il's regime was moving toward the capability to put a nuclear weapon onto an intercontinental ballistic missile. Less than six weeks later, North Korea conducted a small underground nuclear test. A few days later, it fired three more short-range missiles.

These actions prompted the Obama team to reevaluate both the U.S. policy toward North Korea's weapons programs and the underlying assumptions about it. In the past, U.S. officials had often believed that the North Korean leaders, Kim Il-sung and Kim Jong-il, were using the nuclear weapons program as a bargaining chip, one that would eventually be negotiated away in exchange for the right package of benefits, both diplomatic and financial. Now the Obama administration realized it was time to recognize the underlying reality that North Korea had no intention of giving up or bargaining away the nuclear program, because it was essential to the survival of the regime. North Korea was determined to have an operational nuclear capability, the Obama team decided. The Pyongyang regime might make some concessions in negotiations, but only ones that were minor or reversible, so that it could restart or rebuild its nuclear facilities and try to bargain them away again in the future.

Instead, the administration decided in the spring of 2009 on a new approach, one that amounted to an unstated policy of containment, by the account of another senior Obama official. The policy had several elements. First, the United States would try to restrict North Korea's capabilities and its access to technology through economic sanctions and by blocking access to technology. Second, the administration would play for time, waiting until there was a significant change in North Korea's leadership.[8] The Obama team called this part of the policy "strategic patience."

Thirdly, Obama and his advisers decided they would refuse to recognize North Korea as a nuclear weapons state. In public, the objective of American policy would still be to abolish the North Korean nuclear program, even if the Obama team privately recognized that for the time being, under the current regime, the goal was impossible. Maintaining the fiction of a non-nuclear North Korea was of overriding importance to American interests, because if the United States acknowledged the reality that North Korea was already a nuclear weapons state, then Japan and South Korea would feel compelled to respond by trying to develop nuclear weapons of their own.

And if Japan and South Korea went nuclear, then they would no longer be dependent on the United States for their security against nuclear attack. In thinking in this fashion, the Obama administration was not setting down new policy but continuing the approach of past administrations, both Republican and Democratic. The Obama team's commitment to multilateralism and to a more limited role for American military power went only so far; the Obama administration did not welcome the development of nuclear weapons by allies like Japan and South Korea.

The North Koreans began to ask American officials why the United States did not treat their government like India (or Pakistan or Israel), which had developed nuclear weapons without joining the Nuclear Nonproliferation Treaty. In those other cases, the United States had accepted the nuclear weapons capability as a fact. The American answer to the North Koreans was something like Lloyd Bentsen's old quip to Dan Quayle: We know India, and you're no India.

In practical terms, administration officials decided, the new policy meant that Obama would not agree to a peace treaty or to establish diplomatic relations with North Korea, two of Pyongyang's most important priorities in negotiations. These could come only in exchange for North Korea's giving up the nuclear program for good, rather than merely freezing or suspending it. Instead, the Obama administration moved ahead with tighter sanctions, both at the United Nations and on its own. In mid-June, after North Korea's nuclear test, the United States won support for passage of a UN Security Council resolution that imposed new sanctions on the sale of weaponry and luxury goods to North Korea.

Soon afterward, Stuart Levey announced new unilateral sanctions by the United States aimed at cutting off North Korean companies from the global financial system. Levey said North Korea "uses front companies . . . and a range of other deceptive practices to obscure the true nature of its financial dealings, making it nearly impossible for responsible banks and governments to distinguish legitimate from illegitimate North Koran transactions."[9] Levey's implicit message was that "responsible banks" should simply stop doing any kind of business with North Korea.

———

North Korea's leader, Kim Jong-il, suffered a stroke in 2008. Throughout Obama's first years in office, the regime in Pyongyang was swept up in the process of a hurried political succession. In 2010, North Korea's Supreme People's Assembly designated Kim's son Kim Jong-un as the country's next leader, promoting him to the rank of four-star general and vice chairman of the Central Military Commission. Kim Jong-un was not the sort of person who seemed capable of inspiring confidence from North Korea's senior military or civilian leaders. He was thought to be about twenty-seven years old in 2010, and with his callow face and chubby cheeks, he looked younger.

For nine months following the nuclear and missile tests of 2009, North Korea was so preoccupied with the problems of the Kim dynasty that it could do little in dealing with the rest of the world. Then, on March 26, 2010, North Korea entered a new phase of truculence: A North Korean submarine fired a torpedo that sank a South Korean naval ship, the *Cheonan*, killing forty-six South Korean sailors. The North Korean military followed up later in the year by firing a barrage of artillery shells onto a South Korean island. Some analysts interpreted these actions as an effort by Kim Jong-il to pave the way for his son by showing that he was a strong leader and should be given leeway to choose his successor.[10] They were also, more generally, an example of North Korea's distinctive style of provocation and then negotiation—a way of reminding Americans, Japanese and South Koreans of the continuing military threat from North Korea and thus of the need for further talks to restrain it.

Obama himself was infuriated by the sinking of the *Cheonan*—and, particularly, by China's refusal to condemn what North Korea had done. This led to a frosty exchange between the American and Chinese presidents. At an international conference in Toronto, Obama said in public that North Korea had gone "over the line" and suggested that China might be displaying "willful blindness" in refusing to recognize that fact.[11]

In his private meeting with the Chinese president, Obama was much more pointed than he had been in public. China was the principal supplier of energy and food to North Korea. When Hu Jintao spoke of the need to be evenhanded between North and South Korea and urged restraint on all sides, Obama came back hard. According to an American official with first-hand knowledge of the meeting, Obama's message to the Chinese president went roughly like this: "You've been talking about the need for common restraint on the Korean Peninsula. Well, we've been calm and restrained, South Korea's been calm and restrained—and the only one who hasn't been calm and restrained is North Korea. And the only reason they haven't been restrained is that you have their back, and they feel that you protect them. You talk about the need to avoid conflict, but what you're doing is precisely to encourage conflict, because you're showing North Korea that aggressive acts have no consequences."[12]

Obama's arguments failed to turn around the Chinese, who continued to avoid condemnation of North Korea and also continued to provide it with the supplies needed for its survival. Another of Obama's aides acknowledged that while the United States and China might sometimes cooperate in the short run on North Korea, over the long run they have fundamentally different strategic objectives: China wants North Korea to survive, while the United States wants it to be reunited with South Korea. China seeks to prevent the emergence of a new, unified Korean state that would be allied to the United States, knowing America's troops would be just across the border from Chinese Manchuria. It also serves Beijing's interest to pin down American troops in South Korea that might otherwise be used elsewhere, such as in a conflict over Taiwan.[13]

At the end of 2010, North Korea unveiled one more big surprise. A delegation of leading American scientists, including Siegfried Hecker, former director of the Los Alamos labs, was visiting North Korea's Yongbyon nuclear complex when North Korean scientists showed them something new: a sophisticated centrifuge plant, capable of enriching uranium to make nuclear fuel.

North Korea had long ago showed outsiders its plant and equipment for making plutonium, the other, alternative material that can be used to manufacture a nuclear weapon. The significance of the uranium enrichment facilities was that they are much harder to detect; even the United States, with all its intelligence capabilities, would have difficulty finding a small, well-hidden facility to enrich uranium. Once the Hecker team reported what they had been shown, one Obama aide said he no longer believed the United States could ever again be confident of knowing the size and extent of North Korea's nuclear program. Even if North Korea claimed it had halted its nuclear program, no one could know for sure whether it was telling the truth. There could always be some centrifuges buried or hidden somewhere in the country, spinning out more enriched uranium.[14]

As a result, Obama's initial talk of engagement with North Korea never went very far. The real policy, adopted only a few months into the new administration, was to recognize that the current leadership in Pyongyang would never give up or bargain away the nuclear weapons it already had. The United States would simply have to wait for a change in the country's leadership. Meanwhile, North Korea kept on working to improve the one thing it had to guarantee the regime's survival. In early 2011, Defense Secretary Robert Gates told reporters he believed North Korea would have the ability, within five years, to reach the United States with an intercontinental ballistic missile. North Korea "is becoming a direct threat to the United States," Gates said.[15]

———

With Iran, there was a much greater sense of urgency; Obama had little time for "strategic patience." It was not that Iran's nuclear program was ahead of North Korea's—it wasn't—but rather that Iran was in a far more dangerous location. If Iran developed a nuclear weapon, that would alter the strategic calculations throughout the Middle East. Iran would be able to launch a nuclear strike on Israel or Saudi Arabia—and then the Saudis, Egyptians and Turks would want to acquire nuclear weapons because Iran had them. Israel felt particularly threatened. By the time Obama took office, there had already been speculation that Israel might launch a preemptive strike to take out Iran's nuclear facilities, just as Israel had bombed Iraq's Osirak nuclear reactor in 1981.

The Obama appointees charged with stopping the spread of nuclear weapons included several alumni from the Clinton administration: Gary Samore and Daniel Poneman at the National Security Council and Robert Einhorn at the State Department. Back in the 1990s, they had looked upon the North Korean and Iranian nuclear programs in a different way. The United States had then been preoccupied with North Korea, far more than Iran. North Korea's program was advancing rapidly, and the Clinton administration had tried through negotiations to persuade North Korea to freeze the program and then give it up. In the end, these efforts at engagement had failed, both under Clinton and in a renewed attempt during George W. Bush's last years in the White House.

Back then, Iran hadn't even ranked second on the Clinton team's worry list. (That distinction went to Saddam Hussein's Iraq.) In the 1990s, Iran's nuclear program seemed to be at a relatively primitive stage, and Clinton aides such as Samore concentrated on trying to cut off Iran's sources of supply to nuclear technology. In that endeavor, they found at the time that they could get much greater cooperation from China than from Russia.[16]

By the time the Obama administration took office, things had changed. By 2009, North Korea had already acquired the ability to make nuclear weapons and had frustrated all attempts at negotiations to end the program. Iran, meanwhile, still did not have a nuclear weapon, but it had by then acquired so much more nuclear equipment and expertise that it no longer made sense to rely mostly on a strategy of cutting off Iran's access to foreign technology. It was too late for that.

The new Obama team felt that American military action against Iran was not even a viable option, much less a desirable one. In military terms, it would be a difficult operation, and not assured of success. In 2009, the Pentagon was preoccupied with two ongoing wars in Afghanistan and Iraq and was not eager for a third. Moreover, in political terms, the new president would have had an extremely hard time justifying to the public a war to prevent Iran from developing weapons of mass destruction, when he had so recently campaigned against a war in Iraq that had been waged with a similar rationale.

George McGovern accepting the Democratic nomination for president in 1972. In his speech, McGovern, who ran as a passionate opponent of the Vietnam War, issued his famous appeal to "come home, America." (AP Photo)

President Jimmy Carter and his national security adviser, Zbigniew Brzezinski (with Vice President Walter Mondale behind them), meeting at Camp David with Israeli Prime Minister Menachem Begin and Defense Minister Moshe Dayan. The negotiations led to the Camp David accords, a high point for Carter's foreign policy. (Photo by Hulton Archive/Getty Images)

Joe Biden in December 1972, soon after he was first elected to the Senate. He had just celebrated his thirtieth birthday. (AP Photo/Henry Griffin)

Barack Obama during his college days at Columbia University. He took a particular interest in the movement for a freeze on nuclear weapons. (AP Photo/Obama Presidential Campaign)

President Bill Clinton with White House Chief of Staff Leon Panetta and First Lady Hillary Clinton, on November 6, 1996, the day after Clinton won reelection. Fifteen years later, Panetta and Hillary Clinton were serving as secretaries of defense and state, respectively, to President Barack Obama. (AP Photo/Joe Marquette)

Envoy Richard Holbrooke with Yugoslav president Slobodan Milosevic in 1998. Holbrooke, representing the Clinton administration, warned that if Milosevic didn't stop the ongoing crackdown in Kosovo, he would face NATO airstrikes. (AP Photo)

Michèle Flournoy and Kurt Campbell at the founding of the Center for a New American Security in 2007. They and their defense-oriented think tank were at the center of efforts by the Democrats to demonstrate that they were knowledgeable on national security issues and were prepared to take over from the Bush administration. (Ralph Alswang)

Hillary Clinton and Barack Obama locked in debate on July 23, 2007, as both were running for the Democratic presidential nomination. It was at this debate, in Charleston, South Carolina, that Obama seemed to slip by promising to meet in his first year with the leaders of Iran, North Korea, and other authoritarian regimes. Obama and his aides quickly watered down the pledge and turned it to their own advantage. (Photo by Gerry Melendez/*The State*/MCT via Getty Images)

Obama, as the Democratic nominee, meeting with General David Petraeus in Baghdad on July 21, 2008. Antiwar forces had attacked Petraeus for recommending a surge in troops to Iraq. As president, Obama turned toward Petraeus's strategy of counterinsurgency in Afghanistan and appointed him commander of American forces there. Later on, he picked Petraeus as his CIA director. (AP Photo/Ssg. Lorie Jewell, HO)

An inmate prays at the detention center on the U.S. Naval Base at Guantánamo Bay, Cuba. On his second day in the White House, Obama signed an order to have the facility closed within a year. But he retreated in the face of congressional opposition, and Guantánamo remained open under Obama as it was in the Bush years. (AP Photo/Brennan Linsley, File)

Obama at the news conference on December 1, 2008, in which he announced his national security team. From left to right: Eric Holder, Obama's choice for attorney general; Janet Napolitano, secretary of homeland security; Robert Gates, secretary of defense; Vice President Joe Biden; Hillary Clinton, secretary of state; James Jones, national security adviser; and Susan Rice, U.S. ambassador to the United Nations. (AP Photo/Pablo Martinez Monsivais)

Obama with speechwriter Ben Rhodes (left) and Denis McDonough, his closest aide on foreign policy (right), on Air Force One on June 4, 2009. They were on their way to Cairo, where Obama was to deliver a major address to the Islamic world. (Photo by Pete Souza/The White House via Getty Images)

Richard Holbrooke, Obama's special representative for Pakistan and Afghanistan, with Afghan president Hamid Karzai on February 15, 2009. Later that year, Karzai refused to deal with Holbrooke, and the Obama administration began dealing with the Afghan leader through other intermediaries. (AP Photo/Musadeq Sadeq)

Obama shakes hands with Libyan ruler Moammar Gaddafi during an international conference in L'Aquila, Italy, on July 9, 2009. Soon after the fall of Saddam Hussein in Iraq, Gaddafi agreed to give up his nuclear weapons program and revived relations with the United States. The amicable relationship between the two countries lasted until the Arab Spring of 2011. (AP Photo/Michael Gottschalk/Pool)

Obama with Chinese president Hu Jintao at the United Nations in 2009. At the beginning of his presidency, Obama made a concerted effort to avoid conflict with China, hoping to get its help in dealing with Iran and North Korea and in easing the huge trade imbalance between the two countries. But Obama's efforts produced few results, and later on the administration scaled back its hopes and expectations for China. (Photo by John Angelillo-Pool/Getty Images)

Samantha Power, Obama, and Hillary Clinton sitting together at a memorial service for Richard Holbrooke at the Kennedy Center, January 14, 2011. Power had shared with Holbrooke a strong support for U.S. military intervention to stop the killing of civilians in Bosnia. She was an early supporter of Obama's presidential campaign and worked on the National Security Council in his administration. (AP Photo/Carolyn Kaster)

Obama with Deputy National Security Advisor Tom Donilon (left) and National Security Adviser James Jones (right) on October 8, 2010. On that day, Obama announced that Jones would step down and Donilon would replace him. (Photo by White House/Gamma-Rapho via Getty Images)

Deputy National Security Adviser John Brennan, Obama's counterintelligence chief, at a press conference May 2, 2011, about the killing of Osama bin Laden. Brennan, a veteran intelligence official, served as a senior aide to CIA director George Tenet in the Bush administration. After Obama won the 2008 election, he was a leading candidate to be the new CIA director, but was opposed by some liberal groups. Instead, he became a powerful force inside the Obama White House. (Astrid Riecken/MCT via Getty Images)

Four seemingly untroubled Arab leaders at a summit meeting in Sirte, Libya, on October 10, 2010, less than three months before the Arab Spring. From left to right: President Zine el Abidine Ben Ali of Tunisia, President Ali Abdullah Saleh of Yemen, Libyan leader Moammar Gaddafi, and President Hosni Mubarak of Egypt. During 2011, all four leaders fell from power. Gaddafi was killed on October 20, 2011, after being found in a drainage pipe in the same city where this photo was taken. (Khaled Desouki/AFP/Getty Images)

Susan Rice, the U.S. ambassador to the United Nations, casts a vote at the Security Council on March 17, 2011, to approve not only a no-fly zone over Libya but also "all necessary measures" to protect civilians on the ground. Rice was one of Obama's earliest supporters. In his administration, she was a strong voice in favor of humanitarian intervention. (AP Photo/Jason DeCrow)

Obama with his closest advisers in the Oval Office on May 19, 2011. From left to right: National Security Adviser Tom Donilon, Deputy National Security Adviser Denis McDonough, Obama, and (seated at computer) Deputy National Security Adviser and speechwriter Ben Rhodes. (© Pete Souza/White House/Handout/The White House/Corbis)

Obama and his team watching the progress of the raid on the compound in Abbottabad, Pakistan, in which Osama bin Laden was killed. Vice President Joe Biden and Obama watch at the left. Standing, behind the table, are National Security Adviser Tom Donilon; White House Chief of Staff Bill Daley; Biden's top national security aide, Tony Blinken; counterterrorism chief John Brennan; Director of National Intelligence James Clapper; and (seated at table) Mike Mullen, Chairman of the Joint Chiefs of Staff; Deputy National Security Adviser Denis McDonough; Secretary of State Hillary Clinton; and Defense Secretary Robert Gates. (Official White House Photo by Pete Souza)

Still, the Obama team didn't mind keeping Iranian leaders on edge about the possibility of some kind of military action, by Israel if not the United States. In mid-2009, Vice President Joe Biden attracted attention with a vague comment on a Sunday talk show:

Look, Israel can determine for itself—it's a sovereign nation—what's in their interest and what they decide to do relative to Iran and anyone else. . . . If the Netanyahu government decides to take a course of action different than the one being pursued now, that is their sovereign right to do that. That is not our choice.[7]

These remarks were not merely idiosyncratic personal musings by Biden alone. In a private conversation only a few days earlier, another senior Obama aide used strikingly similar language, noting that the United States could not stop Israel from bombing Iran's nuclear facilities, if Israel was really determined to do so.

During his first year in the White House, Obama made a series of overtures to Iran's leadership. He said he would reevaluate how things were going at the end of 2009. Meanwhile, he laid the groundwork for other policies and strategies. Levey's Treasury unit studied how various kinds of sanctions would affect Iran. The White House and the State Department made stopping Iran's nuclear program a high priority in their diplomacy with European governments and with Russia and China.

At one point that fall, President Obama, French president Nicolas Sarkozy and British prime minister Gordon Brown stood side by side at a press conference in Pittsburgh to say that their intelligence services had uncovered proof in Iran of a secret uranium facility Iran had hidden from the International Atomic Energy Agency. The joint event served notice to Iran that the transatlantic frictions over the Iraq War had eased and that American and European leaders were working together.

Obama's drive for engagement with Iran culminated in Geneva on October 1, 2009, when representatives from Iran, the United States, Britain, France, Germany, Russia and China gathered together for talks on Iran's nuclear program. Undersecretary of State William Burns also spoke separately with Iranian negotiator Saeed Jalili in the highest-level bilateral meeting between the two countries since the Iranian Revolution of 1979. The talks ended with an agreement under which Iran would turn over most of its stockpile of enriched uranium to Russia. It would then be converted into reactor fuel, sent onward to France for further processing and finally shipped back to Iran for use in a small nuclear reactor used for medical purposes. Obama called the agreement a "constructive beginning."[18]

Within weeks the deal collapsed. Iran announced it didn't want to ship its enriched uranium out of the country all at once, as the agreement had required. Iran was also unwilling to come to a second round of talks. Negotiating with the Americans would be "naive and perverted," said Iran's supreme leader Ayatollah Ali Khamenei in a speech. "Whenever they smile at the officials of the Islamic revolution, when we carefully look at the situation, we notice that they are hiding a dagger behind their back."[19]

Khamanei's rebuff marked the end of phase one in Obama's Iran policy. The president was now in a position to say to other leaders that he had tried engagement, but that Iran had made no serious effort to respond. This had in fact been one of the unstated purposes of engagement: Even if it didn't work, it would help to get greater support from other countries for taking stronger action against Iran.

As one senior administration official phrased it, the situation was now "teed up" for stage two, a tougher policy. Over the following months, the Obama administration tacked sharply. Having previously held the Green Movement at arm's length, administration officials began to give it more support, hoping to put more pressure on the regime. Secretary of State Hillary Clinton began to warn that Iran was becoming a "military dictatorship."[20] The mood within America's foreign policy community changed, too. Even one of America's leading proponents of engagement, Richard Haass, the president of the Council on Foreign Relations, said he favored a new policy of regime change. The United States, he said, should stop seeking to engage Iran's leaders and instead focus on supporting the Iranian opposition. "I've changed my mind," wrote Haass. "The nuclear talks are going nowhere."[21]

Obama began to move toward sanctions. The administration concentrated on the UN Security Council, hoping to win as much support as possible for internationally imposed sanctions, rather than unilateral American action. The British, French and Germans joined together with the United States in favor of UN sanctions. The Obama administration spent late 2009 and the first half of 2010 in a concerted, intensified drive to obtain the assent of the Russians and Chinese. Asked in the spring of 2010 to name the most important issues confronting the administration at that time, Deputy Secretary of State James Steinberg replied: "Iran, Iran, Iran and Iran."[22]

The administration's strategy was to get the support of Russia first and then China, because if Russia signed on, China would be reluctant to stand alone in casting a veto. The Russians balked, then bargained and finally came around to supporting sanctions. China was much harder. Early on, Obama dispatched Dennis Ross, his Iran and Middle East specialist, to Beijing to make the case that preventing Iran from developing nuclear weapons was in China's own interest. "You're already 50 percent dependent on imports from the Persian Gulf, going up to 70 percent," Ross told Chinese officials. "Do you really believe that a Persian Gulf with three or four nuclear powers is going to be a more secure place as a source of energy for you?"[23] Ross's appeal went unheeded. China forced a series of delays as it watered down the UN sanctions by severely limiting their applicability.

Finally, after months of diplomatic maneuvering, the UN Security Council approved a package of sanctions against Iran. The resolution barred all countries from selling Iran military supplies such as tanks, combat aircraft, helicopters or missile systems. It also prohibited any transfer of technology for Iran's nuclear or missile programs and any financial transactions with Iran's Revolutionary Guard. (One Obama aide observed that the Revolutionary Guard was "the perfect target," because it had an extensive role in the Iranian economy, was directly involved in the nuclear program and, most important, was despised by the Iranian people.)

Soon after the action by the UN Security Council, the Americans and Europeans began to impose additional sanctions of their own that went further than the United Nations'. In Washington, Levey's unit in the Treasury Department kept on pressing private banks overseas to avoid doing business that could help finance Iran's nuclear program. Obama signed a law that penalized companies doing business with Iran's oil industry. Governments in Europe, Canada and Australia imposed sanctions of their own. Within a few months, the combined effect of the UN sanctions and those of individual countries began to have some impact. Iran Air, the country's national airlines, found itself unable to refuel its planes in most locations in Europe.[24] More important, Iran seemed to be having trouble obtaining the specialty materials it needed to produce centrifuges for its nuclear weapons program.

By 2011, two years after Obama's inauguration, he had virtually stopped talking about the need for engagement with Iran. He never went so far as to depict Iran as part of an "axis of evil," as George W. Bush had. But words like "tough" began to make their way into Obama's descriptions of his Iran policy. That year, in an applause line in his State of the Union Address, Obama boasted that "because of a diplomatic effort to insist that Iran meet its obligations, the Iranian government now faces tougher sanctions, tighter sanctions than ever before."[25] Obama was able to obtain stronger sanctions on Iran than his predecessor, because he had been able to obtain greater support from other countries. He had demonstrated that he had first tried to engage with Iran, but it hadn't worked.

In 2011, as the Arab Spring began to spread across the Middle East, Obama's changed Iran policy was on display: He sought to isolate Iran, in order to keep it from trying to influence events in other countries, such as Bahrain. (One aphorism during the Cold War was that the strategy of NATO in Europe was to keep "the Americans in, the Russians out and the Germans down." In 2011, an updated version began making the rounds in Washington: that the right outcome in the Middle East was to keep "the Americans in, the Chinese out and the Iranians down.")

During the Arab Spring, one of Obama's aides admitted privately that the administration hadn't placed as much value on the importance of democratic change in Iran in 2009 as it did in Tunisia and Egypt two years later. In 2011, Obama praised the Iran's Green Movement without hesitation, no longer bothering about the sensitivities of Ayatollah Khamenei or President Ahmadinejad. "Let's remember that the first peaceful protests in the region were in the streets of Tehran, where the government brutalized women and men and threw innocent people in jail," Obama said in a speech about the Middle East. "We still hear the chants echo from the rooftops of Tehran."[26] He hadn't heard those protesters so well two years earlier, and the lingering chants continued to haunt his belated interest in democracy.

On April 8, 2010, during the most intensive phase of his diplomatic campaign to win support for UN sanctions against Iran, Obama met Russian president Dmitry Medvedev in Prague to sign a treaty called New START. The agreement set a new limit of 1,550 strategic warheads for each country, a reduction from the previous ceiling of 2,200.

On the surface, the New START treaty was merely another arms control agreement between Washington and Moscow, a follow-up to the ones negotiated during the Cold War. But there was a difference. Earlier agreements were aimed at reducing the chances of nuclear war between the United States and the Soviet Union. This time, two decades after the end of the Cold War, the New START treaty was prompted less by fear of war between the United States and Russia and much more as part of a broader effort to stop the development of nuclear weapons in other countries.

The treaty was closely connected, in two ways, to Obama's drive for sanctions against Iran. First, the treaty helped in winning support from Russia itself. The New START agreement was one key element in the broader "reset" in relations with Russia, aimed at smoothing over the tensions of the Bush years. "The whole 'reset' with Russia was very calculated, because we knew we had to have Russian support against Iran," explained one of Obama's aides.[27]

Secondly, the treaty was meant to send a message to other countries. The aim was to overcome recurrent charges of American hypocrisy. Whenever the United States tried to convince North Korea or Iran to abandon their nuclear programs and to persuade other countries not to sell them nuclear-related technology, critics charged that the United States didn't practice what it preached: It was preserving a large American stockpile of nuclear weapons while asking others to give up their own, smaller nuclear facilities. The New START was designed, among other reasons, to demonstrate that the United States and Russia were themselves cutting back. "Clinging to nuclear weapons in excess of our security needs does not make the United States safer," Hillary Clinton said in one speech. "And the nuclear status quo is neither desirable nor sustainable. It gives other countries the motivation—or the excuse—to pursue their own nuclear options."[28]

The New START treaty was ratified nine months later, but only after it ran into surprisingly strong opposition from Senate Republicans and from aspiring Republican presidential candidates. Most arms control experts and even some former Bush administration officials described the treaty as modest in scope. It required gradual changes, not transformational ones.[29] Prominent Republican leaders from previous administrations, including Henry Kissinger, Brent Scowcroft, George Shultz, James Baker, Condoleezza Rice and Stephen Hadley, all endorsed the treaty. So did a prominent neoconservative, Robert Kagan, who wrote that blocking the treaty would "set up Republicans as the fall guy if and when U.S.-Russian relations go south."[30]

But most Senate Republicans and potential candidates for the Republican presidential nomination in 2012—including Mitt Romney, Sarah Palin, Newt Gingrich and Tim Pawlenty—denounced the treaty. Romney claimed to have found defects that had somehow managed to elude the collection of secretaries of state and national security advisers from past Republican administrations. New START, Romney contended in an op-ed, "could be his [Obama's] worst foreign policy mistake yet" and "gives Russia a massive nuclear advantage over the United States." On her website, Palin wrote, "Just because we were out-negotiated by the Russians doesn't mean we have to say yes to this." Gingrich called New START "an obsolete approach to national security" and urged a Republican filibuster. "It is clear that President Obama wants America to be popular and well liked around the world, especially by President Medvedev, but I think it's more important to be respected," said Tim Pawlenty.[31]

This opposition to the treaty was baffling to Republican elders like Scowcroft. "I've got to think that it's the increasingly partisan nature and the desire for the president not to have a foreign policy victory," he said. The partisanship was on display when the Senate finally voted, on its final day in session, to approve the treaty. The vote was seventy-one to twenty-six. All of the Senate's Democrats voted in favor, along with thirteen Republicans, while all twenty-six negative votes came from Republicans.

There was also another reason, beyond partisanship, for the Republican opposition. The treaty with Russia was indeed modest (Robert Kagan had called it a "nothingburger"). But Republican opponents in the Senate were trying to put down a firewall to defend against any subsequent effort by Obama to win approval of something much more important: a ban on nuclear testing. Obama had pledged to try to win ratification of the Comprehensive

Nuclear Test Ban Treaty, which Senate Republicans had voted down during the Clinton administration. The Republicans were, in essence, warning that if Obama had had to fight so hard and for so long to get the minor new START with Russia, he would have to spend even more time and energy to get a ban on nuclear testing.

————

Obama had demonstrated an interest in antinuclear causes since his college years at Columbia. In his first big speech after becoming president, delivered in Prague in the spring of 2009, he had voiced the hope for a world without nuclear weapons. His efforts to end the Iranian and North Korean nuclear programs and to ratify the New START treaty were two aspects of this larger goal. As was so often the case, Obama's approach was gradual, offering little in the way of immediate, dramatic change. (It's worth noting that he also said in his Prague speech, "This goal will not be reached quickly, perhaps not in my lifetime." He was, at the time, only forty-eight years old.)[32]

These nuclear issues raised in their clearest form even more fundamental questions: How should the international order be governed or enforced? In seeking to prevent Iran from acquiring a bomb, for example, what countries or international institutions should the Obama administration rely upon? Virtually all Democrats—from whatever faction, administration or wing of the party—expressed a general preference for multilateral approaches.

Should the United States try to deal with the world in concert with its closest allies? That was what happened when Obama, Sarkozy and Brown stood side by side in Pittsburgh in 2009 to denounce Iran's nuclear program. Or should the international order be enforced through the United Nations? Obama had tried that route with sanctions against Iran; for a time in the spring of 2010, the administration's entire diplomacy was dominated by the need to win support at the United Nations for action against Iran. Obama's aides clearly saw those sanctions as a model for similar actions in the future. "This is a test not just of the Obama administration but of the whole approach, whether you can use the international community to solve problems like this," said Steinberg.[33] The sanctions were significantly weakened before they were enacted, although they did turn out to have some impact. So, too, a year later, the major powers—the British, French and eventually the

Americans—went to the UN Security Council to obtain authorization for military action in Libya.

Alternatively, should the Obama administration try to create something new—either by setting up different, stronger international institutions or by reforming existing ones, like the United Nations and the International Monetary Fund? Strobe Talbott, who served as deputy secretary of state in the Clinton administration, argued that one of the most important issues confronting Obama was "global governance." Talbott pointed out that, as president, Bill Clinton had been interested in this issue, but refrained from talking about it either in public or private, because "Clinton's political instincts told him it would be inviting trouble to suggest that the sun might someday set on American preeminence."[34]

Obama didn't use phrases like "global governance," either. If it would have been hard for Bill Clinton in an age of American prosperity and confidence, it would have been all but impossible for Obama, serving at a time when America was far more insecure about its role in the world. Any suggestion that the United States was working in concert with other countries was certain to arouse the anger of populist conservatives. In 2010, during a period when Glenn Beck's ultra-right-wing views dominated Fox News, he accused Obama of having a "World Cup" foreign policy. He added, by way of explanation, "We don't like the World Cup!"[35]

One member of Obama's inner circle said the administration hoped eventually to tackle "global governance issues, related to the Security Council, related to the World Bank and IMF, a whole range of issues." But he said Obama would focus on these questions mostly during his second term in the White House.[36]

15

The Outsiders

In its first months in the White House, the Obama administration seemed remarkably freewheeling and open-minded, particularly in comparison with the outgoing Bush team. The career officials who served in both administrations were astonished by the change. Admiral Mike Mullen, who had begun as chairman of the Joint Chiefs of Staff under Bush, told one friend in the spring of 2009 that the new Obama team was a breath of fresh air.

In the early Bush years, officials such as Colin Powell had sometimes found that the president was making decisions without him, in concert with Dick Cheney. In contrast, Mullen told the associate, when you went into a principals meeting of Obama's top foreign policy advisers, you didn't get that nagging feeling that you were being left out of some other gathering, a more secret one, where the real decisions were being made. Moreover, Mullen said, in discussions within the Obama administration, you could speak your mind. You were even encouraged to do so, whereas in the Bush meetings dissent was all but banned.

These were the impressions formed in Obama's early days. As time passed, however, it turned out that his administration had some foibles of its own. The Obama team wasn't entirely open—far from it—and its tolerance for independent-minded officials had some well-defined limits. Under Obama, too, the final decisions were sometimes made outside of official channels, by the president and the handful of aides closest to and most loyal to him. In foreign policy, Obama's inner circle included Tom Donilon, Denis McDonough, John Brennan and Ben Rhodes from the National Security Council and the White House chiefs of staff, Rahm Emanuel, Peter Rouse and Bill Daley.

The Obama White House seemed to run by two different sets of rules for two different kinds of people. The first were the "team of rivals" rules, which applied to a tiny number of high-profile individuals—notably Hillary Clinton and David Petraeus. Under the "team of rivals" principles, those prominent individuals who might present a potential political problem for the president if allowed to work outside the administration were rewarded with high-level jobs on the inside. The potential "rivals" were treated gingerly, because what counted was keeping them on board. (Joe Biden also qualified under these relatively tolerant rules, not because he was a potential rival to Obama but because he had been elected with Obama. Biden, too, was sometimes given latitude for dissent, even in public—particularly on Afghanistan, where Biden's views were in accord with those of antiwar Democrats, the core constituency that had won Obama the Democratic nomination.)

The second set of rules could be called the "Greg Craig" rules, named for Obama's first White House counsel. Craig had pushed hard for actions to counteract and punish the abuses of the Bush era, and in the process had run into intense opposition from high-ranking officials in the CIA and the Pentagon. Craig seemed to be carrying on the spirit and idealism of Obama's presidential campaign, but his efforts spelled trouble for Obama in trying to run a harmonious, conflict-free administration. Within ten months, Craig had been replaced.

Over the following year, the stricter "Greg Craig" rules were applied, in one fashion or another, to four other high-ranking officials: Director of National Intelligence Dennis Blair, National Security Adviser Jim Jones, special envoy to Afghanistan Richard Holbrooke and Afghan war commander General Stanley McChrystal. All were ultimately replaced except for Holbrooke, whom the Obama White House tried to fire before Hillary Clinton intervened to save his job.

There were special circumstances in each case. McChrystal, for example, stood apart from the others because he was in the military chain of command. Holbrooke was the only one of the four who did not spend most of his career in the military. But the common denominator was that all had run into conflict with Obama or some of his closest aides. The Obama White House didn't like independent actors or internal discord. It also didn't like to be challenged, certainly not in public, and not on the foreign policy issues of greatest sensitivity for Obama: the war in Afghanistan and terrorism.

———

Even Dennis Blair's critics admitted that he had two sterling qualities: He was straightforward and he was intelligent. He was not adroit, however, at White House maneuvering or infighting. Those were skills he had never been required to learn. Blair's style was based on his long and distinguished career in the military, with its formal chain of command: Tell me who I report to, and I'll do that and say what I think, and whoever's in charge of politics can make the political decisions. He was low-key, not arrogant, but also not given to glad-handing. "He's a smart dude," said a foreign policy official who had worked with Blair in a previous administration and come to admire him. "He can let you know it on occasion."

In the Obama administration, Blair confronted two major problems. The first was the president for whom he worked. Obama, too, was uncommonly bright, yet also—unlike Blair—intensely attuned to political considerations. As president, he held the power that Blair lacked. And, self-confident as Obama was, during his early years in office he was a bit edgy toward those who reminded him, intentionally or not, of his lack of foreign policy experience.

Once, during a meeting of administration officials on policy toward Iran's nuclear program, Blair bluntly told Obama that he would have to make a fundamental strategic decision: Was he willing to accept an Iran with nuclear weapons, or not? After the meeting, Obama called Blair aside and told him he didn't want to foreclose any options concerning Iran. Moreover, the president added, he hadn't appreciated Blair saying what he had said, particularly not in front of other people.[1]

Blair's second problem had nothing to do with Obama or his administration. It was institutional, stemming from the peculiar job Blair held: director of national intelligence (or DNI, in Washington lingo). During the Bush years, the Democrats had led the way in creating this new, high-ranking position. After the September 11 attacks, Congress, under Democratic leadership and over George W. Bush's opposition, established a commission to investigate various aspects of the event, including the extensive planning by al-Qaeda and lapses or failures in the U.S. intelligence community. The

9/11 Commission eventually recommended the creation of a new job for a senior official who would make sure that the multitude of U.S. intelligence agencies worked closely together, shared information and functioned as a coherent entity. In 2005, Congress passed a law creating the position.

Until then, the CIA director had been responsible not merely for running his own agency, but also for coordinating the activities of fifteen other bureaucracies in the nation's gargantuan intelligence community. Besides the CIA, that community includes the National Security Agency, the Defense Intelligence Agency, the National Geospatial-Intelligence Agency, the National Reconnaissance Office, the foreign intelligence section of the FBI, the intelligence services of the Treasury, Energy and Homeland Security Departments, the State Department's Bureau of Intelligence and Research, the intelligence specialists for Immigration and Customs Enforcement, and the separate army, navy, air force and coast guard intelligence agencies.

Under the new law, the CIA and its director theoretically lost their primacy within the intelligence community. The statute said that the new director of national intelligence would be the president's "principal adviser" on intelligence. The DNI was the person responsible for briefing the president at the White House each morning on what was happening around the world, a job formerly assigned to the director of the CIA.

But the law also contained some ambiguities and loose wording. It wasn't exactly clear how much authority the new director of national intelligence would have over the CIA itself. Furthermore, the law left uncertain what the CIA director's relationship to the president should be after the new director of national intelligence was in place: Was the CIA director supposed to report to the president through the director of national intelligence, or separately on his own? In short, no one could say where the DNI and the CIA director stood in the pecking order.

Over the previous six decades, the CIA and its director had amassed enormous power, despite the intermittent controversies over its activities. The director of national intelligence and his staff, by contrast, had no history, no legends, no luster and little clout beyond its paper authority under the new law. The national intelligence director didn't work at CIA headquarters in Langley, and CIA agents and operatives were still under the control of the CIA director. Nor did the national intelligence director work inside the

White House, the seat of political power. Instead, he was based in a complex in northern Virginia called Liberty Crossing, with a staff less than a tenth the size of the CIA.[2] His office was removed from the action, floating within the bureaucracy like a ship without an anchor. In the press, the DNI was sometimes called the new "intelligence czar," but this was an imperfect metaphor. He seemed much more like an embattled knight than a czar.

Turf battles between the two intelligence chiefs seemed inevitable. During Bush's final years, CIA Director Michael Hayden and Director of National Intelligence Mike McConnell had occasionally skirmished. Within a few months after Obama took office, the bureaucratic battles resumed, this time more intensely, between Blair and Leon Panetta, Obama's CIA director.

Traditionally, the top American intelligence official in each country came from the ranks of the CIA; he or she was known as the station chief. But Blair argued that there were "rare circumstances" in which some other U.S. intelligence agency had a much larger presence inside a particular country than did the CIA. One classic example was Australia, a close U.S. ally, where there are large installations operated by the National Security Agency and the National Geospatial-Intelligence Agency to collect information from elsewhere around the world. In a few African countries, the CIA had no agents of its own at all, but the Defense Intelligence Agency had a presence. Blair, as the DNI in charge of coordinating all the American intelligence operations, sought the right to name officials from these other agencies, not merely the CIA, as the senior representative from the U.S. intelligence community in a particular capital. Panetta objected, and he persuaded the White House to agree that in every country the CIA's station chief would still be in charge.[3]

Moreover, Blair, who was in charge of the President's Daily Brief, the written document given to the president each day, sought to edit out items submitted by the CIA that seemed to be puff pieces aimed primarily at showing Obama how well the CIA was doing. The CIA wasn't pleased. Blair also sought some authority over the CIA's covert action programs, such as, for example, the drones it was operating in Pakistan. The CIA liked that even less.[4]

Sometimes, both Blair and Panetta would appear at cabinet-level meetings, creating confusion among others about their relative authority. Although

Blair was supposed to be Obama's main intelligence adviser, he found that Panetta was spending a surprising amount of time on his own at the White House. Reflecting on the protracted tug-of-war between the two men, Hayden said, "Leon had all the political juice."[5] In Panetta, it turned out, the CIA had an unusually wily and forceful advocate, one who had previously been White House chief of staff, head of the Office of Management and Budget, a member of Congress and chairman of a congressional committee. Though Panetta had no intelligence experience, he soon won the support of the CIA, particularly its tradition-minded old guard, by vigorously defending the agency inside the administration. Blair had some friends of his own at the White House; he was on good terms with Jim Jones, Obama's first national security adviser. But Jones himself was never part of Obama's inner circle. Panetta, it became clear, had better White House connections than Blair and Jones combined. Rahm Emanuel had essentially learned his job at Panetta's feet, when Emanuel worked under Panetta in Bill Clinton's White House.

As if these weren't enough headaches for Blair, the president also had a close aide with years of intelligence experience, John Brennan, working in the White House less than a minute away from the Oval Office. Brennan had been Obama's own first choice for CIA director, before controversy arose over his former work at the agency. Brennan's formal title was deputy national security adviser and special assistant to the president for counterterrorism. More informally, he was the person to whom the president often turned for advice on intelligence issues. After each morning's intelligence briefing from Blair or one of Blair's aides, the White House officials who regularly stayed behind to talk further about national security issues included Obama, Biden, Donilon, McDonough—and Brennan.

"John Brennan's the actual national intelligence director, and Denny [Blair] can't unwish that," observed Hayden. Brennan himself rejected the idea that he operated as a shadow DNI. He acknowledged that he sometimes gave advice to Obama on issues that went beyond his core assignment of counterterrorism—issues such as Saudi Arabia, where Brennan had been the station chief for six years. But Brennan liked to point out that at the White House, his job was to advise on policy questions, not the intelligence issues for which Blair was responsible.[6]

This setup was not destined to last. The post-9/11 law creating the DNI made for inherent conflict in the intelligence community. The CIA's recalcitrance and the continual maneuvering among Obama's original personnel choices exacerbated the tension. Eventually, after a failed terrorist attack put the intelligence community under renewed scrutiny, Obama would fire Blair.

In the first year of his administration, Obama beefed up the military campaign against al-Qaeda in two ways. First, he decided to step up the use of unmanned drones in Pakistan. The increase became particularly noticeable in late 2009, after the administration's long internal review of the war in Afghanistan. Vice President Joe Biden recommended that the administration rely primarily on drones or missile attacks against al-Qaeda leaders instead of sending more ground troops. While Obama rejected that approach and decided instead on new troop deployments, the president nonetheless expanded the CIA's drone program.[7]

The Obama administration referred to these drone attacks as "targeted killing," rather than "assassinations." The euphemism was of legal significance. The 1970s congressional investigations of the CIA had uncovered the American efforts to assassinate foreign leaders such as Fidel Castro, and in response President Ford issued an executive order that banned assassinations. The order remained in effect in 2009. The administration's formal reasoning for why its overseas killings did not constitute assassination went like this: Congress had authorized the use of force against al-Qaeda. Therefore, America was at war, and under the law of war, America had the right to defend itself "by targeting persons such as high-level al-Qaeda leaders who are planning attacks." Since the laws of war permitted targeted killing, the Obama administration argued, therefore the practice wasn't illegal, and "and hence does not constitute assassination."[8]

Apart from the seeming circularity of the logic, it is worth noting that the Obama administration's reasoning rested on the idea that the United States was at war—if not a "global war on terror" as Bush had called it, then a war on al-Qaeda, as Obama administration officials rephrased it. The administration's rationale for targeted killing also depended on an expanded notion of preemption. Obama did not go so far as Bush, who carried out a full-scale military invasion on the basis of the doctrine of preemptive attack. But

Obama did justify the idea of killing specific individuals on grounds of preemption—that they were said to be "planning attacks"—even if no attacks were imminent.

Secondly, Obama widened the scope of the targeted killings by approving them in areas far beyond Afghanistan and Pakistan, the specific region where American troops were in combat. Once again, the underlying justification was that the war on al-Qaeda had no geographical limits; it was global in nature.[9] In September 2009, U.S. special forces conducted a raid in Somalia that killed Saleh Ali Nabhan, an al-Qaeda leader operating in Somalia and Kenya. Later that fall, the Obama team began to direct its attention to Yemen, where a Bin Laden affiliate known as Al-Qaeda in the Arabian Peninsula was operating. American counterterrorism officials began to focus increasingly on Anwar al-Awlaki, an American-born cleric in Yemen, who had been connected to the 2009 incident in Fort Hood, Texas, in which an army psychiatrist murdered twelve American soldiers and a civilian. Obama authorized an attack carried out on December 24, 2009, in which Yemeni officials, with American advisers, sought to kill al-Awlaki along with some other al-Qaeda leaders. He survived that attack, but was killed two years later in another operation carried out by U.S. special forces and Predator drones.[10]

Since the start of Obama's presidency, Republicans had characterized him and his administration as weak on terrorism. Some of the Republican claims were based on the initial executive order limiting interrogation of detainees and on its decision to proceed with criminal investigations of a few CIA officials who conducted unusually harsh interrogations. Former vice president Dick Cheney led the way, asserting that the policies of the Obama administration were endangering national security.

The partisan disputes over terrorism burst forth again, more intensely, after a terrorism scare on Christmas Day in 2009. A Nigerian man named Umar Farouk Abdulmutallab, whose travel had originated in Yemen, tried to explode a bomb, concealed inside his underwear, aboard a Northwest Airlines flight preparing to land in Detroit. The bomb set his pant leg on fire but failed to explode, and the crew and passengers subdued him. He subsequently told FBI agents he had been trained and given explosives by al-Qaeda operatives in Yemen.

The memories of this Detroit scare have since faded, but the consequences were far-reaching. It was the Abdulmutallab "underwear bomber" case that led to the use of body scans at American airports and the ensuing debates about privacy. ("Keep your hands off my junk," one traveler memorably warned.) In political terms, the incident represented a serious threat for the Obama administration, raising anew the decades-old stereotype that the Democrats were weak on national security.

According to subsequent investigations by the White House and the Senate Select Committee on Intelligence, various parts of the intelligence community had fumbled a series of chances to uncover the plans for the bombing. A few weeks earlier, Abdulmutallab's own father had gone to the American embassy in Nigeria to say he was worried that his son had increasingly radical views, had been associating with dangerous-looking people and had vanished in Yemen. While the embassy passed this information on to Washington, the State Department didn't check to see that Abdulmutallab possessed a valid visa for the United States and thus didn't revoke it. The CIA, meanwhile, had begun to prepare a biographical report on Abdulmutallab, but didn't complete it or disseminate the information in it to other parts of the intelligence community.[11]

Intelligence intercepts from Yemen in November had indicated that a man named Umar Farouk had volunteered for an operation and that he had been in touch with al-Awlaki. On December 22, someone from al-Qaeda said on Al Jazeera that "we carry a bomb for the enemies of God."[12] The CIA and the National Counterterrorism Center (which includes officials from not just the CIA but several other intelligence agencies) began to examine whether the Yemeni branch of al-Qaeda might attack American targets inside Yemen, but had not focused on the possibility it would strike inside the United States. No one in the intelligence community pulled together these disparate pieces of information.

After the flight landed safely in Detroit, Abdulmutallab was turned over to the FBI for questioning. Four months earlier, the Obama administration had announced the creation of a High-Value Detainee Interrogation Group, composed of specialists who would question suspects under the rules set down in the Army Field Manual, the tighter standard Obama had set after he was sworn in. However, this new group was not yet fully operational at the time of the Detroit case and therefore hadn't been available to interrogate Abdulmutallab.

The Republicans had historical reasons for humility on these issues. The Bush administration failed to respond to warnings of the September 11 attacks, which succeeded where the underwear bomber had failed. Nevertheless, Cheney quickly accused Obama of failing to realize that the nation was at war—a charge at variance with the reality that Obama had widened the frequency and scope of "targeted killing." Other Republican charges followed along similar lines. Sarah Palin claimed in an interview on Fox News that Obama had a "lackadaisical approach" to dealing with terrorists. The situation would improve only if Obama would toughen up, she said: "Say he decided to declare war on Iran, or decided to really come out and do whatever he could to support Israel, which I would like him to do."[13]

Many senior officials in the Obama administration had been involved in one way or another in the series of fumbles by the intelligence community leading up to the Christmas Day incident. Obama, who had met with senior intelligence officials on December 22, accepted ultimate responsibility himself. That same day, Brennan had been in a meeting concerning Yemen and the apparent planning there for some sort of attack.[14] Panetta's CIA had slipped up in failing to connect the dots, and so had the National Counterterrorism Center, which operated under Blair. Nevertheless, it was Blair who suffered most as a consequence of the Detroit episode. The problem was not so much Blair's actions before or at the time of the failed bombing; rather, it was the fallout from what happened afterward. Obama had ordered Brennan to conduct a speedy White House review of what had gone wrong; his conclusions (or at least some of them) were to be made public. On January 7, 2010, Blair was shown the final draft of Brennan's report, only a few hours before Obama was scheduled to hold a news conference to announce the results.

Blair didn't like what he read. The report seemed to single out individuals at the National Counterterrorism Center for blame. Intelligence officials at the center were upset, believing they could be fired. Blair argued that the problems were systemic, not personal. He asked for changes in what Brennan had written, even if it meant delaying the president's news conference. Blair added what amounted to a fairly pointed warning: If Brennan's draft was adopted and released without changes, he said, and if he was asked by Congress whether he agreed with the report, he'd be obliged to tell the truth and say no. He couldn't lie. Obama and Brennan were thus faced with the prospect of a highly public disagreement at the highest levels of government concerning the Americans' highest-ranking concern on national security, terrorism. They decided, not surprisingly, to try to accommodate Blair; some of the report's language was changed to de-emphasize the individuals at the counterterrorism center. That afternoon, the news conference was postponed twice, as Brennan and Blair hurriedly worked out new wording. Obama was furious, both at the embarrassingly public last-minute delays in his news conference and, more generally, at the internal bickering within the intelligence community.[15]

Blair stayed on the job, but never recovered his relationship with Brennan or, it turned out, with Obama. On May 18, 2010, the president called Blair in to say he was not satisfied with the way Blair had been overseeing the intelligence community. Blair, maintaining he'd actually run things well, said this couldn't be the real reason for the president's unhappiness. Obama told Blair to write a report giving his own perspective on how the intelligence community had been performing. Blair hurriedly submitted a memo later that day, but to no avail. Two days later, the president called Blair to say he was going to let him go.

Blair was offered an endgame similar to the one for Greg Craig. He was told he could stay in his job for weeks or more while the administration searched for a successor. He would also be permitted to draft his own explanation, or excuse, for why he was leaving—for another job, for health reasons, for whatever reason he chose.

Blair declined the offer.[16] "I have to be honest," he said. "I don't have cancer, my wife's health is okay, I haven't been wanting to return to the private sector." In fact, Blair told the president, "I can't in good conscience say I want to leave. In fact, because there had already been two directors of national intelligence in four years before me, I promised that I'd stay for four years. The truth is that you're firing me." Obama agreed. The White House quickly announced in public that Blair had resigned, leaving out that he had done so at the president's request.

Barely a month later, Obama also fired Stanley McChrystal, his commander in Afghanistan, though the circumstances were quite different. *Rolling Stone* published sarcastic quips by the general and his military aides about American civilian leaders—and about U.S. allies as well. One of McChrystal's top advisers was quoted as saying that during McChrystal's first one-on-one meeting with the president, Obama "clearly didn't know anything about him, who he was. Here's the guy who's going to run his fucking war, but he didn't seem very engaged. The Boss was pretty disappointed." Of the vice president, a McChrystal adviser said, "Biden? Did you say Bite Me?" The McChrystal team offered similar disparaging remarks about Obama's national security adviser (Jim Jones), ambassador to Afghanistan (Karl Eikenberry) and special representative to Pakistan and Afghanistan (Richard Holbrooke).[17]

The ensuing debate over what Obama should do in response did not follow the usual liberal/conservative divisions. Even some of Obama's frequent critics supported him in this instance. Eliot Cohen, a Johns Hopkins professor who had served in the Bush administration, wrote that the remarks by McChrystal and his aides were "an appalling violation of norms of civilian-military relations." Thomas Donnelly, a hawkish military expert at the American Enterprise Institute, declared: "Anyone who understands the challenges of supreme command, particularly in a war where the home front is as important as the battlefront, knows McChrystal has to go."[18] The principal argument made on McChrystal's behalf was that he was an excellent field commander and that replacing him would hinder the war effort. "It takes time for anyone to get up to speed, and right now time is our most precious commodity in Afghanistan," asserted Nathaniel Fick of the Center for a New American Security.[19]

This controversy didn't last long. Within days, the president summoned McChrystal from Afghanistan to Washington and told him he was being relieved of his command. Obama found a way to preempt the arguments that the general would be hard to replace; he appointed McChrystal's own immediate boss, General Petraeus, to go to Afghanistan and run the war. Petraeus was the country's best-known general, the commander who'd helped turn the course of the war in Iraq and the architect of the counterinsurgency strategy that McChrystal had been implementing in Afghanistan.

The McChrystal affair brought to the fore the larger question of how the United States was doing in Afghanistan and how long the war would last. In Congress, liberal Democrats threatened to hold up further appropriations for Afghanistan. Speaking of the change from McChrystal to Petraeus, Massachusetts representative Jim McGovern quipped, "Same menu, different waiter." From the political right, libertarian congressman Ron Paul said, "That McChrystal thing is just a symptom of what we won't face up to, which is that it [Afghanistan] is a totally failed policy. If we were on the verge of a great success, do you think we'd fire the general?"[20]

The White House was not eager to open up a broader public debate on Afghanistan again, only a half year after Obama had, with difficulty, decided on the surge in troops. The truth was that there had not been much progress. The number of American troops in Afghanistan was nearing 100,000, but an early campaign in the southern region around Kandahar, billed as a model for the strategy of counterinsurgency, had slowed down.

That period was by far the deadliest of the decade-long war in Afghanistan. In 2010, a total of 499 American troops were killed, an increase of more than 55 percent over 2009. Gates was pleading with Congress to be patient. "This is not something where we do ourselves any favors by tearing ourselves up by the roots every week to see if we're growing," he told the Senate Appropriations Committee.[21]

The bogged-down war represented an enormous political liability for Obama. "You know, he could lose the presidency on this one," Strobe Talbott said worriedly in the summer of 2010.[22] Antiwar Democrats remained angry about the two troop increases of the previous year and wondered why Obama, the peace candidate of 2008, was spending so much time and money on the conflict. Hawkish Republicans were pointing to Afghanistan to try to raise again the four-decade-old stereotype that the Democrats were weak on national security—a charge that had seemed to disappear in the 2008 campaign because of Bush's war in Iraq. The swaggering commentary by the McChrystal entourage seemed a good opportunity to revive the old stereotype.

Obama and his inner circle worked hard to dispel these impressions. Replacing McChrystal with Petraeus helped greatly. Obama's aides offered the news media a series of insider accounts (called "ticktocks") that portrayed the president as cool and decisive in handling the McChrystal affair.[23] That was not unusual; these ticktocks were offered so often, by Obama as well as his predecessors, that they had become a stereotype all their own.

———

By the fall of 2010, Obama was ready to replace Jim Jones, the former Marine Corps commandant who was serving as his national security adviser. When Obama had first put together his foreign policy team after his election, the appointments of Jones and Blair had served the purpose of fending off accusations that he was too distant from the military. While Obama was confident of his instincts on international relations and diplomacy, he seemed less comfortable in his relations with the military; he recognized that since he hadn't served, he was less familiar with its customs and traditions.[24]

A year later, Jones's military background no longer seemed so important. By that time, the president had his own extensive dealings with military leaders, especially concerning Afghanistan. Obama cared much more about having a smooth-running National Security Council, and since virtually the start of the administration, Jones hadn't fit in well.

The rumors about Jones had begun to spread within ten weeks after the administration took office: Jones, it was said, wasn't working hard enough; he left the office early at night; he let others—principally his deputy Tom Donilon—handle all the flow of paper. Jones didn't help himself with his NSC subordinates when, in responding to the rumors, he told the *New York Times* that he left the office by seven or seven thirty at night, and that was "a reasonable day if you're well organized." Working late into the night "means you're not organized." Those words annoyed his own subordinates, who felt they were staying late not because of disorganization but because of the workload.[25]

Soon, conspiracy theories were being put forward to explain why Jones was under attack. Did the leaks come from someone who wanted to become the next national security adviser? From those who feared some change in policy that Jones was proposing? Jones himself blamed aides Mark Lippert and Denis McDonough, both working under Jones on the National Security Council. At a meeting in the White House Situation Room that Obama didn't attend, Jones was discussing an aspect of foreign policy when Lippert broke in to explain what the president's own view was. One participant was astonished, both because Jones's authority had been undercut and because, as national security adviser, Jones himself was supposed to know what the president thought, not to hear it from a subordinate on the NSC.

After Jones was told repeatedly that Lippert was leaking derogatory information about him, he began asking the president to move Lippert out from the NSC. [26] Obama delayed, but finally went along. The White House announced that Lippert had asked to go back to active duty in the navy. However, that still didn't solidify Jones's hold over his job. The reality was that he didn't get along with the Obama team. He wasn't part of the inner circle that had started in the campaign, like McDonough and Rhodes. He wasn't connected to Obama's network of Democratic operatives, like Tom Donilon, Rahm Emanuel and David Axelrod. He had no strong connection to the president; he had met Obama only twice before his appointment.

Jones began to fly off regularly to overseas meetings. He worked hard, for example, to establish a strong relationship with Pakistan's military and civilian leaders. He was active in the diplomacy with Russia. But he had begun to talk openly about leaving the job, and by the fall of 2010 it seemed likely, if not certain, that Jones would leave in a quiet and orderly way after the midterm elections that November.

In September, however, Bob Woodward's book *Obama's Wars* was published. Woodward, who had known Jones for many years, laid out Jones's astonishingly unflattering view of others on the NSC and elsewhere in the Obama White House. He described Obama's close aides as "like water bugs. They flit around." Jones felt these aides didn't understand foreign policy or war. The book also covered in detail Jones's not entirely positive performance review of Donilon, his own deputy. Jones had informed Donilon that he didn't travel enough and that he lacked credibility with the military. Moreover, Jones was said to have told Donilon, "You frequently pop off with absolute declarations about places you've never been, leaders you've never met, or colleagues you work with."[27]

Those words seemed so bitter and so indiscreet as to make it impossible to have Jones continue to stay on as Obama's national security adviser even until Election Day. Woodward's book was published in late September; in less than two weeks, Obama announced that Jones was stepping down and that Donilon would take his place. McDonough was appointed his deputy.

Tom Donilon had worked on domestic politics longer than he had on foreign policy. He had started his career as an intern in Jimmy Carter's White House immediately after graduation from Catholic University. He had moved quickly into a White House staff job in congressional relations and became Carter's delegate coordinator and convention manager for the 1980 reelection campaign. He had helped Walter Mondale prepare for debating Ronald Reagan in 1984, took part in Joe Biden's abortive presidential race in 1988 and was involved in one way or another in virtually every Democratic presidential campaign since. In 2008, he had worked for Biden during the primaries; during the general election, Donilon was asked to help prepare Obama for the debates with John McCain. Donilon was, in short, a mainstream Democrat's mainstream Democrat.

In the Carter years, Donilon had met Warren Christopher, then the deputy secretary of state. Christopher became his mentor, showing him how to combine politics, law and foreign policy. It was Christopher who gave Donilon a copy of Dean Acheson's book *Present at the Creation* and persuaded Donilon to go to law school.[28] Christopher had helped Donilon land a job in one of Los Angeles's leading law firms, O'Melveny and Myers. When Christopher became secretary of state, he brought Donilon with him as chief of staff and assistant secretary for public affairs. Donilon was at Christopher's side in handling the American intervention in Bosnia, the disputes over the expansion of NATO and human rights in China, the efforts to stop North Korea's nuclear program and a round of frustrating negotiations between Israel and Syria's Hafez al-Assad.

There were some who wondered whether Donilon was knowledgeable enough in foreign policy for a top-level position. "There are lots of people now who spend eight years out of office doing foreign policy, and he [Donilon] is not one of them," said one former official from the Clinton administration. Foreign policy specialists for the party leaving power often land at think tanks or universities, where they can remain closely involved in roughly the same subjects they had worked on while in government. Donilon opted for another not uncommon career path: to take the opportunity to make some serious money. After his stint at the State Department under Clinton, he had returned to his law firm, but then soon went to work as vice president, general counsel and principal lobbyist for Fannie Mae, where several other veterans of Democratic politics, including Jim Johnson and Franklin Raines, also held lucrative positions. Disclosure and lobbying reports and other studies give an indication of Fannie Mae's large compensation packages at the time Donilon was working there, from 1999 to 2005. Donilon's salary alone was more than $600,000 a year. One report shows that between 2001 and 2003, Donilon's annual bonuses were $562,751, $694,983 and $600,000, for a total of about $1.9 million for those three years. In addition to these bonuses, Donilon also received vested options sometimes worth more than his salary or bonus (one block of his options was valued at $900,211 in January 2004).[29] Estimates of his annual compensation package for the year 2002 were $4.3 million.[30] (Fannie Mae's finances collapsed and it had to be taken over by the federal government in 2008.) Few in Washington were surprised when Obama decided to bring in Donilon as deputy national security adviser, a job that didn't require Senate confirmation. (Had he gone to the State Department, he would have faced a nomination hearing in which he could have been grilled about Fannie Mae.)

Others in the administration questioned whether Donilon had core beliefs or philosophy in foreign policy. "He doesn't seem to believe in anything," complained one Obama appointee at the State Department. Yet such criticisms carried little weight at the White House. Donilon had been closely involved in Obama's foreign policy from the outset; he knew Obama's instincts; and as deputy national security adviser, he had already been formally in charge of the day-to-day operations of the National Security Council for nearly two years.

He was a stickler for paperwork and for making sure that government processes ran smoothly. He made sure to vet nearly everything, even his aides' personal speeches, and to keep close track of what was being said about the administration. He had studied the way the National Security Council operated and how it had changed: At one point, when Bob Gates complained about some of the NSC's paperwork, Donilon knew enough to be able to say he was merely following the procedures of George H. W. Bush's administration, in which the deputy national security adviser was none other than Bob Gates.

With Donilon at the top of the NSC and Denis McDonough as his deputy, and with Hillary Clinton and Leon Panetta at State and Defense,

Obama had what was probably the most politically attuned national security team in the modern era. For a president planning to run for reelection, that was of no small importance. A president's longevity in office depends on voters, not on the views of scholars and experts.. Among Donilon's predecessors in the job of national security adviser, Brent Scowcroft and Zbigniew Brzezinski are often accorded the greatest respect for their sober, knowledgeable views on foreign policy. Indeed, the two men have sometimes been grouped together and called "Washington's Elder Statesmen."[31] Yet it is rarely mentioned that, between the two of them, Scowcroft and Brzezinski went zero for three in the task of helping their bosses—Ford, Bush, Carter—win a second term in office. Those three presidents were the only ones since Herbert Hoover to seek another term but lose at the polls. From Obama's own standpoint, then, there was advantage in having a national security adviser who was also a political insider.

16

"Richard Being Richard"

It seemed almost foreordained that Richard Holbrooke would have a difficult, unhappy stint in the Obama administration. He had the wrong history, personality and operating style to fit in with the Obama inner circle, much as Holbrooke struggled in his own fashion to do so. He was of the wrong generation, serving at the wrong time.

Holbrooke would almost certainly have been secretary of state if Hillary Clinton had won the presidency. He might also have landed that job if Al Gore had become president in 2000 or if John Kerry had beaten George Bush in 2004. After Obama appointed Clinton as secretary of state, she hoped to name Holbrooke her deputy, but Obama gave that job to Jim Steinberg, who had been a leading candidate for national security adviser. Instead, Holbrooke was given a lesser job, one that at first seemed to be perfectly suited to his talents but eventually turned out to add to his frustrations.

In dealing with the Obamians, Holbrooke started with two strikes against him. First, he had aggressively campaigned against Obama in the primaries, speaking out vigorously for Clinton and telling those who worked for Obama that they were making a terrible mistake. He warned that Obama was young, inexperienced and destined to fail, and that they were jeopardizing their prospects for a good job in the coming Hillary Clinton administration. Secondly, Holbrooke was a living symbol of the foreign policy establishment against which the Obama team had campaigned. The Obamians saw themselves as insurgents; Holbrooke had always tied himself to power, to worldly, prosperous Democrats like Averell and Pamela Harriman, Clark Clifford and the Clintons.

Holbrooke had been serving Democratic presidents since the 1960s.

When the Democrats lost the White House, he usually returned to New York City, worked for financial firms such as Lehman Brothers and served as a prominent adviser to aspiring presidential candidates and members of Congress. In the lead-up to Bush's Iraq War, he had at first equivocated, along with other Democrats such as Clinton and Biden. Holbrooke told Democrats on Capitol Hill that Saddam Hussein had to be confronted.[1]

In 2009, eager to return to government, Holbrooke took the job he was offered, as the president's special representative for Afghanistan and Pakistan, or "Af-Pak," as he soon called it. He found himself, for the third time in his career, working within but not quite at the top of a Democratic administration, obliged to serve under those who seemed to know less history (and fewer powerful people) than he did. He was working for a secretary of state whom he had tutored in foreign policy and for a president who had been seven years old in 1968, when Holbrooke began working for Averell Harriman at the Paris peace talks on Vietnam. Across the government, in the middle ranks of the Obama administration, were officials who had served under Holbrooke, such as Jeff Bader, the National Security Council staff member in charge of Asia policy, and Chris Hill, the ambassador to Iraq. Even Holbrooke's disciples were no longer young. Holbrooke, the Young Turk of the 1960s and 1970s, was now the old warhorse of the Obama era, ready to do battle again within the Washington bureaucracy.

The rationale for giving Holbrooke the Af-Pak job was that while his outsize personality might create problems in Washington, he was especially good at fixing specific, hands-on problems overseas. Together, the wars against the Taliban in Afghanistan and against al-Qaeda in Pakistan represented the highest priorities for the new administration. The Af-Pak assignment was meant to be a follow-on to the work Holbrooke had done in the Balkans during the Clinton administration. There, Holbrooke had managed to push, shove and cajole the leaders of Bosnia, Serbia and Croatia into accepting the Dayton peace settlement. His aggressive operating style had served him well in dealing with Serbia's Slobodan Milosevic, a tough leader who needed to hear some blunt language and threats along with the standard diplomatic niceties. The logic underlying the Af-Pak appointment went like this: The Balkans had been beset by murderous ethnic tensions and nasty characters; so were Afghanistan and Pakistan; therefore let's put Holbrooke on the job.

Holbrooke's first major setback came in August 2009, when he infuriated Afghanistan's president Hamid Karzai. Afghanistan had just held nation-wide elections. The results were in dispute, but Karzai claimed he had won and would be staying on as president. The Obama administration was eager to make sure the Afghanistan election had been fair, so that the government would be seen as a legitimate one reflecting the will of the Afghan people. A day after the polls closed, Holbrooke met with Karzai at his presidential palace to complain about fraud and other voting irregularities. Holbrooke suggested there should be a runoff election; the United States would remain neutral and would leave it up to Afghanistan's Electoral Complaints Com-mission to decide if a second round of balloting was necessary. Karzai re-acted angrily, maintaining that the voting had been fair and that a second round was unnecessary.

In challenging the election returns, Holbrooke was reflecting the views of the administration, which was increasingly disenchanted with Karzai. The Afghan president was a mercurial figure; his support for the war effort against the Taliban had been intermittent, and his responses to American appeals for action against corruption and for reform of his government were tepid. Holbrooke was not even the first senior official from the Obama ad-ministration to confront him. Shortly before Obama took office, Vice Presi-dent–elect Joe Biden, a critic of Karzai since his days in the Senate, had had a frosty dinner with him in Kabul.

The problem was that Karzai did not stand in the same position as Mi-losevic in the 1990s. The Serbian leader was an adversary; Karzai was a shaky ally. Holbrooke could warn Milosevic that if he balked, he might con-front awesome American military power—and, indeed, the United States and its NATO allies eventually bombed Belgrade. Holbrooke couldn't sim-ilarly threaten Karzai with the bombing of Kabul. Ultimately, the Obama administration needed the help and cooperation of Karzai's government. The applicable historical precedent for dealing with Karzai wasn't Milosevic at all. Rather, the closer comparison was to the leaders aligned with the United States in the Cold War who proved increasingly unpopular at home and obstreperous in dealing with Washington. Both Nguyen Van Thieu in South Vietnam and Ferdinand Marcos in the Philippines fit this description well.

Over the following weeks, Karzai refused to hold a runoff election. He also made it clear to Washington that he was unhappy with Holbrooke. The Obama administration was in the midst of its prolonged review of whether to send more troops to Afghanistan; it didn't need a disputed election to further complicate its problems. In October, a formal investigation of Afghanistan's election concluded that Karzai's share of the vote had been only 46 percent, short of a majority and thus opening the way for a second ballot. But Afghanistan's election commission, controlled by Karzai, at first refused to accept the result.

At this important juncture, the Obama administration urgently needed to persuade Karzai to change his mind and permit a runoff. But Karzai had called Obama to say he refused to deal with Holbrooke anymore. Thus, instead of sending Holbrooke to Kabul, Obama chose to deliver his message through Senator John Kerry, the chairman of the Senate Foreign Relations Committee, a more polite, deferential intermediary. He eventually managed to persuade Karzai to give way.

Kerry, who had hoped to be Obama's secretary of state, was delighted with the new diplomatic role. Holbrooke, however, was hurt. He complained to friends that Obama should have backed him up by telling Karzai that Holbrooke was the administration official responsible for Afghanistan, and that if the Afghan president didn't want to talk with Holbrooke, there would be no other American official with whom he could converse.[2]

There was never a runoff election, because Karzai's opponent, Abdullah Abdullah, withdrew from the race. Karzai stayed on as president for a second five-year term, and his enmity toward Holbrooke persisted. In early 2010, at the annual Wehrkunde Security Conference in Munich for officials involved in defense issues, Karzai refused to appear with Holbrooke on a panel. At one point, Karzai walked up to the American delegation, embraced John McCain and John Kerry and strode past Holbrooke as if he weren't there.

Holbrooke meanwhile ran into even more serious problems in Washington. In the fall of 2009, the underlying tension and mistrust between Holbrooke and the Obama White House first erupted. The precipitating factor was a profile of Holbrooke in *The New Yorker*. Written by George Packer and entitled "The Last Mission," the article told the story of Holbrooke's career from his early days serving in the Vietnam War to his new job in the midst of the war in Afghanistan. There were reflections by Holbrooke on the lessons from Vietnam for Afghanistan, comparisons and contrasts between the two countries, and pictures of Holbrooke in both Vietnam and Afghanistan, all of them introduced by a glossy portrait photograph of Holbrooke covering one and a third pages.

Packer's article was insightful and entirely accurate. Yet there could hardly have been an article more likely to annoy the president and his aides. It pushed every button of sensitivity. It put Holbrooke at the center of the narrative, not Obama or the White House, and it did so on the gravest issue facing the administration, the war in Afghanistan. Worse, it framed the story of Afghanistan against the backdrop of Vietnam—precisely the comparison the Obama inner circle wanted to avoid, preferring to see themselves as the first administration that didn't see every foreign struggle in terms of Vietnam. Moreover, the Vietnam analogy could spur the antiwar wing of the Democratic Party to rise up against the war in Afghanistan, just when the Obama administration was trying to figure out how many more troops to send there. *The New Yorker* piece seemed in line with what the Obama camp had been told about Holbrooke: that he saw life as a drama with himself at center stage, that he was a self-promoter, that he was attracted to glamour, media and celebrity.[3]

Denis McDonough, who rarely said or did anything without the president's approval, summoned Holbrooke to the White House for a strained conversation. Holbrooke and McDonough were probably the two most press-conscious officials in the entire administration; neither was modest about calling reporters to try to shape a story in advance or to complain about something after it appeared. But the similarities stopped there. Holbrooke called the press on matters involving himself or his own causes and issues; McDonough was a staff man who pushed, equally aggressively, on behalf of his boss, Obama. Holbrooke was the embodiment of New York, with its self-identity as the Big Time and its boundless reverence for show business, power and intellectual life. McDonough came from a small Minnesota town and grew up with the disciplined traditions of football and the Catholic Church. He worked loyally for a president whose home base was Chicago, known as the Second City (that is, second in rank to New York). There was, in the milieu of the Obama White House, a distinct wariness toward New York, a determination to look upon it not as the arbiter of American taste and sophistication but as merely an unusually presumptuous locality.

At their meeting, McDonough dressed down Holbrooke, pointing his finger for emphasis. He told Holbrooke that the president was unhappy about the magazine article. It had seemed to give Holbrooke a central role in the foreign policy apparatus. The Obama team wanted to determine the messages and images of the administration, and not have various individual actors send out a cacophony of ideas. In fact, only a couple of months earlier, after the *New York Times Magazine* ran a profile of Obama's senior adviser Valerie Jarrett, administration officials had put out the word that there should be no more profiles of individuals in the administration. But by that time, Holbrooke felt that the impending *New Yorker* profile was too far along to stop. Moreover, he argued to McDonough, he thought the article would be about overall foreign policy from Vietnam to Afghanistan, merely using him as a vehicle for this broader narrative: He hadn't known it would run with such a large, Avedon-style portrait of him.[4] The contretemps with McDonough was merely one of several episodes showing that Holbrooke was out of favor with Obama and his inner circle. In one session with Obama and other senior foreign policy officials conducted by videoconference, Holbrooke began to make a point in dramatic fashion, telling the president how momentous a particular issue was, when Obama cut him short, asking if he was reading from prepared remarks. One official who attended meetings on Afghanistan reported that whenever Holbrooke brought the conversation back to Vietnam, "the rest of us would be rolling our eyes, going, 'All right already.'"[5]

Holbrooke's job description soon began to narrow. After nearly a year in office, he told one audience that his own mandate was merely "the civilian side of the war." He informed another that the term "Af-Pak," which he had vigorously promoted, was being abandoned. "We can't use it anymore because it does not please people in Pakistan, for understandable reasons," Holbrooke explained. Pakistan didn't like being linked only to Afghanistan in the Washington view of the world, just as India, with its larger ambitions, hadn't wanted to be tied to Pakistan.[6] With increasing frequency, the Obama administration, recognizing that the military was the ultimate power in Pakistan and that President Asif Ali Zardari was in a shaky position, began dealing with Pakistan through officials who had spent their own careers in the military: Mike Mullen and James Jones.

The simmering tension over Holbrooke came to a boil in the early months of 2010, when Jones informed the American ambassador in Afghanistan, Karl Eikenberry, that Holbrooke was about to be replaced. The word began to spread through the administration, until Hillary Clinton called Obama and remonstrated on Holbrooke's behalf, arguing vigorously that the administration could not afford to let him go. Even Holbrooke's friends acknowledged that only Clinton had saved him from being forced out.[7] At one point that spring, Holbrooke told friends he might not be in the administration much longer; he might decide to leave and spend more time with his wife, Kati Marton, and to spend the summer at their home on Long Island.

Before long, Obama and his aides were persuaded that it would be politically damaging to have Holbrooke, a media superstar, leave the administration in a big public row. It would be better to have him inside the administration, supporting it, rather than outside, in a position to criticize it. Holbrooke continued to work on Afghanistan, although with diminished authority. After Obama replaced McChrystal as the military commander in Afghanistan, a wave of news stories and columns focused on the broader discord over Afghanistan within the administration. Some commentators suggested the president should replace others beyond McChrystal. "The president should finish cleaning house and fire Ambassador Eikenberry and the special envoy, Richard Holbrooke," wrote Thomas E. Ricks in the *New York Times*. "Richard Holbrooke should be sent packing as well," wrote Fred Kaplan at *Slate*. On Capitol Hill, John McCain embraced these calls for a shake-up.[8]

Holbrooke was working the press, as he had so often in the past, fussing over the wording of even largely positive stories. Doyle McManus, the columnist for the *Los Angeles Times*, wrote a cogent piece arguing that the administration shouldn't lose Holbrooke. "The special envoy is the State Department's most accomplished negotiator—and if negotiations with the

Taliban are coming up, there's an argument for keeping him in his job as long as the lines of authority can be made clear," McManus argued. Holbrooke called him to complain that he was not just a "negotiator" but a strategist and formulator of policy.[9]

Still, the rumors persisted for months: Holbrooke was on the way out; he was going to leave the administration. The focus of Afghan policy turned to Petraeus, McChrystal's successor, the man who had famously called Holbrooke his "wingman." That fall, one senior State Department official predicted that Holbrooke would be allowed a dignified, graceful exit from the administration on his own terms. He would not be fired; Hillary Clinton had made sure of that.[10]

On Sunday, December 5, 2010, Holbrooke played tennis on Long Island with Bill Drozdiak, the president of the American Council on Germany, a former foreign correspondent who became friendly with Holbrooke when both were living in Europe. They played for about an hour. Drozdiak thought Holbrooke seemed unusually pale, pudgy and out of shape, as if he'd been working too hard. When they finished, his breath was labored, his face ashen and his lips a bluish tinge.

They sat, drank some water and talked. Holbrooke said he was in despair over his role in the administration. He simply could not establish a relationship with Obama, Holbrooke said. The president seemed remote and coldblooded, at least in Holbrooke's presence. And, as if that weren't enough, Holbrooke's problem wasn't just with Obama: Holbrooke thought many in the White House were against him, especially McDonough. Still, things weren't all bad. Jones had been replaced as national security adviser, and the impact, Holbrooke told Drozdiak, was "like a giant turd being removed from the center of the room." Holbrooke was an old friend and colleague of Tom Donilon, the new national security adviser. Maybe things will improve, Holbrooke told Drozdiak. He still had hope.[11]

The following Friday, Holbrooke was at a meeting in Hillary Clinton's State Department office when he suddenly became flushed and stricken with pain. He was taken to the State Department medical office, but collapsed and went by ambulance to George Washington University Hospital. He died there three days later of a ruptured aorta.

Holbrooke's death represented, in many ways, a passing of the old guard in American foreign policy. He was the link to the Democratic Party of the post-Vietnam era. His ideas and career reflected the party's prolonged ambivalence about what to say and do in the aftermath of that disaster. In the 1970s, Holbrooke had been among the Democrats' intellectual leaders in trying to fashion America's role in the world after the elder statesmen from the Kennedy and Johnson administrations—the Rusks and McNamaras, Bundys and Rostows—had been discredited.

On the one hand, Holbrooke could sound passionately liberal as he attacked the Republicans during general elections and the periods when the Democrats were out of office. He embraced important causes such as stopping the spread of AIDS. He thought of the Vietnam War as a terrible mistake, one the United States should never repeat. Yet inside the Democratic Party and during Democratic primaries, Holbrooke was not a man of the political left. He did not align himself with antiwar movements or candidates within the party, whether George McGovern in 1972 or Barack Obama in 2008. A year after the end of the Vietnam War, he had denounced "the guilt-ridden anguish of the left."[12] Rather, Holbrooke invariably placed himself close to the Democratic Party's center of gravity, alongside established forces and elites rather than insurgent movements. To a considerable extent, this reflected his ambition and his fascination with power, his perpetual urge to be on the inside, his sense that those in antiwar movements or insurgencies didn't know the way things really worked (nor did they know the right people). Yet along with these personal factors, Holbrooke's determined centrism reflected a set of underlying beliefs. He was not opposed to the use of force, especially not for humanitarian purposes in places like Bosnia and Kosovo. He did not believe America was inherently malign. He argued repeatedly that the United States should continue to play a powerful role in the world.

The great irony was that Barack Obama, the president with whom Holbrooke did not get along, embraced many of these same centrist views himself. After he became president, Obama made clear through his actions that, despite his opposition to the Iraq War, he was no pacifist, and was willing to wield military power and technology on behalf of America's interests and values. And if Holbrooke was respectful of money, comfortable with financial power and the world of Wall Street, Obama was hardly an instinctive populist on economic issues himself.

In their beliefs, then, the two men turned out to be not too far apart. In their personalities, however, they were strikingly different. Holbrooke was aggressive, emotional, dramatic, persistent, preoccupied with the personal and consumed with whatever was happening at that moment. Obama remained cool, restrained, impersonal, far less swept up in the news coverage of the day, more preoccupied with long-term strategy, more driven to challenge established political power.

———

The memorial service for Holbrooke, held at the Kennedy Center, was a Washington event like few others. Its tone was extremely personal; it defied rank and position. By way of comparison, three months later Holbrooke's former boss Warren Christopher died. During his Washington career, Christopher had held two jobs, secretary and deputy secretary of state, that Holbrooke, despite his aspirations, never reached. Christopher had also run the high-level negotiations that brought American hostages home from Iran in early 1981. Yet in the nation's capital, Christopher's death was a one-day story; no big memorial service commemorated his life. Holbrooke, by contrast, had the biggest, mostly highly attended Washington memorial service of any political or foreign policy leader since the state funerals of Ronald Reagan and Gerald Ford. Pakistan's president Asif Ali Zardari flew in from Pakistan for the ceremonies, along with other foreign policy luminaries.

President Obama delivered a eulogy, and so did both Bill and Hillary Clinton. All of them praised Holbrooke, yet there was also a certain undertone to the proceedings, the legacy of his difficult time in the Obama administration. Holbrooke had been one of the stars of the Clinton administration; in the Obama administration, he was forced into the limited role of a character actor. To the Clintons and their associates, Holbrooke was Our Crowd; to the Obama administration he was Their Crowd.

Bill Clinton gave a speech that was typically effusive ("I loved the guy. . . . If you knew him, you had to love him"), but also pointed and obliquely political, with remarks that could have been construed as critical of Obama: Although Holbrooke had a few "rough edges," the former president said, "I could never understand people who didn't appreciate him." (Left unsaid was that Bill Clinton himself had passed over Holbrooke for secretary of state at least twice, in 1992 and 1996—three times, if one includes the time in 1994 that Clinton tried unsuccessfully to bring in Colin Powell as secretary of state.) Hillary Clinton, her face strikingly animated, both warm and sad, spoke of Holbrooke in personal terms, smiling at his foibles: "He'd walk into meetings to which he was not invited, act like he was meant to be there, and just start talking." When he did something no one else would do, she said, she and her associates would just say, "That's Richard being Richard."

It was Obama who sought to put Holbrooke into a broader context, one that went beyond his personality. He depicted Holbrooke against the background of American foreign policy and the generational changes within it. Obama said of Holbrooke:

> In many ways, he was the leading light of a generation of American diplomats who came of age in Vietnam. It was a generation that came to know both the tragic limits and awesome possibilities of American power—born at a time of triumph in World War II, steeped in the painful lessons of Southeast Asia, participants in the struggle that led ultimately to freedom's triumph during the Cold War.[13]

It was hard to escape the implication that Obama, his team and his speechwriters felt that they were of a new and different generation, past Vietnam and the Cold War, facing a new era of constraints that Holbrooke would never see.

In the days afterward, some of Holbrooke's friends and the Clinton crowd murmured privately that Obama had been off-key, that he seemed too aloof in speaking about Holbrooke, that he had been graceful but a bit stinting with his praise. After a few more months, Holbrooke's friends and family became more public in criticizing the Obama White House. He "was effectively gagged, unable to comment on what he saw as missteps of the Obama administration that he served," wrote one columnist.[14]

Holbrooke had indeed been gagged, prevented from appearing on news shows or talking on the record to the news media—although had he been allowed to appear, he would almost certainly have publicly praised and defended the administration in which he served. From the perspective of the Obama White House, Holbrooke had been reined in because, merely by appearing regularly on the talk shows, he would have called attention to himself, assumed more power than the president and his aides were willing to yield. They did not want Holbrooke to shape the stories that were written or told about the administration, the narratives that they wanted to control on their own. It turned out that the only drama in which Holbrooke had the lead role during the Obama administration was his own tragedy.

Holbrooke's widow, Kati Marton, told the columnist Nicholas Kristof that Holbrooke had compared Afghanistan to Vietnam. "He thought that this could become Obama's Vietnam," she said. "Some of the conversations in the Situation Room reminded him of conversations in the Johnson White House. When he raised that, Obama didn't want to hear it." [15]

He certainly didn't.

17

Hillary Clinton's "Miracle" Speech

Hillary Clinton had a rough first year as secretary of state. Five months into her new job, she fractured her right elbow in the basement of the State Department as she was heading to her car for a White House meeting with President Obama. As she recuperated, she was briefly forced to run her department from her home and canceled two trips to Europe, including one with Obama to Moscow. The incident led to a variety of Letterman-style jokes, including one from the president himself. At a big Washington dinner, Obama wished Clinton a speedy recovery and then jibed: "While it's been reported as an accident, there were some suspicious circumstances. Just before the incident, the Secret Service spotted Richard Holbrooke spraying WD-40 all over the driveway."[1]

Clinton had to learn the new job, the tone and idiom required of her as secretary of state, the reactions she would get as she spoke to various audiences. On her first trip to China, she had engendered considerable criticism for her line that she wouldn't dwell on human rights because the Chinese knew what the Americans would say. As she often did, Clinton was focusing on the task immediately at hand, choosing the short-term, tactical approach. She was doing what she felt was necessary to establish an initial relationship with China—almost like a presidential candidate visiting a state and appealing to a constituency by using words it wanted to hear. What she said about human rights wasn't meant to be taken as a major change in policy, her aides later explained; moreover, everyone should have known from her background and long career that she cared about human rights, no matter what she was saying at that moment. When it turned out that quite a few people in the United States and China took her words as a sign the Obama administration would downgrade human rights in dealing with China, she was surprised and avoided repeating the line.[2]

At first she had to be brought up to speed on the details and history underlying many of the issues with which she was dealing. "She's not a foreign policy wonk," observed one old friend. "You know, she started doing foreign policy when she was sixty-one years old. She's basically using her intelligence, her diligence, her strength, her political skills." She relied often on private advice from leading foreign policy figures from Bill Clinton's administration—Holbrooke, Madeleine Albright, Strobe Talbott and Sandy Berger.

Above all, Clinton had to struggle to figure out the Obama White House and to overcome the sense of being kept in check by Obama's inner circle. She took care to avoid outward signs of disagreement with Obama. She had long ago learned, as First Lady of Arkansas and then of the United States, to stand alongside Bill Clinton and nod her head regularly in approval. Now, as secretary of state, she learned how to pepper her speeches with the phrase "As President Obama has said . . . ," demonstrating that she was not an independent actor and knew who was boss. Although she had come close to defeating Obama in the previous year's primaries, she was a loyal, deferential secretary of state.

Still, she sometimes chafed at the limits put on her—if not by Obama, then at least by others in the White House. She battled with the Obama team over appointments, particularly ambassadorships. She wanted to appoint Joseph Nye, a prominent foreign policy specialist with expertise in Asia, to be ambassador to Japan. Instead, Obama appointed John Roos, a California lawyer who had been a leading contributor to the Obama campaign. She gave the White House a list of several other ambassadorial appointments she sought, and only one of them was approved.

That first summer, there was a wave of "Where's Hillary?" stories. They were started by Tina Brown, a longtime admirer of the Clintons, who wrote on her *Daily Beast* website: "It's time for Barack Obama to let Hillary Clinton take off her burqa."

"You could say that Obama is lucky to have such a great foreign policy wife," Brown concluded. Nevertheless, she added, "Those who voted for

Clinton wonder how long she'll be content with an office wifehood of the Saudi variety."[3]

Clinton quickly denied that the Obama White House was muzzling her. "I broke my elbow, not my larynx," she told reporters.[4]

———

In mid-December 2009, Vietnam's defense minister, General Phung Quang Thanh, paid a brief visit to Washington. The United States and Vietnam had agreed to hold top-level defense talks every three years, alternating between Hanoi and Washington, and Thanh's trip was part of the series. Vietnam was eager to improve its military relationship with the United States. It was worried about China's growing assertiveness in the South China Sea, where Vietnam and China (as well as the Philippines, Taiwan, Malaysia, Indonesia, and Brunei) had territorial claims. The underlying issue was economic: The South China Sea has oil and natural gas deposits. That year, China had warned international oil and gas companies to halt exploration in offshore areas near Vietnam. China had also increased its sea patrols and completed a submarine base on Hainan Island. Vietnam was looking overseas for as much military help as possible: At the same time Thanh was in Washington, Vietnam's prime minister, Nguyen Tan Dung, was in Moscow, finishing a deal to buy Russian submarines.[5]

These developments received virtually no media coverage in the United States. The holiday season was approaching, Congress was wrapping up for the year and Obama was off at the UN climate talks in Copenhagen. There was in any event little to report. The talks with Vietnam were of no immediate consequence: There were no arms deals, no major policy pronouncements. Vietnam sought America's explicit support in its bilateral territorial disputes with China. Pentagon officials said they couldn't go that far.[6]

Nevertheless, those talks were an initial step in a chain of events that would cause the Obama administration to stiffen its foreign policy noticeably during its second and third years in office. China would play a prominent role in the story of the administration's gradual turnaround. So would Hillary Clinton.

Some officials in the Pentagon had begun to worry about Obama's incoming China policy. The new administration had been determined to avoid early friction with Beijing. The Chinese read the administration's stance this way: Every issue was negotiable, and now was the time to push. Chinese leaders and the state-controlled press began to describe Taiwan, Tibet and Xinjiang as part of the country's "core interests"—places where China had claims of sovereignty that other countries should recognize.[7] A few weeks before the U.S.-Vietnam defense talks, a scholar at China's National Defense University described the South China Sea as yet another "core interest" that should be accommodated.

Those who wanted Obama to take a firmer line in dealing with China were mistrustful of Deputy Secretary of State Jim Steinberg, who sought to minimize conflict with Beijing. For his own part, Steinberg, who had become involved in China policy for the first time during Bill Clinton's administration, believed he was merely applying the lessons he had learned then: Don't make threats, don't apply public pressure and the Chinese will do at least some of what you want. Pentagon officials were also wary of Deputy National Security Adviser Tom Donilon, who seemed uneasy about antagonizing China at a time when the administration was seeking its help in stopping Iran's nuclear program. Donilon and Steinberg were the two officials most closely involved with day-to-day, working-level decision making in foreign policy. Pentagon officials believed that if they could somehow elevate China policy to the cabinet level of Clinton and Defense Secretary Robert Gates, they could at least get a sympathetic hearing.

On several occasions over the following six months, China flaunted its growing naval power. At one point, Chinese ships made an unprecedented port call in the Middle East. On another, a large flotilla of Chinese destroyers and submarines came close to Japan while en route to the Pacific.[8] Meanwhile, Chinese officials rebuffed both Obama and Gates on military issues. When Obama asked President Hu Jintao to condemn North Korea for its deadly torpedo attack on the South Korean warship *Cheonan*, he got nowhere. Gates sought permission to visit China for military talks, but made little headway on that for months. At a gathering in Singapore of defense officials from twenty-eight countries in Asia and the Pacific, Gates had a chilly public exchange with the deputy chief of general staff of the Chinese People's Liberation Army.

Hillary Clinton had already demonstrated that she was considerably more willing to confront China than she had been on her initial trip there. At the beginning of 2010, she delivered a speech on the increasingly important and contentious issue of Internet freedom around the world. She criticized various countries' barriers to the free flow of information and their detention of bloggers. In particular, she condemned the use of the Internet to monitor and silence the activities of political and religious dissidents.

A year later, this speech would seem particularly prescient, because among the first countries she singled out were Tunisia and Egypt. But the country to which Clinton devoted the most attention in her speech was China. A week before, Google publicly threatened to pull out of China because of cyberattacks on its e-mail system and the targeting of Chinese dissidents and human rights activists. Clinton's response was swift and pointed: She called on the Chinese government to investigate the attacks on Google. Countries that engage in such attacks "should face consequences and international condemnation," she said. (One senior State Department official said there had been internal tensions over the speech; those who were eager to avoid conflict with China, "hated it—absolutely hated it," the official said.)[9]

In the six months following Clinton's Internet speech, China had repeatedly irked the Obama administration. American newspapers, magazines and scholarly journals were beginning to fill up with stories about a new Chinese "assertiveness" in dealing with the world. China rejected requests to revalue its currency, which it held at low values to increase exports. China continued to imprison prominent dissidents such as Liu Xiaobo, a Nobel Prize winner, rebuffing private appeals for their release. It refused to rein in North Korea. At the United Nations, it fought successfully to water down economic sanctions aimed at stopping Iran's nuclear program. It took a harder line in dealing with Japan, Vietnam and the Philippines. Chinese officials and scholars kept declaring that the entire South China Sea represented a "core interest" for China.

On July 23, 2010, Clinton responded. She was attending a routine annual meeting of the Association of Southeast Asian Nations (ASEAN), where there is a forum on security issues. Ordinarily, these gatherings are dull, sleepy affairs in which foreign ministers try as hard as possible to avoid conflict. The most interesting event at ASEAN is usually the end-of-session entertainment in which, by custom, ministers and secretaries of state sing, dance or otherwise perform to help their fellow diplomats overcome their growing sense of ennui.

This particular meeting was held in Hanoi, the capital of the country most concerned about China's expansive maritime claims. Vietnam quickly brought up the subject of the South China Sea, and several other Southeast Asian countries followed. Clinton, speaking last, took her audience by surprise. Freedom of navigation was a "national interest" of the United States, she said—a phrase that sounded like a counter to China's talk about "core interests." She said the United States was determined to maintain open access to the South China Sea, in effect rejecting China's claims to sovereignity there. Much of the world's shipping tonnage—including oil from the Middle East to northeast Asia—passes through the South China Sea. Clinton said the United States would be willing to serve as an intermediary or facilitator for multilateral talks over the competing claims.[10]

China's foreign minister, Yang Jiechi, was his government's most experienced, polished America hand. He had started in the late 1970s, serving as a young escort and translator for out-of-office Republican leaders (a delegation headed by George H. W. Bush and James Baker) on a visit to Tibet. He had become a good friend of the Bush family; as a result, he was designated to carry secret messages from Beijing to the White House after the Tiananmen Square crackdown and served as ambassador to Washington during the presidency of George W. Bush.

At the Hanoi gathering, Hillary Clinton's speech caught Yang off guard. The United States was, in effect, rejecting China's claims in the South China Sea. Its suggestion of multilateral talks also undercut China's strategy of dealing one-on-one with each Southeast Asian country in a way that favored Beijing; it was Vietnam that had most eagerly sought to "internationalize" its dispute with China. Yang was furious. He left the conference for an hour and, on his return, launched into a diatribe against the United States for orchestrating opposition to China. To other Southeast Asian leaders, he warned: "China is a big country, and other countries are small countries, and that's just a fact."[11] Over the following weeks, China felt compelled to repeat its claims to sovereignty over the entire South China Sea.

The impact was considerable. Clinton's initiative helped crystallize a change in the diplomacy of East Asia. Over the previous few years, other governments in Asia had been drifting closer to China, in part attracted by Chinese overtures and also intimidated by China's growing economic and military power. The most prominent example was Japan, where a new ruling party, the Democratic Party of Japan, talked about lessening its dependence on the United States and upgrading its ties with China. Similar dynamics came into play in South Korea and elsewhere.

But by the fall of 2010, after the ASEAN gathering, it was clear that Clinton had thrown this trend into reverse. Asian governments, eager to offset China's power and influence, began moving back closer to the United States. Japan began seeking not to undermine its military alliance with America but to strengthen it. This turnabout in Asia was precisely what the Obama administration had sought to achieve. In one public appearance that fall, Kurt Campbell, assistant secretary of state for East Asia and the Pacific, depicted Clinton's speech as merely one in a series of initiatives by the administration to "deeply step up our game" in Asia and the Pacific. "I think there is now an emerging recognition in Asia that the United States is going to play an important and indeed dominant role in the Asia-Pacific region for the next forty, thirty, fifty years," Campbell said.

Campbell went on to give a global perspective to the message that Clinton's Asia diplomacy was meant to convey. There was some talk that the United States was in decline, but those who accepted this idea were shortsighted, Campbell said. Predictions of American decline had been made before— after the end of the Cold War and after the Vietnam War, for example. They had always proved wrong in the past, and they would prove wrong again.

"I think there is a general recognition," Campbell said, "that you underestimate American power at your peril."[12]

———

Hillary Clinton went one step further—and, in the process, brought out a shade of difference between her own underlying view of America's role in the world and that of Barack Obama.

The two were no longer campaigning against each other; indeed, they had forged a surprisingly smooth working relationship. If there were any specific policy disagreements between them, they remained well concealed. But when they spoke in broader, philosophical terms about American foreign policy, Obama and Clinton sometimes seemed to have different emphases, different priorities and different tones.

On August 31, 2010, in a televised address to the nation, Obama announced the formal end of American combat operations in Iraq. For the president, the speech represented the fulfillment both of a 2008 campaign promise and of the much longer effort to end the Iraq War, a goal he'd laid out as a state senator speaking in Chicago nearly eight years earlier. "It's time to turn the page," Obama said in his speech to the nation. Moving quickly to domestic issues, he declared:

> And so at this moment, as we wind down the war in Iraq, we must tackle those challenges at home with as much energy, and grit, and sense of common purpose as our men and women in uniform who have served abroad. They have met every test that they faced. Now, it's our turn.[13]

Here, Obama was putting forward a new version of the idea he had raised in his West Point speech on Afghanistan nine months earlier. ("The nation that I am most interested in building is our own," he had said back then.) He was also seeking to counteract the predictable criticism, heard whenever any president seems to be spending a lot of time on foreign affairs, that he should instead be addressing problems at home. That line had helped Bill Clinton to oust George H. W. Bush in 1992. In the spring of 2010, the U.S. economy seemed to be on the way to recovery, but it stalled in the summer, and at the time of Obama's announcement about Iraq, America's news media were covering the worrisome economic news far more than the war in Iraq. The news coverage furthered the sense of finality underlying the president's announcement. "Was Obama's Speech 'Mission Accomplished'?" the *Washington Post* asked in a headline, alluding to the phrase that George W. Bush had prematurely used when American troops overran Iraq in 2003.[14]

Something was missing from Obama's speech, and as secretary of state, Hillary Clinton worried about it. Besides Iraq, Obama had mentioned only one other place overseas, Afghanistan—and he did so only in promising that American troops fighting there would come home, too. The president had talked about "making sure that we honor our commitments." That phrase, "our commitments," was regularly used in foreign policy discourse to describe America's obligations to its allies. In this case, however, the only "commitments" Obama mentioned were to the American soldiers coming home, not to other countries.

Clinton was coincidentally scheduled to give a speech of her own eight days later. She wanted to fill the gap and say the things that Obama's speech had left out. The president did not address America's continuing role in the world. She had only recently come back from Asia, where she'd tried to send the message to China's neighbors that the United States would remain an active and powerful nation overseas. Now she wanted to broaden the message and make clear it extended beyond Asia. She didn't want Obama's speech to be misinterpreted overseas as a sign that America was in retreat, that it would bring its troops home and turn inward.

In her own address, given to the Council on Foreign Relations, Clinton began by saying that the world's problems required bringing people together "as only America can." Foreign leaders and ordinary people overseas "look to America not just to engage, but to lead," she said. Then she quickly came to the heart of her speech: "Let me say it clearly: The United States can, must and will lead in this new century."[15]

This was a "New American Moment," Clinton said, the words capitalized in the transcript of the speech to indicate a special phrase meant to be highlighted. It was "a moment when our global leadership is essential, even if we must often lead in new ways." The words seemed reminiscent of Henry Luce's famous 1941 invocation of "the American century," although Clinton made the more modest claim that it was only an American moment and then separately spoke of U.S. leadership through the twenty-first century. She went on to describe the importance of deepening America's alliances, especially NATO. When she extolled the virtues of diplomacy, she immediately added, "Of course, this administration is also committed to maintaining the greatest military in the history of the world and, if needed, to vigorously defend ourselves and our friends."[16]

Her aides said Clinton had taken an unusually active role in drafting this particular speech, not only setting the broad themes but also choosing the specific language. It was Clinton herself who had come up with the passage about "America's Moment." One aide jokingly dubbed it Hillary Clinton's "Miracle" speech, alluding to the 2004 movie *Miracle* about the American hockey team that defeated the Soviets in the 1980 Olympics.[17] (In the movie's climactic scene, American hockey coach Herb Brooks, played by Kurt Russell, gives a pep talk to his players: "Tonight, we are the greatest hockey team in the world. . . . This is your time. Now go out there and take it.")

Looking back, Clinton's speech may have attracted an unusual Republican admirer. In the fall of 2011, when Mitt Romney delivered his first major speech on foreign policy in his campaign for the Republican presidential nomination, he proclaimed, as though it were his personal inspiration, "This is America's moment!" At another point, Romney declared: "This century must be an American century!" He, too, argued that the world needs American leadership. Perhaps he and his speechwriters were borrowing from Clinton and Luce, or perhaps someone on their team had seen the movie *Miracle*.[18]

Clinton's speech was a throwback, a revival of the themes of past administrations and past American leaders dating back to the World War II era. Her assertion that other nations were looking to the United States for leadership recalled the description of America as the "indispensable nation," the phrase Zbigniew Brzezinski had used in the 1970s and that both Madeleine Albright and Bill Clinton had made famous in the 1990s. Hillary Clinton's repeated invocation of American leadership echoed the ideas of presidents from Franklin Roosevelt and Harry Truman to Bill Clinton and George W. Bush. What constituted leadership was, of course, often a matter of dispute; but in general, American presidents and secretaries of state were accustomed to speaking in the same idiom, reminding the American people and other major powers regularly that the United States was the world's predominant (and most benevolent) power.

Clinton drew her inspiration from the past, from the time after World War II when the United States was unquestionably the world's leading military and economic power. She sought to maintain that role and to remind the world of America's continuing strength. If there was a single book that encapsulated the ideas and attitudes underlying Clinton's speech, it would have been *The Wise Men,* an account of the foreign policy leaders, such as Dean Acheson, George Kennan and Averell Harriman, who helped set America's course in the late 1940s and early 1950s.[19]

Obama, by contrast, looked ahead to a time when the United States, with all its economic problems, might no longer be able to maintain predominance. He focused on redirecting America's resources and energy toward domestic renewal. His United States would manage to work out a new, more modest international role in line with its new circumstances: its still awesome military power but diminishing economic power. The ideas underlying Obama's foreign policy were those of Paul Kennedy's book, *The Rise and Fall of the Great Powers.* Kennedy's great powers became overstretched in their military commitments yet were unable to give them up, and they eventually lost their dominant roles. This was the fate of Spain and the Netherlands in the eighteenth and nineteenth centuries and Britain and France in the twentieth.[20] Obama sought to avoid the trap into which these countries fell.

This is not to say that Obama and Clinton gave dueling speeches or offered foreign policies that were in direct conflict with one another. They didn't. In her address to the Council on Foreign Relations, Clinton also spoke about the importance of reviving America's economic strength. Obama, in his Iraq speech, didn't mention the continuing importance of American "leadership," but he did so on other occasions. To some extent, their different perspectives can be explained by the fact that Clinton and Obama were carrying out different jobs: Clinton, as secretary of state, was directly responsible for foreign policy and not the domestic economy; Obama, as president, was accountable to voters for all of American policy, including above all the domestic economy.

Nevertheless, the differences in tone between Obama and Clinton were significant, because they seemed to reflect different sets of ideas for dealing with the world. Obama, both in his campaign for the presidency and early in his presidency, had made "engagement" the central theme of his foreign policy. Under engagement, the United States would focus on dialogue, face-to-face meetings and exchanges of views with other countries, whether Iran or China, Pakistan or Russia.

Clinton, in her first major speech as secretary of state in 2009, had also embraced the idea of what she called "principled engagement." But now, a

year later, she spoke of the limits of engagement and the need for more assertive policies—other countries "look to America *not just to engage, but to
lead*," she said (emphasis hers). So, too, in the first year of the administration
both Obama and Clinton stressed the importance of rising powers such as
China, India, Russia and Brazil. But in her "Miracle" speech Clinton gave
first priority to "our closest allies, the nations that share our most fundamental values and interests, and our commitment to solving common problems."[21]

In short, Clinton's "Miracle" speech envisioned a world in which, despite
its economic difficulties, the United States would continue to lead, would
remain as active and powerful overseas as before and would continue to view
itself as the world's indispensable nation. Obama, in some of his own
speeches, hinted that America's post–World War II role was time-bound and
now in doubt. ("The United States of America has helped underwrite global
security for more than six decades with the blood of our citizens and the
strength of our arms," was Obama's formulation in his address accepting the
Nobel Peace Prize, leaving unanswered how much longer it would do so.
He had said virtually the same thing in his speech announcing the dispatch
of troops to Afghanistan.)[22]

The different emphases between the two leaders reflected the broader
disagreements in America over its role in the world. One high-ranking administration official, who admired both Obama and Clinton and would
speak only anonymously about differences between them, analyzed it this
way: "You can divide up this town into people who believe that the world
revolves around the United States, that other countries wake up in the morning thinking about the United States, and other people who don't think
that. . . . Hillary Clinton thinks of the United States as the world's indispensable nation, as the world's leader. She's still rooted in the Clinton administration of the 1990s. And fundamentally, Barack Obama doesn't think that
way. That's the difference between them."[23]

_____

By late 2010, Obama's own speeches were beginning to evolve. He was never
as comfortable as Clinton with talking about, and embracing, American
power. And when he took office, he was also uncomfortable talking about
the spread of democracy and freedom. Now he was more willing to do so.

At the United Nations General Assembly on September 23, 2010, Obama raised two fundamental questions: "What are we trying to build over the long term? What is the world that awaits us when today's battles are brought to an end?" It was the closest he had ever come to laying out where American policy was headed after the end of the wars in Iraq and Afghanistan.

Obama's answer to his own questions was surprising, particularly in light of the realism he had previously displayed in dealing with countries like Iran, China and Egypt. The United States, he said, believes in human rights, individual freedoms and justice; America would seek to foster these values overseas as "a matter of moral and pragmatic necessity":

> We stand up for universal values because it is the right thing to do. But we also know from experience that those who defend these values for their people have been our closest friends and allies, while those who have denied these rights—whether terrorist groups or tyrannical governments— have chosen to be our adversaries.[24]

Obama also debunked "the false notion that economic growth can come at the expense of freedom" or that human rights should be set aside for the purpose of short-term stability. He proceeded to give a ringing endorsement to the virtues of political liberty and democracy:

> The strongest foundation for human progress lies in open economies, open societies and open governments. To put it simply, democracy, more than any other form of government, delivers for our citizens. . . . The arc of human progress has been shaped by individuals with the freedom to assemble; by organizations outside of government that insisted upon democratic change; and by free media that held the powerful accountable. . . . There is no right more fundamental than the ability to choose your leaders and determine your destiny.[25]

These were not words that would go down easily with those who held power in Beijing or Cairo or Riyadh.

Some of Obama's aides, such as Michael McFaul, a determined proponent of spreading democracy, had been arguing since 2009 that Obama's critics were wrong—that the president believed in the importance of democracy and had in fact said so on a number of occasions; they could supply the citations to prove it. But in the past, democracy and human rights had been discussed only carefully, briefly and gingerly. Obama had not been eager to provoke the leaders of other countries, like China, Egypt and Saudi Arabia. Moreover, in political terms, he sought to avoid sounding too much like George W. Bush. His own close advisers admitted at the time that the UN speech in 2010 did represent a fundamental change, a turning point.

"The most important thing we needed to do, particularly in that first year, was to repair the damage" from the Iraq War, Ben Rhodes, who drafted the speech for Obama, explained a few days later. "We had a long way to come back, to restore America's luster in the world. If we had just come in, guns blazing on democracy, without having taken steps to restore America's appeal and America's example, we'd have been less able to advocate for democracy. So I do think this moment is a natural pivot point."[26]

Still, it was unclear how much Obama really meant by his strong words on human rights and democracy in his UN speech, and how much represented mere rhetoric. Did it signify an actual change in the administration's policies, or would Obama stick to the realist approach he had pursued early in his administration?

No one had the slightest idea then of the tumultuous events that would confront Obama over the following year. Obama's proclaimed belief in the importance of democracy and human rights would be put to the test at a historic moment both for the Middle East and for America's changing role as a superpower.

18

"Now Means Yesterday"

Late in November of 2010, the *New York Times,* the *Guardian* of Great Britain and Germany's *Der Spiegel* began publishing an extensive series of stories based on classified cables obtained by the website Wikileaks. Most of the cables had been sent from American embassies around the world to Washington. They represented the State Department's internal reporting on each country, setting forth both facts and opinions that the U.S. government hadn't offered in public. The news stories based on these cables were long and detailed, with extensive quotes and commentary revealing the State Department's internal views of each country's leaders.

The media reaction to these stories concentrated heavily on Wikileaks itself, its founder, Julian Assange, and the process by which the cables became public. The substance of the cables got much less attention—perhaps because the information was so rich in detail that news organizations found it hard to absorb. The reaction of one editor exemplified the common perception in the United States toward the Wikileaks cables: "I'm not saying they are ho-hum, but there's no huge bombshell that's going to turn everyone's head 180 degrees."[1]

As a result, it was easy to overlook the impact of the Wikileaks cables overseas, particularly in smaller countries where autocratic rulers were described in unflattering terms. America's senior officials recognized the significance of the leaks more easily than the media because they were obliged to deal with the fallout—the furious protests from presidents and prime ministers whose foibles and private conversations were brought to light. Secretary of State Hillary Clinton, who traveled abroad much more often than other senior officials, joked to an aide while on a trip to the Middle East that she should wear a jacket like that of a traveling rock band, bearing an image of a globe with the words "The Apology Tour" surrounding it. "I think I will be answering concerns about Wikileaks for the rest of my life, not just my tenure as secretary of state," Clinton told reporters.[2]

One of the countries in the Wikileaks release was Tunisia. The cables sent from the American embassy in Tunis attracted extremely little press coverage in the United States or Europe. Indeed, in its admirably long and detailed coverage of the Wikileaks files, the *New York Times* did not do a story on Tunisia or even mention it. Neither, at first, did *Der Spiegel* or the *Guardian*.

The Arabic-language press had the time and motivation to look more closely. In early December, a Beirut newspaper called *al-Akhbar* began publishing sets of cables from eight U.S. embassies in the Middle East, including Tunisia.[3] One cable from the American ambassador in Tunisia said that President Zine el Abidine Ben Ali and his regime had "lost touch" with the people of Tunisia. Ben Ali and his family and associates operated like a "quasi mafia," another said. The embassy gave one of its reports to Washington the title "Corruption in Tunisia: What's Yours Is Mine."

In 2008, the embassy in Tunis reported that "seemingly half of the Tunisian business community can claim a Ben Ali connection through marriage, and many of these relations are reported to have made the most of their lineages." In mid-2009, Ambassador Robert Godec wrote:

> Corruption in the inner circle is growing. Even average Tunisians are now keenly aware of it, and the chorus of complaints is rising. Tunisians intensely dislike, even hate, first lady Leila Trabelsi and her family. . . . Meanwhile, anger is growing at Tunisia's high unemployment and regional inequities. As a consequence, the risks to the regime's long-term stability are increasing.[4]

If these damning judgments lacked detail, other embassy cables included those, too. One of them described a dinner at the home of Ben Ali's son-in-law, a leading businessman in Tunisia. The household included a large caged tiger. Ben Ali's daughter served frozen yogurt and ice cream flown in by private plane from St. Tropez, where the couple had recently been on vacation.[5]

Tunisia maintained a system of Internet censorship as extensive as those of China and Iran. When the cables began to appear on the website of *al-Akhbar*, Tunisian authorities blocked the website within a few days. At that point, in early December, the *Guardian* took notice and published a story about Tunisia, first describing the blocking of the Beirut website but then also summarizing what the American embassy had said in its cables. The effect of all these stories, in Arabic and in English, was to give validation from abroad—indeed, indirectly from the United States government itself—to the long-standing grievances of ordinary Tunisians.[6]

On December 17, Mohamed Bouazizi, an unemployed young man working as a peddler of fruits and vegetables, set himself on fire when police seized his goods on grounds that he had no permit. The incident touched off ten days of demonstrations in Bouazizi's town of Sidi Bouzid. The protests soon spread to other cities, where workers and young people, many of them well educated but unemployed, joined in. By the end of December, the demonstrations reached Tunis, the capital, where protesters began to skirmish with police and set fire to police cars and government buildings.[7] The Mideast TV network Al Jazeera began to give extensive, ever increasing coverage to Tunisia.

Washington was caught by surprise, as was the rest of the world, by Tunisia's sudden upheaval. But Obama administration officials had for several months been holding formal discussions on the precise problem of how to foster political reform in the Middle East. The previous summer Obama had signed a document known as Presidential Study Directive 11. It ordered officials from throughout the foreign policy bureaucracy—the State and Defense Departments, the CIA, the National Security Council and others—to study ways of promoting change in various Middle Eastern countries and how to encourage Arab leaders to open up their authoritarian regimes. The directive cited "evidence of growing citizen discontent with the region's regimes." The Middle East was entering a period of transition, the directive said. Administration officials were thinking above all of Egypt, where aging President Hosni Mubarak had spurned all appeals to ease his repression of political opposition.[8]

The genesis of Obama's PSD-11 reflected in many ways the ideas and concerns of the leading proponents of democracy within the National

Security Council, among them Samantha Power, Michael McFaul and Ben Rhodes. The meetings were headed by Dennis Ross, the senior NSC aide with the greatest experience in dealing with the Middle East, who had been a leading player in the administration's overall policy toward the region since Obama's Cairo speech of 2009. As explained by participants, the underlying logic was simple. When the U.S. government thinks about liberalization in the Middle East, it is usually during a crisis, and the need for political change is quickly weighed against competing concerns, notably military or commercial interests. PSD-11 essentially called upon the bureaucracy to put aside the question of trade-offs and to focus on the need for political change itself.

"The premise of the directive was that there were profound costs to allowing the status quo," said Power. "We were going to have to deal soon with the political succession in Egypt, and the social drivers of discontent were becoming uncontainable. It was clear that it was just getting harder and harder to keep a lid on things. We were more and more implicated by our friendships with authoritarian regimes that were using ever more brutal tactics to repress their people."[9]

In short, the Obama team was coming to recognize that authoritarian leaders like Ben Ali (who had run Tunisia for twenty-three years) and Mubarak (who had held power for thirty years) were no longer a force for stability in the Middle East. Their regimes were increasingly shaky, and there was a strong argument that the United States could serve its own long-term interests by identifying itself with the forces for change.

The first clear public indication of these internal deliberations came in a speech by Hillary Clinton. During a visit to the Middle East, Clinton participated in a forum in Doha, Qatar, on the subject of political change. "While some countries have made great strides in governance, in many others people have grown tired of corrupt institutions and a stagnant political order," she said in remarks that were carefully prepared in advance. "This is a critical moment, and this is a test of leadership for all of us." Later on, in response to questions, she drove still harder her message about the impact of corruption:

> It is a costly, frustrating process to open and run a business in many of the countries in [the Middle East and North Africa]. You know this better

than I do. Trying to get a permit, you have to pass money through so many different hands. Trying to open up, you have to pay people off. Trying to stay open, you have to pay people off. Trying to export your goods, you have to pay people off. So by the time you finish paying everyone off, it's not a very profitable venture.[10]

Clinton never mentioned Tunisia, where by this time tanks and security forces were on the streets of the capital, trying to quell the continuing upheaval. But she didn't need to: Tunisia was a near perfect paradigm of the corruption and resistance to change about which she was speaking. News organizations immediately applied Clinton's words to Tunisia. "The United States has tacitly thrown its support behind the protesters," said one typical story.[11]

Two days later, with huge throngs of Tunisians still in the streets even after security forces had tried shooting at them, Ben Ali and his family fled to Saudi Arabia. Obama quickly urged the new government to hold elections that "reflect the true will and aspirations" of the Tunisian people. Those words calling for elections were themselves of some significance, because they went beyond the usual diplomatic message simply welcoming a new government and expressing a willingness to work with it.[12]

Ben Ali was the first Arab leader in modern times to be forced from office by street demonstrations (although Iran, a non-Arab country, had witnessed similar events during the revolution against the Shah thirty-two years earlier). Arab-language television, the Internet and social networks like Facebook and Twitter had all contributed heavily to the protest movement. One protester in Tunis held a sign that said, "Thank you, Al Jazeera."[13]

Immediately, the focus shifted to the question of whether other Middle Eastern leaders might also be vulnerable. Many of the same factors that had played a role in Ben Ali's downfall were also present elsewhere. Al Jazeera was broadcast throughout the region, and social networking had taken hold. People elsewhere were faced with problems similar to Tunisia's, including corruption, political repression, a narrow ruling elite and widespread unemployment.

In the days immediately after Ben Ali fled, there were several cases of self-immolation, similar to the one by Bouazizi, in Algeria, Mauritania and, finally, Egypt. One message on Twitter, posted only minutes after the Tunisian leader had stepped down, caught the spirit of the moment. "Today, Ben Ali," it said. "Tomorrow, Hosni Mubarak."[14]

———

Egypt represented the second major test of Obama's willingness to support democratic change. The first was in 2009, when he had remained steadfastly aloof from Iran's Green Movement, saying as little as possible while large numbers of citizens took to the streets day after day to protest the results of an apparently rigged presidential election. In Egypt in 2011, Obama was confronted with a seemingly similar situation: a growing series of demonstrations aimed at opening the way for democracy.

Yet there were other important respects in which Egypt was not like the Iran of 2009. Egypt was a longtime American ally. Its military had longstanding ties to the Pentagon; many Egyptian military officers had gone to the United States for schooling or training. For decades, Mubarak had supported American positions in the Middle East and peaceful relations with Israel; the same could not be said of Ali Khamenei or Mahmoud Ahmadinejad, Iran's leaders. For Obama, Egypt raised the problem of how to deal with an increasingly unpopular dictator in a country closely tied to the United States. The closest comparison was the Shah of Iran before the Islamic Revolution of 1979. The events there had turned into an object lesson in how a political revolution can turn from liberal reform to religious repression—just what American leaders did not want to happen in Egypt.

The Obama administration was considerably less surprised by the unrest in Egypt than it had been by Tunisia. Because Egypt was of far greater strategic importance, American officials had been watching events there much more closely as Mubarak had repeatedly spurned appeals for change. In 2010, elections for Egypt's parliament had gone badly. Mubarak's security forces had disrupted the campaigns of candidates opposed to the regime and had arrested their supporters. "It was clear from the time of the parliamentary elections that something was going to happen there," said Deputy Secretary of State James Steinberg. "Everyone recognized that Egypt was going to be a crisis sometime in the next couple of years. There was a sense of imminence, but even when you know the underlying dynamics, you don't know exactly when things will come to a head."[15]

When the protests began in Egypt, they were determinedly peaceful. Some of the protesters had been studying the rules and tactics set down by Gene Sharp, an American scholar who had written a series of books describing the theory and practice of nonviolent revolution. Sharp's works, especially his book *From Dictatorship to Democracy*, amounted to a practical guide for how to apply the principles of Mahatma Gandhi. Don't try to fight with violence, because governments have a national advantage there, Sharp wrote. Work to undercut the legitimacy of a regime, so that when it resorts to violence, it is further weakened. "Despite the appearances of strength, all dictatorships have weaknesses," Sharp's book explains.[16]

Sharp had originally written *From Dictatorship to Democracy* in 1993 for the followers of Burma's democratic opposition after the jailing of Aung San Suu Kyi. The ideas in the book were next embraced in Indonesia by opponents of President Suharto and then by protesters in Serbia as they brought down President Slobodan Milosevic in 2000. Serbia was of particular significance because, over the following years, some of the young organizers of the revolution there, from the civic movement called Otpor, began to travel to other countries to train and help leaders of other democratic opposition movements. Sharp's book and Otpor's advice were influential in the "color revolutions" in Georgia and Ukraine and in the Green Movement in Iran in 2009. At the beginning of 2011, some of the Serbians from Otpor traveled to Tunisia to advise the democratic opposition there—and from Tunisia moved on to Egypt. In Cairo's Tahrir Square, protesters were seen distributing photocopies of possible tactics, taken directly out of *From Dictatorship to Democracy*.[17]

The Obama administration's initial reaction to the Egyptian unrest was muted. Officials were not quite so detached as they had been in Iran two years earlier, but nearly so. They proclaimed general support for the principles of freedom of speech and assembly, without saying anything about Mubarak's future. In an interview on the night of Thursday, January 27, 2011, Jim Lehrer of PBS *News Hour* asked Vice President Joe Biden whether Mubarak should step aside. Biden, who had spoken and met with Mubarak fairly often both as chairman of the Senate Foreign Relations Committee and as vice president, replied firmly, "No." When Lehrer asked if the United States should view Mubarak as a dictator, Biden replied that Mubarak had been a "very responsible" ally, particularly on peace with Israel.[18]

The following day, the crisis in Egypt exploded as the demonstrations spread through Egypt and then turned violent. Egyptians in Cairo, Alexandria and Suez emerged from mosques for a new round of protests. Riot police used tear gas and eventually bullets to try to disperse the crowds. In response, the demonstrators torched police stations and the headquarters of Egypt's ruling party. Mubarak called out the army to try to restore calm.[19] American officials were dismayed when some Arab news media reported that a good deal of the weaponry and ammunition used by the Egyptian army was made in America.

Obama met with his senior advisers and decided to step up the pressure by calling for political change in Egypt's government, without asking Mubarak to resign. Clinton was assigned to deliver the public message. That Sunday, in a series of TV news interviews, she called for an "orderly transition" in Egypt. Obama phoned Mubarak beforehand to tell him what the administration was about to say.[20] The president also approved a recommendation from Clinton and the State Department that an emissary be sent to talk privately to Mubarak. The person they selected was Frank Wisner Jr., a former Foreign Service officer who had served as ambassador to Egypt from 1986 to 1991 and knew Mubarak well. At Clinton's suggestion, he was sent to Cairo to give Mubarak a message urging him to move decisively toward that "transition."

Wisner's mission, however, failed to produce the sort of change Obama was seeking. The demonstrations continued to grow. By the decisive day of February 1, there were hundreds of thousands of people in Tahrir Square. That afternoon, at a meeting of the National Security Council, Obama and cabinet-level officials from all the foreign policy agencies wrestled with what to do or say next. Should Obama call Mubarak again? Should he make some further public statement?[21]

In the middle of their meeting, Mubarak went on television to give an address to the Egyptian nation. In the White House Situation Room, Obama and his aides stopped their meeting and silently watched him. Mubarak announced he would not run for president again, but did not go beyond that. That meant he would stay in office until the elections later that year. It also left the door open for Mubarak to stay in effective control in Egypt even after a cosmetic "transition." He would be free to hand over power to Omar

Suleiman, his intelligence chief and newly appointed vice president. He could also rig the election to ensure victory for someone personally loyal to him, such as his son Gamal.

In the speech, Mubarak also denounced foreign interference in Egypt. "The speech was cloaked in so much bombastic rhetoric," said Ben Rhodes, who attended the meeting in the Situation Room. "It wasn't coupled with concrete actions like lifting the emergency law. He didn't say his son wouldn't run for office. It was a very unsatisfying presentation."[22] When the White House meeting resumed, Obama said he thought he should call Mubarak and tell him to resign.

This was the decisive moment. The previous calls for a "transition" had still left that word undefined. It had been unclear whether Mubarak should stay on the job, and there had been continuing disagreements within the administration on that question. Other participants, pointing out that Mubarak had been America's ally, asked the president if he was sure. Obama said he thought there was no way Egypt could go back to the way it was. The opposition to Mubarak was too strong and too far along.

There was no time to prepare talking points for Obama's phone call. The call would have to be made on the fly. The president called Mubarak and said the United States believed it was time for him to step aside. Mubarak resisted. He told Obama the United States did not understand Egyptian culture, that it was necessary for him to remain in power to preside over the "transition," and that, in any case, the protests would probably die down in a few days. The conversation was becoming increasingly tense. "With all due respect," Obama countered, "we have a different analysis. We don't believe the protests are going to die down."

Mubarak argued that there was no way under the constitution for him to resign. "Mr. President," Obama told Mubarak, "I always respect my elders. You've been in politics for a very long time. There are moments in history that, just because things have been the same way in the past, doesn't mean they will be the same way in the future."[23]

Obama told Mubarak he was about to go on television to make a public statement, saying essentially the same thing he had just said in the phone call. The testy conversation came to an end. It was shortly after six p.m. in Washington, after midnight in Cairo.

In the White House, Obama went before television cameras to announce he had told President Mubarak that an orderly transition to a representative government "must begin now." Obama didn't want to say specifically in public that Mubarak should resign, Rhodes explained, because that decision was ultimately up to the Egyptian people and because Obama didn't want to appear to be interfering in Egypt's internal affairs. When reporters the next day rightly focused on the words "must begin now" and asked White House press secretary Robert Gibbs what "now" meant, Gibbs replied simply: "Now means yesterday."

———

As they surveyed the situation, administration officials realized that in dealing with Egypt, they had several advantages. America's biggest asset was the close military relationship between the two countries. Egyptian military leaders clearly did not want to get involved in the domestic crisis. They made plain they did not want Egyptian troops to fire on the demonstrators in Tahrir Square. At the same time, the army also did not want to push Mubarak from power. From the American perspective, the military's reluctance to move against Mubarak wasn't necessarily all bad: It showed that the military was stable and that there weren't some random officers or units ready to stage a coup d'état that might take the United States by surprise and turn in unpredictable directions.

Pentagon officials made regular phone calls to their friends and counterparts in the Egyptian military, utilizing relationships they had made in the past. Defense Secretary Robert Gates made a series of calls to Egyptian defense minister Mohamed Hussein Tantawi; Chairman of the Joint Chiefs of Staff Mike Mullen called Lieutenant General Sami Hafez Enan, the chief of staff of the Egyptian armed forces. "We were encouraging people all the way down the [U.S. military] chain of command, 'If you know an Egyptian officer, call them, tell them to urge restraint,'" recalled Rhodes. Meanwhile, other U.S. officials at the State Department and the American embassy in Cairo were calling Egyptian civilians inside and outside Mubarak's government to deliver similar messages.

Obama's appeals for Mubarak to step aside provoked strong reactions overseas and, to a lesser extent, inside the administration. Senior officials from Saudi Arabia and Israel weighed in hard at the upper levels in Washington.

Obama and Clinton "were really getting earfuls, from long-standing allies," said one senior U.S. official. The Saudis furiously opposed the decision to abandon Mubarak, who had been their close partner in the Middle East, particularly in countering the growing power of Iran. The gist of their message to Obama was: "What are you doing? Thirty years of friendship goes out the window in three days? What kind of friend is that?"[24]

The Israelis were, not surprisingly, worried about what a change in Egypt's government might mean for them: Would Mubarak's successors move to a more distant, even hostile relationship with Israel? The ire of the Israelis led to some unusual politics in the United States; for example, some foreign policy hawks agreed with Israel that it was wrong to push out Mubarak, while other hawks, holding to their generalized belief in spreading democracy, defended the Obama administration's decision to urge Mubarak to step down.

The administration worked out responses to the complaints that it was abandoning a longtime friend. Their case relied upon two old American aphorisms, offered (although in more diplomatic language) to inquiring diplomats and callers from abroad. One was "Friends don't let friends drive drunk." As Egypt's friend, the United States wanted to prevent it from plunging toward widespread violence and chaos. The other old saw was "More pain now, less pain later." Stability in the Middle East was not served by trying to maintain the status quo, American officials argued. Doing nothing about Mubarak would just precipitate more protests in more places.[25]

Nevertheless, inside the administration there were still disagreements. A few days after meeting with Mubarak, Wisner spoke by video link in New York City to an international security conference in Munich and said he thought the Egyptian leader should stay on the job at least for a while to guide the transition. "President Mubarak remains utterly critical in the days ahead as we sort our way towards the future," Wisner said.

Obama heard this at the White House. Aides said he was furious at Wisner. He ordered them to put out the word that Wisner was not speaking for the administration, even though Wisner's mission to Cairo the previous week (and his use of the word "we") might have left that impression. To add to the confusion over American policy, Clinton, at the same Munich conference, warned about unnamed forces that might try to "derail" the movement toward democracy, seeming to refer to Egypt's Muslim Brotherhood. That echoed the concerns of other governments nervous about the direction of change in Egypt, especially the Israelis. Clinton urged support for a transition headed by Suleiman.[26]

Obama and his team had created this confusion. They had called for a transition without defining further what they meant or setting out in detail what they felt should happen next. At first the White House had left unclear if Mubarak should resign or whether he could stay in power to run the transition. Then, after Obama told Mubarak he should step aside, the administration's statements still left ambiguous whether Suleiman, Mubarak's longtime aide, could run Egypt in his place or, possibly, for him.

Clinton's remarks brought to the surface the larger internal debate within the administration. The use of the word "transition" had patched over, but not settled, continuing differences over the question of whether or how much Egypt needed to make a break with the past. Those Obama administration officials with more traditional foreign policy views—including to varying degrees Donilon, Clinton, Biden and Gates—tended to favor a slower, more cautious approach that would allow Suleiman or someone else among Mubarak's ruling elite to continue running the country. These members of the Obama administration were worried about letting go completely from Mubarak's regime; they were concerned that the Muslim Brotherhood could take over Egypt and that a complete break from the Mubarak era could upset American relations with the Saudis, Israelis and other American friends in the Middle East.

On the other side were those members of the administration who had been pushing unsuccessfully over the previous two years for the administration to support democratic change. The group included McFaul, Power, Rhodes and several other lower-ranking aides. All of them were Obamians. This time, the democracy proponents had support from the two top Obamians: Denis McDonough and the president himself.

The Obamians were not so imbued with the more cautious traditions of the State Department, Defense Department and CIA. Just as they looked at themselves as a new generation, the Obamians viewed the events in Tunisia and Egypt as a sign of a new era; the upheavals reflected the beginning of transformational changes in the Middle East, which the United States should not be opposing.

According to Rhodes, the president several times told others in Situation Room meetings that the old American model for dealing with the Middle East was broken. "The way we have been thinking about this region is out of date," Obama had said. U.S. policy had been based upon the assumption that authoritarian regimes like Mubarak's were a force for stability. But after Tunisia, Obama argued, this old paradigm was broken; clinging to the Mubarak regime would not bring stability. "You have U.S. interests that suffer if you are seen to be on the side of counterrevolution," said Rhodes.[27]

What made Obama and his senior officials—so reluctant to voice support for Iran's 2009 Green Movement—so much more willing to do so when it came to Mubarak's Egypt? One reason they put forward, retrospectively, was that the initial policies of 2009 had been a short-term tactic. Obama didn't want to be seen as pushing democratic change during the phase when he was waging an "I'm-not-Bush" campaign, trying to emphasize the differences with his predecessor so he could repair relations with the world. Another reason, Obama officials maintained, was that with its military ties and massive aid programs, the United States had far greater leverage to influence change in Egypt than it had had in Iran.

The third reason was that when it came to Egypt, the lines between realism and idealism, between supporting democratic values and promoting America's strategic interests, were blurred. Pressing for Mubarak to resign could be defended as both idealism (pressing for democratic change) and realism (preventing upheaval and winning popular support in a country of extraordinary strategic importance to the United States).

The truth was that the issues raised by Tunisia and Egypt were not quite so novel as the Obamians sometimes portrayed them. There were good reasons why Donilon was reported to be reading the accounts from former secretary of state George P. Shultz about the Reagan administration's decision to urge Philippine president Ferdinand Marcos to give up power in 1986.[28] That was merely one of several earlier cases in which the United States had to figure out what to do about a dictator who was aligned with the United States but was rapidly losing public support at home. The same problems had arisen with President Suharto in Indonesia in the 1990s, with South Korean president Chun Doo-hwan in the 1980s, with the Shah of Iran in the 1970s. In most cases, American officials sought to persuade the failing dictator to step aside and give way to new leaders. Idealism converged with realism, democratic values with strategic interests.

The phenomenon was relatively new in the Middle East. Nevertheless, there was something of a precedent, an awkward one for Obama. After September 11, George W. Bush and his aides, too, made their own wavering attempt to confront the problem that most of America's allies in the Middle East, including Egypt, were authoritarian regimes. Bush, too, had for a time pressed strongly for democratic change in the Middle East. He backed off after Mubarak resisted strongly. Obama ultimately pushed harder in Egypt, but Obama's own support for democratic change in the Middle East would lag when the issue came up in Bahrain, and it would lurch to a halt well short of Saudi Arabia.

————

While Obama had said the Egyptian president should step down, the statements by Wisner and Clinton had left two questions hanging: Should Mubarak remain in control of the country himself during an interim transition period to new leadership, or could he somehow run the country indirectly through Suleiman? During the week of Monday, February 7, Obama and his aides sought to clarify that the answer to both questions was no. They made their position known through public statements, background quotes and "readouts" in which they informed reporters what senior Obama officials were saying in their private phone calls with Egyptian officials. The Obamians wanted to emphasize that they were unhappy with the limited changes Mubarak was proposing and wanted more specific commitments for change. After Biden spoke by phone to Suleiman, for example, the White House put out the word that the vice president had pressed his Egyptian counterpart for "a clear road map of democratic reforms, linked to a timetable."[29]

Finally, on Thursday, reports from Cairo said Mubarak was about to go on television and announce his resignation. CIA Director Leon Panetta, testifying to Congress, said there was a "strong likelihood" Mubarak would step down that same day. The White House began to prepare. "We had the expectation Mubarak was going to resign," said Rhodes. "We were hearing that from different contacts in the Egyptian government."

Once again, White House officials were reduced to watching television to learn, along with everyone else, what Mubarak would do. What he did confounded everyone. He announced that he was staying on as president, though he said vaguely he would turn over some of his authority to Suleiman. Soon afterward, Suleiman supported Mubarak and told the protesters to end their demonstrations and go back to work. There had still been some lingering notion in Washington that Suleiman could play a role in a new government if Mubarak were really to give up power—but this last speech by Suleiman ended that possibility.[30]

The crowds in Tahrir Square were in an uproar. At the White House, President Obama issued a hurried press statement saying that Mubarak's action wasn't enough. "The Egyptian government must put forward a credible, concrete and unequivocal push toward genuine democracy, and they have not yet seized that opportunity," the statement said.[31]

But by this point, events in Egypt were moving far more quickly than in Washington. The end of the crisis was drawing near. Egypt's military leaders, led by Tantawi and Enan, told Mubarak he should resign.[32] On Friday, February 11, the Egyptian president agreed to step down and fled to his home in the resort town of Sharm el Sheikh. Suleiman made the formal announcement, but within a day, the Egyptian vice president was out of power, too. The Egyptian military took charge of the country for what was said to be a transition period until elections could be held. Arguably, it was a coup d'état, carried out in the name of the Egyptian people and on behalf of democratic change.

19

"We Are All Democrats Now"

The phrase "Arab Spring" was not new in 2011. The phrase had been used on and off for years, whenever it seemed as though political change might sweep the region. It had gained new currency in 2005, following democratic elections in Iraq and Lebanon. ("We are at the dawn of an Arab Spring—the first bloom of democracy in Iraq, Lebanon, Egypt, Palestine, and throughout the greater Middle East," wrote columnist Charles Krauthammer in April 2005.)[1]

After Mubarak's resignation, the old hopes for an Arab Spring were in bloom again. Egypt had quickly followed Tunisia in ousting a longtime dictator. Within a week, there were similar demonstrations throughout the Middle East—in Jordan, Libya, Bahrain, Yemen, Syria and even Iran. "From Tripoli to Tehran, Arab Spring Sprouts New Wave of Protest," announced a *Guardian* headline.[2]

The Obama administration began trying to figure out which country would come next. Administration officials hurriedly made a list of which countries in the Middle East were most at risk of large-scale political turmoil, and which were least at risk. That list turned out to be wrong in many cases. At the top of the list were Yemen and Jordan, the countries where political unrest seemed likely. In the middle tier were Libya, Bahrain and Oman, all countries where it appeared possible. At the bottom were the nations where any widespread demonstrations for democracy were judged to be improbable: Saudi Arabia and Syria. "No one was focused on Syria, because it seemed far less likely than other states in the region," said James Steinberg a few months later.[3]

Meanwhile, Tom Donilon ordered a group of senior officials on his staff to study what had transpired when other countries tried to make the change from an authoritarian regime to democracy. The focus was not so much on which dictators might topple, but rather on what might happen after they did. In essence, the group was trying to figure out how the United States could help bring about transition to stable democratic government in Egypt, and how to prevent Egypt from following the illiberal and bloody path of the Iranian, Russian or French revolutions.

The group studied Poland, Serbia, the Philippines, Chile and several other countries. They gave particular attention to Indonesia, because it was a Muslim country that had succeeded in moving away from authoritarian rule. Indonesia was also, of course, of special interest to Obama because he had lived there.[4] The two countries that administration officials most frequently mentioned as hopeful models for a post-Mubarak Egypt were Indonesia and Turkey. In both places, the army played a continuing, powerful role, yet the countries nevertheless had regular multiparty elections.

The adviser put in charge of these studies was Michael McFaul. That assignment was itself a symbol of how much the Obama team had evolved in its perspective on democracy since the start of the administration. In 2009, McFaul had been on the losing end of internal debates in which the cause of democracy was subordinated to strategic concerns. Now McFaul was in the mainstream. After Tunisia and Egypt, one senior official said he thought the administration's internal wrangling about support for democracy had been settled, at least for a while. He quipped, with self-deprecating humor, "We are all democrats now."[5]

Amid these historical and philosophical debates, the Obama administration meanwhile took more immediate and concrete steps to cushion the impact of Egypt on America's friends in the Middle East. The day after Mubarak resigned, Obama sent two senior officials, Undersecretary of State Bill Burns and Chairman of the Joint Chiefs of Staff Mike Mullen to Jordan to reassure King Abdullah II of America's continuing support. They urged him to move quickly to open up his government and not resist change as Mubarak had. The king quickly announced a package of political and economic reforms. "I want quick results," he said. Those measures succeeded in staving off any political upheaval similar to Egypt's. Nevertheless, street demonstrations in Jordan continued on and off for months.[6]

In contrast, Bahrain, another American ally, was unable to prevent a crisis. The country—a small island with a population of 1.1 million in the Persian Gulf—is the headquarters of the U.S. Navy's Fifth Fleet. It is strategically located just across a causeway from Saudi Arabia and across the Persian Gulf from Iran; commercial flights from Bahrain to Tehran take roughly an hour and a half. Bahrain's ruling family, headed by King Hamad bin Isa al-Khalifa, is Sunni, like the Saudi monarchy; however, a majority of the people are Shiites, as are the leaders of Iran's Islamic Republic.

Demonstrations in Bahrain erupted almost immediately after Mubarak's departure. At first, the protesters called for equal rights for the Shia. On February 17, riot police were called in to try to break up the protests; they used live ammunition, and seven people were killed. At that point, thousands of demonstrators began to call for an end to the monarchy.[7]

Obama and Clinton made calls to Bahrain's leaders to express concern, but they also expressed considerably less support for the Bahraini protesters than they had for those in Egypt's Tahrir Square. In March, still unable to quell the unrest, Bahrain's royal family asked for military help, officially from the multinational Gulf Cooperation Council but in practice from its leading member, Saudi Arabia, which strongly supported the monarchy. About 1,200 troops from Saudi Arabia and another 800 from the United Arab Emirates marched across the causeway to Bahrain.[8] They remained there for months. As Bahrain crushed the protests, American appeals for restraint by the police and security forces went unheeded. To go further and push for democracy in Bahrain, the Obama administration would have had to be willing to risk a rupture in the relationship the United States had built up with Saudi Arabia over the previous seven decades.

Obama and his aides found themselves struggling for some coherent way of explaining the underlying American policy in the Arab Spring, amid all the seeming discrepancies and contradictions. When they had first embraced the demonstrations in Egypt, they were asked why they hadn't done likewise in Iran two years earlier. In private, some officials acknowledged that they had been too tepid in supporting Iran's Green Movement two years earlier, and that in retrospect they might have acted differently—particularly since the attempt to persuade Iran's leaders to give up their nuclear program had been rebuffed. In public, they didn't admit error. Instead, they came up with a workable rationale to differentiate Iran and Egypt: The United States had no ties or leverage in Iran, but lots of both in Egypt.

After Mubarak's resignation, however, they needed some new explanations. What about Bahrain, Jordan or Yemen, where the United States also had close military and diplomatic ties? Should these regimes be encouraged to open up, as Egypt had? Why not give protesters in other countries the same support the United States had given to those in Tahrir Square?

In Washington, several different explanations were offered. One, almost comical in its larger historical implications, was to focus on the distinction between monarchies and other kinds of governments in the Middle East. The monarchies were said to be more stable and therefore less in need of a change in leadership; Arab presidents, like Mubarak or Libya's Moammar Gaddafi, had less legitimacy than the kings. "Arab presidents pretend to be democratically chosen, though most of their elections are rigged," explained the *New York Times* in a perceptive article describing this line of argument.[9] This approach had the benefit of justifying America's more cautious, un-Egyptian approach in dealing with Jordan, Bahrain and Saudi Arabia, all ruled by kings (and, not incidentally, all friendly to the United States). However, the justification had the obvious defect that it contradicted the anti-monarchical principles on which the United States was founded.

The second, more durable rationale was that America stood for the cause of "reform" in the Middle East, specifically political reform. The word "reform" carried positive connotations and some substantial content as well. In pursuit of reform, the Obama administration did, in fact, urge leaders like Jordan's King Abdullah to open up their governments, and to do so quickly. Yet there was also another subtext to the Obama administration's frequent invocation of "reform": The word also meant "*not* revolution" and "*not* regime change." Through its emphasis on reform, then, the administration was sending out the message that it did not want any more Egypts or Tunisias. In the future, it wanted Middle Eastern leaders to make changes on their own; Obama would *not* encourage other leaders to step down, as he had with Mubarak.[10] As one administration official explained it, the private pitch that American officials were making to other leaders in the Middle East went like this: The United States was not hostile to those regimes now in power and, indeed, wanted to remain good allies with them. Therefore, for their own benefit, it was time to move toward some sort of democratic reforms.

Still, this "reform" rationale didn't quite work, either. Bahrain didn't reform. It not only ordered its own troops to fire on demonstrators, but called in Saudi troops to help suppress the demonstrations. Bahrain's rulers were at least as resistant to democratic change as Mubarak had been, if not more so. Saudi Arabia, meanwhile, spurned all American appeals for reform; it actively campaigned against the democratic spirit of the Arab Spring.

At times, the Obamians simply abandoned the search for a rationale and acknowledged that the principles underlying what they were doing varied from country to country. Deputy National Security Adviser Denis McDonough at one point told a reporter that administration officials were not making decisions "based on consistency or precedent. We make them based on how we can best advance our interests in the region."[11]

Such an explanation was hardly unprecedented. Virtually every administration at one point or another throws up its hands and admits that the standards the United States applies to one country don't necessarily apply elsewhere. As secretary of state, Madeleine Albright got so tired of being asked how America could square its engagement policy with China with its refusal to trade or deal with Cuba that she fell back on a catchphrase: We don't have a "cookie-cutter" approach to foreign policy, she said regularly. Ronald Reagan struggled for years to explain how his ringing appeals for political freedom in the Soviet Union and Eastern Europe squared with his support for dictators in Chile, the Philippines and South Korea. (Reagan finally altered his policy toward those authoritarian regimes, but only with great reluctance and after repeated urging by his advisers.)

The problem with the "national interest" rationale was that it made the United States look simply self-serving. Obama wanted to demonstrate America's support for the idea of democratic change in the Middle East; the United States could hardly inspire popular support in the region if it justified its actions as merely doing what was good for the United States. That might work with some American audiences, but not overseas. Indeed, "national interest" was not by itself an adequate explanation for Obama's policies in Egypt, which had been motivated by a combination of strategic and democratic concerns.

Within weeks of Mubarak's downfall, White House officials began to talk about having the president make a major address on the Middle East, one where he could explain to the region where America stood. The goal was to show that America had heard and was responding to the wave of democratic sentiment in the region. But the speech was delayed over and over again. For weeks, officials said Obama knew what he was going to say, but kept putting it off because of one crisis or another, particularly the civil war in Libya.

The Obama speech first discussed in February was finally delivered in May. In it, the president explicitly rejected the idea that his policies in the Middle East were based on American interests. He opted instead for a qualified version of the "reform" rationale.

"It will be the policy of the United States to promote reform across the region, and to support transitions to democracy," Obama declared. He said he would not seek to preserve the existing order of authoritarian regimes. "The status quo is not sustainable," he said. He also gave some further description of what he meant by reform:

> The United States opposes the use of violence and repression against the people of the region. The United States supports a set of universal rights. And these rights include free speech, the freedom of peaceful assembly, the freedom of religion, equality for men and women under the rule of law, and the right to choose your own leaders, whether you live in Baghdad or Damascus, Sanaa or Tehran.[12]

The speech left a loophole that allowed American policy to depart from these principles from time to time, as it had already done in Bahrain. "There will be times when our short-term interests don't align perfectly with our long-term vision for the region," Obama conceded.

Nevertheless, the vision Obama laid out for the Middle East was strikingly idealistic. His words were certainly not what the king and princes of Saudi Arabia wanted to hear or read. Nor was it a speech that Barack Obama himself would have given during his first eighteen months in office. Back then, he would not have talked about "the right to choose your own leaders," particularly in the Middle East. In his Cairo speech in 2009, Obama had mentioned democracy, but without emphasis. It had been fourth on a list of American goals, and as soon as he mentioned it, he quickly followed with the words: "No system of government can or should be imposed by one nation on another." Back then, Obama was speaking against the backdrop of the Iraq War; in 2011, by contrast, he was trying to respond to the passions of the Arab Spring demonstrators.

Obama went on to give a rundown of how these principles applied in individual countries. On Bahrain, he said that "mass arrests and brute force are at odds with the universal rights of Bahrain's citizens. . . . [Y]ou can't have a real dialogue when parts of the opposition are in jail." On Syria, he was similarly forthright: "President Assad now has a choice: He can lead that transition to democracy, or get out of the way."

But in his speech, the president could not come up with the words to reconcile American policy to Saudi Arabia with his expressed desire for change and reform in the Middle East. Concerning the Saudis, Obama said nothing at all.[13]

The assumption underlying the Obama administration's policies was that what had happened in Tunisia and Egypt represented historic change for the Middle East. At one point Donilon told *Washington Post* columnist David Ignatius that the sweeping revolts against dictatorial regimes were comparable in scope to the fall of the Ottoman Empire.[14]

Over the following months, however, the administration's assumption came increasingly into question. Several other Middle Eastern autocrats took from Tunisia and Egypt the perverse lesson that Ben Ali and Mubarak hadn't been brutal enough soon enough. Jordan's King Abdullah, who followed the American advice to adopt quick reforms, was a noteworthy exception. But in Libya, Yemen, Bahrain and Syria, leaders turned to repression, making use of the police, the army, mercenaries or foreign troops. In each country, security forces shot and killed demonstrators.

For opposition movements in these countries, the nonviolent strategies of Gene Sharp or of Serbia's roaming prodemocracy advisers were of little avail, at least in the short term. Their hope was that if leaders needed to resort to violence, they would in the process undermine their own authority. But there had been sad counterexamples, like Burma and China, where the violent suppression of protest movements enabled authoritarian regimes to hold on to power for decades.

Indeed, the course of events in the Arab Spring of 2011 was arguably similar to that in East Asia in the late 1980s. There, too, the notion took hold that authoritarianism was giving way to democracy in one country after another: in the Philippines, South Korea, Taiwan. The initial wave of demonstrations for democracy began to spread to other countries, to the point that the movement threatened other regimes, such as Burma in 1988 and China in 1989. In the latter two countries, leaders cracked down with overwhelming and lethal force, and the regional trend toward democracy came to a halt. Democracy protesters consoled themselves with the notion that although their movements had failed, Burma and China would "never be the same again"—a vague truism that began to be heard once again in 2011 after some of the Arab Spring protests were suppressed.

The consequences of the spreading wave of post-Mubarak crackdowns varied from country to country. In Bahrain, repression succeeded in quelling the demonstrations. In Libya, the result was outright civil war. In Yemen, it was chaos. In Syria, the regime's use of lethal force caused the protests to grow and spread, prompting yet more force and greater opposition to the regime.

In the case of Syria, the Obama administration was once again obliged to come up with new justifications for American policy. Syria had been a longtime adversary of the United States, and in that respect, it differed from Tunisia, Egypt, Jordan, or Bahrain. Assad's continuing use of violence against the Arab Spring protesters eventually surpassed that of any other Middle Eastern leader. In theory, these factors should have made it easier for Obama to call upon President Bashar al-Assad to step down. (Certainly no one would have complained, as with Mubarak, that America was abandoning a friend.) Nevertheless, Obama held back for months from calling for regime change in Syria, repeatedly rejecting appeals from Congress and the press for him to do so. The administration was preoccupied with the strategic implications of rapid change in Syria. Some American officials had voiced the occasional hope that the United States might be able to court Assad in a way that would pull him away from his close relationship with Iran. There was fear that Assad's downfall could lead to sectarian warfare, akin to what had happened after the ouster of Saddam Hussein in Iraq. Moreover, Syria borders on Israel, Turkey, Jordan and Lebanon; the leaders of all these countries were initially worried about instability in Syria and what might come after Assad.

The administration had already settled upon the proposition that its aim in the Middle East was reform, not regime change. While this post-Mubarak policy was derived with the aim of reassuring American friends like Jordan and Saudi Arabia, the administration at first tried to fit Syria under this rubrik, too. Asked at one point why the United States wasn't taking stronger action against Syria, Clinton answered that recent visitors to Syria had felt President Assad was a "reformer."[15] Obama's warning seven weeks later that Assad should "lead that transition to democracy, or get out of the way" was, in effect, a last-ditch appeal for Assad to do something that could qualify him as a reformer.

As Assad spurned these warnings, the Obama team offered another rationale for a hands-off response to Syria. Administration officials pointed out that the United States lacked leverage in dealing with Syria; American military leaders, for example, had no ties with Syria of the sort that they had with Egypt. If that argument sounded familiar, it was. The Obamians had said essentially the same thing in justifying the administration's cool reaction in the face of massive demonstrations in Iran in 2009. It appeared that the president had come full circle, back to downplaying issues of democracy and human rights in the interests of geopolitical strategy.

The administration tried for a time to increase pressure on Assad without questioning his authority to rule. The United States first imposed economic sanctions on Syrian officials associated with Assad, but not the Syrian president himself. A few weeks later, the administration extended the sanctions to cover Assad, too. Syria continued to fire on protesters, sometimes employing tanks to do so. Finally, four months after the Syrian protests had begun to spread, the administration suggested the possibility of regime change. Clinton took the lead. "President Assad is not indispensable, and we have absolutely nothing invested in him remaining in power," she told reporters. "I mean, from our perspective he has lost legitimacy." The following day, Obama offered a notably softer version of the same idea. "You're seeing President Assad lose legitimacy in the eyes of his people," said Obama.[16] Assad remained unmoved and determined to hold on to power, even when the resistance began to grow from peaceful demonstrations to army defections and armed rebellion.

———

The Obamians' attempt to find a set of fundamental principles governing American policy in the Arab Spring was, overall, not particularly successful. They supported popular movements against dictators (Tunisia, Egypt), until they didn't (Bahrain). They called for some authoritarian leaders to step aside, temporized with others (Assad) and went to great lengths to avoid conflict with others (King Abdullah of Jordan, the Saudi royal family).

Obama's rhetoric about democratic change during the Arab Spring was uplifting. It put the United States squarely on the side of altering the status quo in the Middle East, and Obama's withdrawal of support from Mubarak represented a concrete step in line with his rhetoric. Obama's actions were less than critics in the United States would have liked, but also significant enough to infuriate the Saudis, the principal upholders of the existing order in the Middle East.

But after Egypt and Tunisia, Obama's approach was defined not by a policy of democracy for everyone, but rather by circumstance and strategy, country by country, depending on American interests. The Obamians at first saw the Arab Spring as an epochal change in line with their own views of themselves as a new generation. From the standpoint of protesters on the streets of the Middle East, however, Obama's wavering policies could be interpreted not as encouragement of epochal change so much as an effort to continue as long as possible the policies of the past.

———

By late 2011, it was no longer so certain that the Arab Spring represented massive transformational change toward democracy in the Middle East. In some countries, leaders were reverting to the old, familiar ways of doing business. Elsewhere, the events on the streets were turning in unwelcome directions: Security forces were repressing protesters, and the demonstrations were gravitating to causes quite different from the original cries for democracy.

Egypt displayed all these worrisome trends at once. The military government headed by Mohamed Hussein Tantawi slowed the pace of change to civilian rule. The generals also began to invoke and, indeed, expand the emergency laws used against demonstrators by Mubarak. Under these laws, protesters were arrested without cause and tried in military courts. Meanwhile, Egyptian Islamists steadily gained in political strength. At one point, a coalition of religious groups staged a demonstration in Tahrir Square far larger than those of other organizations, with participants shouting slogans like "Islamic, Islamic—Neither secular nor liberal." Other protesters took up another cause: opposition to Israel. In September, thousands of protesters stormed the Israeli embassy and took down the Israeli flag, prompting the embassy to shut down for more than a week. Israel's comfortable relationship with Egypt since the days of Anwar Sadat seemed to be fast eroding.[17]

One midsummer day in Washington, a half year after the demonstrations first began to swell in Cairo's Tahrir Square, a senior Obama administration official seemed to have scaled back the expectations for the Arab Spring. Obama did not view the Middle East with a scorecard, simplistically checking off those countries that had moved to democracy and those that hadn't, this official explained. The administration seemed to be preparing to cast the Arab Spring in the best light, both for domestic audiences and for the benefit of further democratization in the Middle East.

"We want some success stories," mused this Obama adviser. "If Libya winds up messy, we want Benghazi itself to be a place that is a free Libya, an open city. If Egypt deteriorates, it's even more important that the Tunisian experiment succeeds. If the crackdown in Syria continues, then we have an interest in seeing the opposition, whether inside Syria or the émigrés overseas, coalesce in a way that they haven't yet."[18] It was almost like a search for a fallback position, a way to take heart from less than was hoped.

20

Libya: To Fly

L ibya stood apart from the rest of the Arab Spring. Egypt and Tunisia had required the Obama administration to grapple with important but long-standing questions about how much the United States should support the cause of democracy. In Libya, Obama confronted issues not raised elsewhere during the Arab Spring—questions about the proper use of force, about presidential power and, above all, about America's role in the world. It was in Libya that the Obamians gave their clearest definition of themselves, of the ends and the means of American power.

Throughout the 1980s and 1990s, Libya's leader, Colonel Moammar Gaddafi, had been regarded in the United States as at once a terrorist and a lunatic. Ronald Reagan had once labeled him the "madman of the Middle East." Gaddafi's security service had carried out a 1986 terrorist attack that killed two American servicemen and injured seventy-nine other patrons of a West Berlin nightclub. Reagan responded with air strikes against Tripoli and Benghazi, Libya's biggest and second-biggest cities; one of the air strikes came close to killing Gaddafi. Libya countered in 1988 with the bombing of a Pan Am flight from London to New York City; 273 people were killed, most of them Americans.

Nevertheless, in the decade leading up to the Arab Spring, American policy toward Gaddafi and Libya had been steadily easing. Following the Iraq War, Gaddafi emerged as the American-approved counterexample to Saddam Hussein. On April 30, 2003, soon after U.S. forces ousted the Iraqi regime from power, Libya suddenly announced it would take responsibility for the Pan Am bombing and set up a fund to compensate families of the victims. Later that year, Libya volunteered to abandon its nuclear weapons program and gave American, British and UN specialists full access to its covert weapons sites and laboratories. Bush administration officials were doubly delighted. They had hoped that the military action in Iraq would be an intimidating lesson that prompted others in the Middle East to become more careful about challenging American power. Furthermore, U.S. officials hoped that in giving up its nuclear program, Libya might set a positive example for North Korea and Iran: If Gaddafi abandoned programs for weapons of mass destruction and Libya then went on to become a more prosperous, respected member of the international community, perhaps Kim Jong-il or the mullahs in Tehran would change their calculations.

In the Bush years, then, Gaddafi was cast not as a madman but as a chastened leader devoted to establishing ties with the West and attracting foreign investment and technology. The Bush administration reestablished diplomatic relations and took Libya off the list of state sponsors of terrorism. Secretary of State Condoleezza Rice paid a visit to Tripoli, the first by any secretary of state since John Foster Dulles. (Gaddafi referred to her as "Leezza" and "my darling black African woman.")[1] In late 2008, a few weeks before leaving office, Bush phoned Gaddafi, the first American president ever to talk to him.

Obama had no interest in reversing the course Bush had set. The overtures to Libya qualified as the kind of engagement Obama had recommended toward dictatorial regimes during his campaign. In the summer of 2009, at an international gathering in Italy, Obama shook Gaddafi's hand, angering the families of the Lockerbie victims. Obama's right-hand man Denis McDonough explained to reporters that the president would greet the leader of any country in the same fashion. "He doesn't intend to choose which leaders he'll shake hands with and which he won't," McDonough said.

The demonstrations in Libya in early 2011 started much as they had in its two North African neighbors, Tunisia and Egypt. Five days after Mubarak stepped down, Libyan protesters took to the streets to seek the release of a Libyan human rights lawyer. On Facebook and Twitter, Libyans called for nationwide demonstrations seeking Gaddafi's resignation.[2]

The Obama administration, which by this point viewed the Arab Spring as a historic and irreversible wave, at first merely issued the usual call for restraint from the Libyan regime. The Obamians hoped Gaddafi might behave like other Middle Eastern leaders in the early weeks of the Arab Spring, either stepping aside like Mubarak or announcing some immediate reforms like Jordan's King Abdullah. Instead, once the Libyan demonstrations grew large enough and called for Gaddafi's resignation, the regime immediately cracked down hard. Gaddafi's security forces began shooting at protesters in the streets and hunting them down in their homes. Their use of force was so brutal that it seemed clear the intent was not merely to get the protesters off the streets but to terrify them into submission. Early on, a helicopter was used to fire on unarmed civilians. Looking back on these early events a few months later, Samantha Power reflected, "We were trying to convince Gaddafi to act with restraint and moderation, but he had already, right from day one, decided to crush this thing. He was taking the other path, the non-Tunisia choice."[3]

For days, Obama said little. He avoided urging on Gaddafi to step down or acting against him, even as French president Nicolas Sarkozy began calling for international sanctions against Libya. "We did hold off for a couple of days on our statements, until we could get our people out," said Ben Rhodes. "They were very concerned about their personal security." Within minutes after the American diplomats left Libya on the final charter flight out of the country, Obama changed course. The United States froze the assets of the Libyan government in the United States and all assets owned by Gaddafi and all of his children.[4] The following day, the UN Security Council adopted a far-reaching resolution that banned any international travel by Gaddafi and other senior officials, froze Libyan assets, imposed an arms embargo on Libya and referred the actions of Gaddafi and others in Libya to the International Criminal Court for prosecution.

By the time these sanctions were imposed, however, the crisis in Libya had escalated to the point where they seemed almost irrelevant. Over the previous week, the opposition had gathered enough strength to take control of Benghazi. As Gaddafi continued to respond with force, the opposition took up arms. Defecting army officers and troops came to their side. Gathering strength, the rebels came closer and closer to Tripoli. For a few days, it seemed as though the regime was about to collapse.

In one speech in late February, Gaddafi warned that his forces would hunt down opponents "house by house." In another, his son Saif said there would be "rivers of blood" if the armed rebellion continued. "We will take up arms, we will fight to the last bullet," said Saif Gaddafi. His father would "fight until the last man, the last woman, the last bullet" and would "destroy seditious elements."[5]

Gaddafi began to rely heavily on airpower, using planes to bomb rebel forces and helicopters to shoot at civilians. In Washington, the Obama administration received numerous reports of unarmed civilians being shot or simply disappearing.

———

The Obama administration included two prominent officials who had dedicated much of their professional careers to the question of how to prevent mass killings. One of them was Susan Rice. During the mid-1990s, Rice had been a young staff member on the Clinton administration's National Security Council when Hutus slaughtered hundreds of thousands of Tutsis in Rwanda. She visited the country in the aftermath and saw firsthand the decomposed bodies of the victims, many of them hacked to death. "I swore to myself that if I ever faced such a crisis again, I would come down on the side of dramatic action, going down in flames if that was required," she told an interviewer for a 2001 *Atlantic* article called "Bystanders to Genocide."[6]

The author of that *Atlantic* piece happened to be Samantha Power. She was then a young journalist in the process of writing *A Problem from Hell*, her book on America's responses to genocide. Having started her career as a reporter covering atrocities in Bosnia, Power was, through her book, stepping back to examine the broader question of how governments can stop mass slaughter. *A Problem from Hell* made Power one of the most identifiable proponents of humanitarian intervention: the use of force, as a last resort, to prevent atrocities or genocide. Critics sometimes accorded to her some of the stereotypes applied to crusading women since Joan of Arc: a zealot ready to lead troops on behalf of idealistic causes. A thoughtful article about her in *National Interest* was published with a screaming headline on the cover that said, in bloodred type, "Interventionista!" Others, particularly on the political left, called her a "liberal hawk." Such media portrayals were incomplete, because they missed some essential aspects of Power's persona.

She was a policy wonk. Most journalists devote themselves to exposing abuses, but leave it to government officials or others to come up with the unexciting, messy details of a solution. Power wanted to do the latter, too. She had followed up her stint in Bosnia by going to law school, graduating from Harvard eight years after Barack Obama. In book discussions and other public appearances, she sometimes spoke at length about the complex problems of institutions and the dilemmas of government officials, to the surprise of audiences more interested in hearing simple expressions of outrage and condemnations of government malfeasance.

Power joined the Obama administration as the National Security Council staff director for multilateral affairs and human rights. She had a more irreverent title for herself: She was the administration's "conscience mascot." In her government job, Power soon became absorbed in the sorts of problems that are rarely covered at any length in news stories: pressing for interagency meetings, figuring out how to work with the various departments and agencies, persuading career government officials to refocus on new priorities. She learned to talk the lingo of the White House staff: Issues were "teed up" for the president, "transaction costs" were weighed, bureaucracies were "incentivized."

Looking back, Power maintained that her book *A Problem from Hell* had been widely misinterpreted. It was not a treatise on behalf of military intervention, she said, but rather a plea to give American presidents and other world leaders a "toolbox" with a wide range of options to prevent mass killings. As the reports of widespread killings in Libya began to arrive in Washington, Power tried to create such a toolbox for Obama. She and other officials explored the possible benefits and limitations of economic sanctions, asset freezes, travel bans, diplomatic denunciations, "naming and shaming" those who helped the regime, referring Gaddafi to the International Criminal Court. The White House tasked the intelligence community to collect, in a separate channel from its regular reports, all the evidence from a variety of sources relating to possible atrocities in Libya.

In short, Power was, alongside Rice, the second senior official who had come into the Obama administration determined to prevent any future atrocities like those in Bosnia or Rwanda. When Obama decided to take action against Gaddafi, he turned to Samantha Power's toolbox. When Obama went to the UN Security Council to join with the British and French in seeking international sanctions against Libya, he worked through his UN ambassador, Susan Rice.

The first UN resolution against Libya in early March did not authorize armed force. It was drafted in the hope that measures like economic sanctions would deter Gaddafi (and with the knowledge that, in any case, a resolution authorizing force could not win passage at the UN Security Council). Soon, however, Gaddafi's forces began to move toward Benghazi, the main city controlled by the rebels, and it was becoming clear that nothing short of military action could hold him back. The British and French began to propose tougher measures to prevent mass killings. In particular, they called for a no-fly zone over Libya to prevent Gaddafi's planes from killing opposition forces or civilians on the ground.

For the Obama administration, the question of whether to move toward military intervention in Libya was now clearly on the table. Inside the administration, both Rice and Power began to support the use of force if necessary to stop mass killings. There were, however, a multitude of officials on the Obama team with different backgrounds and perspectives from Power and Rice.

———

At the Pentagon, Defense Secretary Robert Gates and military leaders at first looked at Libya as an unnecessary distraction at a time when they were already beset with other important problems. They were worried above all about the war in Afghanistan, which was costing the United States around $10 billion a month and was still not yet on a path to victory. The war in Iraq had not yet come to an end, either. It was not clear whether the White House and Iraqi government would agree on leaving some American troops in Iraq after the existing status-of-forces agreement expired at the end of 2011.

As if all this weren't enough, in early March the Pentagon suddenly found itself with still another new task: helping Japan after the tsunami and the nuclear disaster at Fukushima. The navy sent twenty ships, including the aircraft carrier *Ronald Reagan*, to the waters off Japan; American helicopters delivered food and water to Japanese towns, fire trucks sprayed water to cool down the nuclear fuel rods at Fukushima and U.S. reconnaissance planes kept track of radiation levels.[7] In the news coverage, this military operation was understandably a sideshow to the larger story of what was happening on the ground in Japan. For American military leaders, however, the assistance for Japan was of surpassing importance: Japan was America's military ally, but had also hinted at wanting to reduce its dependence on the United States in favor of a closer relationship with China.

Each of the military services had its own concerns about Libya. The army was of course intensively focused on the war in Afghanistan. The navy was devoting ever more of its time and energy to China and the new problems raised by its increasing maritime power. For the air force, a military operation in Libya would present some practical difficulties; for instance, there were limits on the ability to provide air-to-air refueling for planes going to and from Libyan airspace.

Above all, Libya also raised a series of strategic questions for both civilian and military leaders. Did the United States have any strategic interest in Libya? Or was that the wrong question—should it be whether America had a strategic interest in all of North Africa, which would in turn be affected by Libya? Or should the focus be on the entire Middle East, and how the outcome in Libya would influence the course of the Arab Spring? Meanwhile, what would happen if there was a military intervention in Libya, but Gaddafi managed to withstand it and remain in power? Would he then try to revive the nuclear weapons program he had abandoned? Would he resort once again to terrorism? When it came to Libya, déjà vu would be a particularly bad outcome.

———

The public face for all of the military and strategic misgivings within the Pentagon was Gates. By early 2011, he was by choice a short-timer as defense secretary. He had made it clear both inside the administration and to the public that he would leave later in the year. He had accomplished the feat of serving under both Bush and Obama, winning respect from both presidents and both parties. His calm, straightforward style enabled him to make his points without rancor. He managed to voice dissent, even in public, about policies he didn't like, where others in a similar position would have sounded contentious or self-serving.

He was by this time thinking as much about long-term issues as about day-to-day problems. In speeches and television appearances, he talked about where the Pentagon should be heading in the future. He admonished Congress to stop giving money for pet projects or weapons systems that the Pentagon had not requested. He said bluntly it had been like "pulling teeth" to get the air force to use more drones instead of conventional planes with pilots.[8] On February 25, 2011, in a speech at West Point, Gates argued that the United States should never again try to wage a war like the ones in Iraq and Afghanistan. "In my opinion, any future defense secretary who advises the president to again send a big American land army into Asia or into the Middle East or Africa should 'have his head examined,' as General MacArthur so delicately put it," said Gates.

Throughout early March, Gates repeatedly expressed skepticism about suggestions for American military intervention in Libya. It was more a job for America's European allies, he said. He argued at first that there were no confirmed reports of air strikes by Gaddafi's forces against his opponents and that, in any event, the Libyan opposition hadn't requested any outside help.[9] Within days, when the evidence of air strikes was irrefutable and the opposition did formally request assistance, the defense secretary warned that a no-fly zone over Libya was not nearly so easy as proponents made it sound. It might sound as though a no-fly zone was a step or two short of actual military conflict, but that wasn't true, Gates pointed out.

"Let's just call a spade a spade," Gates testified at one congressional hearing. "A no-fly zone begins with an attack on Libya to destroy the air defenses. That's the way you do a no-fly zone. And then you can fly planes around the country and not worry about our guys being shot down. But that's the way it starts."

Gates's unconcealed skepticism toward humanitarian intervention in Libya was strikingly similar to the attitudes of President George H. W. Bush and his administration toward the Balkans at the beginning of the 1990s. When urged to use force to stop the killing of civilians in Bosnia, Bush, his top advisers Brent Scowcroft and James Baker, and Colin Powell, then chairman of the Joint Chiefs of Staff, said no, in the belief that foreign policy should be based primarily on realistic concerns of national interest, not values or humanitarian concerns. Gates had served all four years of Bush Senior's administration, as deputy national security adviser and CIA director.

He considered Bush and Scowcroft to be his mentors. He believed in foreign policy realism as sincerely as they did.

In early March, when Gaddafi was killing civilians and the British and French began to talk about a no-fly zone, National Security Adviser Tom Donilon ordered the Pentagon to study the military options. "We looked at everything, from no-fly to actual boots on the ground," Donilon later recalled.[10]

———

Obama was thus confronted with conflicting views within his administration between proponents of realism, who urged him to stay out of Libya, and proponents of humanitarian intervention, who wanted him to act. The president and his top advisers at first seemed to side with the realists. Donilon and McDonough often viewed foreign policy through the lens of national interests, rather than values, and were at first inclined to agree with Gates. The intelligence community's assessments did not help the case for intervention. James Clapper, who had succeeded Dennis Blair as director of national intelligence, testified in Congress that Gaddafi possessed so much more in arms and equipment than the opposition that his troops were likely to prevail over the long run.

During the first two weeks of March, Obama offered only cautious responses to what was unfolding. He finally called for Gaddafi to step down, said the Libyan leader had lost his legitimacy and authorized Hillary Clinton to meet with opposition leaders. Obama at one point said that he would not rule out the use of force, apparently hoping to rattle Gaddafi into stepping down or at least stopping the slaughter.

But the president would not go beyond that. In the press, critics were accusing him of indecisiveness or sheer cowardice. "Has Barack Obama ever been brave?" asked the *Economist*. "Perhaps more pertinently, will he ever be?" In an article for the *New York Times*, Anne-Marie Slaughter, who had just stepped down from her post in the administration, spoke of America's "fiddling while Libya burns." In the Senate, not only the hawkish duo of John McCain and Joe Lieberman but even Senate Foreign Relations Committee chairman John Kerry—Obama's closest ally in the Senate—called for a no-fly zone.[11]

A series of developments, both diplomatic and military, gave Obama new reasons to act. First, on March 12, the Arab League, which includes twenty-two Middle East states, came out in favor of a no-fly zone. It issued a statement calling for the UN Security Council to provide the Libyan opposition with "urgent help."[12] Over the following days, on a trip to Paris, Cairo and Tunis, Hillary Clinton met both with Arab leaders and with those of the Libyan opposition. She reported back to Obama that the Arab League resolution wasn't just some meaningless pro forma statement; leaders in the region were serious and, in a few cases, even willing to take part in the military mission. "Essentially, Clinton's read-back to us was, 'People are really prepared to put skin in the game here. This isn't just hollow calls for action,'" Rhodes recalled a few months later.

Secondly, British and French officials privately made clear that they not only wanted but expected America to join with them. The message was simple and direct: We need you on this.[13] It was time for the United States to repay a few favors, they argued. Britain and France had sent troops to Afghanistan to help out the United States; they had joined with the United States in imposing sanctions on North Korea and Iran, which were of greater concern to the United States than to their countries. Now America should help Britain and France in Libya, a country in their own backyard.

Third, amid this flurry of diplomacy Clinton took a decisive step: She came down on the side of intervention, supporting the views of Rice and Power. That meant that Gates, who was frequently aligned with Clinton in cabinet-level discussions on foreign policy, did not have the secretary of state with him on this.[14]

Finally, in Libya itself, Gaddafi's troops began to roll over the opposition. Government forces, with air support, were driving rapidly eastward into and through the parts of Libya that had been controlled by the opposition. They were closing in on Ajdabiya, the last major town before Benghazi, and at the rate they were going would probably be at Benghazi within days.

Benghazi has more than half a million residents. Intelligence reports said that remarkably few civilians from Benghazi had fled eastward to Egypt or otherwise left their homes. This meant that a large urban civilian population could soon be left defenseless at the hands of Libyan troops. Gaddafi and his son Saif had already promised house-to-house searches and rivers of blood.

As Gaddafi's forces drew near, army spokesman Milan Hussein told reporters: "Benghazi doesn't deserve a full-scale military action. They are a group
of rats and vermin, and as soon as we go in, they will raise their hands and
surrender."[15]

This was the sort of decision that a president knows may be remembered
long after his others, particularly if inaction or indecision were to result in
mass slaughter. After leaving the White House, Bill Clinton repeatedly said
in public that the biggest regret of his presidency had been not moving to
prevent genocide in Rwanda. Moreover, the decision confronting Obama
wasn't just about humanitarian intervention. There were other considerations, too. The British and French were by this point not only urging
Obama to act, but moving at the United Nations for a resolution that would
set up a no-fly zone. It was at this point that Obama, on the night of March 15,
approved military action against Libya that would not only set up a no-fly
zone but also authorize "all necessary measures," thus permitting forces to
hit targets on the ground.

When Rice took this measure to the United Nations, there was a round
of intense diplomatic maneuvering. At one point, Obama telephoned South
African president Jacob Zuma to win his country's support. Within two
days, Rice won Security Council approval for the "all necessary measures"
resolution. The vote was ten to zero. Five members of the Security Council
abstained, four of them the BRIC countries of Brazil, Russia, India and
China. The fifth abstention was Germany, a particular disappointment to
the Obama White House.

Only a couple of months earlier, at a State Department farewell party in her
honor, Anne-Marie Slaughter, the outgoing director of policy planning, ven-
tured to raise the subject of gender within Obama's foreign policy team.
She had discovered, she said, that women still got the "soft" jobs in areas
such as human rights, foreign aid and development, while the "hard power"
positions involving the use of force went to men.[16] As a way of analyzing
the administration, it was at best imperfect. One of the senior women
in the administration was Michèle Flournoy, the undersecretary of defense.
The host of Slaughter's good-bye party, standing alongside her as she spoke,
was Hillary Clinton, a former member of the Senate Armed Services

Committee, who might well have been the Democratic nominee for president in 2008 had it not been for the perception that she believed in "hard power" more than Barack Obama did.

After the decision to strike at Libya, the gender-based analyses of the Obama foreign policy team reemerged, but with a new twist. The press pointed out that the leading supporters of military intervention in Libya had been women: Clinton, Power, Rice as well as Gayle Smith, the National Security Council's senior director for global development. *New York Times* columnist Maureen Dowd wrote one piece headlined "Fight of the Valkyries," in which she reported that the four women had also been dubbed the "Amazon Warriors," the "Lady Hawks" and the "Durgas."[17] A few other commentators soon pointed out that these gender-based interpretations were oversimplified and indeed irrelevant. "The women of the administration are individuals with distinctively intellectual histories that are sufficiently explanatory of their views that no further imaginings about some mysterious female factor are required," Garance Franke-Ruta cogently argued on the *Atlantic*'s website. "They were hired for those histories, not because they are women."[18]

————

The intervention in Libya marked a turning point for Obama and his team. With it, the president took a step away from the foreign policy realism that had characterized his first eighteen months in the White House. During his 2008 campaign, Obama had pointed to the administration of George H. W. Bush and his national security adviser, Brent Scowcroft, as models for his approach to foreign policy. But the senior Bush and Scowcroft would not likely have pushed Mubarak to leave office in Egypt, and they would certainly not have intervened in Libya. Indeed, Scowcroft said as much in a television interview with Jim Lehrer immediately after American warplanes went into the skies over Libya. Zbigniew Brzezinski, Scowcroft's counterpart in the Carter administration, disagreed:

> *Lehrer*: Well, what about the other side of the coin, to sit back and have done nothing while people were slaughtered in Benghazi, say?
> *Scowcroft*: Okay. Everywhere that there are people killed, the United States needs to intervene? How about Zimbabwe? You know, you

have the same kind of circumstances. . . . [T]his is not the only place there's violence in the region. There's violence in Yemen, violence in Bahrain. Do we follow the same thing, that we're going to protect the protesters at all cost?

Brzezinski: Well, obviously, if you can't intervene everywhere, you don't conclude that you interfere nowhere.[19]

Gates, Scowcroft's protégé, had argued strenuously against military action, maintaining that Libya was not a vital national interest of the United States. Obama heard these arguments and rejected them.

Aides portrayed Obama's Libya decision as motivated by realistic concerns as well as moral ones. "There is a realist component, which is that a lot of what we have been trying to do is to essentially put forward a model of U.S. leadership," asserted Rhodes. "And the message that we would have sent about U.S. leadership if we were to sit that one out—if we are for democracy, if we are against mass atrocities and we are for collective action on behalf of global security issues, and then we don't step up to the plate in Libya, it would have sent a signal that the U.S. isn't really a leader."[20]

Yet Obama also had, it turned out, a different definition of America's leadership role than the one to which Americans had become accustomed. He worked out his deal with British prime minister David Cameron and French president Nicolas Sarkozy under which the United States would help initiate the air campaign over Libya, and then, after a few days, let Britain, France and other NATO allies and partners take over the work.

The reasons the Obamians put forward for doing this were both political and economic. First, the United States was involved in two wars in Iraq and Afghanistan, and the president was extremely hesitant to take the leading role in a third war against an Islamic nation in the Middle East. (That was, after all, why it had been so important to get the Arab League resolution in favor of action against Gaddafi.) Hillary Clinton at one point offered a variant of this same line of thinking: The administration, she said, wanted to avoid the perception that it had invaded Libya for its oil. No one wanted to revive the rancorous suspicions of the United States that had erupted at the time of the war in Iraq.

Second, by allowing the British and the French to be in the forefront,

Obama greatly reduced the costs of the Libyan operation to the United States. In mid-April, the operations in Libya were costing American taxpayers roughly $1 million to $3 million a day; by contrast, the war in Afghanistan during the same period was costing more than $300 million per day. "American leadership is not simply a matter of going it alone and bearing all of the burden ourselves," said Obama in a speech explaining his decision. "Real leadership creates the conditions and coalitions for others to step up as well; to work with allies and partners so that they bear their share of the burden and pay their share of the costs."[21]

To the Pentagon and others in the national security community, there were important side benefits to America's limited involvement in the Libyan war. In Afghanistan, the United States had virtually begged some of its reluctant NATO allies to join in the military campaign. Here, by contrast, other NATO countries—at least the British and French—were willing to take responsibility for a large share of the war. Moreover, U.S. officials had for years been irked by continuing cutbacks in the defense budgets of its NATO allies, but this time allies were both paying their share and, of equal importance, learning amid wartime what they lacked in military capabilities and equipment. On the other hand, Libya also led to some new friction within NATO: The British and French demonstrated how well they could work together, but Germany was noticeably absent from the NATO campaign.

The symbolism of Obama's decision struck a nerve on the political right, provoking a series of negative commentaries and editorials. While supporting the military action, the *Wall Street Journal* denounced what it called "the first war by global committee." Kori Schake, one of the Republicans' national security experts, wrote, "Stepping back and letting others do the work certainly isn't a bold or brave moment for American foreign policy."[22] These criticisms generally ignored the economic question of whether the United States could afford to wage the war on its own. They also tended to shunt aside the diplomatic question of how America would be perceived if it had been the prime actor in a war in the Islamic world for the third time in eleven years. These were serious considerations, which might in other circumstances have produced an American decision to stay out of the Libyan operation entirely. The mistake of these critics was to assume that the alternative to letting the British and French take the lead in Libya was to wage a military campaign dominated by the United States. But in fact, the more likely alternative was to have done nothing.

The previous administration had decided to go to war in Iraq expecting that its partners in NATO and the Middle East, even if they had at first objected, would eventually close ranks and follow the American lead, just as they had in the Persian Gulf War. That assumption turned out to be wrong. Whatever the merits of Obama's decision for humanitarian intervention in Libya, he found a way to take military action with far greater international support, and at a lower cost as well.

———

Obama faced a separate, sounder line of attack on Libya. He was sending American forces into military conflict without going to Congress under the provisions of the War Powers Resolution. In doing so, he arguably asserted presidential power in warmaking beyond even the claims of George W. Bush.

The War Powers Resolution, passed in 1973 in the shadow of the Vietnam War, requires a president to get congressional authorization when dispatching American forces into hostile action. There is an exception for national emergencies when the United States or American forces are under attack. But in any case, the War Powers Resolution sets a time limit of sixty days for a president to obtain congressional approval. Without it, he is required to bring the military mission to a close within another thirty days.

This provision was the creation of a Democratic Congress, which enacted it by overriding President Nixon's veto. In the nearly four decades since then, Democrats have staunchly invoked the law and insisted that its provisions be followed whenever there was a Republican president in the White House; Presidents Reagan, George H. W. Bush and George W. Bush all notified Congress before sending troops to Lebanon, Grenada, Panama, the Persian Gulf and Iraq. In Democratic administrations, the pattern was often reversed: Bill Clinton resisted following the War Powers procedures in dealing with Haiti and Kosovo, for example, while congressional Republicans in both cases demanded he get legislative approval for military action. Overall, leaders of both parties tend to believe strongly in the requirements of the War Powers Resolution, until they occupy the White House themselves.

Obama conformed to this same pattern of bipartisan hypocrisy. In late

2007, in the midst of his race for the Democratic nomination, he was asked whether the president could bomb Iran without congressional authorization. His answer was categorical: "The president does not have power under the Constitution to unilaterally authorize a military attack in a situation that does not involve stopping an actual or imminent threat to the nation." (Candidates Biden and Clinton gave similar answers.)[23]

Libya was the first military conflict that Obama initiated as president, after inheriting the wars in Iraq and Afghanistan. From the outset, as soon as the American planes and missiles were launched over the Mediterranean, Obama abandoned his campaign position on War Powers. His aides contended that the military action in Libya was too short and too narrow to require congressional authorization. "This is a limited—in terms of scope, duration and task—operation, which does fall in the president's authorities," said National Security Adviser Tom Donilon.[24] In effect, Obama turned his decision to hand over the daily bombing raids to British, French and NATO forces into a rationale for increased presidential power: Administration officials maintained that because NATO had taken over the military campaign, the American military could be sent off to action without congressional authorization. This position on the War Powers Resolution was responsible for some of the verbal contortions the Obamians employed when they talked about Libya. Rhodes, borrowing a Pentagon euphemism, told reporters the campaign did not amount to war or "hostilities," but rather "kinetic military action."

Two months later, Obama went a step further by asserting that he did not need to comply with the law's sixty-day time limit for obtaining congressional authorization, either. Once again, he claimed the War Powers Resolution didn't apply, because the Libya campaign did not amount to war or "hostilities." The close American involvement ended after only a few days, in early April, when the responsibility was handed over to NATO, the Obama team claimed. Over the following two months, American planes hit Libyan air defenses sixty times and drones fired missiles at Gaddafi's forces thirty times.[25] Those drone and air attacks gave rise to another bizarre rationale: Obama administration officials took the position that since there were no American boots on the ground in Libya, the United States was not involved in the war. By that logic, a nuclear attack would not be a war.

The two leaders in advancing these arguments were Harold Koh, the legal adviser to the State Department who, as dean of Yale Law School, had criticized Bush's expansion of presidential powers, and Robert Bauer, who had replaced Greg Craig as White House counsel. Their positions put them, and Obama himself, in unusual company. John Yoo, the former Justice Department attorney who had gained notoriety in the Bush administration for his expansive interpretations on behalf of presidential power, rushed to support the Obama administration's decision not to seek congressional approval on Libya. Meanwhile, some of Koh's former colleagues in academia attacked his views. "Make no mistake: Obama is breaking new ground, moving decisively beyond his predecessors," wrote two Yale law scholars.[26]

The administration resorted to similar verbal evasions in describing the goal of the military action. At Obama's urging, the Security Council had approved "all necessary measures" against Libyan forces—but for the limited purpose of protecting Libyan civilians from Gaddafi's forces. The Obama White House construed this UN resolution as broadly as it interpreted the War Powers Resolution narrowly. Over the following weeks, Obama made clear (along with Cameron and Sarkozy) that there was a much broader purpose: regime change. They wanted Gaddafi to give up power.

Many of the actions of the allies after the initial attacks were devoted to bringing down Gaddafi and those around him. Some of these efforts were psychological operations, aimed at rattling the Libyan loyalists. American, British and French officials encouraged high-level defections from the regime; they sometimes suggested that more defections were coming and often predicted that Gaddafi was about to fall.

But the allies also sought to bring down Gaddafi by force; the bombing was carried out not merely to protect civilians but to aid the opposition forces. On several occasions, warplanes or missiles bombed Gaddafi's own compound in Tripoli. American officials rejected the idea that the aim of these raids was to assassinate Gaddafi. "The compound was a legitimate command-and-control target—and it [the bombing] had the side benefit of making clear the risk to the leadership itself—in effect, to scare him [Gaddafi] a little bit," said Deputy Secretary of State James Steinberg.[27] In this respect, Obama was following down the path of Ronald Reagan, who had authorized bombing attacks on Gaddafi's compound a quarter century earlier.

Obama and his aides offered a series of explanations for why these attacks were compatible with the supposedly limited mission of protecting civilians. One was that so long as Gaddafi was in power, Libyan civilians could never be safe; therefore, the only way to protect civilians was to bring new leadership to the country. A second explanation, equally coherent but at some tension with the first, held that Gaddafi could stay in power if he stopped attacking civilians and pulled his troops back to Tripoli. (The official who made this argument quickly acknowledged that it wasn't so simple: If Gaddafi did this, allowing the rebel troops to control large parts of the country, his regime would probably collapse.) A third argument, followed by many officials, was to draw a distinction between the "military goal" and the "political goal" in Libya: The military aim, officials said, was to protect civilians, while the political aim was regime change. Obama himself offered a version of this argument in his speech to the nation on Libya, saying that he embraced the goal of regime change but would pursue it through "nonmilitary means."[28]

Why didn't the administration simply come out and acknowledge that the goal of the air campaign was to bring Gaddafi down? One reason was that admitting the goal was regime change would have led to a loss of international support, particularly from the nations that had voted for the more limited mission of protecting civilians. "If we tried to overthrow Gaddafi by force, our coalition would splinter," said Obama in his speech. Another reason was that the Obamians didn't want to be perceived, either at home or abroad, as having sought to use military force for the purpose of regime change. To admit to replacing a dictator by force would have been to raise uncomfortable comparisons with George W. Bush. There were important distinctions, to be sure. Obama's use of force came at a time when large numbers of civilians were in imminent danger. It did not involve the use of ground forces. The military campaign in Libya had support in Europe, in the Middle East and at the United Nations; this time, France took a lead role in proposing the use of force, instead of leading the opposition.

Still, there were many in the Middle East who might not have viewed so benignly the acknowledged use of force to overthrow a dictator. The most plausible explanation of this underlying reality came from a television commentator who said on CNN: "The narrative we want to come out of this is that the Libyan people overthrew a dictator, not that we came in and toppled a despot." Ironically, that commentator was Stephen Hadley, formerly national security adviser to George W. Bush.[29]

And so Obama, Cameron and Sarkozy all fudged their war aims. The bombs continued to fall over Tripoli and other parts of Libya controlled by Gaddafi's forces. The Libyan leader, who many predicted would fall within days or weeks after the start of the military campaign, clung to power month after month. In July, the Obama administration decided to grant formal diplomatic recognition to the opposition's Transitional National Council, opening the way for it to receive more than $30 billion in frozen assets of the Libyan government in the United States.

The French meanwhile were trying to negotiate a deal with Gaddafi. French foreign minister Alain Juppé announced in July that Gaddafi would be permitted to stay in Libya if he would give up power. The French had been the most aggressive of all countries in dealing with Libya, but they were also the most frustrated by the long military campaign, which put a considerable strain on equipment and personnel. Gaddafi spurned the deal. By the summer, he had every reason for greater confidence. The civil war seemed to be stalemated, and the rebels were so beset by internal divisions that their top military leader, General Abdul Fattah Younis, was assassinated by rebels from another tribe. But in mid-August, the stalemate broke: The rebel forces, with the considerable help of NATO air strikes, began to push back Gaddafi's troops toward Tripoli. Within a week, they entered the Libyan capital and, again with NATO planes overhead, managed to take control of the city.

Gaddafi disappeared. It took two months for the troops fighting for Libya's new, transitional government to find him. They finally took control of Gaddafi's hometown, Sirte, on October 20, 2011. There, they discovered Gaddafi hiding inside a drainage pipe. In the final moments, he was subjected in captivity to the sort of violent brutality his regime had once handed out. A throng of angry Libyans hit him, spat upon him, taunted him and possibly sodomized him, according to videos taken by bystanders with cell phones. Gaddafi died from a shot to his head.[30] Soon, his body was put on display in a meat locker.

———

The Libyan campaign represented the apotheosis of the Obamian approach to the world. It showed, once again, that Obama was no pacifist; he was willing to use military power. It demonstrated for the first time that he was willing to put the American military to work on behalf of humanitarian goals, in a way that the realists he admired would not.

Above all, it showed the Obama administration's intense commitment to multilateralism. The president approved the use of military force only after the urging of America's closest allies and only after getting formal approval from the Arab League. Moreover, Obama's multilateralism was of a new strain. It went well beyond previous versions, in which the United States simply consulted with its allies. This time, the United States started the military campaign and then stepped aside while allies took over. It was an approach virtually without precedent since World War II. In the Obamian view, the United States should preserve its leadership role in the world in the coming decades, but it could only do so by making some changes, acknowledging the limits of its power and the greater need to share the costs and responsibilities of a military campaign.

During the Cold War, the United States had been the leader of the free world; now, it was less so. After the Soviet collapse, America had been the world's sole superpower, determining what it wanted and then consulting its allies. Now the dynamic was reversed: Its close allies made the initial decisions and then had to beseech the United States to join with them in military action. America would go along, so long as it didn't have to carry the military burden on its own.

On the vague and subjective question of American leadership, the Obama administration said different things to different audiences. To domestic audiences, it often maintained that America's leadership role was unchanged. When *The New Yorker* published an article on Obama's policies during the Arab Spring and quoted an unnamed American official as saying the United States was "leading from behind," the Obamians were irritated and dismayed, insisting this characterization was inaccurate. "The president was shaping the entire operation," said Ben Rhodes. "He was responsible for the Security Council resolution authorizing 'all necessary measures' in Libya. And then it was U.S. firepower that essentially stopped the advance on Benghazi and cleaned out the Gaddafi air defenses, so that we could then hand over responsibility to NATO and the Arab partners." Privately, some of the Obamians even began to belittle France and Britain, saying the no-fly zone they'd favored would have been of little help to civilians on the ground. However, when dealing with overseas audiences that tended to be more suspicious of America's motives and its power, the administration leaned in the opposite direction by minimizing America's role. In Paris on the day the warplanes first appeared over Libya, Clinton said simply: "We did not lead this."[31]

21

New Moon over Pakistan

Back in the summer of 2007, when Obama was still a fledgling presidential candidate, the *Wall Street Journal*'s intensely conservative editorial page offered him a rare bit of (albeit snide) praise. Obama had just declared that if elected, he would send American troops into Pakistan "if we have actionable intelligence about high-value targets," such as al-Qaeda leaders. He would do so even without the assent of Pakistan's top leaders, he said. At the time, Obama's Democratic rivals had disparaged this position and called it proof of his inexperience. The Bush administration had sided with the other Democrats.. White House press secretary Tony Snow had pointedly observed that the Bush administration's approach was to respect Pakistan as a sovereign government and to work in cooperation with it. However, the *Wall Street Journal* demurred, momentarily casting candidate Obama in a positive light. After noting that Defense Secretary Donald Rumsfeld had once vetoed a plan for a commando raid into Pakistan because it would destabilize the government there, the newspaper said of Obama: "Anyone who wants to run to the right of Rummy on counterterrorism can't be all bad."[1]

Four years later, President Obama did almost exactly what he'd said back in the campaign: He dispatched American forces to the Pakistani town of Abbottabad to kill Osama bin Laden. In a sense, Obama went a step further than his campaign position. He didn't merely act without Pakistan's *cooperation*; he acted without Pakistan's *knowledge*, leaving President Asif Ali Zardari and Army Chief of Staff Ashfaq Parvez Kayani completely in the dark until after Bin Laden was killed.

Many of the basic details of the Bin Laden raid, carried out by Navy

SEALs on May 1, 2011, were made public in the immediate aftermath of the attack. It was the culmination of nearly a year of discussions within the Obama administration, at first to gather the intelligence and then to plan the raid. The one aspect that the postmortem accounts left out was that the key question underlying all the planning was how to handle possible military resistance from Pakistan.

When confronted with various options during the preparations, Obama personally and repeatedly chose the riskiest one for relations with Pakistan. As a result, the plan that was carried out included contingencies for direct military conflict with Pakistani forces. These plans went well beyond merely bringing in a few more SEALs or other forces for a localized fight in the town of Abbottabad. "There were other contingencies for further escalation," acknowledged one official directly involved in the planning. "I mean, you can imagine all kinds of scenarios where we would be able to call on any number of different kinds of forces, if the Pakistanis had chosen to oppose us in the air or on the ground."[2] The administration also spent time preparing for the possibility that there would be large-scale Pakistani protests or riots that might endanger personnel at the U.S. embassy in Islamabad or at the consulates in Peshawar, Karachi and Lahore. Fortunately, because the Bin Laden operation went so well and so quickly, none of these dangers materialized. There was no American war with Pakistan, but Obama had been willing to chance it in order to get Bin Laden.

––––––

When he first arrived in the White House, Obama was briefed on the CIA's plans for finding Osama bin Laden.[3] He had made clear he was not particularly impressed, and told Leon Panetta, the incoming CIA director, that the hunt for Bin Laden should be reinvigorated and put at the top of the agency's list of priorities.

In the summer of 2010, the CIA briefed Obama that it had developed a new lead. The agency had begun to track the al-Qaeda courier who would eventually lead them to the compound in Abbottabad. For a time, throughout the fall and early winter, the question preoccupying those who knew about the new intelligence was whether, in fact, Bin Laden himself was inside the compound. For the CIA, this was still merely a "collection project": The task at hand was to gather more intelligence, not to act on it. Officials maintained their detachment; the new information was merely described as one of the most promising leads on Bin Laden that had come in for a long time. "I think the word 'interesting' was used a lot," one of the officials said drily.

At the end of the year and in early 2011, the intelligence began to seem promising enough that, for the first time, CIA officials began to meet with the Pentagon's Joint Special Operations Command to discuss the feasibility of a military attack on the compound. At that point, Obama instructed them to develop specific military options for him to consider. This may have seemed like an obvious course, but it was, in fact, the first of several junctures where Obama chose the more aggressive of the options before him. The CIA was still not sure that Bin Laden was in the compound, and there were some within the administration, including Defense Secretary Robert Gates, who were dubious that military action was warranted. The skeptics suggested holding off for a time until there was greater certainty. The CIA said there were a variety of further avenues to pursue—technical methods, human sources—in order to confirm that Bin Laden was inside the compound. One of these came to light after the raid: The CIA infiltrated a Pakistani doctor into Abbottabad to give vaccinations, hoping to gain access to blood samples from Bin Laden's children so that the DNA could be compared with that of others in Bin Laden's family. The elaborate ruse didn't work.[4]

But the CIA acknowledged that all of these information-gathering efforts would take months to come to fruition. Obama didn't want to delay. If the intelligence wasn't absolutely certain, it was nevertheless the best the United States had gotten since Bin Laden's escape from Tora Bora in 2001. Long delays and more intrusive intelligence collection increased the chance that Bin Laden and his aides might discover they were being watched and would disappear. The hunt for Bin Laden would have to start all over again.

When the Pentagon and CIA brought to Obama their first cut at plans for attacking the compound, he was confronted with his next decision. The ideas included the possibility of some sort of U.S. military action carried out jointly with Pakistan. Obama quickly rejected that approach on grounds of the need to maintain secrecy. Even if only a handful of Pakistani soldiers or operatives were told about the operation, and even if they were informed only hours or minutes before a military strike, there was still fear that someone on the Pakistani side might tip off someone in Abbottabad. To be sure, American and Pakistani officials had cooperated on sensitive counter-terrorism operations in the past, but this one was different: The United States wasn't even telling the British—America's closest ally in the world—and so, the reasoning went, how could we possibly bring in the government of Pakistan? One answer, clearly, was that the operation would take place on Pakistani soil, but the sovereignty issue was shunted aside. Pakistan's leaders had repeatedly assured the United States that Bin Laden was not in Pakistan, raising the extremely awkward questions of whether they were dissembling or didn't know what was going on inside their own country.

Obama's next decision point on Pakistan came as the Joint Special Operations Command began to draw up more detailed plans for a raid on the Bin Laden compound. The military planners were relatively confident that the joint forces could handle any resistance from inside the Abbottabad compound, whether it came from Bin Laden and his associates or from some Pakistanis helping to protect him. The big, hanging question was how to get American forces into and out of Abbottabad without detection.

The Pentagon came up with a solution on how to get into Abbottabad by overcoming Pakistan's air defenses, using special helicopters to carry the commando team. But getting out was more problematic. What would happen if Pakistani forces resisted? "What the president was concerned about was the idea of official Pakistanis, either local police, the ISI [Pakistan's intelligence service] or the military arriving at the compound to try to confront our forces," explained one counterterrorism official. What if, for example, there were enough Pakistani forces to surround the American team, in effect turning the SEALs into hostages?

Initially, the Pentagon developed a plan for handling Pakistani resistance that was dubbed "Talk Your Way Out." The SEALs conducting the strike would try to hold off opposing Pakistani forces as best they could. Meanwhile, President Obama (or Hillary Clinton or some other top-level official) would engage in hurried dialogue with Pakistani leaders to persuade them to let the Americans go. When Obama was briefed on this approach, however, he was not at all optimistic that it would work. He didn't want the fate of the SEALs to rest on his ability to charm or threaten President Zardari, who would then in turn have to persuade Pakistan's powerful army to release American invaders.

Obama asked the Pentagon to develop the details for other options, which were called "Fight Your Way Out." A counterterrorism official explained it this way: "He basically wanted DOD to provide whatever forces were needed to allow our forces to take care of whatever they faced in the way of opposition, and not to rely on Pakistani goodwill. . . . It was more robust, readily available support from a second set of forces that could have come in and provided us that quick reaction force."[5]

The United States thus planned and prepared for a direct military engagement with Pakistan, if necessary, to make sure the Osama bin Laden operation succeeded.

———

The last decision for Obama was left unresolved until only two days before the attack: whether to conduct the raid by the SEALs at all or, as an alternate plan, simply to hit Bin Laden's compound with an air strike. Throughout the months the Pentagon had been developing plans for a commando raid, it had also been drafting and refining other plans for an air attack.

In the early plans for an air strike, the bombing would have been massive. The logic was that, in order to be sure of Bin Laden's death, it would be necessary to destroy not only the entire compound, but also any underground bunkers, tunnels or safe houses beneath it. "You had to really, in a sense, dramatically overachieve in terms of the amount of ordnance you would use," said one of those who reviewed the plans. But a bombing raid of that sort would likely kill people outside the compound as well.

The president asked the Defense Department to develop plans for a more surgical air strike that would cause less collateral damage. Soon the Pentagon came back with a more tailored approach. Only a part of the compound would be hit, the part where intelligence showed that Bin Laden was most likely to be located. The lighter attack would have spared the lives of ordinary citizens living outside the compound, but there would be less certainty of Bin Laden's death.

All of these plans for air attack, heavy or light, had the same inherent defect: The United States might not be able to demonstrate to the rest of the world that Osama bin Laden had been killed. There would likely be no body, no proof. If the Obama administration simply announced that the al-Qaeda leader had been in the compound and that the attack had killed him, many would refuse to believe it. Conspiracy theories would inevitably be put forward: The Americans were lying; the attack had killed only innocent local residents; Bin Laden had found out at the last minute and fled. The United States itself might not know for sure.

On the other hand, a raid by the SEALs also had some disadvantages. Above all, it meant putting American boots on the ground for hostile action inside Pakistan, without approval from its government. An air attack would be easier for Pakistani leaders to accept. It would be, in the abstract, not much different from the air and drone attacks the Obama administration had already been carrying out to kill al-Qaeda or Taliban leaders in the remote tribal areas of Pakistan—operations to which Pakistani leaders had quietly acquiesced (even though this time the attack would not be in the tribal areas, but about thirty miles from the capital of Islamabad).

The worry was that the SEALs could get into some sort of firefight that jeopardized their lives. Even if that didn't happen, and even if the raid was successful, there would be considerable fallout in Pakistan. Indeed, many things could go wrong. In the National Security Council meetings, senior officials, especially Gates, talked about an unhappy precedent: Jimmy Carter's decision in 1980 to dispatch helicopters with troops into Iran in a failed effort to free American hostages there. (The mission had to be aborted when two helicopters were unable to navigate in the desert.) At the working level of the Obama administration, planners came up with a simple phrase to refer to all the messy things that could happen in the Abbottabad operation. It could, they said, turn into a "shit show."

Inside the administration, the planning was carried out in virtually unprecedented secrecy. This was not the sort of decision on which the president could rely on the old network of Obamians from the campaign. Most of them didn't know what was under way. The one Obamian in the center of things was Denis McDonough, who had always worked closely with top counterterrorism adviser John Brennan.

The extreme secrecy within the administration created some awkwardness. Only a handful of people knew what was in the works beyond the president, vice president, the CIA director, and the secretaries of state and defense. Indeed, for a time no one at the State Department was aware of the planning but Clinton. She was traveling overseas regularly during this period, closely involved in international diplomacy on issues like Libya. Ordinarily, senior officials like Clinton took part in National Security Council meetings from overseas by secure videoconference through a system nick-named "sevits" (secure video teleconferencing system). For the Bin Laden raid, however, no video participation was allowed, because of worries that some communications technician helping out with the transmission might overhear what was going on.

This meant that when Clinton was out of town, no one from the State Department would be present at the top-level meetings. Yet the participants realized the State Department needed to be informed in order to take care of its own personnel and facilities in Pakistan. (That sensitivity was reason-able: In 1979, an angry mob inspired by Ayatollah Khomeini in Iran had burned the embassy in Islamabad to the ground, killing one American.) After a time, Obama gave permission for some other officials at State to be "read into" the planning, so that they could participate.

Some cabinet-level officials were not informed until the day of the opera-tion. FBI Director Robert Mueller was preparing to leave for an overseas trip to, of all places, Pakistan, when Brennan called him the night before to tell him not to go; Brennan said he would explain why later. The tight restric-tions applied to the military, too. Admiral William McRaven, the com-mander of the Joint Special Operations Command who was in charge of the raid planning, crossed paths inside the White House with General John Allen, the deputy commander of Centcom. They were old friends, both of four-star rank. "What brings you here?" asked Allen. McRaven mumbled that he had come for lunch with a friend.

The handful of staff members involved in the planning put together a playbook for the top-level participants, a binder with tabs for each of the many difficult issues that had to be addressed. Who would say what to which Pakistani leaders immediately afterward? What would they tell Hamid Karzai, the president of Afghanistan, from whose territory the operation would be launched? What would happen if Bin Laden was captured rather than killed—where would he be detained?

One of the tabs addressed the reverse question: If Bin Laden was killed in the raid, what would be done with his remains? If the SEALs left his body in the compound, there would be uncertainty whether he had really been killed. The SEALs could take a picture of his corpse, but conspiracy theorists would inevitably claim that the photo had been doctored. If, instead, the SEALs brought Bin Laden's remains out from Abbottabad with them, where could it go? Any place Bin Laden was buried would become, in the words of one American official, "a shrine to jihadism and a burden for whatever nation-state on whose territory it would be found." As a result, the planners concluded that if Obama chose the raid option and Bin Laden was killed, he would probably be buried at sea. The administration decided it would check first with Saudi Arabia, where Bin Laden was born, to make sure the government or the Bin Laden family didn't object to this procedure. Brennan, the former CIA station chief in Saudi Arabia, was assigned this task.

By late April, it was time for a decision. The tabs had been leafed through, the contingencies explored. Obama could take any of three actions: (1) a bombing or missile attack; (2) the raid with ground forces; or (3) a delay until the CIA had more intelligence and greater certainty that Bin Laden was inside the Abbottabad compound. The forces were getting ready; Admiral McRaven and the SEALs team had already assembled in Afghanistan, prepared to move if Obama decided on the raid.

On the night of Thursday, April 28, Obama convened his most senior advisers—Biden, Clinton, Gates and Panetta—to get their final thoughts on what he should do. He told them he wouldn't decide during the meeting itself, but afterward, on his own. The conditions were right for attacking the compound soon: Over the following week, there would be a new moon over Pakistan and the skies would be darker than at any time until a month later. While Gates remained skeptical, the advisers supported the idea of an attack without further delay. The participants ran through, once again, the pros and cons of attacking the compound from the air or through a raid by the SEALs.

The following morning, Obama summoned his four senior White House advisers. They amounted to an Irish American band: Tom Donilon, John Brennan, Denis McDonough and Bill Daley. Because the president was about to leave town on a day trip that Friday, the session took only five minutes. The mission was a "go," he told them. He had decided upon the helicopter assault option with the SEALs. He did not want a bombing or missile attack that might leave unclear whether Bin Laden had been killed or even whether he had been inside the compound. Obama was willing to put American boots on the ground, even if it could provoke a conflict with Pakistani forces and would certainly cause a furious reaction inside Pakistan afterward.

It is not clear what the precise rules of engagement were—whether Obama ordered the SEALs, without qualification, to kill Osama bin Laden, or whether there was some circumstance under which he could have instead been taken alive. (The custom in a commando operation targeting a particular individual is for the leader to ask, beforehand, "Is this a kill or is it a capture?"[6]) Afterward, administration officials insisted the SEALs would have been permitted to capture Bin Laden. "If we had the opportunity to take him alive, we would have done that," Brennan told reporters. The fact that they had at least considered where he might be detained indicates that capturing Bin Laden may have at some point been an option.[7] But a number of other facts point to the reverse conclusion. Obama and his aides had made specific, elaborate plans for his sea burial. They had considered, until the very end, the idea of an air attack that would have killed Bin Laden, an approach employed regularly, using drones, for other al-Qaeda figures. They had rejected that option in part because Bin Laden's grave site would have caused too many problems for any government on whose soil it was located. A live Bin Laden in prison would have been far worse; the Obama administration had already discovered how difficult it was to bring far lesser al-Qaeda figures to trial in the United States. If Bin Laden was tried in a military court at Guantánamo and, presumably, executed, that approach would also have reopened the old divisions between the United States and Europe over both Guantánamo and the death penalty. The evidence overwhelmingly suggests that, despite the administration's explanations afterward, Obama sent the SEALs on a mission to kill Bin Laden.

———

Obama left it up to McRaven, commander of the Joint Special Operations Command, to decide exactly when the raid should take place. There had been some casual suggestions that the attack should be delayed past Saturday, April 30, because that was the night of the White House Correspondents' Dinner in Washington, and many senior officials, including Obama, would be at this event. What if something went wrong, while virtually all members of the national security team were off in their tuxedos and gowns at the dinner? Obama said that problem could be handled: Whoever needed to be back at the White House could claim to have come down with a sudden stomachache or find some other excuse for leaving. The timing decision should be made strictly on operational grounds, he said.

But the weather over the flight routes into Pakistan wasn't good on Saturday night. Admiral McRaven scheduled the raid for the following night instead. That Sunday, Obama and the entire national security team assembled at the White House to follow the progress of the raid. (This gathering produced the iconic pictures of the administration during the Bin Laden raid: tense senior officials, some standing, some sitting, some in uniform or jacket and tie, some in shirtsleeves, all staring intensely at a monitor.) The SEALs team made it from Afghanistan into Pakistan without detection. They killed Bin Laden, who was unarmed, and flew out from Abbottabad with his corpse. One of the helicopters went down and had to be left behind, but otherwise, the operation went smoothly. There was no "shit show," no firefight with resisting Pakistani forces.

When it was over, the president and others started making the necessary phone calls, many of which had been on the to-do lists put together well in advance. Obama made the awkward but obligatory phone call to President Asif Ali Zardari. He also phoned other world leaders, starting with British prime minister David Cameron. Brennan called the Saudis, who said to go ahead with the sea burial. The officials in the White House Situation Room relaxed. They began to swap stories of where they had been on September 11.

Next, the president needed to go public with the news. As speechwriter and media strategist, Ben Rhodes had not been brought into the planning until the final weeks. (Some other administration officials who dealt with the news media were informed only in the final hours before the raid.) Late that Sunday, as the president looked over what Rhodes was drafting for him, Rhodes said he couldn't help but think back to the very first campaign speech he had written for the campaign, back in the summer of 2007. In that speech, Obama had pledged to send American forces into Pakistan, even without Pakistan's approval, to attack al-Qaeda personnel there. "Don't think I haven't thought of that, too," Obama replied.[8]

The impact of Osama bin Laden's death was widespread. There were repercussions for national security, for American political life, for intelligence and counterterrorism, for the Islamic world, for Pakistan and for America's war in Afghanistan.

Above all, Bin Laden's death was a milestone in America's path away from September 11, easing the psychological impact of al-Qaeda's successful attack on American soil. A decade after the attacks on the World Trade Center and Pentagon, the United States had finally tracked down and killed the man who'd planned those attacks and led the organization that had carried them out.

Overseas, there were some brief complaints about the way the operation had been carried out. "Which law governs the execution of Bin Laden?" asked one European columnist. But others pointed out that al-Qaeda didn't exactly follow judicial procedures before killing thousands of people, whether in large groups on September 11 or in individual killings such as of journalist Daniel Pearl. No European government was willing to condemn what the Obama administration had done.[9]

Inside the United States, there was virtually no controversy, only rejoicing. The killing of Bin Laden briefly lifted the mood of a nation beset by economic and political problems. It brought forth a sense of national unity and a rare bipartisan consensus. Among Republicans, even Dick Cheney lauded the operation: "I want to congratulate President Obama and the members of his national security team," Cheney said in a statement. Few questioned that the outcome helped Obama's political standing; the debate was over how long the spike in his popularity would last. Skeptics recalled that it had been taken for granted that George H. W. Bush's reelection was assured after American forces won the Persian Gulf War in 1991. Bush lost, however, largely because of the economy.

The commando operation contradicted the stereotype that Democrats were weak on national security and remote from military life. In this instance, in fact, Obama had been willing to use military force in a way that George W. Bush, ever careful to work in tandem with Pakistani authorities, would not. Aides who had served in previous administrations were effusive in their praise. "The stakes could not have been higher. I've never seen a more courageous decision made by a leader," said Tony Blinken. "We had a totally circumstantial case on whether Bin Laden was in fact there. We didn't identify him until we got him. And the president had most of the senior people around him recommending other courses of action."[10]

The Obamians were quick to claim that the Abbottabad operation had a beneficial impact on the Arab Spring and the Islamic world. "Bin Laden is the past; what's happening in the region is the future," Rhodes asserted.[11] In the Obamian narrative, Muslims who had once seen terrorism as the only avenue for bringing about political change in the Arab world were now turning instead to the electoral process, to democracy. It was a coherent and appealing argument, but still an unproven one. It seemed to assume that those who took to the streets for democracy in the Arab Spring were drawn from the same population as those who joined al-Qaeda—as if there were a body of people across the Middle East who somehow functioned like swing voters choosing between political parties in an American election. This perspective also exemplified the Obamians' determinedly optimistic view of how the Arab Spring would come out; they continued to argue that the events of 2011 represented historic change and that political liberalization in the Middle East was inevitable.

The Obama administration had early on narrowed Bush's phrase "war on terror" to simply a war on al-Qaeda. For that war, under whatever name, the death of Bin Laden marked an obvious turning point that required a fundamental change in tactics and focus. Ever since September 11, the counterterrorism efforts had been directed above all at stopping al-Qaeda from sending operatives to the United States from its training camps in Afghanistan or Pakistan. But weeks after Bin Laden's death, Brennan unveiled a new counterterrorism strategy that, for the first time, gave top priority to attacks "from within" the United States.[12]

The administration, Brennan said, would give new emphasis to al-Qaeda "adherents" inside the United States, who in some cases had little or no direct contact with al-Qaeda itself. The change was prompted by events such as the incident in Fort Hood, Texas, in which army psychiatrist Nidal Malik Hasan was accused of killing thirteen people and wounding thirty-two others; he earlier had communicated with Anwar al-Awlaki, the former imam who called for attacks against Americans from his base in Yemen. Brennan warned that al-Qaeda adherents within the United States could be inspired to violence by videos or Internet postings of English-speaking al-Qaeda leaders overseas.[13] The new counterterrorism strategy also called for greater attention to al-Qaeda "affiliates," such as Al-Qaeda in the Arabian Peninsula, the Yemen-based group that had tried to carry out the underwear bombing in the airplane over Detroit.

Meanwhile, administration officials engaged in a largely semantic debate over whether al-Qaeda's core organization in Pakistan and Afghanistan might be on the brink of defeat after Bin Laden's death. The SEALs had brought out from the Abbottabad compound not only Bin Laden's body, but also a large assortment of computer hard drives, flash drives and disks containing Bin Laden's messages to and from others in the organization. It was, overall, a massive collection of new intelligence for the CIA about the inner workings of al-Qaeda. On a trip to Afghanistan two months after Bin Laden's death, Leon Panetta, who by then had taken over from Gates as defense secretary, said the United States was "within reach" of defeating al-Qaeda.[14]

———

Obama administration officials admitted in the months after the raid on Abbottabad that they had underestimated the reaction in Pakistan. They expected Pakistani officials would be upset; the United States had, after all, concealed their plans for the operation, knocked out Pakistani air defenses, put American troops on Pakistani soil and thoroughly embarrassed the Pakistani military. Even so, the Pakistani fury took Washington by surprise. Three months after the Bin Laden operation, one counterterrorism official, speaking slowly and choosing his words carefully, said: "We certainly anticipated that the Pakistani leadership would find what we did unwelcome, and would feel bruised and resentful. I think the depth and breadth of that has probably gone further than we had anticipated."[15]

Immediately after the raid, the United States and Pakistan each had reasons for new grievances with the other. From the American perspective, Bin Laden had been found not far from Pakistan's capital city, in a town that also happens to hold the Pakistan Military Academy and military barracks. Many Americans asked, legitimately, whether Pakistani military or intelligence officials might have been complicit in hiding the al-Qaeda leader and September 11 mastermind. The Obama administration's carefully worded position was that it had no evidence any senior-level Pakistani leader or officer was aware Bin Laden was there. "My supposition is, somebody knew," Gates said. "We don't know whether it was retired people, whether it was low level—pure supposition on our part. It's hard to go to them with an accusation when we have no proof that anybody knew."[16]

From Pakistan's perspective, the United States had intruded on the country's sovereignty in a way that went far beyond anything in the past. In public, its leaders had complained about American drone operations over Pakistan, yet they had been aware of them and allowed them to happen. But this was a secret operation on the ground. The air force had failed to detect the helicopters as they flew into Pakistan. Furious Pakistanis called the raid a national humiliation. Pakistan's intelligence chief, Lieutenant General Ahmed Shuja Pasha, told parliament he had offered his resignation to military authorities, but that it had not been accepted.

In the months before the raid, the two countries had already been at odds over the case of Raymond Davis, an American contractor working for the CIA who shot two armed Pakistani on the streets of Lahore. Davis was thrown into jail in January 2011 and was finally, after American appeals, set free in March. (Davis's release was a factor in Washington's planning for the Bin Laden operation; U.S. officials feared that if he was imprisoned at the time of the raid, he could conceivably have been killed.) Pakistan had also increasingly been protesting the American drone strikes.

The American military operation in Abbottabad amounted to pouring gasoline on a slow-burning fire. Pakistani civilian, military and intelligence leaders lined up to denounce the United States. Days after the raid, Kayani, the army chief of staff, warned that any similar action would cause Pakistan to end its cooperation with the United States.[17] That same week, Pakistani newspapers made public the name of the CIA station chief in the country, after apparently being tipped to do so by Pakistan's intelligence service.

There were other retaliatory actions, too. Pakistan allowed Chinese military engineers to examine the American stealth helicopter that crashed in

Abbottabad during the raid. The defense minister announced that the country had barred U.S. drone flights from a Pakistani air base close to the border with Afghanistan. Authorities arrested several Pakistanis who were found to have been cooperating with the CIA. One of them was the doctor who'd run the vaccination program in Abbottabad. Others were Pakistanis who were said to have given the CIA the pictures or license plate numbers of visitors to the Bin Laden compound.[18]

The Obama administration was willing to retaliate on its own, at least to some extent. In early July, the administration disclosed that it was suspending or canceling hundreds of millions of dollars in security assistance to Pakistan. However, senior U.S. officials also began trying to smooth over the frictions. "The long history of the U.S.-Pakistani relationship has had its ebbs and flows," Gates told reporters in his final news conference as secretary of defense. "We need each other, and we need each other more than just in the context of Afghanistan."[19]

———

Of all the fallout from Bin Laden's death, the most important was its impact on the war in Afghanistan. At the time of the attack on Abbottabad, the Obama administration was eight weeks away from a decision on the future of American deployments in Afghanistan. The raid, it turned out, influenced the administration's deliberations, strengthening the hand of those who wanted to cut back significantly on the number of troops fighting the war. Rhodes acknowledged that Bin Laden's death "did make it easier, I think, for the president to take a position that was more aggressive [in reducing troop strength] than the recommendation from his military commander."[20]

In late 2009, when Obama had ordered his surge of 30,000 more U.S. troops to Afghanistan, he also set a deadline for when those forces would start to come home: July 2011. This was immediately unpopular with defense and military leaders, who believed such a deadline could encourage the Taliban to wait the Americans out. Gates rushed to soften the meaning of the promise, telling Congress that "the pace and character of [the] drawdown . . . will be determined by conditions on the ground."[21]

Within a year, the administration appeared to dilute the significance of the July 2011 deadline still further. Top officials, including Gates, Clinton and Mullen, began to stress the year 2014 in their speeches and public remarks.

America's European allies soon followed suit; at a NATO summit meeting in December 2010, the members agreed to carry forward the mission in Afghanistan until the end of 2014. The two dates were not entirely incompatible; Obama had set July 2011 as the point at which the 30,000 *surge* forces would *start* to come home; 2014 was the time when full responsibility for the war was to be handed over to the government of Afghanistan, and all (or at least most) of the approximately 100,000 American troops in Afghanistan could come home. Still, the switch in emphasis to 2014 carried an unmistakable message: Don't count on too much change in July 2011.

The war, meanwhile, was not going particularly well. With the increase in U.S. deployments, the number of American deaths jumped from 155 in 2008 to 317 in 2009, and to 499 in 2010. "Progress comes slowly and at a very high price in the lives of our men and women in uniform," said Obama a year after he'd ordered the surge. "In many places, the gains we've made are still fragile and reversible."[22]

Military leaders had argued for the surge on grounds that they needed a relatively limited period of time, as in Iraq, to turn the course of the war. But in the early months of 2011, Pentagon officials suggested that very few troops would be pulled out of Afghanistan at the time of the original July deadline. Some military leaders spoke of an array of options ranging from virtually no troop withdrawals at all to a drawdown of at most 5,000. Others said that of the few thousand forces pulled out in July, most or all would be support forces and engineers, not combat troops.[23]

That was where things stood at the time of Bin Laden's death. That event changed the terms of the debate inside the administration. In the White House, the focus was turned away from the military problem of how to defeat the Taliban on the ground in Afghanistan toward the more fundamental strategic question of why the American forces were fighting there. When Obama first ordered the surge, he said the purpose was to "disrupt, dismantle and defeat" al-Qaeda, so that it could no longer threaten the United States or its allies. The Abbottabad operation, along with a series of drone attacks that killed other al-Qaeda leaders in Pakistan, showed that the United States had achieved more than a little success toward reaching this goal—enough, at least, for Obama to draw down the forces more quickly than military leaders had envisioned.

The Pentagon was understandably concentrated on the task of winning the war. It was trying to carry out in Afghanistan the strategy of counterinsurgency it had earlier adopted in Iraq. But the Bin Laden operation raised new doubts about whether that was the right strategy for Afghanistan. Did the United States really need to win over the support of the people of Afghanistan, town by town and province by province, in order to accomplish its larger purpose of defanging al-Qaeda? Or, to put it another way, were there other, more cost-effective means of achieving that goal?

Without quite saying so, Obama was in the process of shifting strategy. He was beginning to turn toward the counterterrorism strategy that Vice President Biden had proposed, unsuccessfully, during the long internal debate in 2009. Counterterrorism meant a greater reliance on drones and special forces to kill al-Qaeda's leaders; it required fewer troops than counterinsurgency. In the year and a half since the surge, American drones and special forces, like the SEALs, had achieved more tangible and certainly more spectacular successes in Pakistan than the ground forces had in their attempts to clear and hold new territory in Afghanistan. (Of course, the relationship between these two approaches was more complex: Without an American military presence to hold ground in Afghanistan, the Joint Special Operations Command would have had no base from which to launch the SEALs attack that killed Bin Laden.)

The truth was that the Obamians were losing their enthusiasm for counterinsurgency, a strategy requiring not only lots of troops, but large amounts of both patience and money. By 2011, the war in Afghanistan was costing roughly $110 billion a year, at a time when Obama was in the midst of intense battles with the Republican-controlled House of Representatives over the federal budget, the debt ceiling and taxes. Once the Obamians confirmed for themselves how expensive and slow a counterinsurgency campaign in Afghanistan would be, it was not surprising that they would look for an alternative.

In the months leading up to the July deadline, senior Pentagon officials along with General Petraeus recommended a cutback of no more than 3,000 to 4,000 of the 30,000 surge troops Obama had decided to send to the country in late 2009.[24] It would have been no more than a token fulfillment of the president's pledge to begin bringing the surge forces home in mid-2011.

This time, Obama chose not to follow the military leaders' advice in the way he had two years earlier. He decided to withdraw 10,000 troops by the end of the year. Even more significantly, he said the remaining 20,000 surge troops should come home by September 2012, a timetable quicker than military leaders would have liked. That would still leave nearly 70,000 American troops in Afghanistan, considerably more than when Obama took office. (He'd already sent more than 20,000 troops to the war during his first months in the White House, before the additional surge of 30,000 at the end of the year.)

Obama's televised speech explaining the cutbacks, delivered from the White House on June 22, 2011, opened with references to Bin Laden's death and returned to it again later, making clear that it provided a rationale (and also political cover) for the drawdown in Afghanistan. The president also touched obliquely on the larger change in his thinking reflected in his decision. "When threatened, we must respond with force," Obama declared. "But when that force can be targeted, we need not deploy large armies overseas."[25]

Those words did not bode well for the future of counterinsurgency in an Obama administration. Indeed, Obama had already paved the way for a change in his approach with a series of high-level personnel decisions made two months earlier. Gates had said he would retire as defense secretary in 2011, after serving for four years in two administrations. Obama had appointed Panetta to replace him, and Petraeus to take over as CIA director. That appointment showed considerable respect for Petraeus and gave further breadth to Petraeus's career. But it also removed Petraeus, by far the nation's most prominent proponent of counterinsurgency, from the ranks of the military and the Pentagon hierarchy. (Although Petraeus was America's best-known general, Obama passed over the option of appointing him to become chairman of the Joint Chiefs of Staff.) The series of personnel changes also brought to the Pentagon a new leader, Panetta, whose primary recent achievement had been in counterterrorism—the drive to find and kill Bin Laden—and whose early career, both in Congress and in the Clinton administration, had been devoted to budgetary issues.

Obama didn't talk much about this change in thinking, his evident shift away from counterinsurgency. Doing so could have led to some frictions or upheaval; the military had only recently and in some cases grudgingly accommodated itself to the doctrine of counterinsurgency. It might also have raised questions about why Obama had changed his mind, and why he had not embraced the counterterrorism strategy before the surge, at the end of 2009, when Biden had recommended it.

The administration clearly hoped to find a way out of the war in Afghanistan through diplomacy rather than a military victory over the Taliban. But that would require a deal with at least some parts of the Taliban. The person originally in charge of such negotiations, Richard Holbrooke, had passed away. And, indeed, two years into his administration, Obama seemed to have turned away from the entire concept of appointing well-known "czars" or special envoys to oversee various problems or regions. George Mitchell, the Middle East peace envoy, quietly stepped down in the spring of 2011. Appointing those czars had been a convenient way of getting top people into their jobs immediately after Obama took office, a way that avoided the ludicrously slow process of Senate confirmation.

Finding the right American negotiator was only the first of Obama's problems in reaching a diplomatic settlement. The larger problem was the worldview and record of the Taliban. In the late 1990s, when the Taliban ruled the country, it had imposed a severe version of Sharia law, repressing political enemies, imposing strict codes for dress and hair, requiring women to wear the burka, prohibiting women from education and jobs and destroying some of the country's best-known art and sculpture.

Nancy Pelosi, the House Democratic minority leader and former Speaker of the House, provided an indication of just how difficult it would be to work out an accommodation with the Taliban. Pelosi was the highest-ranking of any self-identified liberal or progressive in Washington. She was a leader of antiwar forces: She had been one of the main opponents of the war in Iraq and a leading skeptic about the wisdom of Obama's surge in Afghanistan. She was certainly in favor of a diplomatic settlement of the war in Afghanistan. And yet, in an interview for this book, Pelosi indicated that there were some conditions on her support for a settlement, some outcomes in Afghanistan that she could not accept. "We did not go over there for ten years to have women returned to a Taliban state of existence," she said.[26]

Yet the subjugation of women seemed intrinsic to the entire Taliban movement. That posed some dilemmas for the administration: Achieving the commendable goal of protecting Afghan women from being returned to the dark ages might require at least a continuation of the war, if not a complete military victory over the Taliban. Even antiwar leaders like Pelosi have strong views on how a war should end, and what terms for peace would be unacceptable.

In the section of his 2011 Afghanistan speech that attracted the most attention, Obama seemed to offer his own answer to this problem. "America, it is time to focus on nation building at home," he said. This was a frequent refrain for Obama; he had said the same thing, only slightly less forcefully, when he had announced the surge of troops to Afghanistan eighteen months earlier. Obama's words sounded like a milder, more qualified version of George McGovern's "Come Home, America." In a sense, the Democrats had come full circle.

But as Pelosi's appeal not to abandon the women of Afghanistan indicates, the idea that America should turn its attention inward is always easier to accept in the abstract than it is when applied to the most egregious abuses, the most repugnant of societies. Americans will always have ideals to pursue, repression to combat, lives to save beyond their own borders. Obama, an instinctive realist, discovered that sense of idealism for himself in the Arab Spring and in Libya. The United States will also continue to have considerable military might to exert across the globe on behalf of both its interests and its ideals. It remains unclear, in the face of growing economic problems, how much power America will be able to (or will want to) exert in pursuit of its ideals.

Epilogue: Unfinished Business

On January 20, 2012, three years after Barack Obama took the oath of office as president, the world was particularly unsettled. Over the previous months, there had been a series of political convulsions in Egypt, Libya, Syria, North Korea, Pakistan and Russia. The European economy was still in perilous shape and so (for very different reasons) was Iran's. In China, the Communist Party leadership was tightening up its repression and stepping up its shrill condemnations of the West as it sought to make sure an economic slowdown could not lead to a spread in social unrest.

These events served to demonstrate not just what Obama had accomplished, but also how much had eluded him. Obama was in the process of recasting American policy for a new, post-Iraq era, one in which the United States would have to cope with increasing budgetary constraints and diminishing influence over the course of events. Yet the list of unfinished business was a long one.

Obama could point to the death of Osama bin Laden as a triumph. (Indeed, it was already clear at the beginning of 2012 that the Obamians were preparing to showcase the killing of the mastermind of the September 11 attacks as a core element in the president's campaign for reelection.) And indeed, the Bin Laden raid was the prime example of a much larger change: The increased use of drones and special operations had altered the course of the war against al-Qaeda in America's favor.

Yet elsewhere most of Obama's achievements, while real, seemed provisional or preliminary, merely setting the stage for the United States to have to confront more fundamental problems. In finally cutting America loose from Hosni Mubarak in Egypt, for example, Obama succeeded in opening the way for change there, but then found himself facing new quandaries: how to persuade the Egyptian army to give up its control of the country; how to cope with the rise of popular Islamic movements newly empowered by democracy; and how to deal with other longtime American partners in the Middle East, particularly Saudi Arabia, that were just as anti-democratic as Mubarak and were upset that the United States had encouraged his resignation. In similar fashion, Obama had, to his credit, managed to drain the poison out of America's relations with Europe in such a way that European leaders were more able to work with the United States on issues such as economic sanctions against Iran. Yet the cooperation on the Iran sanctions merely highlighted the larger problem, which was Iran itself. As Obama moved into his fourth year in the White House, all efforts to end its nuclear program had been unavailing.

On December 19, 2011, North Korea announced the death of Kim Jong-Il, the leader who had ruled the country and supervised its development of nuclear weapons for the previous seventeen years. Kim was merely the last of several international figures who died, were killed or fell from power in 2011. The list also included Gaddafi in Libya, Mubarak in Egypt, Ben Ali in Tunisia and Silvio Berlusconi in Italy. There was every reason to think that 2012 would be similarly tumultuous. There would be presidential elections not only in the United States but also in France, Russia, Taiwan, Mexico, Venezuela and probably Egypt. China's Communist Party was preparing for a change in leadership. In Iran, President Mahmoud Ahmadinejad was locked in an intense power struggle with the country's supreme leader, Ayatollah Ali Khamenei. In Syria, Bashar al-Assad was clinging to power amid continuing civil strife and growing international isolation. Amid all these other uncertainties, the European financial crisis still threatened to deal another shock to the world's economy.

––––––

Looking around the world, Obama and his aides thought of themselves as having been generally successful. There was one specific foreign-policy problem, however, on which they freely acknowledged things had not gone well: their efforts to move toward an Israeli-Palestinian peace settlement. "We have not gotten the results that we wanted to have in the Arab-Israeli peace process, no doubt," reflected Tom Donilon, Obama's national security adviser. "There are a lot of reasons for that, but I think that if there has been a place where we have not been able to achieve the goals along the path we set out at the beginning, it is there."[1]

The underlying dynamics had been set in motion only a few weeks after Obama's inauguration, when Israeli elections led to the return of the Likud Party's Benjamin Netanyahu as prime minister. Obama, during his presidential campaign, had been recorded on tape telling one private group, "I think there is a strain within the pro-Israel community that says unless you adopt an unwavering pro-Likud approach to Israel that you're anti-Israel, and that can't be the measure of our friendship with Israel."[2]

Obama's mentor Abner Mikva, other Chicago friends, and several members of his new administration, such as Rahm Emanuel, had all emphasized the importance of persuading Israel to stop building new settlements in the occupied territories claimed by the Palestinians. Once in the White House, Obama moved fairly quickly to put this idea into effect. In his Cairo speech in June 2009, he said, without qualification, "It is time for these settlements to stop." On this issue, as with others early in his presidency, Obama seemed to be trying to follow the example of the George H. W. Bush administration, which had also applied strong pressure on Israel to freeze settlements.

But the attempt failed; Netanyahu resisted the pressure. Relations with Israel reached a nadir in March 2010, when Israeli officials announced the construction of new housing in East Jerusalem just as Vice President Joe Biden was in Israel preparing for meetings there. When Netanyahu visited Washington two weeks later, Obama and his aides treated him icily and made sure their displeasure was made public: They allowed no photographs of Netanyahu's meeting with Obama or any news briefings about it. The tensions were eventually smoothed over.

Eventually, frustrated by the Obama administration's diminishing influence over Israel, Mahmoud Abbas, the president of the Palestinian Authority, decided to shift his attention to the United Nations and ask it to recognize the existence of a Palestinian state. Obama sought to dissuade him. In his speech concerning the Arab Spring on May 19, 2011, he said the starting point for negotiations over a new Palestinian state should be the borders that existed in 1967, before Israel captured the West Bank and Gaza Strip in the

Six-Day War. The two sides could then negotiate "mutually agreed swaps" of territory from those 1967 lines, Obama said. Netanyahu, on a trip to the United States, quickly denounced the idea.

Despite Obama's efforts, America's influence with the Palestinian leadership was diminishing, too. In the fall of 2011, Abbas formally asked the U.N. Security Council to grant membership to a Palestinian state, rejecting the Obama administration's pleas to hold off. That in turn forced Obama to reaffirm America's support for Israel; the administration quickly announced that it would veto any resolution for Palestinian membership.

It became increasingly clear that Obama's drive for a Middle East peace settlement were going nowhere. Early in 2011, former Senate majority leader George Mitchell resigned as the president's special envoy to the Middle East. Near the end of the year, Dennis Ross, who had served as Obama's senior adviser on both Iran and the Middle East, also stepped down. "Ultimately there will be no peace without negotiations," Ross wrote in early 2012. "But there should also be no illusions about the prospects of a breakthrough any time soon."[3]

Mitchell and Ross had been two of the three high-level negotiators Obama brought into his new administration. The third was Richard Holbrooke. All had achieved considerable success in the Clinton administration: Mitchell in Northern Ireland, Ross in the Middle East, Holbrooke in the Balkans. None of the three could accomplish anything comparable in the Obama era. While the reasons were different in each case, there was a common underlying factor: the United States simply had a far less dominant role in the world between 2009 and 2012 than it had had in the 1990s.

———

The Obama administration also found itself struggling to keep up with events elsewhere in the Middle East. On the first anniversary of the Arab Spring, Egypt's military leaders were still clinging to power, but Islamic groups had moved toward the forefront of the country's politics.

A year earlier, a series of phone calls from Defense Secretary Robert Gates to Egyptian defense minister Mohamed Hussein Tantawi had helped pave the way for Mubarak's resignation. But Tantawi and other Egyptian military leaders with longstanding ties to the United States had proved no more willing to relinquish control of the country than Mubarak.

They had originally promised a presidential election in September but then put it off for an indefinite period. That fall, they put forward a new constitution that would grant the armed forces special privileges and protection from military control. In November, hundreds of thousands of Egyptians returned to Tahrir Square to demand that the military give way to civilian rule. The armed forces and police countered with a crackdown. Obama condemned the violence and supported the protesters' call for the military to give up power, thus distancing himself from Tantawi and the other generals. The military leadership increasingly blamed the United States for the country's turmoil; a month later, police raided the offices of three large American institutions supporting democratic change in Egypt.

At the beginning of 2012, Egypt completed the last of three rounds of elections for a new parliament, its first since the revolution. The results were striking, if not surprising: Islamist parties won more than 60 percent of the popular vote and a majority of seats. The Islamists were themselves divided, however; the moderate, well-organized Muslim Brotherhood took about 40 percent, while the extremely conservative Salafists garnered more than 20 percent. The Obama administration rushed to forge a working relationship with the Muslim Brotherhood; senior State Department officials and leading congressmen, such as Senator John Kerry, began to pay visits to its leaders, asking basic questions such as whether they would support the Camp David accords with Israel. They said they would.[4]

The Obama administration thus found itself obliged to pin its hopes for Egypt's political future not on a liberalizing military leadership, not on the secular elite or the young people who had taken to Tahrir Square a year earlier but on the ability of the Muslim Brotherhood, a force the United States had opposed for decades, to fend off the challenges of Islamic fundamentalism in Egypt.

―――――

In his inaugural address, Obama had summarized his new policy of engagement by addressing America's adversaries. "We will extend a hand if you are willing to unclench your fist," he said. Iran was at the top of the list of countries for which these words were intended. But over the following three years, the offer of engagement had been first rejected by Iran and then all but abandoned in Washington.

Administration officials were displaying their own clenched fists.

By early 2012, the United States was seeking to weaken Iran through international economic sanctions, diplomatic isolation, covert intelligence operations against its nuclear weapons program and support for a new regime to replace Assad in Syria, Iran's closest ally. Obama's senior aides made little attempt to hide their animosity toward Iran's leaders. "Look at the decisions they've made," asserted Donilon. "They've basically taken a great people and a great civilization, and they've turned it into an isolated state." He was pleased with the role the Obama administration had played in the regime's difficulties. "We have succeeded in isolating, squeezing, putting pressure economically on them, and politically. And turned them into basically as isolated a place as they've ever been, certainly any time since the revolution in 1979."[5]

With Iran, Obama was in a dangerous race against time. He was trying to stave off the moment when Iran acquired nuclear weapons, an event that would probably prompt neighbors like Saudi Arabia, Egypt and Turkey to try to do the same. Obama was, moreover, also trying to avoid allowing Iran to get so close to nuclear capability that Israel might decide to launch an air strike, or so close that he himself might have to decide whether the United States should attack.

In late 2011, the Obama administration imposed new economic sanctions against Iran's petrochemical industry. Moreover, the United States managed to obtain much greater cooperation from allies for tighter sanctions to cut off Iran's access to the international banking system. At the beginning of 2012, the European Union took the first steps toward an embargo on oil from Iran, and Asian nations also seemed to be reducing their oil imports from Iran. The impact on Iran's economy was increasingly severe. The value of Iran's currency, the rial, was in deep decline; imported consumer goods, such as the iPhone, increased in price by more than 30 percent. The dispute increasingly took on a military dimension; Iran threatened to close the Strait of Hormuz and warned that the United States should not send an aircraft carrier nearby.[6]

In Syria, the Obama administration had overcome its reluctance, a half year earlier, to call for the ouster of Assad. By early 2012, Assad's forces had killed at least five thousand Syrians. The United States was working actively to unify the opposition to the regime; it was enforcing severe economic sanctions on Syria and its leaders.

Still, the administration worked against Assad in the distinctive Obamian fashion. It rejected calls for the use of military force on behalf of the opposition. Obama was content, indeed eager, to let other countries, like Turkey, or other groups of countries, like the Arab League, take the front-line role against Assad. Just as in dealing with Libya, he sought to avoid allowing the effort to replace a dictator being perceived as a mostly American operation.

In early January 2012, Assad rebuffed suggestions that he resign and promised to deal with the protests with an "iron hand."7 It seemed extremely unlikely that he would remain in power for another year.

———

The stiffer China policy launched during Hillary Clinton's visit to Hanoi in 2010 was not ephemeral. It marked a fundamental turning point, not just for dealing with China, but in the overall strategy and priorities of the Obama administration.

Since the early days of the administration, the Obamians had been talking about giving higher priority to Asia. ("We are reorienting our focus to Asia," declared Denis McDonough, at a time when the United States still had nearly 200,000 troops engaged in two wars elsewhere.8) At first, the context was largely economic: the Obamians recognized not only that an increasing share of America's trade was with Asia, but that much of the world's economic growth was coming from Asia. With the 2010 dispute over China's extensive claims in the South China Sea, however, the administration began to recognize that it needed to devote much greater attention to Asia in its military and strategic thinking, too. China's neighbors—not only Vietnam, but American allies like Japan, South Korea and Australia— were growing concerned about China's increasing military power. The risk was not that China would begin conquering other countries, but that without an American counterweight, China could intimidate the region; other nations, even major ones like Japan, might eventually fall under China's sway. The Chinese leadership was growing ever more assertive; its mercantilist policies were hurting the economies of other nations; and the

Obama administration's initial efforts at a working accommodation with Beijing had resulted mostly in bolder Chinese policies and demands.

For more than two years, the administration's supposed new emphasis on Asia remained mostly in the realm of rhetoric. But in the fall of 2011, it began to take concrete form. That November, Obama traveled to Honolulu, Australia and Indonesia. As he did, the administration announced that the United States would begin deploying a contingent of 2,500 U.S. Marines to Australia, rotating them in and out every six months so that there would be a permanent American presence. At the same time, the Obama administration began to push for a new free-trade grouping, the Trans-Pacific Partnership, which would spur trade with many countries in Asia and its surroundings, but not, at the outset, with China. The following month, Clinton made a groundbreaking trip to Burma, the first such visit by any top-level American official in a half century.

Administration officials were quick to portray all these steps in strategic terms as part of what they characterized as America's "pivot" to Asia. "The future of the United States is intimately intertwined with the future of the Asia-Pacific," wrote Clinton in a magazine article published that fall. "A strategic turn to the region fits logically into our overall global effort to secure and sustain America's global leadership."9

The administration did not hide the fact that China's growing assertiveness had prompted the new policy. The purpose was to let the world know that China's growing power did not mean it would be able to dominate Asia, and that America's budgetary problems did not mean that it would pull back from the region. "We are here to stay," said Obama during his Asia trip.10 Even before the deal to keep the Marines in Australia was made public, senior administration officials described it as a paradigm for future such arrangements elsewhere in Asia. "We're looking at a number of other places where we can have other kinds of presence in Asia, and not a diminution at all," said Donilon. He also noted that the United States was beginning to invest in new military capabilities that could neutralize China's efforts to keep the U.S. Navy out of the waters near China and Taiwan.

The Obama administration's ideas for Asia were not entirely new. It was following the example of George Shultz, Ronald Reagan's secretary of state.

A decade after President Nixon's opening to China, Shultz had argued that the United States should not worry so much about a close relationship with Beijing and should instead give priority to its ties with allies like Japan and South Korea.

Administration officials insisted this had been their strategy at the very start of the administration. "We focused quite intensively on what has to be a fundamental in Asia, which has to be a restoration of our alliances," Donilon maintained. That was indeed a fair description of Obama's approach in 2011. But such claims glossed over Obama's first eighteen months in office, when he sought above all to conciliate Beijing. It hadn't worked.

———

America's relationship with Pakistan never recovered from the Bin Laden raid. As some Obama administration officials acknowledged, the fallout was much greater than they had anticipated. The very aspects of the operation that had helped make it a success—keeping it secret from Pakistan, choosing a commando raid rather than an air strike, being willing to risk outright military conflict if Pakistani forces resisted—made it, from the perspective of Pakistani military and intelligence leaders, a disaster. The raid seemed to show that the United States could do what it wanted inside Pakistan, with or without the assent of it leaders. It also exposed the inherent contradictions in the ties between America and Pakistan—above all, the fact that it was hard to say whether the two countries were friends or enemies.

Throughout the summer and fall of 2011, the Obama administration made a series of attempts to repair the damage. In late November, however, an American air strike killed approximately twenty-five Pakistani soldiers at an outpost near Pakistan's border with Afghan. U.S. officials explained that the incident resulted from a series of fog-of-war mistakes: the Pakistani forces had supposedly fired on American and Afghan forces in the belief that they were the Taliban, and Americans were said to have countered by calling in air strikes, believing in turn they had been fired on by the Taliban.

In response, Pakistan ordered the CIA to leave an air base from which it was conducting drone operations and restricted the flow of supplies across Pakistan to NATO forces in Afghanistan. For a time, the United States suspended all drone operations from Pakistan. The consequences extended beyond the operational to the strategic: Pakistani officials announced that they were reevaluating the country's entire relationship with the United States. American officials conceded that ties to Pakistan had reached the point of fundamental change. The United States could no longer count on being able to put American soldiers or CIA agents into Pakistan or to launch drone and air attacks from its soil. In turn, Pakistan could no longer count on billions of dollars in American aid.

Pakistan already possessed more than one hundred nuclear weapons and was producing still more. During Obama's first weeks in office, Bruce Riedel, the South Asia expert who had worked in his presidential campaign, warned Obama about the danger of nuclear weapons falling into the wrong hands in a place like Pakistan—a prospect Obama had called "scary." The killing of Bin Laden more than two years later was Obama's greatest triumph. However, the president had to hope that it did not set off a chain of events that could lead to a nuclear-armed Islamic fundamentalist state in Pakistan.

———

Throughout 2011, the governments of the United States and Iraq had negotiated over what would happen at the end of the year. The status-of-forces agreement establishing the legal basis for the American troop presence in Iraq, signed in the final year of the Bush administration, would run out in December. The Pentagon was eager for a new agreement that would keep some U.S. forces there. In the middle of the year, Defense Department officials spoke of maintaining a contingent of about ten thousand troops at a couple of U.S. bases in Iraq. By the fall, American officials scaled back the numbers to five thousand.[11]

But the negotiations broke down because of lack of enthusiasm, first from the Iraqis and then also from the Obamians. Iraqi officials were reluctant to sign a new agreement in which they would, necessarily, have had to grant immunity for the U.S. troops. "Dammit, make a decision," Defense Secretary Leon Panetta exclaimed on a visit to Baghdad in July. Eventually, Obama and his aides decided that if Iraq didn't want a residual American military presence, they didn't either.

U.S. military leaders had worried about the impact of a complete withdrawal from Iraq. But in political terms, making a clean break was much better for Obama than leaving some American troops in the country.

Getting out of Iraq had been the central theme in the campaign that brought him to the White House. He had reaffirmed that commitment within weeks of taking office. In mid-2010, he had announced the formal end of U.S. combat operations in Iraq, declaring that "it's time to turn the page." Obama was preparing to run for reelection in 2012. Any decision to extend the American troop presence there would be portrayed as a violation of these promises and of the "dumb-war" views on which Obama's career in national politics had been based. Furthermore, it would also raise questions about whether Obama would really withdraw American forces from Afghanistan by 2014, as he had also promised. When Iraqi officials resisted the American requests for a new status-of-forces agreement that would allow some troops to stay on, Obama decided not to treat it as a rebuff. At a White House ceremony in October, he said proudly that all the American forces in Iraq would be home for the holidays.

The war in Iraq had lasted more than eight years and cost nearly a trillion dollars. Approximately 4,500 Americans had been killed and another 32,000 had been wounded. With the end of 2011 approaching, both Biden and Panetta paid visits to Iraq to commemorate the impending American departure. "Those lives were not lost in vain," said Panetta. "They gave birth to an independent, free and sovereign Iraq." The end came quietly. At dusk on Saturday, December 17, 2011, the last American forces, a contingent of about 500 troops at what the U.S. military had called Contingency Operating Base Adder near Nasiriyah in southern Iraq, gathered into a convoy of 110 vehicles. The convoy rolled through the desert and, at 2:30 a.m. the following morning, crossed the border into Kuwait. The facility the Americans left behind was renamed Imam Ali Air Base.[12]

On January 5, 2012, Obama traveled across the Potomac River to the Pentagon to unveil a new document, the Defense Strategic Guidance that would set forth American priorities in military strategy defense spending in the coming years. Appearing before reporters in the Pentagon briefing room, Obama was clearly in early campaign mode, setting forth themes that he could use over the following months. "We've ended our war in Iraq. We've decimated al-Qaeda's leadership," he intoned. "We've delivered justice to Osama bin Laden, and we've put that terrorist network on the path to defeat. . . . Now, we're turning the page on a decade of war."[3] Most people assumed the 2012 campaign would be about economics, but Obama seemed to be exploring whether he could make national security a key part of his campaign message.

The eight-page paper released that day described in detail a series of far-reaching changes in defense strategy. They had been prompted in part by previously announced budget cutbacks of $450 billion over the following decade. The army would be cut back from 570,000 to 490,000, the document said. The United States would depart from the longstanding policy of having enough troops and resources to fight and win two wars in two different parts of the world at the same time; instead, the goal would be to be able to win one war while merely fending off and frustrating the ambitions of an adversary in another theater. The new strategy enshrined Obama's recent announcement of a "pivot" to Asia. "We will of necessity rebalance toward the Asia-Pacific region," it said. While defense spending as a whole would be reduced, there would be no cutbacks in Asia. Within days, administration officials let it be known that they planned to withdraw two U.S. army brigades from Europe.

Obama and the new Pentagon document glossed over the biggest change of all, a virtually complete reversal of the views espoused only three years earlier. In 2009, when Obama took office, the Pentagon was swept up in transition to the new doctrine of counterinsurgency, the strategy General David Petraeus had brought to the war in Iraq. Army leaders and troop were being hurriedly trained in how to develop close ties at the village level and how to protect the local population through good works in order to win its loyalty against an insurgent force like the Taliban. Obama had himself embraced the strategy when he sent more troops to Afghanistan in 2009, not realizing what counterinsurgency would mean in time and money.

By 2012, the idea was all but abandoned. Afghanistan had been the graveyard for American counterinsurgency, much as it had earlier been the graveyard for the military aspirations of the British and the Soviets. Once the Bin Laden raid succeeded, Obama quickly shifted to an emphasis on counterterrorism rather than counterinsurgency. In the Pentagon's revised strategy in 2012, "counterterrorism and irregular warfare" was listed at the very top of the list of missions for the U.S. armed forces. Counterinsurgency was all but written off. After Iraq and Afghanistan, the document said, the United States would turn to "non-military means" for handling problems of instability. American forces would "retain" and "refine" the lessons they had learned, the Pentagon said. It then added, in italics: "However, U.S. forces will no longer be sized to conduct large-scale, prolonged stability operations."[14]

In short, Obama had succeeded in changing the Pentagon and its strategy, but only after starting down the wrong path and then reversing course.

———

The drones and the targeted killing did not stop. The United States continued to hold prisoners without trial. The policy of rendition remained in effect. Just as many of Franklin Roosevelt's New Deal reforms didn't become permanent until the Eisenhower administration failed to do away with them, so, too, some of George W. Bush's antiterrorism policies didn't seem like permanent changes until they were perpetuated by Obama.

The prison at Guantánamo remained open, just as it had been three years earlier. Two days after his inauguration, Obama had signed the executive order requiring that the facility be closed within one year—that is, by the beginning of 2010. But his efforts were blocked by a series of obstacles: congressional actions, court decisions and the general apathy of an American public that had once treated closing Guantánamo as a matter of urgency. Sometimes, bringing about change takes more than a president.

Conclusion

In evaluating Obama and his foreign policy, the question of change has several different dimensions. How much did the Obama administration really change from the George W. Bush administration? How much did Obama's generation of Democrats change from the Democrats of the Clinton administration? How much did the Obama administration as a whole change during its time in office? And how much did the president change his own ideas and strategy?

Many people now respond to the first question by claiming Obama was not much different from Bush. That answer comes from both political directions: Liberals mourn the fact that there has not been more change; Republicans such as Dick Cheney gloat about how little of the Bush legacy has been undone. Yet this perception of continuity is too simplistic: Clearly, Obama has *not* been the same as Bush. Indeed, in a few instances Obama has been more hawkish. He vastly expanded both the use of drones for targeted killings and the areas where these drone killings are carried out. Moreover, he was less collaborative and more unilateral than Bush in dealing with Pakistan: Bush's approach was to inform and work with Pakistani leaders; it was Obama who achieved the success of the Bin Laden raid.

More generally, however, the Obama administration relied on multilateralism in its foreign policy where the Bush administration did not, at least during Bush's tumultuous first term. It is hard to imagine George W. Bush intervening in Libya in the fashion that Obama did. Under Bush, the United States either would have spurned the British and French appeals to act against Gaddafi or, if he decided to join them, would have dominated the

335

military operation (and thus paid most of the costs for it). That was how America had always done it since World War II.

Still, on quite a few issues, the continuities from Bush to Obama were striking. Certainly in the field of counterterrorism, Obama changed American policies far less than had been expected when he took office. Few could have predicted, for example, that the prison at Guantánamo would remain open three years into Obama's presidency, or that he would continue so many of Bush's other policies, including targeted killings, rendition and warrantless surveillance.

Why is it that Democratic presidential candidates hold out the prospect of a new American foreign policy, and yet often wind up with ones that are not fundamentally different from the Republicans'? It is worth keeping in mind that during presidential campaigns, both Democrats and Republicans always have an interest in emphasizing the differences between the two parties. Both parties seek to frame foreign policy issues in simplistic ways that will arouse their own supporters. The candidates tend to talk less about the policies of their opponents that they will continue. Moreover, people tend to remember the parts of a candidate's message they like and ignore the parts they don't.

Americans tend to assume that a change in administration represents a wholesale change in personnel and viewpoints. But that is not always true, and especially not in the case of the Obama administration. The new Democratic president kept in place Robert Gates, Bush's secretary of defense. John Brennan, Obama's principal adviser on counterterrorism, had been one of the principal aides to Bush's CIA director at the time the prison at Guantánamo Bay was set up. Stuart Levey, the point man in Obama's efforts to impose economic sanctions on Iran and North Korea, was the same Treasury Department official who had first devised these policies under Bush. Obama appointed David Petraeus, who led the surge in Iraq that the Democrats opposed, to be commander of American forces in Afghanistan and then his CIA director.

Even when the personnel do change with a new administration, that does not automatically produce a change in outlook or assumptions about the world. It would be hard to argue that there was a profound difference in views about America's continuing leadership role in the world between Bush's outgoing national security adviser and secretary of state, Stephen

Hadley and Condoleezza Rice, and their successors, James Jones and Hillary Clinton. Hadley and Clinton had known each other for years; they'd gone to law school together. As secretary of state for Bush, Rice had appointed Jones to be a special envoy in the Middle East.

In short, the people Obama appointed and the assumptions they carried with them into office were far less conducive to far-reaching change than the rhetoric of the Obama presidential campaign had led people to anticipate.

———

During the course of his first three years in the White House, Obama altered some of his own ideas and strategies. His calm demeanor (not to mention the reluctance of any president to admit to reversing course) obscured this reality. In 2009, Obama was determined to avoid sounding like George W. Bush. As one part of that effort, he clearly de-emphasized the importance of promoting democracy overseas, both in his speeches and in dealing with countries like Iran and China. His acknowledged model in foreign policy was the realist approach pursued under President George H. W. Bush and Brent Scowcroft. But Obama gradually changed his ideas and rhetoric during his second year, so that by the time of the Arab Spring of 2011, Obama was openly espousing the importance of democracy and political freedom abroad. It is difficult to believe George H. W. Bush would have told Egyptian president Hosni Mubarak to step down, now rather than later, and to yield to protesters for democracy in the streets. In the case of Libya, Obama sent out military power on a mission justified on humanitarian grounds, not for reasons of a compelling national interest. Scowcroft, the quintessential realist, openly disagreed with Obama.

The president also changed his military strategy in a fundamental way, so that the Obama of 2011 was not the same as the Obama of 2009. At the start of his administration, Obama bought heavily into the strategy of counterinsurgency that had seemed to work for Petraeus in Iraq. He ordered troops to Afghanistan in early 2009 and then more at the end of the year, hoping to win support of the Afghan people in a way that would turn the war. At that time, Obama rejected the arguments of some officials, including Vice President Joe Biden, to rely more heavily on a counterterrorism strategy—using fewer ground troops and relying more heavily on special operations forces, drones and missiles to attack al-Qaeda.

In mid-2011, however, Obama shifted in Afghanistan toward counterter-rorism, the approach that succeeded in killing Osama bin Laden in Pakistan and, five months later, Anwar al-Awlaki in Yemen. The Obama team min-imized the significance of this change in military strategy, probably because calling attention to it would have raised questions about whether he should have sent so many more American troops to Afghanistan in the first place.

———

The senior positions in the Obama administration changed hands often, too. The personnel moves were so gradual that few people bothered to put them all together, but the result was that by the end of Obama's third year in office, only one of the top eight officials in the government's foreign policy appar-atus was in the same job as at the start of the administration: Hillary Clin-ton.[1] By way of comparison, after three years in the Bush administration, all eight of these same positions were filled by the same people as at the start of the administration. The point is not that personnel stability is inherently good. In the Bush years, experience sometimes obscured the ability to see what was new, and long tenure in office sometimes led to stubbornness in acknowledging what went wrong. Rather, it is to say that, in setting his for-eign policy, Obama was often adjusting to different cabinet-level advisers.

By contrast, there was considerably more continuity in Obama's inner circle. Just as he had since 2007, in the early stages of his presidential cam-paign, Obama continued to rely upon Denis McDonough to advise him and make sure that what he wanted in foreign policy would be carried out; and he continued to depend on Ben Rhodes to craft his message and speeches, the themes, narratives and justifications underlying his foreign policy. The one major change in the Obama inner circle brought in from the 2008 cam-paign was the departure of Obama's Senate aide Mark Lippert, who was forced out in White House infighting.

———

How did the Obama administration differ from the *Clinton* administration? Did the Democrats change their views of the world from the 1990s to the Obama era? The answer to that is in some ways as interesting as the more frequent comparison between Barack Obama and George W. Bush.

At the working levels of government, Obama's team included many of the same foreign policy hands who had worked under Clinton. These

Clinton alumni were confronting a changed world, one that the younger Obamians took for granted but the Clinton alumni did not. "The change in the media environment is dramatic—it's had a profound impact," said Tony Blinken, who worked on the National Security Council under Clinton and was Biden's national security adviser under Obama. "In the Clinton administration, we basically stopped work every night at six thirty to watch the national network news. I don't think many people do that anymore. And the other thing everyone did back then was, you got up in the morning and you rushed to see what was above the fold on a physical copy of the *New York Times* and the *Washington Post* and maybe the *LA Times* and the *Wall Street Journal*, which no one does anymore, either. Instead, we're on an intravenous feed of cable and the Internet and blogs, everything else."

Such a change may at first seem inconsequential, but Blinken argued that it has had a profound impact. "You have to resist the temptation to be totally reactive to everything you're hearing minute to minute—so that you're not in an environment where, the minute something pops up on *Morning Joe*, and you haven't figured out a solution by the end of it, you're a failure," he said. He said one of Obama's strengths was that he didn't get "distracted by the daily or hourly turbulence."[2]

All the other changes from Clinton to Obama were dwarfed by the increasing lack of resources. Virtually all the Clinton administration officials who had returned under Obama pointed out that they had less money available to do what they hoped to do overseas. When the Obama administration chose to turn over most of the responsibility for military operations in Libya to its allies, one factor was money. When Obama decided in mid-2011 to begin bringing troops home from Afghanistan sooner rather than later, again one of the reasons cited was financial. The only policy area where a ranking Obama administration official said he did not feel affected by tighter economic constraints was counterterrorism.[3]

During the Arab Spring, when I asked an Obama administration official about the role that Saudi Arabia was playing, the first response was to say, not unexpectedly, that Saudis were trying in country after country to block the movement toward democratic change. But the official's next observation went to economics: "They sure do have a lot of money to throw around."[4] Another administration official, discussing the competition between the

United States and China for influence in Asia, pointed out that over the next few years China is likely to spend tens of billions of dollars in investment and aid to Indonesia, while the United States will spend in the tens of millions. The second official used virtually the same wording as the first, substituting the Chinese in Asia for the Saudis in the Middle East: *They sure do have a lot of money to throw around.* It was the sort of comment that, throughout the last half of the twentieth century, others had made about the United States.

The change in America's economic position gave rise to the most significant difference between the Bill Clinton era and the Obama era: a shift in views on America's role in the world. The words the Americans used in the 1990s were essentially an updated version of what their predecessors had used since World War II: They spoke of America's leadership role; the United States was the indispensable nation, the unchallenged superpower. Obama's rhetoric was much more guarded. He tended to speak of that post–World War II role either as something that was passing away or as something that might be revived through economic changes and renovation. When Obama said in speeches that "the nation we care most about building is our own," the beneficiaries of the Marshall Plan and the postwar reconstruction of Japan got the message.

———

If a single word captured the Obamians' view of their overall strategy in dealing with the world, from the very start of the administration, it was the concept of "rebalancing." They repeated this word again and again in private conversations, in official briefings and in written documents such as their National Security Strategy.

The Obamians used "rebalancing" in a variety of contexts. In general, they said, America should rebalance its priorities toward a greater emphasis on domestic concerns. In foreign policy, America needed to rebalance from an overreliance on the military toward diplomacy and other means of statecraft. The United States also needed to rebalance away from a preoccupation with the Middle East and toward the prosperous region of East Asia. In economics, Obama and his aides spoke of the need to rebalance the international economy, the global markets, the distribution of imports and exports, the values of various countries' currencies. In meetings with Chinese president Hu Jintao, whose government held ever growing foreign exchange reserves, the need for rebalancing was at the heart of Obama's message. "I think we've been trying to make this case to the American people and the world about how we're going to get beyond these wars and we're going to rebalance," explained Ben Rhodes. He was repeating, in a more colloquial fashion, a sentence from the administration's National Security Strategy.[5] In more elegant language, the Obamians were saying that America and the world were out of whack.

To some experienced Washington politicians, the Obamian concept of rebalancing seemed laudable but not exactly right. The word itself seemed to suggest simply a shifting of money and resources from overseas back home—such as, for example, taking $1 billion from the war in Afghanistan and shifting it to pay for rebuilding this nation's transportation system.

"Well, I don't know that that's what he [Obama] is doing, just redirecting resources," said Nancy Pelosi, who was as much in favor of doing so as Obama. She pointed out that the overall resources available to spend were greatly diminished, too. The pie was shrinking. "It's not a question of whether we're going to take the money from that place and spend it over here—I mean, we don't have the money," said Pelosi. She stopped and chuckled. "We had an old expression on the House Appropriations Committee— 'It's not the price, it's the money.' We don't have the money. We just don't have the money."[6]

Did the Obamians' outlook mean that they believed in the idea of America's "decline," as their opponents sometimes claimed? "The ultimate purpose of [Obama's] foreign policy is to make America less hegemonic, less arrogant, less dominant," wrote Charles Krauthammer during Obama's first year. "In a word, it is a foreign policy designed to produce American decline—to make America essentially one nation among many."[7]

Such critiques fail to take account of facts or arguments that don't square with the theory. If Obama's foreign policy was "less hegemonic, less arrogant," as indeed it was, that was because the Obama administration viewed humility as a way to win much greater support from other countries, in a way that would help stave off decline and, indeed, increase American power. The impact of the Iraq War had been such that foreign leaders in countries like France and Germany were unwilling to collaborate with the United

States overseas—and found that even when they wanted to do so, they faced determined and vociferous public opposition at home. That was the situation Obama's less "arrogant" approach was designed to change—as a way of increasing America's power, not reducing it.

"This is the contrary of decline: It's about figuring out, in a more complicated world, with new constraints, how to maximize our power, and that's what we've done," asserted Blinken. Donilon went a step further, arguing that the Obama administration had reversed the decline that had occurred during the Bush years. "We came into office at a period of very significant diminution of American influence, prestige and power in the world," he asserted in an interview. "And our principal strategic goal was the restoration of that position."

––––––––

The related question was whether America *was*, in fact, in decline. Was its international strength plummeting not because the Obama administration wanted that to happen, but as a result of broad international trends, such as the rise of China and India and the erosion of America's financial position?

The Obama administration insisted otherwise, and on this point many of its domestic critics agreed. Again and again over the past several years, officials from both political parties have repeated the same arguments: The United States is still by far the world's leading military power. It continues to have the world's largest economy; even if China catches up within a couple of decades, the United States will still have, in per capita terms, a GNP vastly larger than China's. America's colleges and universities are still the destination of choice for students in China and elsewhere in Asia. The United States still has abundant resources, advanced technology and a knack for innovation beyond that of any other country. America's ingenuity, its inventiveness, its general openness to ideas and people, always enable it to overcome adversity.

Indeed—so the argument goes—warnings of declining American power have been a recurrent theme in modern American life. They come up every few years and then vanish again, in cyclical fashion. Americans worried about declining power at the end of the 1940s, after the Soviet Union acquired the atomic bomb and the Chinese Communist Party came to power; again in the late 1950s, when the Soviets launched Sputnik; and then during the Vietnam War in the 1960s, the oil shocks of the 1970s and the growth of Japanese economic power in the 1980s.

All of these points are valid. Predictions of American decline have repeatedly been wrong in the past, and the United States has often demonstrated an extraordinary ability to adapt and innovate. Still, that does not answer whether the United States will be able to revive itself and fortify its international position now as it has in the past. Those who argue that there has been no decline sometimes ignore or gloss over the objective fact of America's diminishing economic power and resources, compared with other countries. The Obama administration has been able to demonstrate once again America's military strengths and to increase its diplomatic influence, but it has far less in economic and financial clout than any administration for decades.

There is one other striking difference from the past: Never before have America's leaders found it so necessary to proclaim so often, both at home and around the world, that America is *not* in decline.

———

After three years in office, the Obama administration could point to several successes in its foreign policy. The principal one was in counterterrorism, where Obama's overall strategy and the specific choices he made had clearly weakened al-Qaeda's leadership and capabilities. He'd managed to smooth over the animosities with Europe that had been aroused by the Iraq War. By the end of 2011, he had withdrawn American troops from Iraq.

On other goals, he achieved only middling success. He wanted to reorient American policy toward Asia, yet the continuing needs of the war in Afghanistan, which he chose to expand, made it considerably more difficult to achieve this goal. He sought to restore America's standing in the Middle East, but the results were limited; critics remained cynical about American motives, because of the continuing U.S. links to undemocratic regimes in places like Saudi Arabia and Bahrain. The Obama administration had hoped that a conciliatory approach to China would produce a better working relationship, but had to make adjustments after finding that China was emboldened by America's eagerness to avoid conflict. Obama worked hard to forge a relationship with Russian president Dmitry Medvedev, hoping that he could emerge as a leader in his own right with a degree of independence from Prime Minister Vladimir Putin—only to discover in the fall of 2011 that Putin reinstalled himself as president and Russia's unchallenged leader for another twelve years.

There were notable failures, too, in what had been some of Obama's highest priorities at the time he took office. He wanted to bring about significant movement toward a Middle East peace settlement. Yet after three years, his efforts had not yet achieved any substantial change. So, too, Obama wanted to induce Iran to stop its nuclear weapons program and to persuade North Korea to give up the nuclear weapons it already had. Through the end of 2011, he had succeeded in obtaining tighter economic sanctions, but had made little if any headway toward the ultimate goal of persuading the leaders of Iran and North Korea to change course.

Indeed, the events in Libya may well have taught the North Koreans and Iranians a very different lesson: If you give up your nuclear program, you are more vulnerable to military attack. It seems extremely unlikely that the United States and its allies would have bombed nuclear-armed North Korea the way they did Gaddafi's denuclearized Libya, even if North Korea was threatening to kill more civilians than Gaddafi ever did. Kim Jong-il and his associates got the message quickly. Within days after the allied attack on Libya had begun, a senior North Korean official said the agreement Gaddafi had entered into in 2003, giving up his nuclear program in exchange for improved relations with the West, had been a trick. The deal with Libya had been "an invasion tactic to disarm the country," the North Korean official said.[9]

———

Eight years ago, at the end of my book *Rise of the Vulcans*, I asked the question whether the Bush administration's venture into Iraq in 2003 represented "the outer limits of the expansion of American power and ideals." The answer to that question was clearly yes. America discovered that its goal of transforming the Middle East, through the application of unilateral military power, was well beyond its reach.

Does this mean that the Obamians represent the opposite end of a swinging pendulum? If the Bush administration erred by overestimating America's power, could it be that the Obamians are, conversely, underestimating it?

To gauge accurately what power America does or does not possess is one of the essential elements of foreign policy. In the past, both Democrats and

Republicans have sometimes gotten it wrong. Iraq provided a classic example, not once but twice. Before the Persian Gulf War in 1991, Democratic leaders underestimated America's military capabilities. Before the 2003 Iraq War, Republican leaders overestimated them. These judgments seem undeniable, apart from whether one believed in the morality or legitimacy of either conflict.

I don't believe the Obamians represent just another swing of the pendulum, for two reasons. First, its own policies have added up to centrism, not to the mirror image of the Bush administration. Obama's use of drone attacks and his dispatch of more troops to Afghanistan, for instance, seem to have dispelled—at least for now—the decades-old Republican stereotypes that Democrats are weak on national security or unwilling to use force.

More important, I think the entire model of a pendulum doesn't fit. The Obamians don't represent the outer limits of anything. Future presidents of both parties will face the same underlying realities of limited money and diminishing American sway over an increasing number of new powers. The Vulcans of the Bush era reflected a belief in overwhelming American power, one that was linked to the years immediately after the end of the Cold War. The Obamians could not revive that belief, even if they had wanted to do so, and neither will Obama's successors. Rather, Obama's time in office has marked the beginning of a new era in America's relations with the rest of the world, an era when American primacy is no longer taken for granted.

ACKNOWLEDGMENTS

The first person I want to thank for this book is Jessica Einhorn, the dean of the Johns Hopkins University Paul H. Nitze School of Advanced International Studies. She graciously offered me a home at SAIS for this book, as for two previous books. This support has contributed to my work in a variety of ways: the outstanding SAIS library; the stimulation of the school's faculty, students, and events; and not least, her own insights on a variety of subjects.

At SAIS, I benefited from the administrative support of Associate Dean John Harrington, Associate Dean Amir Pasic, Christine Kunkel, and Rosa Bullock. In the SAIS library, Linda Carlson helped me track down information quickly. Finally, I was especially lucky to have the help of three extremely capable researchers, all of them present or former SAIS students: John Gans, Beth Schumaecker and Lena Diesing, each of whom spent months gathering the material I was seeking. I am grateful for their insights and hard work.

Joel Havemann, a superb journalist who worked with me at the *Los Angeles Times*, read and edited the manuscript, chapter after chapter. In the process, he demonstrated once again his talent for eliminating unnecessary words and phrases. My good friends Warren I. Cohen and Nancy Bernkopf Tucker, both of them outstanding historians, read many chapters of the book and offered invaluable suggestions and feedback.

During the course of the book, I conducted roughly 125 interviews, in some instances going back to the same person several times. I'm thankful to all for taking the time to try to answer my questions. I cannot provide a full list of the interviewees, because some of them—principally, officials in the

Obama administration—would speak exclusively on background, meaning that they cannot be identified by name. Thankfully, in some instances, individuals speaking on background would allow portions of their interviews to be put on the record and attributed to them. Here, then, is a necessarily partial list of the individuals who were interviewed: Morton Abramowitz, Warren Bass, Tony Blinken, Bob Borosage, Sam Brown, Zbigniew Brzezinski, Ambassador Heng-Chee Chan, Tom Donilon, Bill Drozdiak, Douglas Frantz, Ambassador Ichiro Fujisaki, Les Gelb, Morton Halperin, David Hawk, Michael Hayden, Robert Kagan, Stephanie Kaplan, Lawrence Korb, Charles Kupchan, Stuart Levey, Tom Malinowski, Michael Mandelbaum, Will Marshall, Denis McDonough, Michael McFaul, Gary Milhollin, Derek Mitchell, Lissa Muscatine, Michael O'Hanlon, Nancy Pelosi, John Podesta, Kenneth Pollack, Samantha Power, Ben Rhodes, Susan Rice, Jeremy Rosner, Gary Samore, Anne-Marie Slaughter, Richard Solomon, Tara Sonenshine, Jim Steinberg, Strobe Talbott, Celeste Ward, and James Woolsey.

At the National Security Council, Caitlin Hayden was especially helpful in coordinating interviews during the crucial last six months, and Ferial Govashiri and Robert Jensen also supplied earlier assistance. Justin Vaïsse, the Brookings University scholar who is on the cutting edge of research into American foreign policy, provided invaluable insight and materials.

My editor Adrian Zackheim showed once again that he knows how to cut to the essence of a book or any of the ideas and story lines in it. My agent, Rafe Sagalyn, provided his usual wise advice. This is the fourth book I have done with each of them, and I realize each time how lucky I was when I first started working with them a decade ago.

At Viking/Penguin, I am particularly thankful to Courtney Young, a talented editor who read the manuscript carefully and was able to pinpoint where it needed revisions. Eric Meyers patiently helped me choose and obtain the photos for the insert and to arrange their layout.

Finally, I am most of all grateful to my expanding family, the bedrock of my happiness. During the three eventful years in which this book was written, Elizabeth married Micah, Ted married Kristin and Nate made his grand entrance into the world. All of them, along with my mother, Peggy, and brother, Andy, managed to provide crucial support, putting up with me or my occasional absence as I went about my research and writing. I have no idea in what form, electronic or printed, Nate will one day read this book, but I can safely predict that when he first sees it, he'll try to chew it.

Caroline, my wife, is in a class all her own, for her supportiveness and, well, class. To her, my thanks are boundless.

NOTES

Introduction

1. This reconstruction of the Libya decision is based on interviews with Tom Donilon, Samantha Power, Ben Rhodes and two other American officials who spoke only on background.
2. Liz Sly, Joby Warrick and Greg Jaffe, "Coalition Hits Libyan Sites from Sea, Air," *Washington Post*, March 20, 2011, p. A-1.
3. Transcript of Barack Obama speech, "Remarks by the President to the Nation on the Way Forward in Afghanistan and Pakistan," delivered at United States Military Academy, December 1, 2009.
4. David Ignatius, "Jim Jones's Team," *Washington Post*, June 7, 2009, p. A-17.

Prologue

1. Kurt M. Campbell and James B. Steinberg, *Difficult Transitions: Foreign Policy Troubles at the Outset of Presidential Power* (Washington: Brookings Institution Press, 2008), p. 140.
2. Interview with John Podesta, February 4, 2010; John Heilemann and Mark Halperin, *Game Change* (New York: HarperCollins, 2010), p. 431.
3. Podesta interview; conversation with an associate of Holbrooke.
4. Jonathan Alter, *The Promise* (New York: Simon & Schuster, 2010), p. 67; Podesta interview.
5. Interview with an Obama campaign source.
6. Robert M. Gates, *From the Shadows* (New York: Simon & Schuster, 1996), p. 27.
7. Dana Milbank, "Senators So Very, Very Not Contrary Towards Gates," *Washington Post*, December 6, 2006, p. A-2.
8. "Transcript: Obama News Conference Announcing Hillary Clinton and National Security Team," CQ Transcripts Wire, December 1, 2008.

Chapter 1: "A Look I Recognized"

1. John Kerry to Council on Foreign Relations, October 26, 2009.
2. "Remarks by the President in Address to the Nation on the Way Forward in Afghanistan and Pakistan," December 1, 2009; interview with Ben Rhodes, October 4, 2010.
3. George McGovern newsletter to constituents, April 1968; David E. Rosenbaum, "Kennedy and Hatfield Disagree at Hearing on Volunteer Army," *New York Times*, February 5, 1971, p. A-12. Over the years, Kennedy was not entirely consistent on the issue;

during his 1980 presidential campaign, he criticized President Carter for reinstituting registration for the draft.

4. Interview with Sam Brown, November 13, 2009.

5. Todd Gitlin, *The Intellectuals and the Flag* (New York: Columbia University Press, 2006), p. 131.

6. McGovern speech quoted in Bruce Miroff, *The Liberals' Moment: The McGovern Insurgency and the Identity Crisis of the Democratic Party* (Lawrence: University Press of Kansas, 2009), p. 128.

7. Carl Bernstein, *A Woman In Charge: The Life of Hillary Rodham Clinton* (New York: Vintage, 2007), p. 85.

8. Miroff, *The Liberals' Moment*, pp. 292, 296.

9. Ibid., p. 133.

10. Paul Taylor, *See How They Run* (New York: Knopf, 1990), p. 96.

11. George Lardner Jr., "Panel Accused of Rushing New Intelligence Charter," *Washington Post*, March 26, 1980, p. A-14.

12. Marcus G. Raskin, "Democracy Versus the National Security State," *Law and Contemporary Problems* 40:3 (Summer 1976), p. 219; Sidney Blumenthal, "The Left Stuff: IPS and the Long Road Back," *Washington Post*, July 30, 1986, p. D-1.

13. Richard Holbrooke, "A Sense of Drift, a Time for Calm," *Foreign Policy* 23 (Summer 1976), pp. 98–100.

14. Ibid., pp. 107, 111.

15. See Justin Vaïsse, *Neoconservatism: The Biography of a Movement* (Cambridge: Harvard University Press, 2010), p. 99.

16. Ibid., p. xxi.

17. Anthony Lake, ed., *The Vietnam Legacy* (New York: Council on Foreign Relations/New York University Press, 1976), p. xxviii.

18. Zbigniew Brzezinski, "America in a Hostile World," *Foreign Policy* 23 (Summer 1976), pp. 90–92.

19. Zbigniew Brzezinski, *Power and Principle* (New York: Farrar, Straus and Giroux, 1983), p. 5; Leslie H. Gelb, "Brzezinski Viewed as Key Adviser to Carter," *New York Times*, October 6, 1976, p. 24.

20. Briefing book for Jimmy Carter in debate with President Ford in 1976 Presidential Campaign Files, Zbigniew Brzezinski papers, Library of Congress, obtained through researcher Justin Vaïsse of the Brookings Institution.

21. Gelb, "Brzezinski Viewed as Key Adviser."

22. Anatoly Dobrynin, *In Confidence* (New York: Times Books, 1995), p. 461.

23. Gates, *From the Shadows*, pp. 176–78.

24. Arthur Schlesinger, "Human Rights and the American Tradition," *Foreign Affairs* 57:3 (1978), p. 514.

25. Interview with Jeane Kirkpatrick, April 24, 2002.

26. Vaïsse, *Neoconservatism*, pp. 125–33.

27. Jeane Kirkpatrick, "Dictatorships and Double Standards," *Commentary* 68 (November 1979), p. 41.

28. Charles Jones, *Boys of '67* (Mechanicsburg, PA: Stackpole Books, 2007), p. 184.

29. Colin Powell, *My American Journey* (New York: Ballantine Books, 1995), pp. 242–43.

30. Karen Bennett, "Democrats Say They Must Prove Unafraid to Use Military Power," Associated Press, May 3, 1986; Phil Gailey, "From Biden to Babbitt to Nunn," *New York Times Magazine*, May 18, 1986, p. 70.

31. Interview with Will Marshall, September 16, 2009.

32. Ibid., May 22, 2009.

33. Ibid.

34. Barney Frank, "So Call It a Victory Dividend," *New York Times*, May 1, 1991, p. A-25.
35. E. J. Dionne, "Gulf Crisis Rekindles Democrats' Old Debate but with New Focus," *Washington Post*, January 3, 1991, p. A-16.
36. "Confrontation in the Gulf, Day 2: Lawmakers Debate War and More Time for Sanctions," *New York Times*, January 12, 1991, p. 6.
37. George Bush and Brent Scowcroft, *A World Transformed* (New York: Knopf, 1998), pp. 389, 445; "A Sampling from the Debate on Capitol Hill," *New York Times*, January 11, 1991, p. A-8.

Chapter 2: "I'm Running Out of Demons"

1. See editorial, "Don't Shoot Down Iraqi Aircraft," *New York Times*, February 19, 1992, p. A-20; Andrew Rosenthal, "Stressing Foreign Policy Could Cut Both Ways," *New York Times*, February 16, 1992, section 4, p. 2; Michael Kramer, "The Cost of Removing Saddam Hussein," *Time*, October 24, 1994, p. 39; Philip Shenon, "U.S. Quietly Intensifies Attacks on Iraq, Destroying Radar Sites," May 5, 1999, p. A-6.
2. Marshall interview, May 22, 2009; Michael Kelly, "Clinton Defends Position on Iraqi War," *New York Times*, July 31, 1992, p. A-13.
3. Thomas L. Friedman, "Clinton Asserts Bush Is Too Eager to Befriend the World's Dictators," *New York Times*, October 2, 1992, p. A-1.
4. Jim Wolffe, "Powell: I'm Running Out of Demons," *Army Times*, April 5, 1991.
5. Elaine Sciolino, "Christopher Sees a Place for Force," *New York Times*, January 14, 1993, p. A-11.
6. Daniel Williams and John M. Goshko, "Reduced U.S. World Role Outlined but Soon Altered; High-Level Disavowals Follow Official's Talk," *Washington Post*, May 26, 1993, p. A-1.
7. Susan Bennett, "Clinton's Allies Push Him to Act Against 'Ethnic Cleansing,'" *Houston Chronicle*, April 21, 1993, p. A-15.
8. Colin Powell, *My American Journey* (New York: Ballantine Books, 2005), p. 561.
9. Taylor Branch, *The Clinton Tapes* (New York: Simon & Schuster, 2009), p. 187.
10. Derek Chollet and James Goldgeier, *America Between the Wars* (New York: Public-Affairs, 2008), pp. 65–70.
11. Ibid., pp. 147–48.
12. Ibid., p. 102.
13. David Halberstam, *War in a Time of Peace* (New York: Scribner, 2001), p. 352.
14. Ibid., p. 421.
15. Andrew J. Bacevich, *American Empire* (Cambridge: Harvard University Press, 2002), pp. 154–55.
16. Halberstam, *War in a Time of Peace*, pp. 423–25.
17. Bill Clinton press conference with Jiang Zemin, January 28, 1997.
18. "Clinton Criticizes Bush Decision to Renew China's Most Favored Nation Status," press release, June 3, 1992.
19. Interview with Nancy Pelosi, May 21, 1996, quoted in James Mann, *About Face: A History of America's Curious Relationship with China, from Nixon to Clinton* (New York: Knopf, 1999), p. 308.
20. Memo to Interested Parties from Greg Craig, March 11, 2008.

Chapter 3: Democrats in Exile

1. Jeffrey Goldberg, "The CIA and the Pentagon Take Another Look at Al Qaeda and Iraq," *The New Yorker*, February 10, 2003, p. 40.
2. See Michael Isikoff and David Corn, *Hubris* (New York: Crown, 2006), pp. 125–26.
3. Richard C. Holbrooke, "Give Diplomacy More Time," *Washington Post*, September 7, 2002, p. A-17; Richard C. Holbrooke, "It Didn't Have to Be This Way," *Washington Post*, February 23, 2003, p. B-7.
4. Samuel R. Berger, "Foreign Policy for a Democratic President," *Foreign Affairs* 83:3 (May/June 2004), p. 47.
5. Dan Balz, "Bush Assails Kerry on Iraq Remarks," *Washington Post*, August 11, 2004, p. A-4.
6. Interview with John Podesta, February 4, 2010; Bill Keller, "The Sunshine Warrior," *New York Times Magazine*, September 22, 2002, p. 48.
7. According to Podesta, the principal donors helping to launch CAP were Herbert Sandler, George Soros and Peter Lewis, along with their families.
8. Podesta interview.
9. Lawrence J. Korb, "Trim Fat from Pentagon Budget to Help Pay for Katrina Relief," *Baltimore Sun*, October 13, 2005, p. A-15; Caroline P. Wadhams and Lawrence J. Korb, "The Forgotten Front," report by Center for American Progress, November 6, 2007.
10. Lawrence J. Korb and Brian Katulis, "Strategic Redeployment," report by Center for American Progress, September 29, 2005.
11. Kurt M. Campbell and Michael E. O'Hanlon, *Hard Power* (New York: Basic Books, 2006), pp. 7–8.
12. Podesta interview; interview with Lawrence J. Korb, December 1, 2009.

Chapter 4: The Trout Fishers

1. Interview with Morton Abramowitz, December 21, 2009.
2. "Statement on Postwar Iraq," issued by Project for a New American Century, March 17, 2003; interview with James Steinberg, November 13, 2009.
3. Bill Keller, "The I-Can't-Believe-I'm-a-Hawk Club," *New York Times*, February 8, 2003, p. A-17; Bill Keller, "My Unfinished 9/11 Business," *New York Times Magazine*, September 11, 2011, p. 34, http://www.dlc.org/documents/Progressive_Internationalism_1003.pdf.
4. "Progressive Internationalism: A Democratic National Security Strategy," October 30, 2003, pp. 3–4, http://www.dlc.org/documents/Progressive_Internationalism_1003.pdf.
5. Ibid., p. 5.
6. www.trumanproject.org/about/mission/values.
7. Nancy Pelosi, "Power and Principle," David A. Morse Lecture to Council on Foreign Relations, March 7, 2003; Steinberg interview, November 13, 2009.
8. Remarks by Al Gore to MoveOn PAC, May 26, 2004.
9. Ceci Connolly, "U.S. Combat Death Rate Lowest Ever," *Washington Post*, December 9, 2004, p. A-24.
10. Interview with Kenneth Pollack, March 2, 2010.
11. Peter Baker and Shailagh Murray, "Democrats Split over Position on Iraq War," *Washington Post*, August 22, 2005, p. A-1.

12. Adam Nagourney, "Democrats Turned War into an Ally," *New York Times*, November 9, 2006, p. 1.
13. This account is based on David Remnick, *The Bridge* (New York: Knopf, 2010), pp. 344–48.
14. Transcript of Barack Obama speech against the Iraq War, October 2, 2002, from NPR, www.npr.org/templates/story/story.php?storyId=99591469.
15. Kurt M. Campbell and Michael E. O'Hanlon, "Creating a Lasting Shift on Defense," *Washington Post*, Think Tank Town, October 3, 2006, www.washingtonpost.com/wpdyn/content/article/2006/10/02/AR2006100200842.html.

Chapter 5: The Obamians

1. This section is based upon interviews with Ben Rhodes, July 14 and October 4, 2010.
2. This section is based upon interviews with Denis McDonough, July 14 and October 22, 2010. See also Albert Eisele, "At Home in the West Wing," *St. John's University Alumni Magazine*, Winter 2009, p. 22.
3. Michael Mandelbaum, *The Frugal Superpower* (New York: PublicAffairs, 2010).
4. Interview with an Obama administration official.
5. See Dinesh D'Souza, "Obama's Problems with Business," *Forbes*, September 27, 2010, pp. 84–94; and Robert Costa, "Gingrich: Obama's 'Kenyan, Anti-Colonial' Worldview," *National Review Online*, September 10, 2010, www.nationalreview.com/corner/246302/gingrich-obama-s-kenyan-anti-colonial-worldview-robert-costa.
6. McDonough interview, July 14, 2010.
7. Bill Clinton press conference with Jiang Zemin, January 28, 1997.
8. Steven Pearlstein, "Can 'Old Europe' Preserve Its Prosperity?" *Washington Post*, August 6, 2004, p. E-1.

Chapter 6: "Join Us"

1. Abner Mikva and Anthony Lake, "What Rules Do We Play By?" *Boston Globe*, July 22, 2002, p. A-11.
2. Interview with Tony Lake, April 23, 2009.
3. For details of Rice's background, see Martha Brant, "Into Africa," *Stanford Magazine*, January/February 2000, and Lonnae O'Neal Parker, "She's on Top of the World," *Washington Post*, March 30, 1998, p. C-1.
4. Interview with former Clinton administration official, November 19, 2008.
5. Interview with Michael O'Hanlon, April 26, 2009.
6. Interview with Michael McFaul, June 29, 2010.
7. McFaul and Lake interviews; interview with Tara Sonenshine, May 20, 2009.
8. This section is based on an interview with Jeffrey Bader, July 14, 2010, and on author conversations with Bader during his career in government.
9. Michael Hirsh, "The Talent Primary," *Newsweek*, September 15, 2007, p. 36.
10. Bruce Riedel discussion at Johns Hopkins School of Advanced International Studies, March 10, 2010.
11. Author conversation with an Obama adviser in 2007.
12. Barack Obama, *The Audacity of Hope* (New York: Three Rivers, 2006), pp. 300–301;

Monica Langley, "From the Campaign to the Battlefield," *Wall Street Journal*, September 22, 2007, p. A-1.

13. See Bob Woodward, *Obama's Wars* (New York: Simon & Schuster, 2010), pp. 197–99.
14. Transcript of fourth Democratic debate, Charleston, South Carolina, July 24, 2007.
15. David Plouffe, *The Audacity to Win* (New York: Viking, 2009), pp. 84–85.
16. Interview with Ben Rhodes, July 31, 2009.
17. Plouffe, *The Audacity to Win*, p. 85.

Chapter 7: "To Track Down, Capture or Kill"

1. Barack Obama speech at Woodrow Wilson International Center, August 1, 2007.
2. Transcript of Democratic Candidates Forum sponsored by the AFL-CIO, Chicago, August 8, 2007.
3. Rhodes interview, October 4, 2010.
4. Conversations with two Obama campaign officials; see also Michael Hirsh, "The Talent Primary."
5. Interview with confidential source.
6. Gerri Peev, "Hillary's a Monster," *The Scotsman*, March 7, 2008.
7. Harry Kreisler, "Genocide and U.S. Foreign Policy: Conversation with Samantha Power," April 29, 2002, http://globetrotter.berkeley.edu/people2/Power/power-con1 .html.
8. Stephen Holmes, "The War of the Liberals," *The Nation*, November 14, 2005.
9. "Statement from Senator Obama on the Olympics," April 9, 2008.
10. "Remarks by Senator Obama at Alliance for American Manufacturing," April 14, 2008.
11. Interview with Tony Blinken, September 27, 2011.
12. Interview with an associate of Petraeus.
13. James Mann, *The Rebellion of Ronald Reagan* (New York: Viking, 2009), pp. 129–30.
14. Gregor Peter Schmitz, "Obama Reacts to Debate in Berlin," *Spiegel Online*, July 10, 2008.
15. Author conversation with Peter Schneider, December 14, 2008.
16. Plouffe, *The Audacity to Win*, p. 273.
17. Anne E. Kornblut, "Obama Group on Security Meets," *Washington Post*, June 19, 2008, p. A-6.
18. Interview with Obama campaign official.
19. Michael D. Shear and Alec MacGillis, "On Georgia Crisis, McCain's Tone Grows Sharper," *Washington Post*, August 13, 2008, p. A-3.
20. Interview with Obama campaign official.
21. McFaul interview.
22. Transcript of first presidential debate, Oxford, Mississippi, September 26, 2008.
23. Interviews with Ben Rhodes, October 4, 2010, and Denis McDonough, October 20, 2010.

Chapter 8: CIA and the "Aw, Shit!" Campaign

1. This account of the December 9 meeting is based on interviews with Michael Hayden, May 27, 2010, and Denis McDonough, July 14, 2010.

2. Statement by Barack Obama, released by Obama campaign, October 4, 2007.

3. Interview with John Brennan, July 29, 2010.

4. R. Jeffrey Smith, "Obama Taps CIA Veteran as Adviser on Terror; Brennan Has Drawn Fire on Interrogations," *Washington Post*, January 9, 2009, p. A-1.

5. "Open Letter to President-elect Obama: Break with the Dark Side," www.common dreams.org/newswire/2008/11/22.

6. Interview with Nancy Pelosi, June 7, 2011.

7. Joby Warrick and Walter Pincus, "CIA Nominee Vows an End to Disputed Tactics," *Washington Post*, February 6, 2009, p. A-2.

8. Michael Hayden, address at Duquesne University Commencement, May 4, 2007, www .cia.gov/news-information/speeches-testimony/2007/cia-directors-address-at-duquesne -university-commencement.html.

9. John A. Herfort, "HUC Will Ask Faculty for Parietal Extension," *Harvard Crimson*, October 24, 1966, from www.thecrimson.com.

10. Richard Blumenthal, "Rusk Meets the Students, but the 'New Middle' Leaves Unsatisfied," *Harvard Crimson*, February 11, 1967, and Patrick Y. Mitchell, "Two Secret Meetings: Student Moderates Debate Johnson Administration on the War," October 10, 1967; both articles obtained from www.thecrimson.com.

11. Barack Obama, inaugural address, January 20, 2009.

12. Hayden interview; "Obama Reverses Bush Policies on Detention and Interrogation," *Washington Post*, January 23, 2009, p. A-6; Scott Shane, Mark Mazzetti and Helene Cooper, "Obama Reverses Key Bush Policy, but Questions on Detainees Remain," *New York Times*, January 23, 2009, p. A-16.

13. Barack Obama, "Protecting Our Security and Our Values," speech at National Archives Museum, May 21, 2009.

14. White House transcript, "Remarks by the President at West Point Commencement," United States Military Academy, May 22, 2010.

15. National Security Strategy, May 2010.

16. John Brennan, "A New Approach for Safeguarding Americans," speech to Center for Strategic and International Studies, August 6, 2009.

17. Harold Hongju Koh, speech to the Annual Meeting of the American Society of International Law, Washington D.C., March 25, 2010.

18. Eugene Robinson, "So Much to Be Undone," *Washington Post*, January 23, 2009, p. A-15.

19. Charlie Savage, "Closing Guantánamo Fades as a Priority," *New York Times*, June 27, 2010, p. A-13.

20. Peter Finn and Greg Miller, "Panetta Outlines Plan for Bin Laden's Detention," *Washington Post*, February 16, 2001.

21. Obama, "Protecting Our Security and Our Values."

22. Brennan interview; R. Jeffrey Smith, Michael D. Shear and Walter Pincus, "In Obama's Inner Circle, Debate over Memos' Release Was Intense," *Washington Post*, April 24, 2009, p. A-1.

23. Jeff Zeleny and Thom Shanker, "Obama Reversal on Abuse Photos," *New York Times*, May 14, 2009, p. A-1.

24. Dana Priest, "CIA Avoids Scrutiny of Detainee Treatment," *Washington Post*, March 3, 2005, p. A-1.

25. The seven were James Schlesinger, William Webster, James Woolsey, John Deutch, George Tenet, Porter Goss and Michael Hayden.

26. Peter Baker, "Chiefs Ask Obama to Abandon Abuse Inquiry," *New York Times*, September 19, 2009, p. A-6.

27. Eric Holder, testimony to Senate Judiciary Committee, November 8, 2011; Peter Finn

and Julie Tate, "U.S. Looking into 2 Detainee Deaths," *Washington Post*, July 1, 2011, p. 1.

28. Evan Perez, "White House Counsel's Job at Stake," *Wall Street Journal*, August 4, 2009, p. A-4.

29. Background interview.

30. The Kennedy sensibility that Craig symbolized was that of Bobby and Ted Kennedy in the late 1960s and 1970s. Earlier, when John Kennedy took office, he and his brothers viewed themselves as hard-nosed and pragmatic. They thought of Adlai Stevenson as representative of an older generation of liberals, and they treated Stevenson more shabbily than the Obama team did Greg Craig.

31. Brown interview.

32. Dick Cheney, speech to American Enterprise Institute, May 21, 2009.

33. "Former Vice President Dick Cheney Sits Down with Jamie Gangel," NBC News, January 18, 2011; "Cheney Makes Surprise Appearance at CPAC," Associated Press, February 10, 2011.

Chapter 9: Afghanistan: Flip of the COIN

1. Conversation with Bruce Riedel, March 10, 2010.

2. Louis Uchitelle and Edmund L. Andrews, "Economy Slides at Fastest Rate Since Late 1950s," *New York Times*, April 30, 2009, p. A-1.

3. Barack Obama, "Responsibly Ending the War in Iraq," speech at Camp Lejeune, North Carolina, February 27, 2009.

4. Dan Balz, "Have We Forgotten?" *Washington Post*, July 1, 2009, p. A-4; Ross Douthat, "The War We'd Like to Forget," *New York Times*, July 27, 2009, www.nytimes.com/2009/07/27/opinion/27douthat.html.

5. Peter Baker, "With Pledges to Troops and Iraqis, Obama Details Pullout," *New York Times*, February 28, 2009, p. A-6.

6. Alter, *The Promise*, p. 229.

7. Karen DeYoung, "More Troops Headed to Afghanistan," *Washington Post*, February 18, 2009, p. A-1.

8. Carlos Lozada, "Outspoken: An Interview with David Kilcullen," *Washington Post*, March 22, 2009, p. B-2.

9. Celeste Ward, "Countering the Military's Latest Mantra," *Washington Post*, May 17, 2009, p. B-1; interview with Celeste Ward, June 2, 2009.

10. Robert F. Kennedy, "Counterinsurgency," speech before the International Police Academy graduating class, July 9, 1965.

11. Presentation by Eric Edelman at Johns Hopkins School of Advanced International Studies, September 21, 2010; conversation with Peter Schneider, Berlin, December 8, 2008.

12. Farhan Bokhari and Daniel Dombey, "Kabul Attack Sends Signal to U.S. Aide," *Financial Times*, February 12, 2009, p. 5; Karen DeYoung, "17,000 More Troops Headed to Afghanistan," *Washington Post*, February 18, 2009, p. A-1.

13. Emily Wax, "U.S. Removes Kashmir from Envoy's Mandate; India Exults," *Washington Post*, January 30, 2009, p. A-9.

14. Interview with a friend of Richard Holbrooke; Michael Crowley, "Hillary's State," *New Republic*, March 4, 2009, p. 17; transcript of remarks by General David Petraeus at Harvard University, April 22, 2009.

15. Bob Woodward, *Obama's Wars* (New York: Simon & Schuster, 2010), p. 90; Bruce Rie-

del, *The Search for al Qaeda*, first edition (Washington D.C.: Brookings Institution Press, 2008).

16. White House transcript, "Press Briefing by Bruce Riedel, Ambassador Richard Holbrooke and Michèle Flournoy on the New Strategy for Afghanistan and Pakistan," March 27, 2009.

17. Pelosi interview, June 7, 2011.

18. Leslie H. Gelb, "How to Leave Afghanistan," *New York Times*, March 13, 2009, p. A-27; interview with Leslie Gelb, June 18, 2009.

19. Michael D. Shear, "Obama Says He Is Sharpening Focus of War in Afghanistan," *Washington Post*, March 30, 2009, p. A-6.

20. Ibid.; White House transcript, "Press Briefing by Bruce Riedel."

21. Ann Scott Tyson, "Top U.S. Commander in Afghanistan Is Fired," *Washington Post*, May 12, 2009, p. A-1.

Chapter 10: "It's Not Like This Ghost in His Head"

1. Jodi Wilgoren, "Fed Up, Kerry Says Bush Lets Group 'Do His Dirty Work,'" *New York Times*, August 20, 2004, p. A-18.

2. Transcript, "Senator Obama's Remarks Before VFW Convention in Orlando," August 19, 2008.

3. White House transcript, "President Obama's Remarks to the VFW Convention," August 17, 2009.

4. Woodward, *Obama's Wars*, pp. 131–34, 156.

5. Yaroslav Trofimov, "Soviets' Afghan Ordeal Vexed Gates on Troop-Surge Plan," *Wall Street Journal*, November 30, 2009, p. A-1.

6. Gordon M. Goldstein, *Lessons in Disaster: McGeorge Bundy and the Path to War in Vietnam* (New York: Times Books, 2008); Richard Holbrooke, "The Doves Were Right," *New York Times Book Review*, November 28, 2008, p. 1.

7. Peter Spiegel and Jonathan Weisman, "Behind Afghan War Debate, a Battle of Two Books Rages," *Wall Street Journal*, October 7, 2009, p. A-1.

8. Ibid.

9. McDonough interview, July 14, 2010.

10. Interview with Susan Rice, January 28, 2011.

11. Rhodes interview, October 4, 2010.

12. Michael D. Shear and Paul Kane, "President vs. Party on Troop Increase," *Washington Post*, November 26, 2009, p. A-1.

13. Background interview with an administration official involved in the Afghanistan policy review.

14. Alter, *The Promise*, pp. 376–80; Michael Gerson, "In Afghanistan, No Choice But to Try," *Washington Post*, September 4, 2009, p. A-23.

15. Powell, *My American Journey*, p. 561.

16. Ben Smith, "Obama 'Realism' Faces Afghan Test," *Politico*, November 29, 2009.

17. Interview with a participant in these discussions.

18. "Remarks by the President in Address to the Nation on the Way Forward in Afghanistan and Pakistan," December 1, 2009.

19. Ibid.

20. Conversation with a German correspondent.

Chapter 11: The Speeches: "Evil Does Exist"

1. This account is based upon background interviews with several officials at the White House and State Department.
2. The account was provided by an official with knowledge of the meeting.
3. See, for example, Peter Baker, "Following a Different Map to a Similar Direction," *New York Times*, June 9, 2009, p. A-10.
4. White House transcript, "Remarks by the President on a New Beginning," Cairo, June 4, 2009.
5. Ibid.
6. "Obama Gives a Bush Speech; U.S. Talking Points on Islam Haven't Changed," *Washington Times*, June 5, 2009, p. A-20.
7. Frank J. Gaffney Jr., "America's First Muslim President? Obama Aligns with the Policies of Shariah Adherents," *Washington Times*, June 9, 2009, p. A-19.
8. White House transcript, "Remarks by President Obama," Prague, April 5, 2009.
9. White House transcript, "Remarks by the President to the Ghanian Parliament," Accra, July 11, 2009.
10. White House transcript, "Remarks by the President at the New Economic School Graduation," Moscow, July 7, 2009.
11. Background interview with an aide to President Obama.
12. Gerald F. Seib, "Capital Journal: What Should Obama Say in Egypt?" *Wall Street Journal*, June 2, 2009, p. A-2.
13. Confidential conversation with an Obama aide.
14. "The Nobel Peace Prize for 2009," press release, Nobelprize.org.
15. This account of the internal workup of the Nobel speech was supplied in background interviews by an administration official and by a senior Democrat with ties to the administration.
16. White House transcript, "Remarks by the President at the Acceptance of the Nobel Peace Prize," Oslo, December 10, 2009.
17. Ibid.
18. Ibid.

Chapter 12: The Scowcroft Democrats

1. "Remarks by the President on a New Beginning," Cairo, June 4, 2009.
2. "Remarks by President Obama," Prague, April 5, 2009.
3. "Foreign Press Center Briefing on Overview of the Obama Administration's Nonproliferation Agenda," April 20, 2010.
4. Podesta interview.
5. White House transcript, "President Obama's Address to the United Nations General Assembly," September 23, 2010.
6. "Remarks by the President on a New Beginning," Cairo, June 4, 2009.
7. Glenn Kessler, "Clinton's Candor Abroad Draws Mixed Reviews," *Washington Post*, February 23, 2009, p. A-12.
8. Mark Landler, "A New Iran Overture, with Hot Dogs," *New York Times*, June 2, 2009, p. A-4.
9. "Remarks by the President on a New Beginning," Cairo, June 4, 2009.
10. Thomas Erdbrink, "Iran Election in Dispute as Both Sides Claim Victory," *Washington Post*, June 13, 2009, p. A-1; and Thomas Erdbrink, "Ahmadinejad Vows New Start as Clashes Flare," *Washington Post*, June 14, 2009, p. A-1.

11. Martin Fletcher, "'Torture, Murder and Rape'—Iran's Way of Breaking the Opposition," *The Times*, September 18, 2009, p. 12.
12. White House transcript, "Press Conference by the President," June 23, 2009.
13. Background interview with a senior administration official, June 30, 2009.
14. Thomas Erdbrink and Liz Sly, "Egypt's Revolt Stokes Fires Regionwide," *Washington Post*, February 15, 2011, p. A-1; White House transcript, "Press Conference by the President," February 5, 2011.
15. James P. Rubin, "The Principle of the Thing: How America's Commitment to Democratic Values Is Waning in the Age of Obama," *Newsweek*, December 14, 2009, p. 44.
16. Leon Wieseltier, "In Which We Engage," *New Republic*, April 1, 2009, p. 48.
17. Interview with Brent Scowcroft, June 6, 2002.
18. David Brooks, "Obama Admires Bush," *New York Times*, May 16, 2008, p. A-23.
19. Interview with a friend of Gates.
20. Peter Baker, "Obama Puts His Own Mark on Foreign Policy Issues," *New York Times*, April 13, 2010, p. A-1.
21. McDonough interview, July 14, 2010.
22. "Brent Scowcroft Supports Obama's Missile Defense Decision," Atlantic Council press release, September 18, 2009; Eli Lake, "Newsmaker Interview: Scowcroft Lauds Obama's Foreign Diplomacy," *Washington Times*, October 6, 2009, p. A-1.
23. Background interview with an administration official.
24. Michael McFaul, *Advancing Democracy Abroad: Why We Should and How We Can* (Lanham, MD: Rowman & Littlefield, 2010), p. 233; McFaul interview.
25. Richard Nixon, "Remarks at the Dedication of the Woodrow Wilson International Center for Scholars," February 18, 1971.

Chapter 13: No Roosevelt, No Churchill, No Brandy

1. The belief that George W. Bush's China policy merits inclusion on this list alongside Reagan and Clinton is widespread, but untrue. While running for president, Bush had labeled China a "strategic competitor," but had proposed no far-reaching policy changes as Reagan and Clinton had. In the early months of the Bush administration, Donald Rumsfeld's Pentagon pressed for harder policies toward China, but at the White House the president himself and National Security Adviser Condoleezza Rice favored more traditional approaches.
2. Campbell and Steinberg, *Difficult Transitions*, pp. 59–60.
3. Dennis Wilder, "How a 'G-2' Would Hurt," *Washington Post*, April 2, 2009, p. A-21.
4. Transcript, "Barack Obama at the G-20 Summit, London," Federal News Service, April 2, 2009.
5. The members of the G-20 are Argentina, Australia, Brazil, Canada, China, the European Union, France, Germany, India, Indonesia, Italy, Japan, Mexico, Russia, Saudi Arabia, South Africa, South Korea, Turkey, the United Kingdom and the United States.
6. See "Another BRIC in the Wall," *The Economist*, April 21, 2008.
7. Hillary Rodham Clinton, "Foreign Policy Address at the Council on Foreign Relations," July 15, 2009.
8. Keith B. Richburg, "A New Economic World Order?" *Washington Post*, April 15, 2011, p. A-17.
9. Ian Wilhelm, "Ford Foundation Links Parents of Obama and Treasury Secretary Nominee," *Chronicle of Philanthropy*, December 3, 2008.

10. Daniel Dombey and Alan Beattie, "Clinton Signals Broader Focus on Beijing," *Financial Times*, January 28, 2009, p. 7.

11. John Pomfret, "Obama's Meeting with the Dalai Lama Is Delayed," *Washington Post*, October 5, 2009, p. A-1.

12. Background interview with a close aide to President Obama.

13. Background interview with an Obama administration official, July 14, 2010.

14. Mark Landler and David E. Sanger, "China Seeks Assurances That U.S. Will Cut Deficit," *New York Times*, July 29, 2009, p. A-6.

15. Glenn Kessler, "U.S.-Chinese Meeting Renews the Dialogue," *Washington Post*, July 28, 2009, p. A-8.

16. David Wessel, "Free-Trade Winds May Be Picking Up Again," *Wall Street Journal*, July 1, 2010, p. A-2; background interviews with two administration officials.

17. White House transcript, "Remarks by President Barack Obama at Town Hall Meeting with Future Chinese Leaders," November 16, 2009.

18. "Obama Interview Irks China," *Los Angeles Times*, November 20, 2009, p. A-29; Jason Dean, "Obama's China Interview Mystery," *Wall Street Journal*, China Real Time Report, November 19, 2009, blogs.wsj.com/chinarealtime.

19. Michael Wines and Sharon LaFraniere, "As Weight of Relationship Tilts East, Obama Opts for Nuance and Deference," *New York Times*, November 18, 2009, p. A-14.

20. Keith Bradsher, "U.S. Deal with Taiwan Has China Retaliating," *New York Times*, January 31, 2010, p. A-14.

21. Joseph S. Nye Jr., "The U.S., Japan and China: Focus on the Long Term," speech delivered to Pacific Forum CSIS, Honolulu, February 23, 2010.

22. Author notes from Dmitry Medvedev meeting with members of Council on Foreign Relations, Washington D.C., November 15, 2008.

23. It is true that Obama, as a child, was in Indonesia not long after the bloody purges against alleged communists there. But he witnessed none of the violence, which in any case was far removed from the U.S.-Soviet competition at the heart of the Cold War.

24. Obama, *The Audacity of Hope*, p. 313.

25. Medvedev meeting with Council on Foreign Relations.

26. Philip P. Pan, "Kyrgyzstan Threatens to Close U.S. Base," *Washington Post*, February 4, 2009, p. A-12.

27. Background interview with Obama administration official, June 29, 2010.

28. Michael Schwirtz and Clifford J. Levy, "In Reversal, Kyrgyzstan Won't Close a U.S. Base," *New York Times*, June 24, 2009, p. A-6.

29. In late 2011, the newly elected president of Kyrgyzstan, Almazbek Atambayev, announced he would try once more to close the U.S. base at Manas, but only after its current lease runs out in 2014. That is the year in which American forces are supposed to be withdrawn from Afghanistan. Michael Schwirtz, "New Leader Says U.S. Base in Kyrgyzstan Will Be Shut," *New York Times*, November 2, 2011, p. A-6.

30. Amy Argetsinger and Roxanne Roberts, "Off the List, but Somehow on the South Lawn," *Washington Post*, November 26, 2009, p. A-1.

31. Henry Kissinger memo to Richard Nixon, from Mann, *About Face*, p. 63.

32. Interview with Ben Rhodes, October 4, 2010.

Chapter 14: "Iran, Iran, Iran and Iran"

1. Dafna Linzer, "The Money Man in the Terror Fight," *Washington Post*, July 5, 2006, p. A-11.

2. The Republican Party's views of economic sanctions have also wavered, though in different ways (for example, its leaders opposed sanctions against South Africa and against China in the 1980s). I single out the Democrats here simply because they are the focus of this book.

3. See www.usaengage.org.

4. Interview with Gary Milhollin, October 2, 2009.

5. Robin Wright, "Stuart Levey's War," *New York Times Magazine*, November 2, 2008, p. 29.

6. David E. Sanger, James Glanz and Jo Becker, "From Arabs and Israelis, Sharp Distress over a Nuclear Iran," *New York Times*, November 29, 2010, p. A-1.

7. Interview with James Steinberg, June 23, 2009.

8. The description of the policy review and policy changes was supplied in an interview with Gary Samore, the special assistant to the president in charge of arms control and nonproliferation.

9. Glenn Kessler, "U.S. Targets Firms Tied to North Korea Arms Trade," *Washington Post*, July 1, 2009, p. A-10.

10. Emma Chanlett-Avery and Mi Ae Taylor, "North Korea: U.S. Relations, Nuclear Diplomacy, and Internal Situation," Congressional Research Service, November 10, 2010, p. 6.

11. Na Jeong-ju, "Obama Criticizes China for 'Willful Blindness' to North Korean Provocation," *Korea Times*, June 28, 2010.

12. Background interview with a senior administration official, July 16, 2010.

13. Background interview with a senior administration official, June 30, 2009; interview with Gary Samore, February 10, 2011.

14. Samore interview.

15. Elisabeth Bumiller and David E. Sanger, "North Korea Could Strike Continental U.S. with a Missile Within Five Years, Gates Says," *New York Times*, January 12, 2011, p. A-8.

16. Samore interview.

17. "Interview with Vice President Joe Biden Discussing Events in the Middle East," *This Week*, ABC News, July 5, 2009.

18. Glenn Kessler, "Iran, Major Powers Reach Agreement on Series of Points; Obama Sees a Constructive Beginning," *Washington Post*, October 2, 2009, p. A-1.

19. Thomas Erdbrink and William Branigan, "Iran's Khamenei Rejects U.S. Outreach; Obama Efforts Disdained," *Washington Post*, November 4, 2009, p. A-12.

20. Paul Richter, "U.S. Changing Focus of Its Iran Policy," *Los Angeles Times*, March 10, 2010, p. A-4.

21. Richard N. Haass, "Enough Is Enough," *Newsweek*, February 1, 2010, pp. 440–41.

22. Interview with James Steinberg, April 28, 2010.

23. Interview with a senior administration official, October 7, 2010.

24. Thomas Erdbrink, "U.S. Deal with European Oil Firms Hobbles Iran Air," *Washington Post*, October 17, 2010, p. A-14.

25. Text of President Obama's State of the Union Address, January 26, 2011.

26. White House transcript, "Remarks by the President on the Middle East and North Africa," May 19, 2011.

27. Background interview with Obama administration official, July 16, 2010.

28. Text of speech by Secretary of State Hillary Clinton, "Remarks at the U.S. Institute of Peace," October 21, 2009.

29. Mary Beth Sheridan, "New Nuclear Policy Shows Limits," *Washington Post*, April 7, 2010, p. A-6.

30. Robert Kagan, "The New START Trap for the GOP," *Washington Post*, November 12, 2010, p. A-17.

31. Mitt Romney, "Obama's Worst Foreign Policy Mistake," *Washington Post*, July 6, 2010, p. A-13; Sarah Palin, "Delink Missile Defense, Defeat New START," December 17, 2010, http://sarah palininformation.wordpress.com/2010/12/18/sarah-palin-new-start-treaty-deeply-flawed-not-in-americas-best-interest; Newt Gingrich, "New START Can Wait," *National Review Online*, December 13, 2010, www.nationalreview.com/articles/255169/new-start-can-wait-newt-gin
grich; Tim Pawlenty, "Skeptical of New START," *National Review Online*, September 15, 2010, www.nationalreview.com/articles/246662/skeptical-new-start-nro-symposium; Scowcroft quoted in Abby Phillip and Carol E. Lee, "START Puts Lugar on the Spot," *Politico*, November 27, 2010, http://dyn.politico.com/printstory.cfm?uuid=8B55BDF1-BF68-FF90-A66565772982D5E4.
32. "Remarks by President Obama," Prague, April 5, 2009.
33. Steinberg interview, April 28, 2010.
34. Interview with Strobe Talbott, July 13, 2010; Strobe Talbott, *The Great Experiment* (New York: Simon & Schuster, 2008), p. 330.
35. See www.youtube.com/watch?v=GPpxvOAVx5M. Glenn Beck left Fox News in 2011.
36. Interview with an aide to President Obama.

Chapter 15: The Outsiders

1. Background interview with an intelligence official.
2. The actual numbers are classified. Various estimates put the size of the CIA at roughly 20,000 and that of the Office of the Director of National Intelligence at well below 2,000.
3. Background interview with an intelligence official.
4. Marc Ambinder, "The Real Intelligence Wars," *The Atlantic*, November 2009, www.theatlantic.com/politics/archive/2009/11/the-real-intelligence-wars-oversight-and-access/30334. Woodward, *Obama's Wars*, pp. 370–71.
5. Hayden interview.
6. Brennan interview; Hayden interview.
7. Scott Shane, "CIA Drone Use Is Set to Expand Inside Pakistan," *New York Times*, December 4, 2009, p. A-1.
8. Harold Hongju Koh, speech to American Society of International Law.
9. The Bush administration had carried out one attack on an al-Qaeda official in Somalia in 2002, but all other targeted killings were in Pakistan or Afghanistan.
10. Dana Priest, "U.S. Playing a Key Role in Yemen Attacks," *Washington Post*, January 27, 2010, p. A-1.
11. Karen DeYoung and Michael Fletcher, "Report: Focus Was on al-Qaeda Plans Overseas," *Washington Post*, January 8, 2010, p. A-1; Greg Miller, "Spy Agencies Faulted for Missing Airline Bomb Threat," *Washington Post*, May 19, 2010, p. A-2.
12. Eric Lipton, Eric Schmitt and Mark Mazzetti, "Review of Jet Bomb Shows More Missed Clues," *New York Times*, January 18, 2010, p. A-1.
13. Edward Luce, "Palin Says U.S. 'Ready for Another Revolution,'" *Financial Times*, February 8, 2010, p. 3.
14. Lipton, Schmitt and Mazzetti, "Review."
15. Background interview with an intelligence official.
16. Ibid.
17. Michael Hastings, "The Runaway General," *Rolling Stone*, July 8, 2010, p. 92.

18. Eliot A. Cohen, "Why McChrystal Has to Go," *Wall Street Journal*, June 23, 2010, p. A-17; Gordon Lubed and Carol E. Lee, "President Obama: Stanley McChrystal Showed 'Poor Judgment,'" *Politico*, June 23, 2010, www.politico.com/news/stories/0610/38837.html.

19. Greg Jaffe and Ernesto Londoño, "Angered Obama Orders McChrystal to Return," *Washington Post*, June 23, 2010, p. A-1.

20. Jonathan Allen and Marin Cogan, "Obama Losing Hill Liberals on War," *Politico*, June 25, 2010, www.politico.com/news/stories/0610/39010.html.

21. Thom Shanker and Elisabeth Bumiller, "Military and Pentagon Leaders Urge Patience for Afghan Mission," *New York Times*, June 17, 2010, p. 10; casualty figures based on official reports from http://icasualties.org/oef.

22. Talbott interview.

23. Mike Allen, "The Tick-Tock: How Obama Took Command of the McChrystal Situation," *Politico*, June 24, 2010, www.politico.com/news/stories/0610/38962.html; Mark Landler, "Short, Tense Deliberation, Then a General Is Gone," *New York Times*, June 24, 2010, p. A-14.

24. Interview with an aide to President Obama, July 31, 2009.

25. Helene Cooper, "National Security Adviser Takes Less Visible Approach to His Job," *New York Times*, May 7, 2009, p. A-10.

26. Woodward, *Obama's Wars*, pp. 197–99.

27. Ibid., pp. 138, 199–200.

28. See Jason Horowitz, "Is the Donilon Doctrine the New New World Order?" *Washington Post*, December 21, 2010, p. C-1.

29. "Report of the Special Examination of Fannie Mae," published by Office of Federal Housing Enterprise Oversight, May 2006, http://fhfa.gov/webfiles/747/FNMSPECIAL EXAM, pp. 64, 78.

30. See Albert B. Crenshaw, "High Pay at Fannie Mae for the Well-Connected," *Washington Post*, December 23, 2004, p. E-3; Rob Blackwell, "Fannie Defends Big Paychecks for Its Leaders," *The American Banker*, April 27, 2004.

31. See "Zbigniew Brzezinski and Brent Scowcroft Discuss Turmoil in the Arab World," PBS *News Hour*, March 21, 2011; Brent Scowcroft and Zbigniew Brzezinski, moderated by David Ignatius, *America and the World: Conversations on the Future of American Foreign Policy* (New York: Basic Books, 2008).

Chapter 16: *"Richard Being Richard"*

1. Isikoff and Corn, *Hubris*, p. 127.

2. Background interview with a friend of Holbrooke, February 15, 2011; Karen DeYoung, "For Kerry, a Growing Role on Foreign Policy Stage," *Washington Post*, October 23, 2009, p. A-1.

3. George Packer, "The Last Mission: Richard Holbrooke's Plan to Avoid the Mistakes of Vietnam in Afghanistan," *The New Yorker*, September 28, 2009, p. 38.

4. Conversation with a Holbrooke associate, April 19, 2010; Robert Draper, "The Ultimate Obama Insider," *New York Times Magazine*, July 26, 2009, p. 30.

5. Background conversation with a senior administration official.

6. Richard Holbrooke, "U.S. Policy on Afghanistan," speech to Council on Foreign Relations, Washington D.C., December 15, 2009, transcribed by Federal News Service; Holbrooke speech to Women's Foreign Policy Group, January 8, 2010, reported by Josh Robin, "Team Obama Scuttles the Term AfPak," *Foreign Policy*, January 20,

2010, thecable.foreignpolicy.com/posts/2010/01/20/team_obama_scuttles_the_term_ afpak.

7. Interview with a Holbrooke associate; see also Helene Cooper, Thom Shanker and Dexter Filkins, "General's Job Is in Doubt in Exposing Afghan Rifts," *New York Times*, June 23, 2010, p. A-1.

8. Thomas E. Ricks, "Lose a General, Win a War," *New York Times*, June 24, 2010, p. A-33; Fred Kaplan, "McChrystal: Gone and Soon Forgotten," *Slate*, June 23, 2010, www.slate.com/articles/news_and_politics/war_stories/2010/06/mcchrystal _gone_and_soon_forgotten.html.

9. Doyle McManus, "Who's in Charge in Afghanistan?" *Los Angeles Times*, June 27, 2010, p. A-32; conversation with Doyle McManus, August 26, 2010.

10. Conversation with senior State Department official, October 19, 2010.

11. Interview with Bill Drozdiak, February 16, 2011.

12. Holbrooke, "A Sense of Drift," pp. 98–100.

13. White House transcript, "Remarks by the President at a Memorial Service for Richard Holbrooke," January 14, 2011; State Department transcript, "Hillary Rodham Clinton Remarks at Memorial Service for Richard Holbrooke," January 14, 2011; Federal News Service transcript, "Remarks by Former President Bill Clinton at the Memorial Service for Richard Holbrooke," January 14, 2011.

14. Nicholas Kristof, "What Holbrooke Knew," *New York Times*, Week in Review, May 15, 2011, p. 10.

15. Ibid.

Chapter 17: Hillary Clinton's "Miracle" Speech

1. Transcript, "Remarks by President Barack Obama at the Radio and Television Correspondents' Association," June 19, 2009.

2. Background conversation with an aide to Secretary Clinton.

3. Tina Brown, "Hillary: Take Off Your Burqa," *The Daily Beast*, July 13, 2009, www .thedailybeast.com/articles/2009/07/13/obamas-other-wife-1.html.

4. Anne Applebaum, "No Burqa for Clinton," *Washington Post*, July 28, 2009, p. A-17.

5. Greg Torode, "Vietnam Buys Submarines to Counter China," *South China Morning Post*, December 17, 2009, p. 1.

6. Viola Gienger, "Vietnam, U.S. Will Expand Military Links, Hold Talks Next Year," Bloomberg News Service, December 16, 2009.

7. "Scholar Urges U.S. to Respect China's 'Four Core Interests,'" BBC Monitoring Service, November 14, 2009.

8. Edward Wong, "Chinese Military Seeks to Extend Its Naval Power," *New York Times*, April 24, 2010, p. A-1.

9. State Department transcript, "Secretary Clinton's Remarks on Internet Freedom," delivered at the Newseum, January 21, 2010; background interview with a senior State Department official, April 14, 2010.

10. Mark Landler, "Offering to Aid Talks, U.S. Challenges China on Disputed Islands," *New York Times*, July 24, 2010, p. A-4; John Pomfret, "U.S. Takes Tougher Stance with China," *Washington Post*, July 30, 2010, p. A-1.

11. Pomfret, op. cit.

12. Kurt Campbell remarks at Schieffer Series Dialogue, "South China Sea: A Key Indica-

tor for Asian Security Cooperation for the 21st Century," Center for Strategic and International Studies, September 28, 2010.

13. White House transcript, "Remarks by the President in Address to the Nation on the End of Combat Operations in Iraq," August 31, 2010.

14. Dan Balz, "Was Obama's Speech 'Mission Accomplished'?'" *Washington Post*, September 1, 2010, http://www.washingtonpost.com/wp-dyn/content/article/2010/09/01/AR2010090103045_2.html?sid=ST2010090105699.

15. State Department transcript, "Hillary Rodham Clinton Remarks to Council on Foreign Relations," September 8, 2010.

16. Ibid.

17. Background interviews with two former State Department officials.

18. Transcript, "Mitt Romney Delivers Remarks on U.S. Foreign Policy," speech at the Citadel, Charleston, South Carolina, October 7, 2011.

19. Walter Isaacson and Evan Thomas, *The Wise Men* (New York: Simon & Schuster, 1986).

20. Paul Kennedy, *The Rise and Fall of the Great Powers* (New York: Random House, 1987).

21. "Hillary Rodham Clinton Remarks to Council on Foreign Relations."

22. "Remarks by the President at the Acceptance of the Nobel Peace Prize," December 10, 2009; "Remarks by the President in Address on the Way Forward in Afghanistan and Pakistan," December 1, 2009.

23. Background interview with senior administration official.

24. "President Obama's Address to the United Nations General Assembly," September 23, 2010.

25. Ibid.

26. Interview with Ben Rhodes, October 4, 2010.

Chapter 18: *"Now Means Yesterday"*

1. Dave Gilson, senior editor of *Mother Jones*, quoted in Daniel Denvir, "Wikileaks and the Cult of Secrets," *Huffington Post*, December 23, 2010, www.huffingtonpost.com/daniel-denvir/wikileaks-and-the-cult-of_b_800570.html.

2. Joby Warrick, "In Mideast, Clinton Cites Harm from Leaks," *Washington Post*, January 10, 2011, p. A-11.

3. *Al-Akhbar* is an opposition newspaper in Lebanon with close links to Hezbollah, the radical Shiite party. It claimed to have obtained the cables on its own, separately from the three main international papers publishing the cables. See "*Al-Akhbar* Releases 183 Exclusive U.S. Diplomatic Cables," *Middle East Reporter*, December 4, 2010; Bassem Mroue, "Lebanese Paper's Website Attacked over Wikileaks," Associated Press, December 9, 2010.

4. Ian Black, "The U.S. Embassy Cables North Africa: Tunisia's Repressive Regime Blocks U.S. Account of President's Corrupt Lifestyle," *The Guardian*, December 8, 2010, p. 7.

5. Ibid.

6. Jillian York, "Tunisia's Comprehensive Internet System," Al Jazeera, January 9, 2011, published by BBC Monitoring Service; Black, "The U.S. Embassy Cables"; Mroue, "Lebanese Paper's Website."

7. Julian Borger, "Crackdown Threat in Tunisia After Graduate Protests," *The Guardian*, December 30, 2010, p. 22.

8. Mark Landler, "Secret Report Ordered by Obama Identified Potential Arab Uprisings," *New York Times*, February 17, 2011, p. A-14; David Ignatius, "Obama's Low-Key Strategy for the Middle East," *Washington Post*, March 6, 2011, p. A-21.

9. Interview with Samantha Power, February 22, 2011.

10. State Department transcript, "Secretary of State Hillary Rodham Clinton Remarks to 'Forum for the Future,'" Doha, Qatar, January 13, 2011.

11. "Deadly Unrest in Tunisia Continues," *Los Angeles Times*, January 13, 2011, p. A-4.

12. Edward Cody and Joby Warrick, "Tunisia's President Flees the Country," *Washington Post*, January 15, 2011, p. A-1.

13. David D. Kirkpatrick, "President of Tunisia Flees, Capitulating to Protesters," *New York Times*, January 15, 2011, p. A-1.

14. Sam Jones, "Self Immolations Across North Africa Follow Suicide in Tunisia," *The Guardian*, January 18, 2011, www.guardian.co.uk/world/2011/jan/17/self-immolation-protests-north-africa; Liz Sly and Leila Fadel, "Overthrow Delivers a Jolt to Arab Region," *Washington Post*, January 17, 2011, p. A-11.

15. Interview with James Steinberg, July 5, 2011; "Egypt's Parliamentary Elections," press statement, U.S. Department of State, November 29, 2010.

16. Gene Sharp, *From Dictatorship to Democracy* (Boston: Albert Einstein Institution, 2002), pp. 28–29; Ruaridh Arrow, "Gene Sharp: Author of the Nonviolent Revolution Rulebook," BBC News, February 21, 2011, www.bbc.co.uk/news/world-middle-east-12522848; David D. Kirkpatrick and David E. Sanger, "A Tunisian-Egyptian Link That Shook Arab History," *New York Times*, February 14, 2011, p. A-1.

17. Arrow, "Gene Sharp."

18. Transcript, "Jim Lehrer Interview with Vice President Joe Biden," PBS *News Hour*, January 27, 2011.

19. David D. Kirkpatrick, "Mubarak Orders Crackdown, with Revolt Sweeping Egypt," *New York Times*, January 29, 2011, p. A-1.

20. Mark Landler, Helene Cooper and David D. Kirkpatrick, "A Diplomatic Scramble as an Ally Is Pushed to the Exit," *New York Times*, February 2, 2011, p. A-1.

21. The account of the February 1 events is based on an interview with Ben Rhodes, July 15, 2011.

22. Ibid.

23. This quote was taken from the memorandum of conversation between President Obama and President Mubarak.

24. Background interview with an aide to President Obama.

25. Ibid.

26. Griff Witte, Mary Beth Sheridan and Karen DeYoung, "Rifts Stall Egypt Talks," *Washington Post*, February 6, 2011, p. A-1.

27. Rhodes interview, July 15, 2011.

28. David Ignatius, "Obama's Low-Key Strategy for the Middle East," *Washington Post*, March 6, 2011, p. A-21.

29. Helene Cooper and David E. Sanger, "In Egypt, U.S. Weighs Push for Change with Stability," *New York Times*, February 8, 2011, p. A-1.

30. Rhodes interview, July 15, 2011.

31. Scott Wilson, "Mubarak's Decision Puts Obama on Defensive," *Washington Post*, February 11, 2011, p. A-6.

32. Joby Warrick, "Defiance Threatens White House, Threatens Chaos," *Washington Post*, February 12, 2011, p. A-1.

Chapter 19: "We are All Democrats Now"

1. Charles Krauthammer, "Syria and the New Axis of Evil," *Washington Post*, April 1, 2005, p. A-27.
2. "From Tripoli to Tehran, Arab Spring Sprouts New Wave of Protest," *The Guardian,* February 17, 2011, p. 22.
3. Steinberg interview, July 5, 2011.
4. See Scott Wilson, "Obama Administration Studies Recent Revolutions for Lessons Applicable in Egypt," *Washington Post*, February 14, 2011, p. A-12.
5. Background interview, late February 2011.
6. Massoud A. Derhally, "Jordan's King Abdullah Seeks Rapid Change from New Government Amid Protest," Bloomberg News Service, February 21, 2011; Bill Spindle, "Jordan, Too, Feels Heat of Arab Spring Protests," *Wall Street Journal*, July 13, 2011, p. A-12.
7. "Bahrain Mourners Call for an End to Monarchy," Associated Press, February 18, 2011, available at www.guardian.co.uk/world/2011/feb/18/bahrain-mourners-call-downfall-monarchy.
8. Ethan Bronner and Michael D. Slackman, "Saudis, Fearful of Iran, Sent Troops to Bahrain to Quell Protests," *New York Times*, March 15, 2011, p. A-1.
9. Mark Landler and Helene Cooper, "Trying to Pick the Winners in the Middle East," *New York Times*, February 25, 2001, p. A-1.
10. One obvious exception here was Libya, which is described in the next chapter.
11. Joby Warrick and Michael Birnbaum, "Questions Mount as Bahrain Stifles Revolt," *Washington Post*, April 15, 2011, p. A-1.
12. "Remarks by the President on the Middle East and North Africa," May 19, 2011.
13. Ibid.
14. David Ignatius, "The Pol and the Policy," *Washington Post*, April 27, 2011, p. A-17.
15. Transcript, "Interview with Hillary Clinton and Robert Gates," CBS *Face the Nation*, March 27, 2011.
16. Mark Landler and David E. Sanger, "White House, in Shift, Turns Against Syrian Leader," *New York Times*, July 13, 2011.
17. Anthony Faiola, "Egypt's Military Tightens Reins," *Washington Post*, September 17, 2011, p. A-1; Anthony Shadid, "Egypt's Islamists Show Their Might and Numbers," *New York Times*, July 30, 2011, p. A-4.
18. Background interview with a senior Obama administration official.

Chapter 20: Libya: To Fly

1. Glenn Kessler, "Rice and Gaddafi Hammer at Wall Built by Decades of Animosity," *Washington Post*, September 6, 2008, p. A-10. In her own memoir, Rice describes Gaddafi's apparent obsession with her: *No Higher Honor: A Memoir of My Years in Washington* (New York: Random House, 2011), pp. 701–3.
2. Alan Cowell, "Protests Take Aim at Leader of Libya," *New York Times*, February 17, 2011, p. A-14.
3. Interview with Samantha Power, July 26, 2011.
4. Rhodes interview, July 14, 2011; Karen DeYoung and Colum Lynch, "U.S. Ratchets Up Pressure on Gaddafi," *Washington Post*, February 26, 2011, p. A-1.
5. Kareem Fahim and David D. Kirkpatrick, "Qaddafi Orders Brutal Crackdown as Revolt Grows," *New York Times*, February 23, 2011, p. A-1; "Gaddafi's Son Warns of

'Rivers of Blood' in Libya," Al Arabiya, February 22, 2011, www.alarabiya.net/arti cles/2011/02/21/138515.html.

6. Samantha Power, "Bystanders to Genocide," *The Atlantic*, September 2001, pp. 84–108.

7. Martin Fackler, "Helping Hands Rebuild Lives and United States Ties to Japan," *New York Times*, March 23, 2011, p. A-13.

8. Thom Shanker, "Gates Ratchets Up His Campaign of Candor," *New York Times*, March 5, 2011, p. A-4.

9. Karen DeYoung and Craig Whitlock, "U.S. Defense Leaders Warn of Risks in Enforcing No-Fly Zone," *Washington Post*, March 2, 2011, p. A-8.

10. Interview with Tom Donilon, October 4, 2011.

11. "The Courage Factor," *The Economist*, March 19, 2011, p. 42; Anne-Marie Slaughter, "Fiddling While Libya Burns," *New York Times*, March 14, 2011, p. A-25.

12. Diaa Hadid, "Arab League Asks UN for No-Fly Zone," Associated Press, March 12, 2011.

13. Donilon interview.

14. Rhodes interview, July 14, 2011; Helene Cooper and Steven Lee Myers, "Shift by Clinton Helped Persuade President to Take a Harder Line," *New York Times*, March 19, 2011, p. A-1.

15. Paul Schemm and Zeina Karam, "Gaddafi Forces Drive Rebels from Key Oil Town," Associated Press, March 13, 2011.

16. Author observation at State Department event, January 27, 2011.

17. Maureen Dowd, "Fight of the Valkyries," *New York Times*, March 23, 2011, p. A-27.

18. Garance Franke-Ruta, "On the Idiocy of Framing the Libya Intervention as a Battle of the Sexes," *The Atlantic*, March 22, 2011, www.theatlantic.com/politics/archive/2011/03/on-the-idiocy-of-framing-the-libya-intervention-as-a-battle-of-the-sexes/72779.

19. PBS *News Hour*, March 21, 2011.

20. Rhodes interview, July 14, 2011.

21. White House transcript, "Remarks by the President in Address to the Nation on Libya," delivered at National Defense University, March 28, 2011.

22. "War by Global Committee," *Wall Street Journal*, March 21, 2011, p. A-16; Kori Schake, "The U.S. Sits One Out," *Foreign Policy*, March 18, 2011, http://shadow.foreignpolicy.com/posts/2011/03/18/the_us_sits_one_out.

23. See Glenn Kessler, "On Libya, Where You Stand Depends on Where You Sit," *Washington Post*, March 29, 2011, www.washingtonpost.com/blogs/fact-checker/post/onlibya-where-you-stand-depends-on-where-you-sit/2011/03/28/AFBONgrB_blog.html.

24. Charlie Savage, "Attack Renews Debate over Congressional Consent," *New York Times*, March 22, 2011, p. A-14.

25. Charlie Savage and Thom Shanker, "Scores of U.S. Strikes in Libya Followed Handoff to NATO," *New York Times*, June 21, 2011, p. A-8.

26. John Yoo, "Antiwar Senator, War-Powers President," *Wall Street Journal*, March 25, 2011, p. A-17; Bruce Ackerman and Oona Hathaway, "Libya's Looming Deadline," *Washington Post*, May 18, 2011, p. A-17.

27. Steinberg interview, July 5, 2011.

28. "Remarks by the President in Address to the Nation on Libya," March 28, 2011.

29. Candy Crowley, "Interview with Stephen J. Hadley and Jane Harman," CNN *State of the Union*, May 1, 2011.

30. Mary Beth Sheridan, "Gaddafi Buried in Secret Desert Grave, Libyan Officials Say," *Washington Post*, October 26, 2011, p. A-10.

31. Rhodes interview, July 14, 2011; Mary Beth Sheridan and Scott Wilson, "Administration

Plays Down Its Role in Assault," *Washington Post*, March 20, 2011, p. A-1; Ryan Lizza, "The Consequentialist," *The New Yorker*, May 2, 2011, p. 45.

Chapter 21: "New Moon over Pakistan"

1. "Barack Obama, Neocon," *Wall Street Journal*, August 3, 2007, p. A-8.
2. Interview with a senior official who took part in the planning for the Bin Laden raid.
3. The following lengthy account is based on interviews with three senior administration officials involved in the planning for the raid.
4. Julian E. Barnes, "Basic Training: How Gates Grew," *Wall Street Journal*, June 20, 2011, p. B-6; Saeed Shah, "CIA Organised Fake Vaccination Drive to Get Osama Bin Laden's Family DNA," *The Guardian*, July 12, 2011, p. 1.
5. Background interview with senior counterterrorism official.
6. Hayden interview.
7. Yochi Dreazen, Aamer Madhani and Marc Ambinder, "For Obama, Killing—Not Capturing—Bin Laden Was Goal," *National Journal*, May 3, 2011, www.nationaljournal.com/for-obama-killing-not-capturing-nobr-bin-laden-nobr-was-goal-20110503.
8. Rhodes interview, July 15, 2011.
9. Steven Erlanger, "In Europe, Disquiet over Pakistan Raid," *New York Times*, May 6, 2011, p. A-16.
10. Interview with Tony Blinken, September 27, 2011.
11. Mark Landler, "Obama Seeks Reset in Arab World," *New York Times*, May 12, 2011, p. A-12.
12. White House transcript, "Remarks of John O. Brennan, Assistant to the President for Homeland Security and Counterterrorism, on Ensuring al-Qaeda's Demise," Johns Hopkins University School of Advanced International Studies, June 29, 2011.
13. Ibid.
14. Craig Whitlock, "Panetta Eager to Seize Chance to Defang al-Qaeda," *Washington Post*, July 10, 2011, p. A-7.
15. Background interview with a counterterrorism official.
16. Elisabeth Bumiller, "Gates Says There Is No Sign Top Pakistanis Knew About Bin Laden," *New York Times*, May 19, 2011, p. A-9.
17. Farhan Bokhari, "Pakistani Army Warns U.S. on Repeat Strike," *Financial Times*, May 6, 2011, p. 10.
18. Anna Fifield, "Pakistan Let China See Secret U.S. Aircraft," *Financial Times*, August 15, 2011, p. 1; Farhan Bokhari, "Pakistan Closes Air Base to U.S. Drones," *Financial Times*, June 30, 2011, p. 8; Karen DeYoung and Griff Witte, "Pakistan Relations Reach a New Low," *Washington Post*, June 16, 2011, p. A-1.
19. Elisabeth Bumiller and Thom Shanker, "Gates Stresses the Importance of Ties with Pakistan," *New York Times*, June 17, 2011, p. A-12.
20. Rhodes interview, July 15, 2011.
21. Robert M. Gates testimony to Senate Foreign Relations Committee, December 3, 2009.
22. http://icasualties.org/oef; White House transcript, "Statement of the President on the Afghanistan-Pakistan Annual Review," December 16, 2010.
23. Rajiv Chandrasekaran, "Battle Looms over Pace of Afghanistan Pullout," *Washington Post*, March 31, 2011, p. A-1; Thom Shanker and Elisabeth Bumiller, "First to Leave Afghanistan Will Be Noncombatants," *New York Times*, March 15, 2011, p. A-21.

24. David S. Cloud and Christi Parsons, "Obama Expected to Announce Major Afghan Drawdown," *Los Angeles Times*, June 21, 2011, www.latimes.com/news/nationworld/world/la-fg-afghan-withdrawal-20110621,0,6964197.story.
25. White House transcript, "Remarks by the President on the Way Forward in Afghanistan," June 22, 2011.
26. Pelosi interview, June 7, 2011.

Epilogue: Unfinished Business

1. Interview with Tom Donilon, October 4, 2011.
2. Glenn Kessler, "Obama's Signals on Middle East Scrutinized by All Sides," *Washington Post*, January 24, 2009, p. A-9.
3. Dennis Ross, "How to Break a Middle East Stalemate," *Washington Post*, Outlook section, January 8, 2002, p. B-3.
4. Leila Fadel, "Islamists Secure Lead in Egyptian Election," *Washington Post*, January 8, 2012, p. A-12; David D. Kirkpatrick, "Islamists in Egypt Back Timing of Military Handover," January 9, 2012, *New York Times*, January 9, 2012, p. A-1.
5. Donilon interview.
6. Steven Erlanger, "In Bold Step, Europe Nears Embargo on Iran Oil," *New York Times*, Jan. 5, 2012, p. A-1; Thomas Erdbrink and Joby Warrick, "Iran Fears the Worst as West Steps Up Pressure," *Washington Post*, January 6, 2002, p. A-1.
7. Zeina Karam, "Assad Vows 'Iron Hand' Against Opponents," Associated Press, January 10, 2012.
8. Interview with Denis McDonough, July 14, 2010.
9. Hillary Clinton, "America's Pacific Century," *Foreign Policy*, November 2011.
10. David Nakamura, "Marines Will Be Sent to Australia, Obama Announces," *Washington Post*, November 17, 2011, p. A-10.
11. David S. Cloud and Ned Parker, "U.S. Is Open to Leaving a Force in Iraq; American Officials Say Up to 10,000 Troops Could Remain Past the Withdrawal Deadline If Baghdad Wants Them," *Los Angeles Times*, July 6, 2011, p. A-3; Tim Arango and Michael S. Schmidt, "Despite Difficult Talks, Both Sides Had Expected Some American Troops to Stay," *New York Times*, October 22, 2011, p. A-8.
12. Greg Jaffe, "Last American Troops Cross Border into Kuwait, *Washington Post*, December 18, 2011, p. A-10.
13. White House transcript, "Remarks by the President on the Defense Strategic Review"; "Sustaining Global Leadership: Priorities for 21st Century Defense," U.S. Department of Defense, January 2012.
14. "Sustaining Global Leadership."

Conclusion

1. The eight jobs referred to here are the secretaries and deputy secretaries of State and Defense, the national security adviser and his deputy, and the director and deputy director of the CIA.
2. Blinken interview, September 27, 2011.
3. Background interview.
4. Background conversations with two administration officials.

5. "We must rebalance our long-term priorities so that we successfully move beyond to-day's wars, and focus our attention and resources on a broader set of countries and challenges," U.S. National Security Strategy, May 2010, p. 9; Rhodes interview, July 15, 2011.

6. Pelosi interview, June 7, 2011.

7. Charles Krauthammer, "Decline Is a Choice," *The Weekly Standard*, October 19, 2009.

8. Blinken interview, September 27, 2011; interview with Tom Donilon, October 4, 2011.

9. Mark McDonald, "North Korea Sees Nuclear Error by Libya," *New York Times*, March 25, 2011, p. A-12.

INDEX